C000181958

Jane Shaw

**Ordained to the Office and Work of a Deacon
in The Church of God in Ripon Cathedral on**

1ˢᵀ July 2001

+ Joh Ripon . Leeds

THE
REVISED ENGLISH
BIBLE

THE NEW TESTAMENT

THE REVISED ENGLISH BIBLE

was planned and directed by representatives of

THE BAPTIST UNION OF GREAT BRITAIN

THE CHURCH OF ENGLAND

THE CHURCH OF SCOTLAND

THE COUNCIL OF CHURCHES FOR WALES

THE IRISH COUNCIL OF CHURCHES

THE LONDON YEARLY MEETING OF THE
RELIGIOUS SOCIETY OF FRIENDS

THE METHODIST CHURCH OF GREAT BRITAIN

THE MORAVIAN CHURCH IN GREAT BRITAIN AND IRELAND

THE ROMAN CATHOLIC CHURCH IN ENGLAND AND WALES

THE ROMAN CATHOLIC CHURCH IN IRELAND

THE ROMAN CATHOLIC CHURCH IN SCOTLAND

THE SALVATION ARMY

THE UNITED REFORMED CHURCH

THE BIBLE SOCIETY

THE NATIONAL BIBLE SOCIETY OF SCOTLAND

THE
REVISED ENGLISH
BIBLE

THE NEW TESTAMENT

OXFORD UNIVERSITY PRESS

Oxford University Press, Great Clarendon Street, Oxford OX2 6DP

Oxford New York

Athens Auckland Bangkok Bogota Bombay
Buenos Aires Calcutta Cape Town Dar es Salaam
Delhi Florence Hong Kong Istanbul Karachi
Kuala Lumpur Madras Madrid Melbourne
Mexico City Nairobi Paris Singapore
Taipei Tokyo Toronto

and associated companies in
Berlin Ibadan

Oxford is a trade mark of Oxford University Press

© Oxford University Press and Cambridge University Press 1989

The Revised English Bible
First published 1989
This reprint 1997

The Revised English Bible is a revision of The New English Bible;
The New English Bible New Testament was first published by
the Oxford and Cambridge University Presses in 1961,
and the complete Bible in 1970

British Library Cataloguing in Publication Data

Revised English Bible: the New Testament
I. Title   II. Bible. N.T. English
225.5208

ISBN 0-19-101254-8 (Standard edition)
ISBN 0-19-101251-3 (Presentation edition)

Printed in Great Britain by
Clays Ltd
Bungay, Suffolk

PREFACE

THE second half of the twentieth century has produced many new versions of the Bible. One of the pioneers was The New English Bible, which was distinctive inasmuch as it was a new translation from the ancient texts and was officially commissioned by the majority of the British Churches.

The translators themselves were chosen for their ability as scholars, without regard to Church affiliation. Literary advisers read and criticized the translators' drafts.

The translation of the New Testament appeared in 1961. The Old Testament and the Apocrypha were published with a limited revision of the New Testament in 1970; The New English Bible was then complete. Two years later a new impression appeared with some very minor corrections, and The New English Bible has remained substantially as it was first produced until the present day. It has proved to be of great value throughout the English-speaking world and is very widely used.

The debt of the Churches to those who served on the various committees and panels is very considerable and has been gladly acknowledged on many occasions. One name that will always be associated with The New English Bible is that of Dr C. H. Dodd, who as Director from start to finish brought to the enterprise outstanding leadership, sensitivity, and scholarship. It is fitting also to recall with gratitude the roles of Professor Sir Godfrey Driver, Joint Director from 1965, and Professor W. D. McHardy, Deputy Director from 1968.

It was right that The New English Bible in its original form, like any other version, should be subject to critical examination and discussion, and especially the Old Testament, which had not had the advantage of even a limited general revision. From the beginning helpful suggestions and criticisms had come in from many quarters. Moreover the widespread enthusiasm for The New English Bible had resulted in its being frequently used for reading aloud in public worship, the implications of which had not been fully anticipated by the translators. As a result it became desirable to review the translation, and in 1974 the Joint Committee of the Churches decided to set in train what was to become a major revision of the text.

New translators' panels were constituted under the chairmanship of Professor W. D. McHardy, who was appointed Director of Revision. The result of their work is The Revised English Bible, a translation standing firmly in the tradition established by The New English Bible. This substantial revision expresses the mind and conviction of biblical scholars and translators of the 1980s, as The New English Bible expressed the mind of a previous generation of such specialists, and it is fortunate that some distinguished scholars have been able to give their services throughout the entire process. To them we owe a great deal, and to none more than to Professor McHardy, who has served with great devotion throughout and made this a large part of his life's work.

The original initiative for making the New English Bible translation had come from the Church of Scotland in 1946, and a number of other Churches later joined them and formed a committee which was to plan and direct a new translation in contemporary language. The Joint Committee comprised representatives of the Baptist Union of Great Britain and Ireland, the Church of England, the Church of Scotland, the Congregational Church of England and Wales, the Council of Churches for Wales, the Irish Council of Churches, the London Yearly Meeting of the Religious Society of Friends, the Methodist Church of Great Britain, and the Presbyterian Church of England, as well as of the British and Foreign Bible Society and the National Bible Society of Scotland. Roman Catholic representatives later attended as observers.

After publication of the complete translation, there were changes in the composition of the Joint Committee. The Roman Catholic Church entered into full membership, with representatives from the hierarchies of England and Wales, Scotland, and Ireland. Following the union of the Presbyterian Church of England with the Congregational Church as the United Reformed Church, the united church was represented on the Committee. After the review began, the Committee was joined by representatives of the Salvation Army and the Moravian Church.

The progress of the work of the revisers has been regularly reported to meetings of the Joint Committee, taking place once and sometimes twice a year in the Jerusalem Chamber, Westminster Abbey. The Committee has much appreciated the courtesy of the Dean and Chapter in making the Chamber available for these meetings.

Members of the Joint Committee have given guidance and support to the Director of Revision throughout, and have had the opportunity of inspecting drafts as the work on each book approached its final stage, in many cases making detailed comments and criticisms for the consideration of the Director and revisers.

Care has been taken to ensure that the style of English used is fluent and of appropriate dignity for liturgical use, while maintaining intelligibility for worshippers of a wide range of ages and backgrounds. The revisers have sought to avoid complex or technical terms where possible, and to provide sentence structure and word order, especially in the Psalms, which will facilitate congregational reading but will not misrepresent the meaning of the original texts. As the 'you'-form of address to God is now commonly used, the 'thou'-form which was preserved in the language of prayer in The New English Bible has been abandoned. The use of male-oriented language, in passages of traditional versions of the Bible which evidently apply to both genders, has become a sensitive issue in recent years; the revisers have preferred more inclusive gender reference where that has been possible without compromising scholarly integrity or English style.

The revision is characterized by a somewhat more extensive use than in The New English Bible of textual subheadings printed in italic type. These headings are used, for example, to mark broad structural divisions in the writing or substantial changes of direction or theme. They should not be regarded in any way as part of the biblical text. The headings in the Psalms are a special case; these have been translated from those prefixed in ancient times to the Hebrew Psalms.

The traditional verse numbering of the Authorized (King James) Version is retained in The Revised English Bible for ease of reference. Where the Authorized Version contains passages which are found in the manuscripts on which that version rests, but which are absent from those followed by The Revised English Bible, these passages are reproduced in footnotes, in order to explain gaps in the verse numbering.

A table of measures, weights, and values will be found on pages xi–xii. The ancient terms usually appear in the text, but modern equivalents have been used when it seemed appropriate to do so.

In the Introduction to the Apocrypha mention is made of the views held by different Churches with regard to the canonicity and authority of the books here included within the Apocrypha.

The Joint Committee commends The Revised English Bible to the Churches and to the English-speaking world with due humility, but with confidence that God has yet new light and truth to break forth from his word. The Committee prays that the new version will prove to be a means to that end.

DONALD COGGAN

Chairman of the Joint Committee

CONTENTS

INTRODUCTION

TO THE NEW TESTAMENT

THE Revised English Bible, a revision of The New English Bible, carries forward the aim of its predecessor to provide English-speaking readers with a faithful rendering of the best available Greek text into modern English, incorporating the gains of modern biblical scholarship.

The earliest manuscripts of the books of the New Testament were written down within a generation of their first composition. But the transmission of the text has not been altogether straightforward, and there is no scholarly Greek text of the New Testament which commands universal acceptance at the present time. Those who prepared the first draft of The New English Bible New Testament usually started with the text originally published by Eberhard Nestle at the end of the nineteenth century. The translators considered variant readings on their merits and, having weighed the evidence, selected for translation in each passage the reading which, to the best of their judgement, seemed most likely to represent what the author wrote. In assessing the evidence, the translators took into account (a) manuscripts of the New Testament in Greek, (b) early translations into other languages, and (c) quotations from the New Testament by early Christian writers. These three sources of evidence were referred to as 'witnesses'. The complete text eventually followed was edited by R. V. G. Tasker and published as The Greek New Testament (Oxford and Cambridge University Presses, 1964). A notable contribution to New Testament biblical studies after the completion of The New English Bible was the publication of Novum Testamentum Graece, edited by Kurt Aland and others (Deutsche Bibelstiftung, Stuttgart, 26th edn 1979), and this was a major point of reference for those engaged in the revision. The translators and revisers have taken into consideration not only the evidence presented in recent editions of the Greek text, but also the work of exegetical and literary scholarship, which is continuing all the time. The revisers have drawn attention in footnotes to variant readings which may result in significant alternative understanding or interpretation of the text, and in particular to those readings which were followed in The New English Bible, but which now seem to the revisers to be less probable than those used in this revision. They are well aware that their judgement is provisional, but they believe the text they have adopted to be an improvement on that underlying earlier translations.

In accordance with the original decision of the Joint Committee of the

Churches, the translators and revisers attempted to use consistently the idiom of contemporary English, employing its natural vocabulary, constructions, and rhythms to convey the meaning of the Greek. The revision has been concerned to avoid archaisms, technical terms, and pretentious language as far as possible. The New English Bible and its revisers adopted the wholesome practice of the translators of the Authorized (King James) Version, who recognized no obligation to render the same Greek word everywhere by the same English word. This version claims to be a translation rather than a paraphrase, observing faithfulness to the meaning of the text without necessarily reproducing grammatical structure or translating word for word.

The revisers are conscious of the limitations and imperfections of their work. Anyone who has tried it will know that it is impossible to make a perfect translation. Only those who have long meditated on the Greek original are aware of the richness and subtlety of meaning that may lie even within what appears to be the most simple of sentences, or know the despair that can attend efforts to bring it out through the medium of a different language. All who have been involved in the work trust that under the providence of Almighty God this revision may build on the achievement of The New English Bible in opening yet further the truth of the scriptures.

THE
NEW TESTAMENT

THE GOSPEL ACCORDING TO
MATTHEW

The ancestry of the Messiah

1 THE genealogy of Jesus Christ, son of David, son of Abraham.

2 Abraham was the father of Isaac, Isaac of Jacob, Jacob of Judah and his brothers, 3 Judah of Perez and Zarah (their mother was Tamar), Perez of Hezron, Hezron of Ram, 4 Ram of Amminadab, Amminadab of Nahshon, Nahshon of Salmon, 5 Salmon of Boaz (his mother was Rahab), Boaz of Obed (his mother was Ruth), Obed of Jesse; 6 and Jesse was the father of King David.

David was the father of Solomon (his mother had been the wife of Uriah), 7 Solomon of Rehoboam, Rehoboam of Abijah, Abijah of Asa, 8 Asa of Jehoshaphat, Jehoshaphat of Joram, Joram of Uzziah, 9 Uzziah of Jotham, Jotham of Ahaz, Ahaz of Hezekiah, 10 Hezekiah of Manasseh, Manasseh of Amon, Amon of Josiah; 11 and Josiah was the father of Jeconiah and his brothers at the time of the deportation to Babylon.

12 After the deportation Jeconiah was the father of Shealtiel, Shealtiel of Zerubbabel, 13 Zerubbabel of Abiud, Abiud of Eliakim, Eliakim of Azor, 14 Azor of Zadok, Zadok of Achim, Achim of Eliud, 15 Eliud of Eleazar, Eleazar of Matthan, Matthan of Jacob, 16 Jacob of Joseph, the husband of Mary, who gave birth to Jesus called Messiah.

17 There were thus fourteen generations in all from Abraham to David, fourteen from David until the deportation to Babylon, and fourteen from the deportation until the Messiah.

The birth and infancy of Jesus

18 THIS is how the birth of Jesus Christ came about. His mother Mary was betrothed to Joseph; before their marriage she found she was going to have a child through the Holy Spirit. 19 Being a man of principle, and at the same time wanting to save her from exposure, Joseph made up his mind to have the marriage contract quietly set aside. 20 He had resolved on this, when an angel of the Lord appeared to him in a dream and said, 'Joseph, son of David, do not be afraid to take Mary home with you to be your wife. It is through the Holy Spirit that she has conceived. 21 She will bear a son; and you shall give him the name Jesus, for he will save his people from their sins.' 22 All this happened in order to fulfil what the Lord declared through the prophet: 23 'A virgin will conceive and bear a son, and he shall be called Emmanuel,' a name which means 'God is with us'. 24 When he woke Joseph did as the angel of the Lord had directed him; he took Mary home to be his wife, 25 but had no intercourse with her until her son was born. And he named the child Jesus.

2 JESUS was born at Bethlehem in Judaea during the reign of Herod. After his birth astrologers from the east arrived in Jerusalem, 2 asking, 'Where is the newborn king of the Jews? We observed the rising of his star, and we have come to pay him homage.' 3 King Herod was greatly perturbed when he heard this, and so was the whole of Jerusalem. 4 He called together the chief priests and scribes of Jews, and asked them where the Messiah was to be born. 5 'At Bethlehem in Judaea,' they replied, 'for this is what the prophet wrote: 6 "Bethlehem in the land of Judah, you are by no means least among the rulers of Judah; for out of you shall come a ruler to be the shepherd of my people Israel."'

7 Then Herod summoned the astrologers to meet him secretly, and ascertained from them the exact time when the star had appeared. 8 He sent them to Bethlehem, and said, 'Go and make a careful search for the child, and when you have found him, bring me word, so that I may go myself and pay him homage.'

9-10 After hearing what the king had to say they set out; there before them was the star they had seen rising, and it went ahead of them until it stopped above the

1:21 **Jesus:** *that is* Saviour.

place where the child lay. They were overjoyed at the sight of it [11] and, entering the house, they saw the child with Mary his mother and bowed low in homage to him; they opened their treasure chests and presented gifts to him: gold, frankincense, and myrrh. [12] Then they returned to their own country by another route, for they had been warned in a dream not to go back to Herod.

[13] After they had gone, an angel of the Lord appeared to Joseph in a dream, and said, 'Get up, take the child and his mother and escape with them to Egypt, and stay there until I tell you; for Herod is going to search for the child to kill him.' [14] So Joseph got up, took mother and child by night, and sought refuge with them in Egypt, [15] where he stayed till Herod's death. This was to fulfil what the Lord had declared through the prophet: 'Out of Egypt I have called my son.'

[16] When Herod realized that the astrologers had tricked him he flew into a rage, and gave orders for the massacre of all the boys aged two years or under, in Bethlehem and throughout the whole district, in accordance with the time he had ascertained from the astrologers. [17] So the words spoken through Jeremiah the prophet were fulfilled: [18] 'A voice was heard in Rama, sobbing in bitter grief; it was Rachel weeping for her children, and refusing to be comforted, because they were no more.'

[19] After Herod's death an angel of the Lord appeared in a dream to Joseph in Egypt [20] and said to him, 'Get up, take the child and his mother, and go to the land of Israel, for those who threatened the child's life are dead.' [21] So he got up, took mother and child with him, and came to the land of Israel. [22] But when he heard that Archelaus had succeeded his father Herod as king of Judaea, he was afraid to go there. Directed by a dream, he withdrew to the region of Galilee, [23] where he settled in a town called Nazareth. This was to fulfil the words spoken through the prophets: 'He shall be called a Nazarene.'

John the Baptist and Jesus

3 IN the course of time John the Baptist appeared in the Judaean wilderness, proclaiming this message: [2] 'Repent, for the kingdom of Heaven is upon you!' [3] It was of him that the prophet Isaiah spoke when he said,

A voice cries in the wilderness,
'Prepare the way for the Lord;
clear a straight path for him.'

[4] John's clothing was a rough coat of camel's hair, with a leather belt round his waist, and his food was locusts and wild honey. [5] Everyone flocked to him from Jerusalem, Judaea, and the Jordan valley, [6] and they were baptized by him in the river Jordan, confessing their sins.

[7] When he saw many of the Pharisees and Sadducees coming for baptism he said to them: 'Vipers' brood! Who warned you to escape from the wrath that is to come? [8] Prove your repentance by the fruit you bear; [9] and do not imagine you can say, "We have Abraham for our father." I tell you that God can make children for Abraham out of these stones. [10] The axe lies ready at the roots of the trees; every tree that fails to produce good fruit is cut down and thrown on the fire. [11] I baptize you with water, for repentance; but the one who comes after me is mightier than I am, whose sandals I am not worthy to remove. He will baptize you with the Holy Spirit and with fire. [12] His winnowing-shovel is ready in his hand and he will clear his threshing-floor; he will gather the wheat into his granary, but the chaff he will burn on a fire that can never be put out.'

[13] Then Jesus arrived at the Jordan from Galilee, and came to John to be baptized by him. [14] John tried to dissuade him. 'Do you come to me?' he said. 'It is I who need to be baptized by you.' [15] Jesus replied, 'Let it be so for the present; it is right for us to do all that God requires.' Then John allowed him to come. [16] No sooner had Jesus been baptized and come up out of the water than the heavens were opened and he saw the Spirit of God descending like a dove to alight on him. [17] And there came a voice from heaven saying, 'This is my beloved Son, in whom I take delight.'

The temptation of Jesus

4 JESUS was then led by the Spirit into the wilderness, to be tempted by the devil.

[2] For forty days and nights he fasted, and at the end of them he was famished.

3:17 **This ... Son:** *or* This is my only Son.   4:1 **tempted:** *or* tested.

³ The tempter approached him and said, 'If you are the Son of God, tell these stones to become bread.' ⁴ Jesus answered, 'Scripture says, "Man is not to live on bread alone, but on every word that comes from the mouth of God."'

⁵ The devil then took him to the Holy City and set him on the parapet of the temple. ⁶ 'If you are the Son of God,' he said, 'throw yourself down; for scripture says, "He will put his angels in charge of you, and they will support you in their arms, for fear you should strike your foot against a stone."' ⁷ Jesus answered him, 'Scripture also says, "You are not to put the Lord your God to the test."'

⁸ The devil took him next to a very high mountain, and showed him all the kingdoms of the world in their glory. ⁹ 'All these', he said, 'I will give you, if you will only fall down and do me homage.' ¹⁰ But Jesus said, 'Out of my sight, Satan! Scripture says, "You shall do homage to the Lord your God and worship him alone."'

¹¹ Then the devil left him; and angels came and attended to his needs.

The first disciples

¹² WHEN he heard that John had been arrested, Jesus withdrew to Galilee; ¹³ and leaving Nazareth he went and settled at Capernaum on the sea of Galilee, in the district of Zebulun and Naphtali. ¹⁴ This was to fulfil the words of the prophet Isaiah about ¹⁵ 'the land of Zebulun, the land of Naphtali, the road to the sea, the land beyond Jordan, Galilee of the Gentiles':

¹⁶ The people that lived in darkness
  have seen a great light;
  light has dawned on those
  who lived in the land of death's dark
    shadow.

¹⁷ From that day Jesus began to proclaim the message: 'Repent, for the kingdom of Heaven is upon you.'

¹⁸ JESUS was walking by the sea of Galilee when he saw two brothers, Simon called Peter and his brother Andrew, casting a net into the lake; for they were fishermen. ¹⁹ Jesus said to them, 'Come with me, and I will make you fishers of men.' ²⁰ At once they left their nets and followed him.

²¹ Going on farther, he saw another pair of brothers, James son of Zebedee and his brother John; they were in a boat with their father Zebedee, mending their nets. He called them, ²² and at once they left the boat and their father, and followed him.

²³ He travelled throughout Galilee, teaching in the synagogues, proclaiming the good news of the kingdom, and healing every kind of illness and infirmity among the people. ²⁴ His fame spread throughout Syria; and they brought to him sufferers from various diseases, those racked with pain or possessed by demons, those who were epileptic or paralysed, and he healed them all. ²⁵ Large crowds followed him, from Galilee and the Decapolis, from Jerusalem and Judaea, and from Transjordan.

The Sermon on the Mount

5 WHEN he saw the crowds he went up a mountain. There he sat down, and when his disciples had gathered round him ² he began to address them. And this is the teaching he gave:

³ 'Blessed are the poor in spirit;
  the kingdom of Heaven is theirs.
⁴ Blessed are the sorrowful;
  they shall find consolation.
⁵ Blessed are the gentle;
  they shall have the earth for their
    possession.
⁶ Blessed are those who hunger and
    thirst to see right prevail;
  they shall be satisfied.
⁷ Blessed are those who show mercy;
  mercy shall be shown to them.
⁸ Blessed are those whose hearts are
    pure;
  they shall see God.
⁹ Blessed are the peacemakers;
  they shall be called God's children.
¹⁰ Blessed are those who are persecuted
    in the cause of right;
  the kingdom of Heaven is theirs.

¹¹ 'Blessed are you, when you suffer insults and persecution and calumnies of every kind for my sake. ¹² Exult and be glad, for you have a rich reward in heaven; in the same way they persecuted the prophets before you.

¹³ 'You are salt to the world. And if salt becomes tasteless, how is its saltness to be

5:6 to ... prevail: *or* to do what is right.

3

restored? It is good for nothing but to be thrown away and trodden underfoot.

¹⁴ 'You are light for all the world. A town that stands on a hill cannot be hidden. ¹⁵ When a lamp is lit, it is not put under the meal-tub, but on the lampstand, where it gives light to everyone in the house. ¹⁶ Like the lamp, you must shed light among your fellows, so that, when they see the good you do, they may give praise to your Father in heaven.

¹⁷ 'DO NOT suppose that I have come to abolish the law and the prophets; I did not come to abolish, but to complete. ¹⁸ Truly I tell you: so long as heaven and earth endure, not a letter, not a dot, will disappear from the law until all that must happen has happened. ¹⁹ Anyone therefore who sets aside even the least of the law's demands, and teaches others to do the same, will have the lowest place in the kingdom of Heaven, whereas anyone who keeps the law, and teaches others to do so, will rank high in the kingdom of Heaven. ²⁰ I tell you, unless you show yourselves far better than the scribes and Pharisees, you can never enter the kingdom of Heaven.

²¹ 'You have heard that our forefathers were told, "Do not commit murder; anyone who commits murder must be brought to justice." ²² But what I tell you is this: Anyone who nurses anger against his brother must be brought to justice. Whoever calls his brother "good for nothing" deserves the sentence of the court; whoever calls him "fool" deserves hellfire. ²³ So if you are presenting your gift at the altar and suddenly remember that your brother has a grievance against you, ²⁴ leave your gift where it is before the altar. First go and make your peace with your brother; then come back and offer your gift. ²⁵ If someone sues you, come to terms with him promptly while you are both on your way to court; otherwise he may hand you over to the judge, and the judge to the officer, and you will be thrown into jail. ²⁶ Truly I tell you: once you are there you will not be let out until you have paid the last penny.

²⁷ 'You have heard that they were told, "Do not commit adultery." ²⁸ But what I tell you is this: If a man looks at a woman

with a lustful eye, he has already committed adultery with her in his heart. ²⁹ If your right eye causes your downfall, tear it out and fling it away; it is better for you to lose one part of your body than for the whole of it to be thrown into hell. ³⁰ If your right hand causes your downfall, cut it off and fling it away; it is better for you to lose one part of your body than for the whole of it to go to hell.

³¹ 'They were told, "A man who divorces his wife must give her a certificate of dismissal." ³² But what I tell you is this: If a man divorces his wife for any cause other than unchastity he involves her in adultery; and whoever marries her commits adultery.

³³ 'Again, you have heard that our forefathers were told, "Do not break your oath," and "Oaths sworn to the Lord must be kept." ³⁴ But what I tell you is this: You are not to swear at all—not by heaven, for it is God's throne, ³⁵ nor by the earth, for it is his footstool, nor by Jerusalem, for it is the city of the great King, ³⁶ nor by your own head, because you cannot turn one hair of it white or black. ³⁷ Plain "Yes" or "No" is all you need to say; anything beyond that comes from the evil one.

³⁸ 'You have heard that they were told, "An eye for an eye, a tooth for a tooth." ³⁹ But what I tell you is this: Do not resist those who wrong you. If anyone slaps you on the right cheek, turn and offer him the other also. ⁴⁰ If anyone wants to sue you and takes your shirt, let him have your cloak as well. ⁴¹ If someone in authority presses you into service for one mile, go with him two. ⁴² Give to anyone who asks; and do not turn your back on anyone who wants to borrow.

⁴³ 'You have heard that they were told, "Love your neighbour and hate your enemy." ⁴⁴ But what I tell you is this: Love your enemies and pray for your persecutors; ⁴⁵ only so can you be children of your heavenly Father, who causes the sun to rise on good and bad alike, and sends the rain on the innocent and the wicked. ⁴⁶ If you love only those who love you, what reward can you expect? Even the tax-collectors do as much as that. ⁴⁷ If you greet only your brothers, what is there extraordinary about that? Even the

---

5:18 *until ... happened: or* before all that it stands for is achieved.

heathen do as much. [48] There must be no limit to your goodness, as your heavenly Father's goodness knows no bounds.

6 'BE careful not to parade your religion before others; if you do, no reward awaits you with your Father in heaven.

[2] 'So, when you give alms, do not announce it with a flourish of trumpets, as the hypocrites do in synagogues and in the streets to win the praise of others. Truly I tell you: they have their reward already. [3] But when you give alms, do not let your left hand know what your right is doing; [4] your good deed must be secret, and your Father who sees what is done in secret will reward you.

[5] 'Again, when you pray, do not be like the hypocrites; they love to say their prayers standing up in synagogues and at street corners for everyone to see them. Truly I tell you: they have their reward already. [6] But when you pray, go into a room by yourself, shut the door, and pray to your Father who is in secret; and your Father who sees what is done in secret will reward you.

[7] 'In your prayers do not go babbling on like the heathen, who imagine that the more they say the more likely they are to be heard. [8] Do not imitate them, for your Father knows what your needs are before you ask him.

[9] 'This is how you should pray:

Our Father in heaven,
may your name be hallowed;
[10] your kingdom come,
your will be done,
on earth as in heaven.
[11] Give us today our daily bread.
[12] Forgive us the wrong we have done,
as we have forgiven those who have
wronged us.
[13] And do not put us to the test,
but save us from the evil one.

[14] 'For if you forgive others the wrongs they have done, your heavenly Father will also forgive you; [15] but if you do not forgive others, then your Father will not forgive the wrongs that you have done.

[16] 'So too when you fast, do not look gloomy like the hypocrites: they make their faces unsightly so that everybody may see that they are fasting. Truly I tell you: they have their reward already. [17] But when you fast, anoint your head and wash your face, [18] so that no one sees that you are fasting, but only your Father who is in secret; and your Father who sees what is done in secret will give you your reward.

[19] 'DO NOT store up for yourselves treasure on earth, where moth and rust destroy, and thieves break in and steal; [20] but store up treasure in heaven, where neither moth nor rust will destroy, nor thieves break in and steal. [21] For where your treasure is, there will your heart be also.

[22] 'The lamp of the body is the eye. If your eyes are sound, you will have light for your whole body; [23] if your eyes are bad, your whole body will be in darkness. If then the only light you have is darkness, how great a darkness that will be.

[24] 'No one can serve two masters; for either he will hate the first and love the second, or he will be devoted to the first and despise the second. You cannot serve God and Money.

[25] 'This is why I tell you not to be anxious about food and drink to keep you alive and about clothes to cover your body. Surely life is more than food, the body more than clothes. [26] Look at the birds in the sky; they do not sow and reap and store in barns, yet your heavenly Father feeds them. Are you not worth more than the birds? [27] Can anxious thought add a single day to your life? [28] And why be anxious about clothes? Consider how the lilies grow in the fields; they do not work, they do not spin; [29] yet I tell you, even Solomon in all his splendour was not attired like one of them. [30] If that is how God clothes the grass in the fields, which is there today and tomorrow is thrown on the stove, will he not all the more clothe you? How little faith you have! [31] Do not ask anxiously, "What are we to eat? What are we to drink? What shall we wear?" [32] These are the things that occupy the minds of the heathen, but

---

6:11 **our ... bread:** *or* our bread for the morrow.   6:13 **from the evil one:** *or* from evil. *Some witnesses add* For yours is the kingdom and the power and the glory, for ever. Amen.   6:27 **add ... life:** *or* add one foot to your height.   6:28 **Consider ... spin:** *one witness reads* Consider the lilies: they neither card, nor spin, nor work.

your heavenly Father knows that you need them all. ³³ Set your mind on God's kingdom and his justice before everything else, and all the rest will come to you as well. ³⁴ So do not be anxious about tomorrow; tomorrow will look after itself. Each day has troubles enough of its own.

7 'Do NOT judge, and you will not be judged. ² For as you judge others, so you will yourselves be judged, and whatever measure you deal out to others will be dealt to you. ³ Why do you look at the speck of sawdust in your brother's eye, with never a thought for the plank in your own? ⁴ How can you say to your brother, "Let me take the speck out of your eye," when all the time there is a plank in your own? ⁵ You hypocrite! First take the plank out of your own eye, and then you will see clearly to take the speck out of your brother's.

⁶ 'Do not give dogs what is holy; do not throw your pearls to the pigs: they will only trample on them, and turn and tear you to pieces.

⁷ 'Ask, and you will receive; seek, and you will find; knock, and the door will be opened to you. ⁸ For everyone who asks receives, those who seek find, and to those who knock, the door will be opened.

⁹ 'Would any of you offer his son a stone when he asks for bread, ¹⁰ or a snake when he asks for a fish? ¹¹ If you, bad as you are, know how to give good things to your children, how much more will your heavenly Father give good things to those who ask him!

¹² 'Always treat others as you would like them to treat you: that is the law and the prophets.

¹³ 'Enter by the narrow gate. Wide is the gate and broad the road that leads to destruction, and many enter that way; ¹⁴ narrow is the gate and constricted the road that leads to life, and those who find them are few.

¹⁵ 'Beware of false prophets, who come to you dressed up as sheep while underneath they are savage wolves. ¹⁶ You will recognize them by their fruit. Can grapes be picked from briars, or figs from thistles? ¹⁷ A good tree always yields sound fruit, and a poor tree bad fruit. ¹⁸ A good tree cannot bear bad fruit, or a poor tree sound fruit. ¹⁹ A tree that does not yield sound fruit is cut down and thrown on the fire.

²⁰ That is why I say you will recognize them by their fruit.

²¹ 'Not everyone who says to me, "Lord, Lord" will enter the kingdom of Heaven, but only those who do the will of my heavenly Father. ²² When the day comes, many will say to me, "Lord, Lord, did we not prophesy in your name, drive out demons in your name, and in your name perform many miracles?" ²³ Then I will tell them plainly, "I never knew you. Out of my sight; your deeds are evil!"

²⁴ 'So whoever hears these words of mine and acts on them is like a man who had the sense to build his house on rock. ²⁵ The rain came down, the floods rose, the winds blew and beat upon that house; but it did not fall, because its foundations were on rock. ²⁶ And whoever hears these words of mine and does not act on them is like a man who was foolish enough to build his house on sand. ²⁷ The rain came down, the floods rose, the winds blew and battered against that house; and it fell with a great crash.'

²⁸ When Jesus had finished this discourse the people were amazed at his teaching; ²⁹ unlike their scribes he taught with a note of authority.

Miracles and teaching

8 WHEN he came down from the mountain great crowds followed him. ² And now a leper approached him, bowed before him, and said, 'Sir, if only you will, you can make me clean.' ³ Jesus stretched out his hand and touched him, saying, 'I will; be clean.' And his leprosy was cured immediately. ⁴ Then Jesus said to him, 'See that you tell nobody; but go and show yourself to the priest, and make the offering laid down by Moses to certify the cure.'

⁵ As Jesus entered Capernaum a centurion came up to ask his help. ⁶ 'Sir,' he said, 'my servant is lying at home paralysed and racked with pain.' ⁷ Jesus said, 'I will come and cure him.' ⁸ But the centurion replied, 'Sir, I am not worthy to have you under my roof. You need only say the word and my servant will be cured. ⁹ I know, for I am myself under orders, with soldiers under me. I say to one, "Go," and he goes; to another, "Come here," and he comes; and to my servant, "Do this," and he does it.' ¹⁰ Jesus heard him with astonishment, and said to the people who were

following him, 'Truly I tell you: nowhere in Israel have I found such faith. ¹¹ Many, I tell you, will come from east and west to sit with Abraham, Isaac, and Jacob at the banquet in the kingdom of Heaven. ¹² But those who were born to the kingdom will be thrown out into the dark, where there will be wailing and grinding of teeth.' ¹³ Then Jesus said to the centurion, 'Go home; as you have believed, so let it be.' At that very moment the boy recovered.

¹⁴ Jesus then went to Peter's house and found Peter's mother-in-law in bed with fever. ¹⁵ So he took her by the hand; the fever left her, and she got up and attended to his needs.

¹⁶ That evening they brought to him many who were possessed by demons; and he drove the spirits out with a word and healed all who were sick, ¹⁷ to fulfil the prophecy of Isaiah: 'He took our illnesses from us and carried away our diseases.'

¹⁸ At the sight of the crowd surrounding him Jesus gave word to cross to the other side of the lake. ¹⁹ A scribe came up and said to him, 'Teacher, I will follow you wherever you go.' ²⁰ Jesus replied, 'Foxes have their holes and birds their roosts; but the Son of Man has nowhere to lay his head.' ²¹ Another man, one of his disciples, said to him, 'Lord, let me go and bury my father first.' ²² Jesus replied, 'Follow me, and leave the dead to bury their dead.'

²³ Jesus then got into the boat, and his disciples followed. ²⁴ All at once a great storm arose on the lake, till the waves were breaking right over the boat; but he went on sleeping. ²⁵ So they came and woke him, saying: 'Save us, Lord; we are sinking!' ²⁶ 'Why are you such cowards?' he said. 'How little faith you have!' With that he got up and rebuked the wind and the sea, and there was a dead calm. ²⁷ The men were astonished at what had happened, and exclaimed, 'What sort of man is this? Even the wind and the sea obey him.'

²⁸ When he reached the country of the Gadarenes on the other side, two men came to meet him from among the tombs; they were possessed by demons, and so violent that no one dared pass that way. ²⁹ 'Son of God,' they shouted, 'what do you want with us? Have you come here to

torment us before our time?' ³⁰ In the distance a large herd of pigs was feeding; ³¹ and the demons begged him: 'If you drive us out, send us into that herd of pigs.' ³² 'Go!' he said. Then they came out and went into the pigs, and the whole herd rushed over the edge into the lake, and perished in the water. ³³ The men in charge of them took to their heels, and made for the town, where they told the whole story, and what had happened to the madmen. ³⁴ Then the whole town came out to meet Jesus; and when they saw him they begged him to leave the district. ¹ So he got into the boat and crossed over, and came to his own town.

9

² Some men appeared, bringing to Jesus a paralysed man on a bed. When he saw their faith Jesus said to the man, 'Take heart, my son; your sins are forgiven.' ³ At this some of the scribes said to themselves, 'This man is blaspheming!' ⁴ Jesus realized what they were thinking, and said, 'Why do you harbour evil thoughts? ⁵ Is it easier to say, "Your sins are forgiven," or to say, "Stand up and walk"? ⁶ But to convince you that the Son of Man has authority on earth to forgive sins'— he turned to the paralysed man—'stand up, take your bed, and go home.' ⁷ And he got up and went off home. ⁸ The people were filled with awe at the sight, and praised God for granting such authority to men.

⁹ As he went on from there Jesus saw a man named Matthew at his seat in the custom-house, and said to him, 'Follow me'; and Matthew rose and followed him.

¹⁰ When Jesus was having a meal in the house, many tax-collectors and sinners were seated with him and his disciples. ¹¹ Noticing this, the Pharisees said to his disciples, 'Why is it that your teacher eats with tax-collectors and sinners?' ¹² Hearing this he said, 'It is not the healthy who need a doctor, but the sick. ¹³ Go and learn what this text means, "I require mercy, not sacrifice." I did not come to call the virtuous, but sinners.'

¹⁴ Then John's disciples came to him with the question: 'Why is it that we and the Pharisees fast but your disciples do not?' ¹⁵ Jesus replied, 'Can you expect the bridegroom's friends to be sad while the bridegroom is with them? The time will

come when the bridegroom will be taken away from them; then they will fast. [16] 'No one puts a patch of unshrunk cloth on an old garment; for then the patch tears away from the garment, and leaves a bigger hole. [17] Nor do people put new wine into old wineskins; if they do, the skins burst, and then the wine runs out and the skins are ruined. No, they put new wine into fresh skins; then both are preserved.'

[18] EVEN as he spoke, an official came up, who bowed before him and said, 'My daughter has just died; but come and lay your hand on her, and she will live.' [19] Jesus rose and went with him, and so did his disciples.

[20] Just then a woman who had suffered from haemorrhages for twelve years came up from behind, and touched the edge of his cloak; [21] for she said to herself, 'If I can only touch his cloak, I shall be healed.' [22] But Jesus turned and saw her, and said, 'Take heart, my daughter; your faith has healed you.' And from that moment she recovered.

[23] When Jesus arrived at the official's house and saw the flute-players and the general commotion, [24] he said, 'Go away! The girl is not dead: she is asleep'; and they laughed at him. [25] After turning them all out, he went into the room and took the girl by the hand, and she got up. [26] The story became the talk of the whole district.

[27] As he went on from there Jesus was followed by two blind men, shouting, 'Have pity on us, Son of David!' [28] When he had gone indoors they came to him, and Jesus asked, 'Do you believe that I have the power to do what you want?' 'We do,' they said. [29] Then he touched their eyes, and said, 'As you have believed, so let it be'; [30] and their sight was restored. Jesus said to them sternly, 'See that no one hears about this.' [31] But as soon as they had gone out they talked about him all over the region.

[32] They were on their way out when a man was brought to him, who was dumb and possessed by a demon; [33] the demon was driven out and the dumb man spoke. The crowd was astonished and said,

'Nothing like this has ever been seen in Israel.'

[35] So JESUS went round all the towns and villages teaching in their synagogues, proclaiming the good news of the kingdom, and curing every kind of illness and infirmity. [36] The sight of the crowds moved him to pity: they were like sheep without a shepherd, harassed and helpless. [37] Then he said to his disciples, 'The crop is heavy, but the labourers too few; [38] you must ask the owner to send labourers to bring in the harvest.'

The Twelve are commissioned

10 THEN he called his twelve disciples to him and gave them authority to drive out unclean spirits and to cure every kind of illness and infirmity.

[2] These are the names of the twelve apostles: first Simon, also called Peter, and his brother Andrew; James son of Zebedee, and his brother John; [3] Philip and Bartholomew, Thomas and Matthew the tax-collector, James son of Alphaeus, Thaddaeus, [4] Simon the Zealot, and Judas Iscariot, the man who betrayed him.

[5] These twelve Jesus sent out with the following instructions: 'Do not take the road to gentile lands, and do not enter any Samaritan town; [6] but go rather to the lost sheep of the house of Israel. [7] And as you go proclaim the message: "The kingdom of Heaven is upon you." [8] Heal the sick, raise the dead, cleanse lepers, drive out demons. You received without cost; give without charge.

[9] 'Take no gold, silver, or copper in your belts, [10] no pack for the road, no second coat, no sandals, no stick; the worker deserves his keep.

[11] 'Whatever town or village you enter, look for some suitable person in it, and stay with him until you leave. [12] Wish the house peace as you enter it; [13] if it is welcoming, let your peace descend on it, and if it is not, let your peace come back to you. [14] If anyone will not receive you or listen to what you say, then as you leave that house or that town shake the dust of it off your feet. [15] Truly I tell you: on the day of judgement it will be more bearable for the land of Sodom and Gomorrah than for that town.

9:20 edge: *or* tassel.   9:33 in Israel: *some witnesses add* [34] But the Pharisees said, 'He drives out devils by the prince of devils.'   10:3 Thaddaeus: *some witnesses read* Lebbaeus.

[16] 'I send you out like sheep among wolves; be wary as serpents, innocent as doves.

[17] 'Be on your guard, for you will be handed over to the courts, they will flog you in their synagogues, [18] and you will be brought before governors and kings on my account, to testify before them and the Gentiles. [19] But when you are arrested, do not worry about what you are to say, for when the time comes, the words you need will be given you; [20] it will not be you speaking, but the Spirit of your Father speaking in you.

[21] 'Brother will hand over brother to death, and a father his child; children will turn against their parents and send them to their death. [22] Everyone will hate you for your allegiance to me, but whoever endures to the end will be saved. [23] When you are persecuted in one town, take refuge in another; truly I tell you: before you have gone through all the towns of Israel the Son of Man will have come.

[24] 'No pupil ranks above his teacher, no servant above his master. [25] The pupil should be content to share his teacher's lot, the servant to share his master's. If the master has been called Beelzebul, how much more his household!

[26] 'So do not be afraid of them. There is nothing covered up that will not be uncovered, nothing hidden that will not be made known. [27] What I say to you in the dark you must repeat in broad daylight; what you hear whispered you must shout from the housetops. [28] Do not fear those who kill the body, but cannot kill the soul. Fear him rather who is able to destroy both soul and body in hell.

[29] 'Are not two sparrows sold for a penny? Yet without your Father's knowledge not one of them can fall to the ground. [30] As for you, even the hairs of your head have all been counted. [31] So do not be afraid; you are worth more than any number of sparrows.

[32] 'Whoever will acknowledge me before others, I will acknowledge before my Father in heaven; [33] and whoever disowns me before others, I will disown before my Father in heaven.

[34] 'You must not think that I have come to bring peace to the earth; I have not come to bring peace, but a sword. [35] I have come to set a man against his father, a daughter against her mother, a daughter-in-law against her mother-in-law; [36] and a man will find his enemies under his own roof.

[37] 'No one is worthy of me who cares more for father or mother than for me; no one is worthy of me who cares more for son or daughter; [38] no one is worthy of me who does not take up his cross and follow me. [39] Whoever gains his life will lose it; whoever loses his life for my sake will gain it.

[40] 'To receive you is to receive me, and to receive me is to receive the One who sent me. [41] Whoever receives a prophet because he is a prophet will be given a prophet's reward, and whoever receives a good man because he is a good man will be given a good man's reward. [42] Truly I tell you: anyone who gives so much as a cup of cold water to one of these little ones because he is a disciple of mine, will certainly not go unrewarded.'

11 When Jesus had finished giving instructions to his twelve disciples, he went from there to teach and preach in the neighbouring towns.

Recognizing the Messiah

[2] JOHN, who was in prison, heard what Christ was doing, and sent his own disciples [3] to put this question to him: 'Are you the one who is to come, or are we to expect someone else?' [4] Jesus answered, 'Go and report to John what you hear and see: [5] the blind recover their sight, the lame walk, lepers are made clean, the deaf hear, the dead are raised to life, the poor are brought good news— [6] and blessed are those who do not find me an obstacle to faith.'

[7] When the messengers were on their way back, Jesus began to speak to the crowds about John: 'What was the spectacle that drew you to the wilderness? A reed swaying in the wind? [8] No? Then what did you go out to see? A man dressed in finery? Fine clothes are to be found in palaces. [9] But why did you go out? To see a prophet? Yes indeed, and far more than a prophet. [10] He is the man of whom scripture says,

Here is my herald, whom I send
   ahead of you,
and he will prepare your way before
   you.

¹¹ 'Truly I tell you: among all who have ever been born, no one has been greater than John the Baptist, and yet the least in the kingdom of Heaven is greater than he.

¹² 'Since the time of John the Baptist the kingdom of Heaven has been subjected to violence and violent men are taking it by force. ¹³ For until John, all the prophets and the law foretold things to come; ¹⁴ and John is the destined Elijah, if you will but accept it. ¹⁵ If you have ears, then hear.

¹⁶ 'How can I describe this generation? They are like children sitting in the market-place and calling to each other,

¹⁷ We piped for you and you would not dance.

We lamented, and you would not mourn.

¹⁸ 'For John came, neither eating nor drinking, and people say, "He is possessed"; ¹⁹ the Son of Man came, eating and drinking, and they say, "Look at him! A glutton and a drinker, a friend of tax-collectors and sinners!" Yet God's wisdom is proved right by its results.'

²⁰ Then he spoke of the towns in which most of his miracles had been performed, and denounced them for their impenitence. ²¹ 'Alas for you, Chorazin!' he said. 'Alas for you, Bethsaida! If the miracles performed in you had taken place in Tyre and Sidon, they would have repented long ago in sackcloth and ashes. ²² But it will be more bearable, I tell you, for Tyre and Sidon on the day of judgement than for you. ²³ As for you, Capernaum, will you be exalted to heaven? No, you will be brought down to Hades! For if the miracles performed in you had taken place in Sodom, Sodom would be standing to this day. ²⁴ But it will be more bearable, I tell you, for the land of Sodom on the day of judgement than for you.'

²⁵ At that time Jesus spoke these words: 'I thank you, Father, Lord of heaven and earth, for hiding these things from the learned and wise, and revealing them to the simple. ²⁶ Yes, Father, such was your choice. ²⁷ Everything is entrusted to me by my Father; and no one knows the Son but the Father, and no one knows the Father

but the Son and those to whom the Son chooses to reveal him.

²⁸ 'Come to me, all who are weary and whose load is heavy; I will give you rest. ²⁹ Take my yoke upon you, and learn from me, for I am gentle and humble-hearted; and you will find rest for your souls. ³⁰ For my yoke is easy to wear, my load is light.'

Opposition to Jesus

12 About that time Jesus was going through the cornfields on the sabbath; and his disciples, feeling hungry, began to pluck some ears of corn and eat them. ² When the Pharisees saw this, they said to him, 'Look, your disciples are doing what is forbidden on the sabbath.' ³ He answered, 'Have you not read what David did when he and his men were hungry? ⁴ He went into the house of God and ate the sacred bread, though neither he nor his men had a right to eat it, but only the priests. ⁵ Or have you not read in the law that on the sabbath the priests in the temple break the sabbath and they are not held to be guilty? ⁶ But I tell you, there is something greater than the temple here. ⁷ If you had known what this text means, "It is mercy I require, not sacrifice," you would not have condemned the innocent. ⁸ For the Son of Man is lord of the sabbath.'

⁹ He went on to another place, and entered their synagogue. ¹⁰ A man was there with a withered arm, and they asked Jesus, 'Is it permitted to heal on the sabbath?' (They wanted to bring a charge against him.) ¹¹ But he said to them, 'Suppose you had one sheep, and it fell into a ditch on the sabbath; is there a single one of you who would not catch hold of it and lift it out? ¹² Surely a man is worth far more than a sheep! It is therefore permitted to do good on the sabbath.' ¹³ Then he said to the man, 'Stretch out your arm.' He stretched it out, and it was made sound again like the other. ¹⁴ But the Pharisees, on leaving the synagogue, plotted to bring about Jesus's death.

¹⁵ Jesus was aware of it and withdrew, and many followed him. He healed all who were ill, ¹⁶ and gave strict instructions that they were not to make him known. ¹⁷ This was to fulfil Isaiah's prophecy:

11:12 has been ... force: *or* has been forcing its way forward, and men of force are seizing it.   11:26 Yes ... such: *or* Yes, I thank you, Father, that such.

¹⁸ Here is my servant, whom I have
     chosen,
   my beloved, in whom I take delight;
   I will put my Spirit upon him,
   and he will proclaim justice among
     the nations.
¹⁹ He will not strive, he will not shout,
   nor will his voice be heard in the
     streets.
²⁰ He will not snap off a broken reed,
   nor snuff out a smouldering wick,
   until he leads justice on to victory.
²¹ In him the nations shall put their
     hope.

²² THEN they brought him a man who was possessed by a demon; he was blind and dumb, and Jesus cured him, restoring both speech and sight. ²³ The bystanders were all amazed, and the word went round: 'Can this be the Son of David?' ²⁴ But when the Pharisees heard it they said, 'It is only by Beelzebul prince of devils that this man drives the devils out.'

²⁵ Knowing what was in their minds, he said to them, 'Every kingdom divided against itself is laid waste; and no town or household that is divided against itself can stand. ²⁶ And if it is Satan who drives out Satan, he is divided against himself; how then can his kingdom stand? ²⁷ If it is by Beelzebul that I drive out devils, by whom do your own people drive them out? If this is your argument, they themselves will refute you. ²⁸ But if it is by the Spirit of God that I drive out the devils, then be sure the kingdom of God has already come upon you.

²⁹ 'Or again, how can anyone break into a strong man's house and make off with his goods, unless he has first tied up the strong man? Then he can ransack the house.

³⁰ 'He who is not with me is against me, and he who does not gather with me scatters.

³¹ 'So I tell you this: every sin and every slander can be forgiven, except slander spoken against the Spirit; that will not be forgiven. ³² Anyone who speaks a word against the Son of Man will be forgiven; but if anyone speaks against the Holy Spirit, for him there will be no forgiveness, either in this age or in the age to come.

³³ 'Get a good tree and its fruit will be good; get a bad tree and its fruit will be bad. You can tell a tree by its fruit. ³⁴ Vipers' brood! How can your words be good when you yourselves are evil? It is from the fullness of the heart that the mouth speaks. ³⁵ Good people from their store of good produce good; and evil people from their store of evil produce evil.

³⁶ 'I tell you this: every thoughtless word you speak you will have to account for on the day of judgement. ³⁷ For out of your own mouth you will be acquitted; out of your own mouth you will be condemned.'

³⁸ At this some of the scribes and the Pharisees said, 'Teacher, we would like you to show us a sign.' ³⁹ He answered: 'It is a wicked, godless generation that asks for a sign, and the only sign that will be given it is the sign of the prophet Jonah. ⁴⁰ Just as Jonah was in the sea monster's belly for three days and three nights, so the Son of Man will be three days and three nights in the bowels of the earth. ⁴¹ The men of Nineveh will appear in court when this generation is on trial, and ensure its condemnation, for they repented at the preaching of Jonah; and what is here is greater than Jonah. ⁴² The queen of the south will appear in court when this generation is on trial, and ensure its condemnation; for she came from the ends of the earth to listen to the wisdom of Solomon, and what is here is greater than Solomon.

⁴³ 'When an unclean spirit comes out of someone it wanders over the desert sands seeking a resting-place, and finds none. ⁴⁴ Then it says, "I will go back to the home I left." So it returns and finds the house unoccupied, swept clean, and tidy. ⁴⁵ It goes off and collects seven other spirits more wicked than itself, and they all come in and settle there; and in the end that person's plight is worse than before. That is how it will be with this wicked generation.'

⁴⁶ He was still speaking to the crowd when his mother and brothers appeared; they stood outside, wanting to speak to him. ⁴⁷ Someone said, 'Your mother and your brothers are standing outside; they want to speak to you.' ⁴⁸ Jesus turned to the man who brought the message, and said, 'Who is my mother? Who are my brothers?' ⁴⁹ and pointing to his disciples,

12:41 will appear ... trial: *or* will rise again with this generation at the judgement.   12:42 The queen ...
trial: *or* The queen of the south will be raised to life with this generation at the judgement.

he said, 'Here are my mother and my brothers. [50] Whoever does the will of my heavenly Father is my brother and sister and mother.'

Parables

13 THAT same day Jesus went out and sat by the lakeside, [2] where so many people gathered round him that he had to get into a boat. He sat there, and all the people stood on the shore. [3] He told them many things in parables.

He said: 'A sower went out to sow. [4] And as he sowed, some of the seed fell along the footpath; and the birds came and ate it up. [5] Some fell on rocky ground, where it had little soil, and it sprouted quickly because it had no depth of earth; [6] but when the sun rose it was scorched, and as it had no root it withered away. [7] Some fell among thistles; and the thistles grew up and choked it. [8] And some of the seed fell on good soil, where it produced a crop, some a hundredfold, some sixtyfold, and some thirtyfold. [9] If you have ears, then hear.'

[10] The disciples came to him and asked, 'Why do you speak to them in parables?' [11] He replied, 'To you it has been granted to know the secrets of the kingdom of Heaven, but not to them. [12] For those who have will be given more, till they have enough and to spare; and those who have not will forfeit even what they have. [13] That is why I speak to them in parables; for they look without seeing, and listen without hearing or understanding. [14] The prophecy of Isaiah is being fulfilled in them: "You may listen and listen, but you will never understand; you may look and look, but you will never see. [15] For this people's mind has become dull; they have stopped their ears and shut their eyes. Otherwise, their eyes might see, their ears hear, and their mind understand, and then they might turn to me, and I would heal them."

[16] 'But happy are your eyes because they see, and your ears because they hear! [17] Truly I tell you: many prophets and saints longed to see what you now see, yet never saw it; to hear what you hear, yet never heard it.

[18] 'Hear then the parable of the sower. [19] When anyone hears the word that tells of the Kingdom, but fails to understand it, the evil one comes and carries off what has been sown in his heart; that is the seed sown along the footpath. [20] The seed sown on rocky ground stands for the person who hears the word and accepts it at once with joy; [21] it strikes no root in him and he has no staying-power; when there is trouble or persecution on account of the word he quickly loses faith. [22] The seed sown among thistles represents the person who hears the word, but worldly cares and the false glamour of wealth choke it, and it proves barren. [23] But the seed sown on good soil is the person who hears the word and understands it; he does bear fruit and yields a hundredfold, or sixtyfold, or thirtyfold.'

[24] Here is another parable he gave them: 'The kingdom of Heaven is like this. A man sowed his field with good seed; [25] but while everyone was asleep his enemy came, sowed darnel among the wheat, and made off. [26] When the corn sprouted and began to fill out, the darnel could be seen among it. [27] The farmer's men went to their master and said, "Sir, was it not good seed that you sowed in your field? So where has the darnel come from?" [28] "This is an enemy's doing," he replied. "Well then," they said, "shall we go and gather the darnel?" [29] "No," he answered; "in gathering it you might pull up the wheat at the same time. [30] Let them both grow together till harvest; and at harvest time I will tell the reapers, 'Gather the darnel first, and tie it in bundles for burning; then collect the wheat into my barn.'"'

[31] This is another parable he gave them: 'The kingdom of Heaven is like a mustard seed, which a man took and sowed in his field. [32] Mustard is smaller than any other seed, but when it has grown it is taller than other plants; it becomes a tree, big enough for the birds to come and roost among its branches.'

[33] He told them also this parable: 'The kingdom of Heaven is like yeast, which a woman took and mixed with three measures of flour till it was all leavened.'

[34] In all this teaching to the crowds Jesus spoke in parables; indeed he never spoke to them except in parables. [35] This was to fulfil the saying of the prophet:

13:35 *prophet: some witnesses add* Isaiah.

I will open my mouth in parables;
I will utter things kept secret since
　　the world was made.

36 Then he sent the people away, and
went into the house, where his disciples
came to him and said, 'Explain to us the
parable of the darnel in the field.' 37 He
replied, 'The sower of the good seed is the
Son of Man. 38 The field is the world; the
good seed stands for the children of the
Kingdom, the darnel for the children of
the evil one, 39 and the enemy who sowed
the darnel is the devil. The harvest is the
end of time, and the reapers are angels.
40 As the darnel is gathered up and burnt,
so at the end of time 41 the Son of Man will
send his angels, who will gather out of his
kingdom every cause of sin, and all whose
deeds are evil; 42 these will be thrown into
the blazing furnace, where there will be
wailing and grinding of teeth. 43 Then the
righteous will shine like the sun in the
kingdom of their Father. If you have ears,
then hear.

44 'The kingdom of Heaven is like
treasure which a man found buried in a
field. He buried it again, and in joy went
and sold everything he had, and bought
the field.

45 'Again, the kingdom of Heaven is like
this. A merchant looking out for fine
pearls 46 found one of very special value;
so he went and sold everything he had
and bought it.

47 'Again the kingdom of Heaven is like
a net cast into the sea, where it caught
fish of every kind. 48 When it was full, it
was hauled ashore. Then the men sat
down and collected the good fish into
baskets and threw the worthless away.
49 That is how it will be at the end of time.
The angels will go out, and they will
separate the wicked from the good, 50 and
throw them into the blazing furnace,
where there will be wailing and grinding
of teeth.

51 'Have you understood all this?' he
asked; and they answered, 'Yes.' 52 So he
said to them, 'When, therefore, a teacher
of the law has become a learner in the
kingdom of Heaven, he is like a householder who can produce from his store
things new and old.'

53 WHEN Jesus had finished these parables
he left that place, 54 and came to his home

town, where he taught the people in their
synagogue. In amazement they asked,
'Where does he get this wisdom from, and
these miraculous powers? 55 Is he not the
carpenter's son? Is not his mother called
Mary, his brothers James, Joseph, Simon,
and Judas? 56 And are not all his sisters
here with us? Where does he get all this
from?' 57 So they turned against him.
Jesus said to them, 'A prophet never lacks
honour, except in his home town and in
his own family.' 58 And he did not do
many miracles there, such was their want
of faith.

Death of John the Baptist

14 IT was at that time that reports
about Jesus reached Herod the
tetrarch. 2 'This is John the Baptist,' he
said to his attendants; 'he has been raised
from the dead, and that is why these
miraculous powers are at work in him.'

3 Now Herod had arrested John, put
him in chains, and thrown him into
prison, on account of Herodias, his
brother Philip's wife; 4 for John had told
him: 'You have no right to her.' 5 Herod
would have liked to put him to death, but
he was afraid of the people, in whose eyes
John was a prophet. 6 But at his birthday
celebrations the daughter of Herodias
danced before the guests, and Herod was
so delighted 7 that he promised on oath
to give her anything she asked for.
8 Prompted by her mother, she said, 'Give
me here on a dish the head of John the
Baptist.' 9 At this the king was distressed,
but because of his oath and his guests, he
ordered the request to be granted, 10 and
had John beheaded in prison. 11 The head
was brought on a dish and given to the
girl; and she carried it to her mother.
12 Then John's disciples came and took
away the body, and buried it; and they
went and told Jesus.

More miracles and teaching

13 WHEN he heard what had happened
Jesus withdrew privately by boat to a
remote place; but large numbers of people
heard of it, and came after him on foot
from the towns. 14 When he came ashore
and saw a large crowd, his heart went out
to them, and he healed those who were
sick. 15 As evening drew on, the disciples
came up to him and said, 'This is a remote
place and the day has gone; send the

people off to the villages to buy themselves food.' [16] Jesus answered, 'There is no need for them to go; give them something to eat yourselves.' [17] 'All we have here', they said, 'is five loaves and two fish.' [18] 'Bring them to me,' he replied. [19] So he told the people to sit down on the grass; then, taking the five loaves and the two fish, he looked up to heaven, said the blessing, broke the loaves, and gave them to the disciples; and the disciples gave them to the people. [20] They all ate and were satisfied; and twelve baskets were filled with what was left over. [21] Some five thousand men shared in this meal, not counting women and children.

[22] As soon as they had finished, he made the disciples embark and cross to the other side ahead of him, while he dismissed the crowd; [23] then he went up the hill by himself to pray. It had grown late, and he was there alone. [24] The boat was already some distance from the shore, battling with a head wind and a rough sea. [25] Between three and six in the morning he came towards them, walking across the lake. [26] When the disciples saw him walking on the lake they were so shaken that they cried out in terror: 'It is a ghost!' [27] But at once Jesus spoke to them: 'Take heart! It is I; do not be afraid.'

[28] Peter called to him: 'Lord, if it is you, tell me to come to you over the water.' [29] 'Come,' said Jesus. Peter got down out of the boat, and walked over the water towards Jesus. [30] But when he saw the strength of the gale he was afraid; and beginning to sink, he cried, 'Save me, Lord!' [31] Jesus at once reached out and caught hold of him. 'Why did you hesitate?' he said. 'How little faith you have!' [32] Then they climbed into the boat; and the wind dropped. [33] And the men in the boat fell at his feet, exclaiming, 'You must be the Son of God.'

[34] So they completed the crossing and landed at Gennesaret. [35] The people there recognized Jesus and sent word to all the country round. They brought to him all who were ill [36] and begged him to let them simply touch the edge of his cloak; and all who touched it were completely cured.

15 THEN Jesus was approached by a group of Pharisees and scribes from Jerusalem, with the question:

[2] 'Why do your disciples break the ancient tradition? They do not wash their hands before eating.' [3] He answered them: 'And what about you? Why do you break God's commandment in the interest of your tradition? [4] For God said, "Honour your father and mother," and "Whoever curses his father or mother shall be put to death." [5] But you say, "Whoever says to his father or mother, 'Anything I have which might have been used for your benefit is set apart for God'," [6] must not honour his father or his mother." You have made God's law null and void out of regard for your tradition. [7] What hypocrites! How right Isaiah was when he prophesied about you: [8] "This people pays me lip-service, but their heart is far from me; [9] they worship me in vain, for they teach as doctrines the commandments of men."'

[10] He called the crowd and said to them, 'Listen and understand! [11] No one is defiled by what goes into his mouth; only by what comes out of it.'

[12] Then the disciples came to him and said, 'Do you know that the Pharisees have taken great offence at what you have been saying?' [13] He answered: 'Any plant that is not of my heavenly Father's planting will be rooted up. [14] Leave them alone; they are blind guides, and if one blind man guides another they will both fall into the ditch.'

[15] Then Peter said, 'Tell us what that parable means.' [16] Jesus said, 'Are you still as dull as the rest? [17] Do you not see that whatever goes in by the mouth passes into the stomach and so is discharged into the drain? [18] But what comes out of the mouth has its origins in the heart; and that is what defiles a person. [19] Wicked thoughts, murder, adultery, fornication, theft, perjury, slander—these all proceed from the heart; [20] and these are the things that defile a person; but to eat without first washing his hands, that cannot defile him.'

[21] JESUS then withdrew to the region of Tyre and Sidon. [22] And a Canaanite woman from those parts came to meet him crying, 'Son of David! Have pity on me; my daughter is tormented by a devil.' [23] But he said not a word in reply. His

14:36 edge: *or* tassel.   15:14 blind guides: *some witnesses add* of blind men.

14

disciples came and urged him: 'Send her away! See how she comes shouting after us.' [24] Jesus replied, 'I was sent to the lost sheep of the house of Israel, and to them alone.' [25] But the woman came and fell at his feet and cried, 'Help me, sir.' [26] Jesus replied, 'It is not right to take the children's bread and throw it to the dogs.' [27] 'True, sir,' she answered, 'and yet the dogs eat the scraps that fall from their master's table.' [28] Hearing this Jesus replied, 'What faith you have! Let it be as you wish!' And from that moment her daughter was restored to health.

[29] After leaving that region Jesus took the road by the sea of Galilee, where he climbed a hill and sat down. [30] Crowds flocked to him, bringing with them the lame, blind, dumb, and crippled, and many other sufferers; they put them down at his feet, and he healed them. [31] Great was the amazement of the people when they saw the dumb speaking, the crippled made strong, the lame walking, and the blind with their sight restored; and they gave praise to the God of Israel.

[32] Jesus called his disciples and said to them, 'My heart goes out to these people; they have been with me now for three days and have nothing to eat. I do not want to send them away hungry; they might faint on the way.' [33] The disciples replied, 'Where in this remote place can we find bread enough to feed such a crowd?' [34] 'How many loaves have you?' Jesus asked. 'Seven,' they replied, 'and a few small fish.' [35] So he ordered the people to sit down on the ground; [36] then he took the seven loaves and the fish, and after giving thanks to God he broke them and gave them to the disciples, and the disciples gave them to the people. [37] They all ate and were satisfied; and seven baskets were filled with what was left over. [38] Those who were fed numbered four thousand men, not counting women and children. [39] After dismissing the crowd, he got into a boat and went to the neighbourhood of Magadan.

16 The Pharisees and Sadducees came, and to test him they asked him to show them a sign from heaven. [2] He answered: [4] 'It is a wicked, godless generation that asks for a sign; and the only sign that will be given it is the sign of Jonah.' With that he left them and went away.

[5] In crossing to the other side the disciples had forgotten to take any bread. [6] So when Jesus said to them, 'Take care; be on your guard against the leaven of the Pharisees and Sadducees,' [7] they began to say to one another, 'We have brought no bread!' [8] Knowing what they were discussing, Jesus said, 'Why are you talking about having no bread? Where is your faith? [9] Do you still not understand? Have you forgotten the five loaves for the five thousand, and how many basketfuls you picked up? [10] Or the seven loaves for the four thousand, and how many basketfuls you picked up? [11] How can you fail to see that I was not talking about bread? Be on your guard, I said, against the leaven of the Pharisees and Sadducees.' [12] Then they understood: they were to be on their guard, not against baker's leaven, but against the teaching of the Pharisees and Sadducees.

Jesus the Son of God

[13] WHEN he came to the territory of Caesarea Philippi, Jesus asked his disciples, 'Who do people say that the Son of Man is?' [14] They answered, 'Some say John the Baptist, others Elijah, others Jeremiah, or one of the prophets.' [15] 'And you,' he asked, 'who do you say I am?' [16] Simon Peter answered: 'You are the Messiah, the Son of the living God.' [17] Then Jesus said: 'Simon son of Jonah, you are favoured indeed! You did not learn that from any human being; it was revealed to you by my heavenly Father. [18] And I say to you: you are Peter, the Rock; and on this rock I will build my church, and the powers of death shall never conquer it. [19] I will give you the keys of the kingdom of Heaven; what you forbid on earth shall be forbidden in heaven, and what you allow on earth shall be allowed in heaven.' [20] He then gave his disciples strict orders not to tell anyone that he was the Messiah.

[21] From that time Jesus began to make it

16:2 **He answered**: *some witnesses here insert* 'In the evening you say, "It will be fine weather, for the sky is red"; [3] and in the morning you say, "It will be stormy today; the sky is red and lowering." You know how to interpret the appearance of the sky; can you not interpret the signs of the times?'   16:18 **powers of death**: *lit.* gates of Hades.

clear to his disciples that he had to go to Jerusalem, and endure great suffering at the hands of the elders, chief priests, and scribes; to be put to death, and to be raised again on the third day. ²²At this Peter took hold of him and began to rebuke him: 'Heaven forbid!' he said. 'No, Lord, this shall never happen to you.' ²³Then Jesus turned and said to Peter, 'Out of my sight, Satan; you are a stumbling block to me. You think as men think, not as God thinks.'

²⁴Jesus then said to his disciples, 'Anyone who wishes to be a follower of mine must renounce self; he must take up his cross and follow me. ²⁵⁻²⁶Whoever wants to save his life will lose it, but whoever loses his life for my sake will find it. What will anyone gain by winning the whole world at the cost of his life? Or what can he give to buy his life back? ²⁷For the Son of Man is to come in the glory of his Father with his angels, and then he will give everyone his due reward. ²⁸Truly I tell you: there are some of those standing here who will not taste death before they have seen the Son of Man coming in his kingdom.'

17 Six days later Jesus took Peter, James, and John the brother of James, and led them up a high mountain by themselves. ²And in their presence he was transfigured; his face shone like the sun, and his clothes became a brilliant white. ³And they saw Moses and Elijah appear, talking with him. ⁴Then Peter spoke: 'Lord,' he said, 'it is good that we are here. Would you like me to make three shelters here, one for you, one for Moses, and one for Elijah?' ⁵While he was still speaking, a bright cloud suddenly cast its shadow over them, and a voice called from the cloud: 'This is my beloved Son, in whom I take delight; listen to him.' ⁶At the sound of the voice the disciples fell on their faces in terror. ⁷Then Jesus came up to them, touched them, and said, 'Stand up; do not be afraid.' ⁸And when they raised their eyes there was no one but Jesus to be seen.

⁹On their way down the mountain, Jesus commanded them not to tell anyone of the vision until the Son of Man had been raised from the dead. ¹⁰The disciples put a question to him: 'Why then do the scribes say that Elijah must come first?' ¹¹He replied, 'Elijah is to come and set everything right. ¹²But I tell you that Elijah has already come, and they failed to recognize him, and did to him as they wanted; in the same way the Son of Man is to suffer at their hands.' ¹³Then the disciples understood that he meant John the Baptist.

¹⁴When they returned to the crowd, a man came up to Jesus, fell on his knees before him, and said, ¹⁵'Have pity, sir, on my son: he is epileptic and has bad fits; he keeps falling into the fire or into the water. ¹⁶I brought him to your disciples, but they could not cure him.' ¹⁷Jesus answered, 'What an unbelieving and perverse generation! How long shall I be with you? How long must I endure you? Bring him here to me.' ¹⁸Then Jesus spoke sternly to him; the demon left the boy, and from that moment he was cured.

¹⁹Afterwards the disciples came to Jesus and asked him privately, 'Why could we not drive it out?' ²⁰He answered, 'Your faith is too small. Truly I tell you: if you have faith no bigger than a mustard seed, you will say to this mountain, "Move from here to there!" and it will move; nothing will be impossible for you.'

²²THEY were going about together in Galilee when Jesus said to them, 'The Son of Man is to be handed over into the power of men, ²³and they will kill him; then on the third day he will be raised again.' And they were filled with grief.

²⁴On their arrival at Capernaum the collectors of the temple tax came up to Peter and asked, 'Does your master not pay temple tax?' ²⁵'He does,' said Peter. When he went indoors Jesus forestalled him by asking, 'Tell me, Simon, from whom do earthly monarchs collect tribute money? From their own people, or from aliens?' ²⁶'From aliens,' said Peter. 'Yes,' said Jesus, 'and their own people are exempt. ²⁷But as we do not want to cause offence, go and cast a line in the lake; take the first fish you catch, open its mouth, and you will find a silver coin; take that and pay the tax for us both.'

17:5 **This ... Son:** *or* This is my only Son. 17:20 **impossible for you:** *some witnesses add* ²¹But there is no means of driving out this sort but prayer and fasting.

Teaching about the kingdom

18 AT that time the disciples came to Jesus and asked, 'Who is the greatest in the kingdom of Heaven?' [2] He called a child, set him in front of them, [3] and said, 'Truly I tell you: unless you turn round and become like children, you will never enter the kingdom of Heaven. [4] Whoever humbles himself and becomes like this child will be the greatest in the kingdom of Heaven, [5] and whoever receives one such child in my name receives me. [6] But if anyone causes the downfall of one of these little ones who believe in me, it would be better for him to have a millstone hung round his neck and be drowned in the depths of the sea. [7] Alas for the world that any of them should be made to fall! Such things must happen, but alas for the one through whom they happen!

[8] 'If your hand or your foot causes your downfall, cut it off and fling it away; it is better for you to enter into life maimed or lame, than to keep two hands or two feet and be thrown into the eternal fire. [9] And if your eye causes your downfall, tear it out and fling it away; it is better to enter into life with one eye than to keep both eyes and be thrown into the fires of hell.

[10] 'See that you do not despise one of these little ones; I tell you, they have their angels in heaven, who look continually on the face of my heavenly Father.

[12] 'What do you think? Suppose someone has a hundred sheep, and one of them strays, does he not leave the other ninety-nine on the hillside and go in search of the one that strayed? [13] Truly I tell you: if he should find it, he is more delighted over that sheep than over the ninety-nine that did not stray. [14] In the same way, it is not your heavenly Father's will that one of these little ones should be lost.

[15] 'If your brother does wrong, go and take the matter up with him, strictly between yourselves. If he listens to you, you have won your brother over. [16] But if he will not listen, take one or two others with you, so that every case may be settled on the evidence of two or three witnesses. [17] If he refuses to listen to them, report the matter to the congregation; and if he will not listen even to the congregation, then treat him as you would a pagan or a tax-collector.

[18] 'Truly I tell you: whatever you forbid on earth shall be forbidden in heaven, and whatever you allow on earth shall be allowed in heaven.

[19] 'And again I tell you: if two of you agree on earth about any request you have to make, that request will be granted by my heavenly Father. [20] For where two or three meet together in my name, I am there among them.'

[21] Then Peter came to him and asked, 'Lord, how often am I to forgive my brother if he goes on wronging me? As many as seven times?' [22] Jesus replied, 'I do not say seven times but seventy times seven.

[23] 'The kingdom of Heaven, therefore, should be thought of in this way: There was once a king who decided to settle accounts with the men who served him. [24] At the outset there appeared before him a man who owed ten thousand talents. [25] Since he had no means of paying, his master ordered him to be sold, with his wife, his children, and everything he had, to meet the debt. [26] The man fell at his master's feet. "Be patient with me," he implored, "and I will pay you in full"; [27] and the master was so moved with pity that he let the man go and cancelled the debt. [28] But no sooner had the man gone out than he met a fellow-servant who owed him a hundred denarii; he took hold of him, seizing him by the throat, and said, "Pay me what you owe." [29] The man fell at his fellow-servant's feet, and begged him, "Be patient with me, and I will pay you"; [30] but he refused, and had him thrown into jail until he should pay the debt. [31] The other servants were deeply distressed when they saw what had happened, and they went to their master and told him the whole story. [32] Then he sent for the man and said, "You scoundrel! I cancelled the whole of your debt when you appealed to me; [33] ought you not to have shown mercy to your fellow-servant just as I showed mercy to you?" [34] And so angry was the master that he condemned the man to be tortured until he should pay the debt in full. [35] That is how my heavenly Father

18:10 **Father**: *some witnesses add* [11] For the Son of Man came to save the lost.   18:15 **wrong**: *some witnesses add* to you.   18:22 **seventy times seven**: *or* seventy-seven times.   18:24 **talents**: *see p. xi.*   18:28 **denarii**: *see p. xi.*

will deal with you, unless you each forgive your brother from your hearts.'

On the road to Jerusalem

19 WHEN Jesus had finished this discourse he left Galilee and came into the region of Judaea on the other side of the Jordan. ²Great crowds followed him, and he healed them there.

³Some Pharisees came and tested him by asking, 'Is it lawful for a man to divorce his wife for any cause he pleases?' ⁴He responded by asking, 'Have you never read that in the beginning the Creator made them male and female?' ⁵and he added, 'That is why a man leaves his father and mother, and is united to his wife, and the two become one flesh. ⁶It follows that they are no longer two individuals: they are one flesh. Therefore what God has joined together, man must not separate.' ⁷'Then why', they objected, 'did Moses lay it down that a man might divorce his wife by a certificate of dismissal?' ⁸He answered, 'It was because of your stubbornness that Moses gave you permission to divorce your wives; but it was not like that at the beginning. ⁹I tell you, if a man divorces his wife for any cause other than unchastity, and marries another, he commits adultery.'

¹⁰The disciples said to him, 'If that is how things stand for a man with a wife, it is better not to marry.' ¹¹To this he replied, 'That is a course not everyone can accept, but only those for whom God has appointed it. ¹²For while some are incapable of marriage because they were born so, or were made so by men, there are others who have renounced marriage for the sake of the kingdom of Heaven. Let those accept who can.'

¹³They brought children for him to lay his hands on them with prayer. The disciples rebuked them, ¹⁴but Jesus said, 'Let the children come to me; do not try to stop them; for the kingdom of Heaven belongs to such as these.' ¹⁵And he laid his hands on the children, and went on his way.

¹⁶A man came up and asked him, 'Teacher, what good must I do to gain eternal life?' ¹⁷'Good?' said Jesus. 'Why

do you ask me about that? One alone is good. But if you wish to enter into life, keep the commandments.' ¹⁸'Which commandments?' he asked. Jesus answered, 'Do not murder; do not commit adultery; do not steal; do not give false evidence; ¹⁹honour your father and mother; and love your neighbour as yourself.' ²⁰The young man answered, 'I have kept all these. What do I still lack?' ²¹Jesus said to him, 'If you wish to be perfect, go, sell your possessions, and give to the poor, and you will have treasure in heaven; then come and follow me.' ²²When the young man heard this, he went away with a heavy heart; for he was a man of great wealth.

²³Jesus said to his disciples, 'Truly I tell you: a rich man will find it hard to enter the kingdom of Heaven. ²⁴I repeat, it is easier for a camel to pass through the eye of a needle than for a rich man to enter the kingdom of God.' ²⁵The disciples were astonished when they heard this, and exclaimed, 'Then who can be saved?' ²⁶Jesus looked at them and said, 'For men this is impossible; but everything is possible for God.'

²⁷Then Peter said, 'What about us? We have left everything to follow you. How shall we fare?' ²⁸Jesus replied, 'Truly I tell you: in the world that is to be, when the Son of Man is seated on his glorious throne, you also will sit on twelve thrones, judging the twelve tribes of Israel. ²⁹And anyone who has left houses, or brothers or sisters, or father or mother, or children, or land for the sake of my name will be repaid many times over, and gain eternal life. ³⁰But many who are first will be last, and the last first.

20 'The kingdom of Heaven is like this. There was once a landowner who went out early one morning to hire labourers for his vineyard; ²and after agreeing to pay them the usual day's wage he sent them off to work. ³Three hours later he went out again and saw some more men standing idle in the market-place. ⁴"Go and join the others in the vineyard," he said, "and I will pay you a fair wage"; so off they went. ⁵At midday he went out again, and at three in the afternoon, and made the same

---

19:9 **adultery:** *some witnesses add* And the man who marries a woman so divorced commits adultery.
20:2 **the … wage:** *lit.* one denarius for the day.

arrangement as before. ⁶An hour before sunset he went out and found another group standing there; so he said to them, "Why are you standing here all day doing nothing?" ⁷"Because no one has hired us," they replied; so he told them, "Go and join the others in the vineyard." ⁸When evening fell, the owner of the vineyard said to the overseer, "Call the labourers and give them their pay, beginning with those who came last and ending with the first." ⁹Those who had started work an hour before sunset came forward, and were paid the full day's wage. ¹⁰When it was the turn of the men who had come first, they expected something extra, but were paid the same as the others. ¹¹As they took it, they grumbled at their employer: ¹²"These latecomers did only one hour's work, yet you have treated them on a level with us, who have sweated the whole day long in the blazing sun!" ¹³The owner turned to one of them and said, "My friend, I am not being unfair to you. You agreed on the usual wage for the day, did you not? ¹⁴Take your pay and go home. I choose to give the last man the same as you. ¹⁵Surely I am free to do what I like with my own money? Why be jealous because I am generous?" ¹⁶So the last will be first, and the first last.'

¹⁷JESUS was journeying towards Jerusalem, and on the way he took the Twelve aside and said to them, ¹⁸'We are now going up to Jerusalem, and the Son of Man will be handed over to the chief priests and the scribes; they will condemn him to death ¹⁹and hand him over to the Gentiles, to be mocked and flogged and crucified; and on the third day he will be raised to life again.'

²⁰The mother of Zebedee's sons then approached him with her sons. She bowed before him and begged a favour. ²¹'What is it you want?' asked Jesus. She replied, 'Give orders that in your kingdom these two sons of mine may sit next to you, one at your right hand and the other at your left.' ²²Jesus turned to the brothers and said, 'You do not understand what you are asking. Can you drink the cup that I am to drink?' 'We can,' they

replied. ²³'You shall indeed drink my cup,' he said; 'but to sit on my right or on my left is not for me to grant; that honour is for those to whom it has already been assigned by my Father.'

²⁴When the other ten heard this, they were indignant with the two brothers. ²⁵So Jesus called them to him and said, 'You know that, among the Gentiles, rulers lord it over their subjects, and the great make their authority felt. ²⁶It shall not be so with you; among you, whoever wants to be great must be your servant, ²⁷and whoever wants to be first must be the slave of all—²⁸just as the Son of Man did not come to be served but to serve, and to give his life as a ransom for many.'

²⁹As they were leaving Jericho he was followed by a huge crowd. ³⁰At the roadside sat two blind men. When they heard that Jesus was passing by they shouted, 'Have pity on us, Son of David.' ³¹People told them to be quiet, but they shouted all the more, 'Sir, have pity on us; have pity on us, Son of David.' ³²Jesus stopped and called the men. 'What do you want me to do for you?' ³³he asked. 'Sir,' they answered, 'open our eyes.' ³⁴Jesus was deeply moved, and touched their eyes. At once they recovered their sight and followed him.

Jesus in the temple

21 THEY were approaching Jerusalem, and when they reached Bethphage at the mount of Olives Jesus sent off two disciples, ²and told them: 'Go into the village opposite, where you will at once find a donkey tethered with her foal beside her. Untie them, and bring them to me. ³If anyone says anything to you, answer, "The Master needs them"; and he will let you have them at once.' ⁴This was to fulfil the prophecy which says, ⁵'Tell the daughter of Zion, "Here is your king, who comes to you in gentleness, riding on a donkey, on the foal of a beast of burden."'

⁶The disciples went and did as Jesus had directed, ⁷and brought the donkey and her foal; they laid their cloaks on them and Jesus mounted. ⁸Crowds of people carpeted the road with their cloaks, and some cut branches from the

20:9 **the ... wage:** *lit.* one denarius each.　　20:13 **You ... day:** *lit.* You agreed on a denarius.　　21:3 **The Master ... once:** *or* "The Master needs them and will send them back without delay."

19

trees to spread in his path. ⁹ Then the crowds in front and behind raised the shout: 'Hosanna to the Son of David! Blessed is he who comes in the name of the Lord! Hosanna in the heavens!'

¹⁰ When he entered Jerusalem the whole city went wild with excitement. 'Who is this?' people asked, ¹¹ and the crowds replied, 'This is the prophet Jesus, from Nazareth in Galilee.'

¹² Jesus went into the temple and drove out all who were buying and selling in the temple precincts; he upset the tables of the money-changers and the seats of the dealers in pigeons, ¹³ and said to them, 'Scripture says, "My house shall be called a house of prayer"; but you are making it a bandits' cave.'

¹⁴ In the temple the blind and the crippled came to him, and he healed them. ¹⁵ When the chief priests and scribes saw the wonderful things he did, and heard the boys in the temple shouting, 'Hosanna to the Son of David!' they were indignant ¹⁶ and asked him, 'Do you hear what they are saying?' Jesus answered, 'I do. Have you never read the text, "You have made children and babes at the breast sound your praise aloud"?' ¹⁷ Then he left them and went out of the city to Bethany, where he spent the night.

¹⁸ Next morning on his way to the city he felt hungry; ¹⁹ and seeing a fig tree at the roadside he went up to it, but found nothing on it but leaves. He said to the tree, 'May you never bear fruit again!' and at once the tree withered away. ²⁰ The disciples were amazed at the sight. 'How is it', they asked, 'that the tree has withered so suddenly?' ²¹ Jesus answered them, 'Truly I tell you: if only you have faith and have no doubts, you will do what has been done to the fig tree. And more than that: you need only say to this mountain, "Be lifted from your place and hurled into the sea," and what you say will be done. ²² Whatever you pray for in faith you will receive.'

²³ He entered the temple, and, as he was teaching, the chief priests and elders of the nation came up to him and asked: 'By what authority are you acting like this? Who gave you this authority?' ²⁴ Jesus replied, 'I also have a question for you. If you answer it, I will tell you by what authority I act. ²⁵ The baptism of John:

was it from God, or from men?' This set them arguing among themselves: 'If we say, "From God," he will say, "Then why did you not believe him?" ²⁶ But if we say, "From men," we are afraid of the people's reaction, for they all take John for a prophet.' ²⁷ So they answered, 'We do not know.' And Jesus said: 'Then I will not tell you either by what authority I act.

²⁸ 'But what do you think about this? There was a man who had two sons. He went to the first, and said, "My son, go and work today in the vineyard." ²⁹ "I will, sir," the boy replied; but he did not go. ³⁰ The father came to the second and said the same. "I will not," he replied; but afterwards he changed his mind and went. ³¹ Which of the two did what his father wanted?' 'The second,' they replied. Then Jesus said, 'Truly I tell you: tax-collectors and prostitutes are entering the kingdom of God ahead of you. ³² For when John came to show you the right way to live, you did not believe him, but the tax-collectors and prostitutes did; and even when you had seen that, you did not change your minds and believe him.

³³ 'Listen to another parable. There was a landowner who planted a vineyard: he put a wall round it, hewed out a wine-press, and built a watch-tower; then he let it out to vine-growers and went abroad. ³⁴ When the harvest season approached, he sent his servants to the tenants to collect the produce due to him. ³⁵ But they seized his servants, thrashed one, killed another, and stoned a third. ³⁶ Again, he sent other servants, this time a larger number; and they treated them in the same way. ³⁷ Finally he sent his son. "They will respect my son," he said. ³⁸ But when they saw the son the tenants said to one another, "This is the heir; come on, let us kill him, and get his inheritance." ³⁹ So they seized him, flung him out of the vineyard, and killed him. ⁴⁰ When the owner of the vineyard comes, how do you think he will deal with those tenants?' ⁴¹ 'He will bring those bad men to a bad end,' they answered, 'and hand the vineyard over to other tenants, who will give him his share of the crop when the season comes.' ⁴² Jesus said to them, 'Have you never read in the scriptures: "The stone which the builders rejected has become the main corner-stone. This is the Lord's doing, and it is wonderful in

our eyes"? ⁴³ Therefore, I tell you, the kingdom of God will be taken away from you, and given to a nation that yields the proper fruit.'

⁴⁵ When the chief priests and Pharisees heard his parables, they saw that he was referring to them. ⁴⁶ They wanted to arrest him, but were afraid of the crowds, who looked on Jesus as a prophet.

22 JESUS spoke to them again in parables: ² 'The kingdom of Heaven is like this. There was a king who arranged a banquet for his son's wedding; ³ but when he sent his servants to summon the guests he had invited, they refused to come. ⁴ Then he sent other servants, telling them to say to the guests, "Look! I have prepared this banquet for you. My bullocks and fatted beasts have been slaughtered, and everything is ready. Come to the wedding." ⁵ But they took no notice; one went off to his farm, another to his business, ⁶ and the others seized the servants, attacked them brutally, and killed them. ⁷ The king was furious; he sent troops to put those murderers to death and set their town on fire. ⁸ Then he said to his servants, "The wedding banquet is ready; but the guests I invited did not deserve the honour. ⁹ Go out therefore to the main thoroughfares, and invite everyone you can find to the wedding." ¹⁰ The servants went out into the streets, and collected everyone they could find, good and bad alike. So the hall was packed with guests.

¹¹ 'When the king came in to watch them feasting, he observed a man who was not dressed for a wedding. ¹² "My friend," said the king, "how do you come to be here without wedding clothes?" But he had nothing to say. ¹³ The king then said to his attendants, "Bind him hand and foot; fling him out into the dark, the place of wailing and grinding of teeth." ¹⁴ For many are invited, but few are chosen.'

¹⁵ THEN the Pharisees went away and agreed on a plan to trap him in argument. ¹⁶ They sent some of their followers to him, together with members of Herod's party. 'Teacher,' they said, 'we know you are a sincere man; you teach in all

sincerity the way of life that God requires, courting no man's favour, whoever he may be. ¹⁷ Give us your ruling on this: are we or are we not permitted to pay taxes to the Roman emperor?' ¹⁸ Jesus was aware of their malicious intention and said, 'You hypocrites! Why are you trying to catch me out? ¹⁹ Show me the coin used for the tax.' They handed him a silver piece. ²⁰ Jesus asked, 'Whose head is this, and whose inscription?' ²¹ 'Caesar's,' they replied. He said to them, 'Then pay to Caesar what belongs to Caesar, and to God what belongs to God.' ²² Taken aback by this reply, they went away and left him alone.

²³ The same day Sadducees, who maintain that there is no resurrection, came to him and asked: ²⁴ 'Teacher, Moses said that if a man dies childless, his brother shall marry the widow and provide an heir for his brother. ²⁵ We know a case involving seven brothers. The first married and died, and as he was without issue his wife was left to his brother. ²⁶ The same thing happened with the second, and the third, and so on with all seven. ²⁷ Last of all the woman died. ²⁸ At the resurrection, then, whose wife will she be, since they had all married her?' ²⁹ Jesus answered: 'How far you are from the truth! You know neither the scriptures nor the power of God. ³⁰ In the resurrection men and women do not marry; they are like angels in heaven.

³¹ 'As for the resurrection of the dead, have you never read what God himself said to you: ³² "I am the God of Abraham, the God of Isaac, the God of Jacob"? God is not God of the dead but of the living.' ³³ When the crowds heard this, they were amazed at his teaching.

³⁴ Hearing that he had silenced the Sadducees, the Pharisees came together in a body, ³⁵ and one of them tried to catch him out with this question: ³⁶ 'Teacher, which is the greatest commandment in the law?' ³⁷ He answered, '"Love the Lord your God with all your heart, with all your soul, and with all your mind." ³⁸ That is the greatest, the first commandment. ³⁹ The second is like it: "Love your neighbour as yourself." ⁴⁰ Everything in the law and the prophets hangs on these two commandments.'

21:43 **proper fruit:** *some witnesses add* ⁴⁴ Any man who falls on this stone will be dashed to pieces; and if it falls on a man he will be crushed by it.   22:35 **one of them:** *some witnesses add* an expert in the law.

⁴¹ Turning to the assembled Pharisees Jesus asked them, ⁴² 'What is your opinion about the Messiah? Whose son is he?' 'The son of David,' they replied. ⁴³ 'Then how is it', he asked, 'that David by inspiration calls him "Lord"? For he says, ⁴⁴ "The Lord said to my Lord, 'Sit at my right hand until I put your enemies under your feet.'" ⁴⁵ If then David calls him "Lord", how can he be David's son?' ⁴⁶ Nobody was able to give him an answer; and from that day no one dared to put any more questions to him.

23 Jesus then addressed the crowds and his disciples ² in these words: 'The scribes and the Pharisees occupy Moses' seat; ³ so be careful to do whatever they tell you. But do not follow their practice; for they say one thing and do another. ⁴ They make up heavy loads and pile them on the shoulders of others, but will not themselves lift a finger to ease the burden. ⁵ Whatever they do is done for show. They go about wearing broad phylacteries and with large tassels on their robes; ⁶ they love to have the place of honour at feasts and the chief seats in synagogues, ⁷ to be greeted respectfully in the street, and to be addressed as "rabbi".

⁸ 'But you must not be called "rabbi", for you have one Rabbi, and you are all brothers. ⁹ Do not call any man on earth "father", for you have one Father, and he is in heaven. ¹⁰ Nor must you be called "teacher"; you have one Teacher, the Messiah. ¹¹ The greatest among you must be your servant. ¹² Whoever exalts himself will be humbled; and whoever humbles himself will be exalted.

¹³ 'Alas for you, scribes and Pharisees, hypocrites! You shut the door of the kingdom of Heaven in people's faces; you do not enter yourselves, and when others try to enter, you stop them.

¹⁵ 'Alas for you, scribes and Pharisees, hypocrites! You travel over sea and land to win one convert; and when you have succeeded you make him twice as fit for hell as you are yourselves.

¹⁶ 'Alas for you, blind guides! You say, "If someone swears by the sanctuary, that is nothing; but if he swears by the gold in the sanctuary, he is bound by his oath." ¹⁷ Blind fools! Which is the more important, the gold, or the sanctuary which sanctifies the gold? ¹⁸ Or you say, "If someone swears by the altar, that is nothing; but if he swears by the offering that lies on the altar, he is bound by his oath." ¹⁹ What blindness! Which is the more important, the offering, or the altar which sanctifies it? ²⁰ To swear by the altar, then, is to swear both by the altar and by whatever lies on it; ²¹ to swear by the sanctuary is to swear both by the sanctuary and by him who dwells there; ²² and to swear by Heaven is to swear both by the throne of God and by him who sits upon it.

²³ 'Alas for you, scribes and Pharisees, hypocrites! You pay tithes of mint and dill and cummin; but you have overlooked the weightier demands of the law—justice, mercy, and good faith. It is these you should have practised, without neglecting the others. ²⁴ Blind guides! You strain off a midge, yet gulp down a camel!

²⁵ 'Alas for you, scribes and Pharisees, hypocrites! You clean the outside of a cup or a dish, and leave the inside full of greed and self-indulgence! ²⁶ Blind Pharisee! Clean the inside of the cup first; then the outside will be clean also.

²⁷ 'Alas for you, scribes and Pharisees, hypocrites! You are like tombs covered with whitewash; they look fine on the outside, but inside they are full of dead men's bones and of corruption. ²⁸ So it is with you: outwardly you look like honest men, but inside you are full of hypocrisy and lawlessness.

²⁹ 'Alas for you, scribes and Pharisees, hypocrites! You build up the tombs of the prophets and embellish the monuments of the saints, ³⁰ and you say, "If we had been living in the time of our forefathers, we should never have taken part with them in the murder of the prophets." ³¹ So you acknowledge that you are the sons of those who killed the prophets. ³² Go on then, finish off what your fathers began! ³³ Snakes! Vipers' brood! How can you escape being condemned to hell?

³⁴ 'I am sending you therefore prophets and wise men and teachers of the law; some of them you will kill and crucify, others you will flog in your synagogues

23:13 **you stop them:** *some witnesses add* ¹⁴ Alas for you, scribes and Pharisees, hypocrites! You eat up the property of widows, while for appearance' sake you say long prayers. You will receive the severest sentence. 23:32 **Go on ... began:** *or* You too must come up to your fathers' standards.

and hound from city to city. [35] So on you will fall the guilt of all the innocent blood spilt on the ground, from the blood of innocent Abel to the blood of Zechariah son of Berachiah, whom you murdered between the sanctuary and the altar. [36] Truly I tell you: this generation will bear the guilt of it all.

[37] 'O Jerusalem, Jerusalem, city that murders the prophets and stones the messengers sent to her! How often have I longed to gather your children, as a hen gathers her brood under her wings; but you would not let me. [38] Look! There is your temple, forsaken by God and laid waste. [39] I tell you, you will not see me until the time when you say, "Blessed is he who comes in the name of the Lord!"'

Warnings about the end

24 Jesus left the temple and was walking away when his disciples came and pointed to the temple buildings. [2] He answered, 'Yes, look at it all. Truly I tell you: not one stone will be left upon another; they will all be thrown down.'

[3] As he sat on the mount of Olives the disciples came to speak to him privately. 'Tell us,' they said, 'when will this happen? And what will be the sign of your coming and the end of the age?'

[4] Jesus replied: 'Take care that no one misleads you. [5] For many will come claiming my name and saying, "I am the Messiah," and many will be misled by them. [6] The time is coming when you will hear of wars and rumours of wars. See that you are not alarmed. Such things are bound to happen; but the end is still to come. [7] For nation will go to war against nation, kingdom against kingdom; there will be famines and earthquakes in many places. [8] All these things are the first birth-pangs of the new age.

[9] 'You will then be handed over for punishment and execution; all nations will hate you for your allegiance to me. [10] At that time many will fall from their faith; they will betray one another and hate one another. [11] Many false prophets will arise, and will mislead many; [12] and as lawlessness spreads, the love of many will grow cold. [13] But whoever endures to the end will be saved. [14] And this gospel of the kingdom will be proclaimed through-

out the earth as a testimony to all nations; and then the end will come.

[15] 'So when you see "the abomination of desolation", of which the prophet Daniel spoke, standing in the holy place (let the reader understand), [16] then those who are in Judaea must take to the hills. [17] If anyone is on the roof, he must not go down to fetch his goods from the house; [18] if anyone is in the field, he must not turn back for his coat. [19] Alas for women with child in those days, and for those who have children at the breast! [20] Pray that it may not be winter or a sabbath when you have to make your escape. [21] It will be a time of great distress, such as there has never been before since the beginning of the world, and will never be again. [22] If that time of troubles were not cut short, no living thing could survive; but for the sake of God's chosen it will be cut short.

[23] 'If anyone says to you then, "Look, here is the Messiah," or "There he is," do not believe it. [24] Impostors will come claiming to be messiahs or prophets, and they will produce great signs and wonders to mislead, if possible, even God's chosen. [25] See, I have forewarned you. [26] If therefore they tell you, "He is there in the wilderness," do not go out; or if they say, "He is there in the inner room," do not believe it. [27] Like a lightning-flash, that lights the sky from east to west, will be the coming of the Son of Man.

[28] 'Wherever the carcass is, there will the vultures gather.

[29] 'As soon as that time of distress has passed,

the sun will be darkened,
the moon will not give her light;
the stars will fall from the sky,
the celestial powers will be shaken.

[30] 'Then will appear in heaven the sign that heralds the Son of Man. All the peoples of the world will make lamentation, and they will see the Son of Man coming on the clouds of heaven with power and great glory. [31] With a trumpet-blast he will send out his angels, and they will gather his chosen from the four winds, from the farthest bounds of heaven on every side.

[32] 'Learn a lesson from the fig tree.

23:38 *Some witnesses omit* and laid waste.

When its tender shoots appear and are breaking into leaf, you know that summer is near. ³³ In the same way, when you see all these things, you may know that the end is near, at the very door. ³⁴ Truly I tell you: the present generation will live to see it all. ³⁵ Heaven and earth will pass away, but my words will never pass away.

³⁶ 'Yet about that day and hour no one knows, not even the angels in heaven, not even the Son; no one but the Father alone.

³⁷ 'As it was in the days of Noah, so will it be when the Son of Man comes. ³⁸ In the days before the flood they ate and drank and married, until the day that Noah went into the ark, ³⁹ and they knew nothing until the flood came and swept them all away. That is how it will be when the Son of Man comes. ⁴⁰ Then there will be two men in the field: one will be taken, the other left; ⁴¹ two women grinding at the mill: one will be taken, the other left.

⁴² 'Keep awake, then, for you do not know on what day your Lord will come. ⁴³ Remember, if the householder had known at what time of night the burglar was coming, he would have stayed awake and not let his house be broken into. ⁴⁴ Hold yourselves ready, therefore, because the Son of Man will come at the time you least expect him.

⁴⁵ 'Who is the faithful and wise servant, charged by his master to manage his household and supply them with food at the proper time? ⁴⁶ Happy that servant if his master comes home and finds him at work! ⁴⁷ Truly I tell you: he will be put in charge of all his master's property. ⁴⁸ But if he is a bad servant and says to himself, "The master is a long time coming," ⁴⁹ and begins to bully the other servants and to eat and drink with his drunken friends, ⁵⁰ then the master will arrive on a day when the servant does not expect him, at a time he has not been told. ⁵¹ He will cut him in pieces and assign him a place among the hypocrites, where there is wailing and grinding of teeth.

25 'When the day comes, the kingdom of Heaven will be like this. There were ten girls, who took their lamps and went out to meet the bridegroom. ² Five of them were foolish, and five prudent; ³ when the foolish ones took their lamps, they took no oil with them, ⁴ but the others took flasks of oil with their lamps. ⁵ As the bridegroom was a long time in coming, they all dozed off to sleep. ⁶ But at midnight there came a shout: "Here is the bridegroom! Come out to meet him." ⁷ Then the girls all got up and trimmed their lamps. ⁸ The foolish said to the prudent, "Our lamps are going out; give us some of your oil." ⁹ "No," they answered; "there will never be enough for all of us. You had better go to the dealers and buy some for yourselves." ¹⁰ While they were away the bridegroom arrived; those who were ready went in with him to the wedding banquet; and the door was shut. ¹¹ Later the others came back. "Sir, sir, open the door for us," they cried. ¹² But he answered, "Truly I tell you: I do not know you." ¹³ Keep awake then, for you know neither the day nor the hour.

¹⁴ 'It is like a man going abroad, who called his servants and entrusted his capital to them; ¹⁵ to one he gave five bags of gold, to another two, to another one, each according to his ability. Then he left the country. ¹⁶ The man who had the five bags went at once and employed them in business, and made a profit of five bags, ¹⁷ and the man who had the two bags made two. ¹⁸ But the man who had been given one bag of gold went off and dug a hole in the ground, and hid his master's money. ¹⁹ A long time afterwards their master returned, and proceeded to settle accounts with them. ²⁰ The man who had been given the five bags of gold came and produced the five he had made: "Master," he said, "you left five bags with me; look, I have made five more." ²¹ "Well done, good and faithful servant!" said the master. "You have proved trustworthy in a small matter; I will now put you in charge of something big. Come and share your master's joy." ²² The man with the two bags then came and said, "Master, you left two bags with me; look, I have made two more." ²³ "Well done, good and faithful servant!" said the master. "You have proved trustworthy in a small matter; I will now put you in charge of something big. Come and share your master's joy." ²⁴ Then the man who

24:33 that ... near: *or* that he is near.

had been given one bag came and said, "Master, I knew you to be a hard man: you reap where you have not sown, you gather where you have not scattered; [25] so I was afraid, and I went and hid your gold in the ground. Here it is—you have what belongs to you." [26] "You worthless, lazy servant!" said the master. "You knew, did you, that I reap where I have not sown, and gather where I have not scattered? [27] Then you ought to have put my money on deposit, and on my return I should have got it back with interest. [28] Take the bag of gold from him, and give it to the one with the ten bags. [29] For everyone who has will be given more, till he has enough and to spare; and everyone who has nothing will forfeit even what he has. [30] As for the useless servant, throw him out into the dark, where there will be wailing and grinding of teeth!"

[31] 'When the Son of Man comes in his glory and all the angels with him, he will sit on his glorious throne, [32] with all the nations gathered before him. He will separate people into two groups, as a shepherd separates the sheep from the goats; [33] he will place the sheep on his right hand and the goats on his left. [34] Then the king will say to those on his right, "You have my Father's blessing; come, take possession of the kingdom that has been ready for you since the world was made. [35] For when I was hungry, you gave me food; when thirsty, you gave me drink; when I was a stranger, you took me into your home; [36] when naked, you clothed me; when I was ill, you came to my help; when in prison, you visited me." [37] Then the righteous will reply, "Lord, when was it that we saw you hungry and fed you, or thirsty and gave you drink, [38] a stranger and took you home, or naked and clothed you? [39] When did we see you ill or in prison, and come to visit you?" [40] And the king will answer, "Truly I tell you: anything you did for one of my brothers here, however insignificant, you did for me." [41] Then he will say to those on his left, "A curse is on you; go from my sight to the eternal fire that is ready for the devil and his angels. [42] For when I was hungry, you gave me nothing to eat; when thirsty, nothing to drink; [43] when I was a stranger, you did not welcome me; when I was naked, you did not clothe me; when I was ill and in prison, you did not

come to my help." [44] And they in their turn will reply, "Lord, when was it that we saw you hungry or thirsty or a stranger or naked or ill or in prison, and did nothing for you?" [45] And he will answer, "Truly I tell you: anything you failed to do for one of these, however insignificant, you failed to do for me." [46] And they will go away to eternal punishment, but the righteous will enter eternal life.'

The trial and crucifixion of Jesus

26 WHEN Jesus had finished all these discourses he said to his disciples, [2] 'You know that in two days' time it will be Passover, when the Son of Man will be handed over to be crucified.'

[3] Meanwhile the chief priests and the elders of the people met in the house of the high priest, Caiaphas, [4] and discussed a scheme to seize Jesus and put him to death. [5] 'It must not be during the festival,' they said, 'or there may be rioting among the people.'

[6] JESUS was at Bethany in the house of Simon the leper, [7] when a woman approached him with a bottle of very costly perfume; and she began to pour it over his head as he sat at table. [8] The disciples were indignant when they saw it. 'Why this waste?' they said. [9] 'It could have been sold for a large sum and the money given to the poor.' [10] Jesus noticed, and said to them, 'Why make trouble for the woman? It is a fine thing she has done for me. [11] You have the poor among you always, but you will not always have me. [12] When she poured this perfume on my body it was her way of preparing me for burial. [13] Truly I tell you: wherever this gospel is proclaimed throughout the world, what she has done will be told as her memorial.'

[14] THEN one of the Twelve, the man called Judas Iscariot, went to the chief priests [15] and said, 'What will you give me to betray him to you?' They weighed him out thirty silver pieces. [16] From that moment he began to look for an opportunity to betray him.

[17] On the first day of Unleavened Bread the disciples came and asked Jesus, 'Where would you like us to prepare the Passover for you?' [18] He told them to go to

a certain man in the city with this message: 'The Teacher says, "My appointed time is near; I shall keep the Passover with my disciples at your house."' [19] The disciples did as Jesus directed them and prepared the Passover.

[20] In the evening he sat down with the twelve disciples; [21] and during supper he said, 'Truly I tell you: one of you will betray me.' [22] Greatly distressed at this, they asked him one by one, 'Surely you do not mean me, Lord?' [23] He answered, 'One who has dipped his hand into the bowl with me will betray me. [24] The Son of Man is going the way appointed for him in the scriptures; but alas for that man by whom the Son of Man is betrayed! It would be better for that man if he had never been born.' [25] Then Judas spoke, the one who was to betray him: 'Rabbi, surely you do not mean me?' Jesus replied, 'You have said it.'

[26] During supper Jesus took bread, and having said the blessing he broke it and gave it to the disciples with the words: 'Take this and eat; this is my body.' [27] Then he took a cup, and having offered thanks to God he gave it to them with the words: 'Drink from it, all of you. [28] For this is my blood, the blood of the covenant, shed for many for the forgiveness of sins. [29] I tell you, never again shall I drink from this fruit of the vine until that day when I drink it new with you in the kingdom of my Father.'

[30] After singing the Passover hymn, they went out to the mount of Olives. [31] Then Jesus said to them, 'Tonight you will all lose faith because of me; for it is written: "I will strike the shepherd and the sheep of his flock will be scattered." [32] But after I am raised, I shall go ahead of you into Galilee.' [33] Peter replied, 'Everyone else may lose faith because of you, but I never will.' [34] Jesus said to him, 'Truly I tell you: tonight before the cock crows you will disown me three times.' [35] Peter said, 'Even if I have to die with you, I will never disown you.' And all the disciples said the same.

[36] JESUS then came with his disciples to a place called Gethsemane, and he said to them, 'Sit here while I go over there to pray.' [37] He took with him Peter and the two sons of Zebedee. Distress and anguish overwhelmed him, [38] and he said to them,

'My heart is ready to break with grief. Stop here, and stay awake with me.' [39] Then he went on a little farther, threw himself down, and prayed, 'My Father, if it is possible, let this cup pass me by. Yet not my will but yours.'

[40] He came back to the disciples and found them asleep; and he said to Peter, 'What! Could none of you stay awake with me for one hour? [41] Stay awake, and pray that you may be spared the test. The spirit is willing, but the flesh is weak.'

[42] He went away a second time and prayed: 'My Father, if it is not possible for this cup to pass me by without my drinking it, your will be done.' [43] He came again and found them asleep, for their eyes were heavy. [44] So he left them and went away again and prayed a third time, using the same words as before.

[45] Then he came to the disciples and said to them, 'Still asleep? Still resting? The hour has come! The Son of Man is betrayed into the hands of sinners. [46] Up, let us go! The traitor is upon us.'

[47] He was still speaking when Judas, one of the Twelve, appeared, and with him a great crowd armed with swords and cudgels, sent by the chief priests and the elders of the nation. [48] The traitor had given them this sign: 'The one I kiss is your man; seize him.' [49] Going straight up to Jesus, he said, 'Hail, Rabbi!' and kissed him. [50] Jesus replied, 'Friend, do what you are here to do.' Then they came forward, seized Jesus, and held him fast.

[51] At that moment one of those with Jesus reached for his sword and drew it, and struck the high priest's servant, cutting off his ear. [52] But Jesus said to him, 'Put up your sword. All who take the sword die by the sword. [53] Do you suppose that I cannot appeal for help to my Father, and at once be sent more than twelve legions of angels? [54] But how then would the scriptures be fulfilled, which say that this must happen?'

[55] Then Jesus spoke to the crowd: 'Do you take me for a bandit, that you have come out with swords and cudgels to arrest me? Day after day I sat teaching in the temple, and you did not lay hands on me. [56] But this has all happened to fulfil what the prophets wrote.'

Then the disciples all deserted him and ran away.

⁵⁷ JESUS was led away under arrest to the house of Caiaphas the high priest, where the scribes and elders were assembled. ⁵⁸ Peter followed him at a distance till he came to the high priest's courtyard; he went in and sat down among the attendants, to see how it would all end.

⁵⁹ The chief priests and the whole Council tried to find some allegation against Jesus that would warrant a death sentence; ⁶⁰ but they failed to find one, though many came forward with false evidence. Finally two men ⁶¹ alleged that he had said, 'I can pull down the temple of God, and rebuild it in three days.' ⁶² At this the high priest rose and said to him, 'Have you no answer to the accusations that these witnesses bring against you?' ⁶³ But Jesus remained silent. The high priest then said, 'By the living God I charge you to tell us: are you the Messiah, the Son of God?' ⁶⁴ Jesus replied, 'The words are yours. But I tell you this: from now on you will see the Son of Man seated at the right hand of the Almighty and coming on the clouds of heaven.' ⁶⁵ At these words the high priest tore his robes and exclaimed, 'This is blasphemy! Do we need further witnesses? You have just heard the blasphemy. ⁶⁶ What is your verdict?' 'He is guilty,' they answered; 'he should die.' ⁶⁷ Then they spat in his face and struck him with their fists; some said, as they beat him, ⁶⁸ 'Now, Messiah, if you are a prophet, tell us who hit you.'

⁶⁹ Meanwhile Peter was sitting outside in the courtyard when a servant-girl accosted him; 'You were with Jesus the Galilean,' she said. ⁷⁰ Peter denied it in front of them all. 'I do not know what you are talking about,' he said. ⁷¹ He then went out to the gateway, where another girl, seeing him, said to the people there, 'He was with Jesus of Nazareth.' ⁷² Once again he denied it, saying with an oath, 'I do not know the man.' ⁷³ Shortly afterwards the bystanders came up and said to Peter, 'You must be one of them; your accent gives you away!' ⁷⁴ At this he started to curse and declared with an oath: 'I do not know the man.' At that moment a cock crowed; ⁷⁵ and Peter remembered how Jesus had said, 'Before the cock crows you will disown me three times.' And he went outside, and wept bitterly.

27 WHEN morning came, the chief priests and the elders of the nation all met together to plan the death of Jesus. ² They bound him and led him away, to hand him over to Pilate, the Roman governor.

³ When Judas the traitor saw that Jesus had been condemned, he was seized with remorse, and returned the thirty silver pieces to the chief priests and elders. ⁴ 'I have sinned,' he said; 'I have brought an innocent man to his death.' But they said, 'What is that to us? It is your concern.' ⁵ So he threw the money down in the temple and left; he went away and hanged himself.

⁶ The chief priests took up the money, but they said, 'This cannot be put into the temple fund; it is blood-money.' ⁷ So after conferring they used it to buy the Potter's Field, as a burial-place for foreigners. ⁸ This explains the name Blood Acre, by which that field has been known ever since; ⁹ and in this way fulfilment was given to the saying of the prophet Jeremiah: 'They took the thirty silver pieces, the price set on a man's head (for that was his price among the Israelites), ¹⁰ and gave the money for the potter's field, as the Lord directed me.'

¹¹ Jesus was now brought before the governor; 'Are you the king of the Jews?' the governor asked him. 'The words are yours,' said Jesus; ¹² and when the chief priests and elders brought charges against him he made no reply. ¹³ Then Pilate said to him, 'Do you not hear all this evidence they are bringing against you?' ¹⁴ but to the governor's great astonishment he refused to answer a single word.

¹⁵ At the festival season it was customary for the governor to release one prisoner chosen by the people. ¹⁶ There was then in custody a man of some notoriety, called Jesus Barabbas. ¹⁷ When the people assembled Pilate said to them, 'Which would you like me to release to you—Jesus Barabbas, or Jesus called Messiah?' ¹⁸ For he knew it was out of malice that Jesus had been handed over to him. ¹⁹ While Pilate was sitting in court a

---

26:64 **The words are yours:** *or* It is as you say.   27:9 **They took:** *or* I took.   27:11 **The words are yours:** *or* It is as you say.   27:16,17 **Jesus Barabbas:** *many witnesses omit* Jesus *in both verses.*

message came to him from his wife: 'Have nothing to do with that innocent man; I was much troubled on his account in my dreams last night.'

²⁰ Meanwhile the chief priests and elders had persuaded the crowd to ask for the release of Barabbas and to have Jesus put to death. ²¹ So when the governor asked, 'Which of the two would you like me to release to you?' they said, 'Barabbas.' ²² 'Then what am I to do with Jesus called Messiah?' asked Pilate; and with one voice they answered, 'Crucify him!' ²³ 'Why, what harm has he done?' asked Pilate; but they shouted all the louder, 'Crucify him!'

²⁴ When Pilate saw that he was getting nowhere, and that there was danger of a riot, he took water and washed his hands in full view of the crowd. 'My hands are clean of this man's blood,' he declared. 'See to that yourselves.' ²⁵ With one voice the people cried, 'His blood be on us and on our children.' ²⁶ He then released Barabbas to them; but he had Jesus flogged, and then handed him over to be crucified.

²⁷ THEN the soldiers of the governor took Jesus into his residence, the Praetorium, where they collected the whole company round him. ²⁸ They stripped him and dressed him in a scarlet cloak; ²⁹ and plaiting a crown of thorns they placed it on his head, and a stick in his right hand. Falling on their knees before him they jeered at him: 'Hail, king of the Jews!' ³⁰ They spat on him, and used the stick to beat him about the head. ³¹ When they had finished mocking him, they stripped off the cloak and dressed him in his own clothes.

Then they led him away to be crucified. ³² On their way out they met a man from Cyrene, Simon by name, and pressed him into service to carry his cross.

³³ Coming to a place called Golgotha (which means 'Place of a Skull'), ³⁴ they offered him a drink of wine mixed with gall; but after tasting it he would not drink.

³⁵ When they had crucified him they shared out his clothes by casting lots, ³⁶ and then sat down there to keep watch. ³⁷ Above his head was placed the inscription giving the charge against him: 'This is Jesus, the king of the Jews.' ³⁸ Two bandits were crucified with him, one on his right and the other on his left.

³⁹ The passers-by wagged their heads and jeered at him, ⁴⁰ crying, 'So you are the man who was to pull down the temple and rebuild it in three days! If you really are the Son of God, save yourself and come down from the cross.' ⁴¹ The chief priests with the scribes and elders joined in the mockery: ⁴² 'He saved others,' they said, 'but he cannot save himself. King of Israel, indeed! Let him come down now from the cross, and then we shall believe him. ⁴³ He trusted in God, did he? Let God rescue him, if he wants him—for he said he was God's Son.' ⁴⁴ Even the bandits who were crucified with him taunted him in the same way.

⁴⁵ From midday a darkness fell over the whole land, which lasted until three in the afternoon; ⁴⁶ and about three Jesus cried aloud, 'Eli, Eli, lema sabachthani?' which means, 'My God, my God, why have you forsaken me?' ⁴⁷ Hearing this, some of the bystanders said, 'He is calling Elijah.' ⁴⁸ One of them ran at once and fetched a sponge, which he soaked in sour wine and held to his lips on the end of a stick. ⁴⁹ But the others said, 'Let us see if Elijah will come to save him.'

⁵⁰ Jesus again cried aloud and breathed his last. ⁵¹ At that moment the curtain of the temple was torn in two from top to bottom. The earth shook, rocks split, ⁵² and graves opened; many of God's saints were raised from sleep, ⁵³ and coming out of their graves after his resurrection entered the Holy City, where many saw them. ⁵⁴ And when the centurion and his men who were keeping watch over Jesus saw the earthquake and all that was happening, they were filled with awe and said, 'This must have been a son of God.'

⁵⁵ A NUMBER of women were also present, watching from a distance; they had followed Jesus from Galilee and looked after him. ⁵⁶ Among them were Mary of Magdala, Mary the mother of James and Joseph, and the mother of the sons of Zebedee.

⁵⁷ When evening fell, a wealthy man from Arimathaea, Joseph by name, who had himself become a disciple of Jesus,

27: 54 **a son of God:** *or* the Son of God.

58 approached Pilate and asked for the body of Jesus; and Pilate gave orders that he should have it. 59 Joseph took the body, wrapped it in a clean linen sheet, 60 and laid it in his own unused tomb, which he had cut out of the rock. He then rolled a large stone against the entrance, and went away. 61 Mary of Magdala was there, and the other Mary, sitting opposite the grave.

62 Next day, the morning after the day of preparation, the chief priests and the Pharisees came in a body to Pilate. 63 'Your excellency,' they said, 'we recall how that impostor said while he was still alive, "I am to be raised again after three days." 64 We request you to give orders for the grave to be made secure until the third day. Otherwise his disciples may come and steal the body, and then tell the people that he has been raised from the dead; and the final deception will be worse than the first.' 65 'You may have a guard,' said Pilate; 'go and make the grave as secure as you can.' 66 So they went and made it secure by sealing the stone and setting a guard.

The resurrection

28 ABOUT daybreak on the first day of the week, when the sabbath was over, Mary of Magdala and the other Mary came to look at the grave. 2 Suddenly there was a violent earthquake; an angel of the Lord descended from heaven and came and rolled away the stone, and sat down on it. 3 His face shone like lightning; his garments were white as snow. 4 At the sight of him the guards shook with fear and fell to the ground as though dead.

5 The angel spoke to the women: 'You', he said, 'have nothing to fear. I know you are looking for Jesus who was crucified. 6 He is not here; he has been raised, as he said he would be. Come and see the place where he was laid, 7 and then go quickly and tell his disciples: "He has been raised from the dead and is going ahead of you into Galilee; there you will see him." That is what I came to tell you.'

8 They hurried away from the tomb in awe and great joy, and ran to bring the news to the disciples. 9 Suddenly Jesus was there in their path, greeting them. They came up and clasped his feet, kneeling before him. 10 'Do not be afraid,' Jesus said to them. 'Go and take word to my brothers that they are to leave for Galilee. They will see me there.'

11 While the women were on their way, some of the guard went into the city and reported to the chief priests everything that had happened. 12 After meeting and conferring with the elders, the chief priests offered the soldiers a substantial bribe 13 and told them to say, 'His disciples came during the night and stole the body while we were asleep.' 14 They added, 'If this should reach the governor's ears, we will put matters right with him and see you do not suffer.' 15 So they took the money and did as they were told. Their story became widely known, and is current in Jewish circles to this day.

16 The eleven disciples made their way to Galilee, to the mountain where Jesus had told them to meet him. 17 When they saw him, they knelt in worship, though some were doubtful. 18 Jesus came near and said to them: 'Full authority in heaven and on earth has been committed to me. 19 Go therefore to all nations and make them my disciples; baptize them in the name of the Father and the Son and the Holy Spirit, 20 and teach them to observe all that I have commanded you. I will be with you always, to the end of time.'

29

THE GOSPEL ACCORDING TO

MARK

John the Baptist and Jesus

1 THE beginning of the gospel of Jesus Christ the Son of God.

[2] IN the prophet Isaiah it stands written:

I am sending my herald ahead of you;
he will prepare your way.
[3] A voice cries in the wilderness,
'Prepare the way for the Lord;
clear a straight path for him.'

[4] John the Baptist appeared in the wilderness proclaiming a baptism in token of repentance, for the forgiveness of sins; [5] and everyone flocked to him from the countryside of Judaea and the city of Jerusalem, and they were baptized by him in the river Jordan, confessing their sins. [6] John was dressed in a rough coat of camel's hair, with a leather belt round his waist, and he fed on locusts and wild honey. [7] He proclaimed: 'After me comes one mightier than I am, whose sandals I am not worthy to stoop down and unfasten. [8] I have baptized you with water; he will baptize you with the Holy Spirit.'

[9] It was at this time that Jesus came from Nazareth in Galilee and was baptized in the Jordan by John. [10] As he was coming up out of the water, he saw the heavens break open and the Spirit descend on him, like a dove. [11] And a voice came from heaven: 'You are my beloved Son; in you I take delight.'

[12] At once the Spirit drove him out into the wilderness, [13] and there he remained for forty days tempted by Satan. He was among the wild beasts; and angels attended to his needs.

Proclaiming the kingdom

[14] AFTER John had been arrested, Jesus came into Galilee proclaiming the gospel of God: [15] 'The time has arrived; the kingdom of God is upon you. Repent, and believe the gospel.'

[16] Jesus was walking by the sea of Galilee when he saw Simon and his brother Andrew at work with casting-nets in the lake; for they were fishermen. [17] Jesus said to them, 'Come, follow me, and I will make you fishers of men.' [18] At once they left their nets and followed him.

[19] Going a little farther, he saw James son of Zebedee and his brother John in a boat mending their nets. [20] At once he called them; and they left their father Zebedee in the boat with the hired men and followed him.

[21] They came to Capernaum, and on the sabbath he went to the synagogue and began to teach. [22] The people were amazed at his teaching, for, unlike the scribes, he taught with a note of authority. [23] Now there was a man in their synagogue possessed by an unclean spirit. He shrieked at him: [24] 'What do you want with us, Jesus of Nazareth? Have you come to destroy us? I know who you are—the Holy One of God.' [25] Jesus rebuked him: 'Be silent', he said, 'and come out of him.' [26] The unclean spirit threw the man into convulsions and with a loud cry left him. [27] They were all amazed and began to ask one another, 'What is this? A new kind of teaching! He speaks with authority. When he gives orders, even the unclean spirits obey.' [28] His fame soon spread far and wide throughout Galilee.

[29] On leaving the synagogue, they went straight to the house of Simon and Andrew; and James and John went with them. [30] Simon's mother-in-law was in bed with a fever. As soon as they told him about her, [31] Jesus went and took hold of her hand, and raised her to her feet. The fever left her, and she attended to their needs.

[32] That evening after sunset they brought to him all who were ill or possessed by demons; [33] and the whole town was there, gathered at the door. [34] He healed many who suffered from various diseases, and drove out many

1:1 *Some witnesses omit* the Son of God.   1:11 **You are** ... **Son:** *or* You are my only Son.   1:24 **Have you:** *or* You have.

30

demons. He would not let the demons speak, because they knew who he was.

35 Very early next morning he got up and went out. He went away to a remote spot and remained there in prayer. 36 But Simon and his companions went in search of him, 37 and when they found him, they said, 'Everybody is looking for you.' 38 He answered, 'Let us move on to the neighbouring towns, so that I can proclaim my message there as well, for that is what I came out to do.' 39 So he went through the whole of Galilee, preaching in their synagogues and driving out demons.

40 On one occasion he was approached by a leper, who knelt before him and begged for help. 'If only you will,' said the man, 'you can make me clean.' 41 Jesus was moved to anger; he stretched out his hand, touched him, and said, 'I will; be clean.' 42 The leprosy left him immediately, and he was clean. 43 Then he dismissed him with this stern warning: 44 'See that you tell nobody, but go and show yourself to the priest, and make the offering laid down by Moses for your cleansing; that will certify the cure.' 45 But the man went away and made the whole story public, spreading it far and wide, until Jesus could no longer show himself in any town. He stayed outside in remote places; yet people kept coming to him from all quarters.

2 After some days he returned to Capernaum, and news went round that he was at home; 2 and such a crowd collected that there was no room for them even in the space outside the door. While he was proclaiming the message to them, 3 a man was brought who was paralysed. Four men were carrying him, 4 but because of the crowd they could not get him near. So they made an opening in the roof over the place where Jesus was, and when they had broken through they lowered the bed on which the paralysed man was lying. 5 When he saw their faith, Jesus said to the man, 'My son, your sins are forgiven.'

6 Now there were some scribes sitting there, thinking to themselves, 7 'How can the fellow talk like that? It is blasphemy! Who but God can forgive sins?' 8 Jesus knew at once what they were thinking,

and said to them, 'Why do you harbour such thoughts? 9 Is it easier to say to this paralysed man, "Your sins are forgiven," or to say, "Stand up, take your bed, and walk"? 10 But to convince you that the Son of Man has authority on earth to forgive sins'—he turned to the paralysed man—11 'I say to you, stand up, take your bed, and go home.' 12 And he got up, and at once took his bed and went out in full view of them all, so that they were astounded and praised God. 'Never before', they said, 'have we seen anything like this.'

13 Once more he went out to the lakeside. All the crowd came to him there, and he taught them. 14 As he went along, he saw Levi son of Alphaeus at his seat in the custom-house, and said to him, 'Follow me'; and he rose and followed him.

15 When Jesus was having a meal in his house, many tax-collectors and sinners were seated with him and his disciples, for there were many of them among his followers. 16 Some scribes who were Pharisees, observing the company in which he was eating, said to his disciples, 'Why does he eat with tax-collectors and sinners?' 17 Hearing this, Jesus said to them, 'It is not the healthy who need a doctor, but the sick; I did not come to call the virtuous, but sinners.'

18 Once, when John's disciples and the Pharisees were keeping a fast, some people came and asked him, 'Why is it that John's disciples and the disciples of the Pharisees are fasting, but yours are not?' 19 Jesus replied, 'Can you expect the bridegroom's friends to fast while the bridegroom is with them? As long as he is with them, there can be no fasting. 20 But the time will come when the bridegroom will be taken away from them; that will be the time for them to fast.

21 'No one sews a patch of unshrunk cloth on to an old garment; if he does, the patch tears away from it, the new from the old, and leaves a bigger hole. 22 No one puts new wine into old wineskins; if he does, the wine will burst the skins, and then wine and skins are both lost. New wine goes into fresh skins.'

23 One sabbath he was going through the cornfields; and as they went along his disciples began to pluck ears of corn.

1:41 to anger: *many witnesses read* with pity.

²⁴ The Pharisees said to him, 'Why are they doing what is forbidden on the sabbath?' ²⁵ He answered, 'Have you never read what David did when he and his men were hungry and had nothing to eat? ²⁶ He went into the house of God, in the time of Abiathar the high priest, and ate the sacred bread, though no one but a priest is allowed to eat it, and even gave it to his men.'

²⁷ He also said to them, 'The sabbath was made for man, not man for the sabbath: ²⁸ so the Son of Man is lord even of the sabbath.'

3 On another occasion when he went to synagogue, there was a man in the congregation who had a withered arm; ² and they were watching to see whether Jesus would heal him on the sabbath, so that they could bring a charge against him. ³ He said to the man with the withered arm, 'Come and stand out here.' ⁴ Then he turned to them: 'Is it permitted to do good or to do evil on the sabbath, to save life or to kill?' They had nothing to say; ⁵ and, looking round at them with anger and sorrow at their obstinate stupidity, he said to the man, 'Stretch out your arm.' He stretched it out and his arm was restored. ⁶ Then the Pharisees, on leaving the synagogue, at once began plotting with the men of Herod's party to bring about Jesus's death.

⁷ JESUS went away to the lakeside with his disciples. Great numbers from Galilee, Judaea ⁸ and Jerusalem, Idumaea and Transjordan, and the neighbourhood of Tyre and Sidon, heard what he was doing and came to him. ⁹ So he told his disciples to have a boat ready for him, to save him from being crushed by the crowd. ¹⁰ For he healed so many that the sick all came crowding round to touch him. ¹¹ The unclean spirits too, when they saw him, would fall at his feet and cry aloud, 'You are the Son of God'; ¹² but he insisted that they should not make him known.

¹³ Then he went up into the hill-country and summoned the men he wanted; and they came and joined him. ¹⁴ He appointed twelve to be his companions and to be sent out to proclaim the gospel, ¹⁵ with authority to drive out demons. ¹⁶ The Twelve he appointed were: Simon, whom he named Peter; ¹⁷ the sons of Zebedee, James and his brother John,

whom he named Boanerges, Sons of Thunder; ¹⁸ Andrew, Philip, Bartholomew, Matthew, Thomas, James son of Alphaeus, Thaddaeus, Simon the Zealot, ¹⁹ and Judas Iscariot, the man who betrayed him.

He entered a house, ²⁰ and once more such a crowd collected round them that they had no chance even to eat. ²¹ When his family heard about it they set out to take charge of him. 'He is out of his mind,' they said.

²² The scribes, too, who had come down from Jerusalem, said, 'He is possessed by Beelzebul,' and, 'He drives out demons by the prince of demons.' ²³ So he summoned them, and spoke to them in parables: 'How can Satan drive out Satan? ²⁴ If a kingdom is divided against itself, that kingdom cannot stand; ²⁵ if a household is divided against itself, that house cannot stand; ²⁶ and if Satan is divided and rebels against himself, he cannot stand, and that is the end of him.

²⁷ 'On the other hand, no one can break into a strong man's house and make off with his goods unless he has first tied up the strong man; then he can ransack the house.

²⁸ 'Truly I tell you: every sin and every slander can be forgiven; ²⁹ but whoever slanders the Holy Spirit can never be forgiven; he is guilty of an eternal sin.' ³⁰ He said this because they had declared that he was possessed by an unclean spirit.

³¹ Then his mother and his brothers arrived; they stayed outside and sent in a message asking him to come out to them. ³² A crowd was sitting round him when word was brought that his mother and brothers were outside asking for him. ³³ 'Who are my mother and my brothers?' he replied. ³⁴ And looking round at those who were sitting in the circle about him he said, 'Here are my mother and my brothers. ³⁵ Whoever does the will of God is my brother and sister and mother.'

Parables

4 ON another occasion he began to teach by the lakeside. The crowd that gathered round him was so large that he had to get into a boat on the lake and sit there, with the whole crowd on the beach right down to the water's edge. ² And he taught them many things by parables.

As he taught he said:

[3] 'Listen! A sower went out to sow. [4] And it happened that as he sowed, some of the seed fell along the footpath; and the birds came and ate it up. [5] Some fell on rocky ground, where it had little soil, and it sprouted quickly because it had no depth of earth; [6] but when the sun rose it was scorched, and as it had no root it withered away. [7] Some fell among thistles; and the thistles grew up and choked the corn, and it produced no crop. [8] And some of the seed fell into good soil, where it came up and grew, and produced a crop; and the yield was thirtyfold, sixtyfold, even a hundredfold.' [9] He added, 'If you have ears to hear, then hear.'

[10] When Jesus was alone with the Twelve and his other companions they questioned him about the parables. [11] He answered, 'To you the secret of the kingdom of God has been given; but to those who are outside, everything comes by way of parables, [12] so that (as scripture says) they may look and look, but see nothing; they may listen and listen, but understand nothing; otherwise they might turn to God and be forgiven.'

[13] He went on: 'Do you not understand this parable? How then are you to understand any parable? [14] The sower sows the word. [15] With some the seed falls along the footpath; no sooner have they heard it than Satan comes and carries off the word which has been sown in them. [16] With others the seed falls on rocky ground; as soon as they hear the word, they accept it with joy, [17] but it strikes no root in them; they have no staying-power, and when there is trouble or persecution on account of the word, they quickly lose faith. [18] With others again the seed falls among thistles; they hear the word, [19] but worldly cares and the false glamour of wealth and evil desires of all kinds come in and choke the word, and it proves barren. [20] But there are some with whom the seed is sown on good soil; they accept the word when they hear it, and they bear fruit thirtyfold, sixtyfold, or a hundredfold.'

[21] He said to them, 'Is a lamp brought in to be put under the measuring bowl or under the bed? No, it is put on the lampstand. [22] Nothing is hidden except to be disclosed, and nothing concealed except to be brought into the open. [23] If you have ears to hear, then hear.'

[24] He also said to them, 'Take note of what you hear; the measure you give is the measure you will receive, with something more besides. [25] For those who have will be given more, and those who have not will forfeit even what they have.'

[26] He said, 'The kingdom of God is like this. A man scatters seed on the ground; [27] he goes to bed at night and gets up in the morning, and meanwhile the seed sprouts and grows—how, he does not know. [28] The ground produces a crop by itself, first the blade, then the ear, then full grain in the ear; [29] but as soon as the crop is ripe, he starts reaping, because harvest time has come.'

[30] He said, 'How shall we picture the kingdom of God, or what parable shall we use to describe it? [31] It is like a mustard seed; when sown in the ground it is smaller than any other seed, [32] but once sown, it springs up and grows taller than any other plant, and forms branches so large that birds can roost in its shade.'

[33] With many such parables he used to give them his message, so far as they were able to receive it. [34] He never spoke to them except in parables; but privately to his disciples he explained everything.

Miracles

[35] THAT day, in the evening, he said to them, 'Let us cross over to the other side of the lake.' [36] So they left the crowd and took him with them in the boat in which he had been sitting; and some other boats went with him. [37] A fierce squall blew up and the waves broke over the boat until it was all but swamped. [38] Now he was in the stern asleep on a cushion; they roused him and said, 'Teacher, we are sinking! Do you not care?' [39] He awoke and rebuked the wind, and said to the sea, 'Silence! Be still!' The wind dropped and there was a dead calm. [40] He said to them, 'Why are you such cowards? Have you no faith even now?' [41] They were awestruck and said to one another, 'Who can this be? Even the wind and the sea obey him.'

5 So they came to the country of the Gerasenes on the other side of the lake. [2] As he stepped ashore, a man possessed by an unclean spirit came up to him from among the tombs [3] where he had made his home. Nobody could control him any longer; even chains were useless, [4] for he had often been fettered

and chained up, but had snapped his chains and broken the fetters. No one was strong enough to master him. [5] Unceasingly, night and day, he would cry aloud among the tombs and on the hillsides and gash himself with stones. [6] When he saw Jesus in the distance, he ran up and flung himself down before him, [7] shouting at the top of his voice, 'What do you want with me, Jesus, son of the Most High God? In God's name do not torment me.' [8] For Jesus was already saying to him, 'Out, unclean spirit, come out of the man!' [9] Jesus asked him, 'What is your name?' 'My name is Legion', he said, 'there are so many of us.' [10] And he implored Jesus not to send them out of the district. [11] There was a large herd of pigs nearby, feeding on the hillside, [12] and the spirits begged him, 'Send us among the pigs; let us go into them.' [13] He gave them leave; and the unclean spirits came out and went into the pigs; and the herd, of about two thousand, rushed over the edge into the lake and were drowned.

[14] The men in charge of them took to their heels and carried the news to the town and countryside; and the people came out to see what had happened. [15] When they came to Jesus and saw the madman who had been possessed by the legion of demons, sitting there clothed and in his right mind, they were afraid. [16] When eyewitnesses told them what had happened to the madman and what had become of the pigs, [17] they begged Jesus to leave the district. [18] As he was getting into the boat, the man who had been possessed begged to go with him. [19] But Jesus would not let him. 'Go home to your own people,' he said, 'and tell them what the Lord in his mercy has done for you.' [20] The man went off and made known throughout the Decapolis what Jesus had done for him; and everyone was amazed.

[21] As soon as Jesus had returned by boat to the other shore, a large crowd gathered round him. While he was by the lakeside, [22] there came a synagogue president named Jairus; and when he saw him, he threw himself down at his feet [23] and pleaded with him. 'My little daughter is at death's door,' he said. 'I beg you to come and lay your hands on her so that her life may be saved.' [24] So Jesus went with him, accompanied by a great crowd which pressed round him.

[25] Among them was a woman who had suffered from haemorrhages for twelve years; [26] and in spite of long treatment by many doctors, on which she had spent all she had, she had become worse rather than better. [27] She had heard about Jesus, and came up behind him in the crowd and touched his cloak; [28] for she said, 'If I touch even his clothes, I shall be healed.' [29] And there and then the flow of blood dried up and she knew in herself that she was cured of her affliction. [30] Aware at once that power had gone out of him, Jesus turned round in the crowd and asked, 'Who touched my clothes?' [31] His disciples said to him, 'You see the crowd pressing round you and yet you ask, "Who touched me?"' [32] But he kept looking around to see who had done it. [33] Then the woman, trembling with fear because she knew what had happened to her, came and fell at his feet and told him the whole truth. [34] He said to her, 'Daughter, your faith has healed you. Go in peace, free from your affliction.'

[35] While he was still speaking, a message came from the president's house, 'Your daughter has died; why trouble the teacher any more?' [36] But Jesus, overhearing the message as it was delivered, said to the president of the synagogue, 'Do not be afraid; simply have faith.' [37] Then he allowed no one to accompany him except Peter and James and James's brother John. [38] They came to the president's house, where he found a great commotion, with loud crying and wailing. [39] So he went in and said to them, 'Why this crying and commotion? The child is not dead: she is asleep'; [40] and they laughed at him. After turning everyone out, he took the child's father and mother and his own companions into the room where the child was. [41] Taking hold of her hand, he said to her, 'Talitha cum,' which means, 'Get up, my child.' [42] Immediately the girl got up and walked about—she was twelve years old. They were overcome with amazement; [43] but he gave them strict instructions not to let anyone know about it, and told them to give her something to eat.

6 From there he went to his home town accompanied by his disciples. [2] When the sabbath came he began to teach in the synagogue; and the large congregation who heard him asked in amazement,

'Where does he get it from? What is this wisdom he has been given? How does he perform such miracles? [3] Is he not the carpenter, the son of Mary, the brother of James and Joses and Judas and Simon? Are not his sisters here with us?' So they turned against him. [4] Jesus said to them, 'A prophet never lacks honour except in his home town, among his relations and his own family.' [5] And he was unable to do any miracle there, except that he put his hands on a few sick people and healed them; [6] and he was astonished at their want of faith.

Death of John the Baptist

As HE went round the villages teaching,[7] he summoned the Twelve and sent them out two by two with authority over unclean spirits. [8] He instructed them to take nothing for the journey except a stick—no bread, no pack, no money in their belts. [9] They might wear sandals, but not a second coat. [10] 'When you enter a house,' he told them, 'stay there until you leave that district. [11] At any place where they will not receive you or listen to you, shake the dust off your feet as you leave, as a solemn warning.' [12] So they set out and proclaimed the need for repentance; [13] they drove out many demons, and anointed many sick people with oil and cured them.

[14] Now King Herod heard of Jesus, for his fame had spread, and people were saying, 'John the Baptist has been raised from the dead, and that is why these miraculous powers are at work in him.' [15] Others said, 'It is Elijah.' Others again, 'He is a prophet like one of the prophets of old.' [16] But when Herod heard of it, he said, 'This is John, whom I beheaded, raised from the dead.'

[17] It was this Herod who had sent men to arrest John and put him in prison at the instance of his brother Philip's wife, Herodias, whom he had married. [18] John had told him, 'You have no right to take your brother's wife.' [19] Herodias nursed a grudge against John and would willingly have killed him, but she could not, [20] for Herod went in awe of him, knowing him to be a good and holy man; so he gave him his protection. He liked to listen to

him, although what he heard left him greatly disturbed.

[21] Herodias found her opportunity when Herod on his birthday gave a banquet to his chief officials and commanders and the leading men of Galilee. [22] Her daughter came in and danced, and so delighted Herod and his guests that the king said to the girl, 'Ask me for anything you like and I will give it to you.' [23] He even said on oath: 'Whatever you ask I will give you, up to half my kingdom.' [24] She went out and said to her mother, 'What shall I ask for?' She replied, 'The head of John the Baptist.' [25] The girl hurried straight back to the king with her request: 'I want you to give me, here and now, on a dish, the head of John the Baptist.' [26] The king was greatly distressed, yet because of his oath and his guests he could not bring himself to refuse her. [27] He sent a soldier of the guard with orders to bring John's head; and the soldier went to the prison and beheaded him; [28] then he brought the head on a dish, and gave it to the girl; and she gave it to her mother.

[29] When John's disciples heard the news, they came and took his body away and laid it in a tomb.

Miracles of feeding and their significance

[30] THE apostles rejoined Jesus and reported to him all that they had done and taught. [31] He said to them, 'Come with me, by yourselves, to some remote place and rest a little.' With many coming and going they had no time even to eat. [32] So they set off by boat privately for a remote place. [33] But many saw them leave and recognized them, and people from all the towns hurried round on foot and arrived there first. [34] When he came ashore and saw a large crowd, his heart went out to them, because they were like sheep without a shepherd; and he began to teach them many things. [35] It was already getting late, and his disciples came to him and said, 'This is a remote place and it is already very late; [36] send the people off to the farms and villages round about, to buy themselves something to eat.' [37] 'Give them something to eat yourselves,' he answered. They replied, 'Are we to go and

6:3 the carpenter ... Mary: *some witnesses read* the son of the carpenter and Mary.   6:14 and ... saying: *some witnesses read* and he said.

spend two hundred denarii to provide them with food?' [38] 'How many loaves have you?' he asked. 'Go and see.' They found out and told him, 'Five, and two fish.' [39] He ordered them to make the people sit down in groups on the green grass, [40] and they sat down in rows, in companies of fifty and a hundred. [41] Then, taking the five loaves and the two fish, he looked up to heaven, said the blessing, broke the loaves, and gave them to the disciples to distribute. He also divided the two fish among them. [42] They all ate and were satisfied; [43] and twelve baskets were filled with what was left of the bread and the fish. [44] Those who ate the loaves numbered five thousand men.

[45] As soon as they had finished, he made his disciples embark and cross to Bethsaida ahead of him, while he himself dismissed the crowd. [46] After taking leave of them, he went up the hill to pray. [47] It was now late and the boat was already well out on the water, while he was alone on the land. [48] Somewhere between three and six in the morning, seeing them labouring at the oars against a head wind, he came towards them, walking on the lake. He was going to pass by them; [49] but when they saw him walking on the lake, they thought it was a ghost and cried out; [50] for they all saw him and were terrified. But at once he spoke to them: 'Take heart! It is I; do not be afraid.' [51] Then he climbed into the boat with them, and the wind dropped. At this they were utterly astounded, [52] for they had not understood the incident of the loaves; their minds were closed.

[53] So they completed the crossing and landed at Gennesaret, where they made fast. [54] When they came ashore, he was recognized at once; [55] and the people scoured the whole countryside and brought the sick on their beds to any place where he was reported to be. [56] Wherever he went, to village or town or farm, they laid the sick in the market-place and begged him to let them simply touch the edge of his cloak; and all who touched him were healed.

7 A GROUP of Pharisees, with some scribes who had come from Jerusalem, met him [2] and noticed that some of his disciples were eating their food with defiled hands—in other words, without washing them. [3] (For Pharisees and Jews in general never eat without washing their hands, in obedience to ancient tradition; [4] and on coming from the market-place they never eat without first washing. And there are many other points on which they maintain traditional rules, for example in the washing of cups and jugs and copper bowls.) [5] These Pharisees and scribes questioned Jesus: 'Why do your disciples not conform to the ancient tradition, but eat their food with defiled hands?' [6] He answered, 'How right Isaiah was when he prophesied about you hypocrites in these words: "This people pays me lip-service, but their heart is far from me: [7] they worship me in vain, for they teach as doctrines the commandments of men." [8] You neglect the commandment of God, in order to maintain the tradition of men.'

[9] He said to them, 'How clever you are at setting aside the commandment of God in order to maintain your tradition! [10] Moses said, "Honour your father and your mother," and again, "Whoever curses his father or mother shall be put to death." [11] But you hold that if someone says to his father or mother, "Anything I have which might have been used for your benefit is Corban,"' (that is, set apart for God) [12] 'he is no longer allowed to do anything for his father or mother. [13] In this way by your tradition, handed down among you, you make God's word null and void. And you do many other things just like that.'

[14] On another occasion he called the people and said to them, 'Listen to me, all of you, and understand this: [15] nothing that goes into a person from outside can defile him; no, it is the things that come out of a person that defile him.'

[17] When he had left the people and gone indoors, his disciples questioned him about the parable. [18] He said to them, 'Are you as dull as the rest? Do you not see that nothing that goes into a person from outside can defile him, [19] because it does not go into the heart but into the stomach, and so goes out into the drain?' By saying this he declared all foods clean.

6: 37 **denarii**: *see p. xi.*   6: 56 **edge**: *or tassel.*   7: 3 **washing their hands**: *some witnesses add* with the fist; *others add* frequently; *or* thoroughly.   7: 9 **maintain**: *some witnesses read* establish.   7: 15 **that defile him**: *some witnesses here add* [16] If you have ears to hear, then hear.

²⁰ He went on, 'It is what comes out of a person that defiles him. ²¹ From inside, from the human heart, come evil thoughts, acts of fornication, theft, murder, ²² adultery, greed, and malice; fraud, indecency, envy, slander, arrogance, and folly; ²³ all these evil things come from within, and they are what defile a person.'

²⁴ He moved on from there into the territory of Tyre. He found a house to stay in, and would have liked to remain unrecognized, but that was impossible. ²⁵ Almost at once a woman whose small daughter was possessed by an unclean spirit heard of him and came and fell at his feet. ²⁶ (The woman was a Gentile, a Phoenician of Syria by nationality.) She begged him to drive the demon out of her daughter. ²⁷ He said to her, 'Let the children be satisfied first; it is not right to take the children's bread and throw it to the dogs.' ²⁸ 'Sir,' she replied, 'even the dogs under the table eat the children's scraps.' ²⁹ He said to her, 'For saying that, go, and you will find the demon has left your daughter.' ³⁰ And when she returned home, she found the child lying in bed; the demon had left her.

³¹ On his journey back from Tyrian territory he went by way of Sidon to the sea of Galilee, well within the territory of the Decapolis. ³² They brought to him a man who was deaf and had an impediment in his speech, and begged Jesus to lay his hand on him. ³³ He took him aside, away from the crowd; then he put his fingers in the man's ears, and touched his tongue with spittle. ³⁴ Looking up to heaven, he sighed, and said to him, 'Ephphatha', which means 'Be opened.' ³⁵ With that his hearing was restored, and at the same time the impediment was removed and he spoke clearly. ³⁶ Jesus forbade them to tell anyone; but the more he forbade them, the more they spread it abroad. ³⁷ Their astonishment knew no bounds: 'All that he does, he does well,' they said; 'he even makes the deaf hear and the dumb speak.'

8 THERE was another occasion about this time when a huge crowd had collected, and, as they had no food, Jesus called his disciples and said to them, ² 'My heart goes out to these people; they have been with me now for three days and have nothing to eat. ³ If I send them home hungry, they will faint on the way, and some of them have a long way to go.' ⁴ His disciples answered, 'How can anyone provide these people with bread in this remote place?' ⁵ 'How many loaves have you?' he asked; and they answered, 'Seven.' ⁶ So he ordered the people to sit down on the ground; then he took the seven loaves, and after giving thanks to God he broke the bread and gave it to his disciples to distribute; and they distributed it to the people. ⁷ They had also a few small fish, which he blessed and ordered them to distribute. ⁸ They ate and were satisfied, and seven baskets were filled with what was left over. ⁹ The people numbered about four thousand. Then he dismissed them, ¹⁰ and at once got into the boat with his disciples and went to the district of Dalmanutha.

¹¹ Then the Pharisees came out and began to argue with him. To test him they asked him for a sign from heaven. ¹² He sighed deeply and said, 'Why does this generation ask for a sign? Truly I tell you: no sign shall be given to this generation.' ¹³ With that he left them, re-embarked, and made for the other shore.

¹⁴ Now they had forgotten to take bread with them, and had only one loaf in the boat. ¹⁵ He began to warn them: 'Beware,' he said, 'be on your guard against the leaven of the Pharisees and the leaven of Herod.' ¹⁶ So they began to talk among themselves about having no bread. ¹⁷ Knowing this, he said to them, 'Why are you talking about having no bread? Have you no inkling yet? Do you still not understand? Are your minds closed? ¹⁸ You have eyes: can you not see? You have ears: can you not hear? Have you forgotten? ¹⁹ When I broke the five loaves among five thousand, how many basketfuls of pieces did you pick up?' 'Twelve,' they said. ²⁰ 'And how many when I broke the seven loaves among four thousand?' 'Seven,' they answered. ²¹ He said to them, 'Do you still not understand?'

²² They arrived at Bethsaida. There the people brought a blind man to Jesus and begged him to touch him. ²³ He took the blind man by the hand and led him out of

8:10 *Dalmanutha: some witnesses read* Magedan; *others read* Magdala.

the village. Then he spat on his eyes, laid his hands upon him, and asked whether he could see anything. [24] The man's sight began to come back, and he said, 'I see people—they look like trees, but they are walking about.' [25] Jesus laid his hands on his eyes again; he looked hard, and now he was cured and could see everything clearly. [26] Then Jesus sent him home, saying, 'Do not even go into the village.'

The cross foreshadowed

[27] JESUS and his disciples set out for the villages of Caesarea Philippi, and on the way he asked his disciples, 'Who do people say I am?' [28] They answered, 'Some say John the Baptist, others Elijah, others one of the prophets.' [29] 'And you,' he asked, 'who do you say I am?' Peter replied: 'You are the Messiah.' [30] Then he gave them strict orders not to tell anyone about him; [31] and he began to teach them that the Son of Man had to endure great suffering, and to be rejected by the elders, chief priests, and scribes; to be put to death, and to rise again three days afterwards. [32] He spoke about it plainly. At this Peter took hold of him and began to rebuke him. [33] But Jesus, turning and looking at his disciples, rebuked Peter. 'Out of my sight, Satan!' he said. 'You think as men think, not as God thinks.'

[34] Then he called the people to him, as well as his disciples, and said to them, 'Anyone who wants to be a follower of mine must renounce self; he must take up his cross and follow me. [35] Whoever wants to save his life will lose it, but whoever loses his life for my sake and for the gospel's will save it. [36] What does anyone gain by winning the whole world at the cost of his life? [37] What can he give to buy his life back? [38] If anyone is ashamed of me and my words in this wicked and godless age, the Son of Man will be ashamed of him, when he comes in the glory of his Father with the holy angels.'

9 He said to them, 'Truly I tell you: there are some of those standing here who will not taste death before they have seen the kingdom of God come with power.'

[2] Six days later Jesus took Peter, James, and John with him and led them up a high mountain by themselves. And in their presence he was transfigured; [3] his clothes became dazzling white, with a whiteness no bleacher on earth could equal. [4] They saw Elijah appear and Moses with him, talking with Jesus. [5] Then Peter spoke: 'Rabbi,' he said, 'it is good that we are here! Shall we make three shelters, one for you, one for Moses, and one for Elijah?' [6] For he did not know what to say; they were so terrified. [7] Then a cloud appeared, casting its shadow over them, and out of the cloud came a voice: 'This is my beloved Son; listen to him.' [8] And suddenly, when they looked around, only Jesus was with them; there was no longer anyone else to be seen.

[9] On their way down the mountain, he instructed them not to tell anyone what they had seen until the Son of Man had risen from the dead. [10] They seized upon those words, and discussed among themselves what this 'rising from the dead' could mean. [11] And they put a question to him: 'Why do the scribes say that Elijah must come first?' [12] He replied, 'Elijah does come first to set everything right. How is it, then, that the scriptures say of the Son of Man that he is to endure great suffering and be treated with contempt? [13] However, I tell you, Elijah has already come and they have done to him what they wanted, as the scriptures say of him.'

[14] When they came back to the disciples they saw a large crowd surrounding them and scribes arguing with them. [15] As soon as they saw Jesus the whole crowd were overcome with awe and ran forward to welcome him. [16] He asked them, 'What is this argument about?' [17] A man in the crowd spoke up: 'Teacher, I brought my son for you to cure. He is possessed by a spirit that makes him dumb. [18] Whenever it attacks him, it flings him to the ground, and he foams at the mouth, grinds his teeth, and goes rigid. I asked your disciples to drive it out, but they could not.' [19] Jesus answered: 'What an unbelieving generation! How long shall I be with you? How long must I endure you? Bring him to me.' [20] So they brought the boy to him; and as soon as the spirit saw him it threw the boy into convulsions, and he fell on

8:26 Do ... village: *some witnesses read* Do not tell anyone in the village.   8:38 me and my words: *some witnesses read* me and mine. Father ... angels: *some witnesses read* Father and of the holy angels.   9:7 This ... Son: *or* This is my only Son.

the ground and rolled about foaming at the mouth. ²¹ Jesus asked his father, 'How long has he been like this?' 'From childhood,' he replied; ²² 'it has often tried to destroy him by throwing him into the fire or into water. But if it is at all possible for you, take pity on us and help us.' ²³ 'If it is possible!' said Jesus. 'Everything is possible to one who believes.' ²⁴ At once the boy's father cried: 'I believe; help my unbelief.' ²⁵ When Jesus saw that the crowd was closing in on them, he spoke sternly to the unclean spirit. 'Deaf and dumb spirit,' he said, 'I command you, come out of him and never go back!' ²⁶ It shrieked aloud and threw the boy into repeated convulsions, and then came out, leaving him looking like a corpse; in fact, many said, 'He is dead.' ²⁷ But Jesus took hold of his hand and raised him to his feet, and he stood up.

²⁸ Then Jesus went indoors, and his disciples asked him privately, 'Why could we not drive it out?' ²⁹ He said, 'This kind cannot be driven out except by prayer.'

Learning what discipleship means

³⁰ THEY left that district and made their way through Galilee. Jesus did not want anyone to know, ³¹ because he was teaching his disciples, and telling them, 'The Son of Man is now to be handed over into the power of men, and they will kill him; and three days after being killed he will rise again.' ³² But they did not understand what he said, and were afraid to ask.

³³ So they came to Capernaum; and when he had gone indoors, he asked them, 'What were you arguing about on the way?' ³⁴ They were silent, because on the way they had been discussing which of them was the greatest. ³⁵ So he sat down, called the Twelve, and said to them, 'If anyone wants to be first, he must make himself last of all and servant of all.' ³⁶ Then he took a child, set him in front of them, and put his arm round him. ³⁷ 'Whoever receives a child like this in my name,' he said, 'receives me; and whoever receives me, receives not me but the One who sent me.'

³⁸ John said to him, 'Teacher, we saw someone driving out demons in your name, and as he was not one of us, we tried to stop him.' ³⁹ Jesus said, 'Do not stop him, for no one who performs a miracle in my name will be able the next moment to speak evil of me. ⁴⁰ He who is not against us is on our side. ⁴¹ Truly I tell you: whoever gives you a cup of water to drink because you are followers of the Messiah will certainly not go unrewarded.

⁴² 'If anyone causes the downfall of one of these little ones who believe, it would be better for him to be thrown into the sea with a millstone round his neck. ⁴³ If your hand causes your downfall, cut it off; it is better for you to enter into life maimed than to keep both hands and go to hell, to the unquenchable fire. ⁴⁵ If your foot causes your downfall, cut it off; it is better to enter into life crippled than to keep both your feet and be thrown into hell. ⁴⁷ And if your eye causes your downfall, tear it out; it is better to enter into the kingdom of God with one eye than to keep both eyes and be thrown into hell, ⁴⁸ where the devouring worm never dies and the fire is never quenched.

⁴⁹ 'Everyone will be salted with fire.

⁵⁰ 'Salt is good; but if the salt loses its saltness, how will you season it?

'You must have salt within yourselves, and be at peace with one another.'

10 ON leaving there he came into the regions of Judaea and Transjordan. Once again crowds gathered round him, and he taught them as was his practice. ² He was asked: 'Is it lawful for a man to divorce his wife?' This question was put to test him. ³ He responded by asking, 'What did Moses command you?' ⁴ They answered, 'Moses permitted a man to divorce his wife by a certificate of dismissal.' ⁵ Jesus said to them, 'It was because of your stubbornness that he made this rule for you. ⁶ But in the beginning, at the creation, "God made them male and female." ⁷ "That is why a man leaves his father and mother, and is united to his wife, ⁸ and the two become one flesh." It follows that they are no longer two individuals: they are one flesh.

9:29 **by prayer:** *some witnesses add* and fasting.   9:43 **unquenchable fire:** *some witnesses add* ⁴⁴ where the devouring worm never dies and the fire is never quenched.   9:45 **into hell:** *some witnesses add* ⁴⁶ where the devouring worm never dies and the fire is never quenched.   10:2 **He was asked:** *some witnesses read* Pharisees approached and asked him.

⁹ Therefore what God has joined together, man must not separate.'

¹⁰ When they were indoors again, the disciples questioned him about this. ¹¹ He said to them, 'Whoever divorces his wife and remarries commits adultery against her; ¹² so too, if she divorces her husband and remarries, she commits adultery.'

¹³ They brought children for him to touch. The disciples rebuked them, ¹⁴ but when Jesus saw it he was indignant, and said to them, 'Let the children come to me; do not try to stop them; for the kingdom of God belongs to such as these. ¹⁵ Truly I tell you: whoever does not accept the kingdom of God like a child will never enter it.' ¹⁶ And he put his arms round them, laid his hands on them, and blessed them.

¹⁷ As he was starting out on a journey, a stranger ran up, and, kneeling before him, asked, 'Good Teacher, what must I do to win eternal life?' ¹⁸ Jesus said to him, 'Why do you call me good? No one is good except God alone. ¹⁹ You know the commandments: "Do not murder; do not commit adultery; do not steal; do not give false evidence; do not defraud; honour your father and mother."' ²⁰ 'But Teacher,' he replied, 'I have kept all these since I was a boy.' ²¹ As Jesus looked at him, his heart warmed to him. 'One thing you lack,' he said. 'Go, sell everything you have, and give to the poor, and you will have treasure in heaven; then come and follow me.' ²² At these words his face fell and he went away with a heavy heart; for he was a man of great wealth.

²³ Jesus looked round at his disciples and said to them, 'How hard it will be for the wealthy to enter the kingdom of God!' ²⁴ They were amazed that he should say this, but Jesus insisted, 'Children, how hard it is to enter the kingdom of God! ²⁵ It is easier for a camel to pass through the eye of a needle than for a rich man to enter the kingdom of God.' ²⁶ They were more astonished than ever, and said to one another, 'Then who can be saved?' ²⁷ Jesus looked at them and said, 'For men it is impossible, but not for God; everything is possible for God.'

²⁸ 'What about us?' said Peter. 'We have left everything to follow you.' ²⁹ Jesus said, 'Truly I tell you: there is no one who has given up home, brothers or sisters, mother, father or children, or land, for my sake and for the gospel, ³⁰ who will not receive in this age a hundred times as much—houses, brothers and sisters, mothers and children, and land—and persecutions besides; and in the age to come eternal life. ³¹ But many who are first will be last, and the last first.'

³² THEY were on the road going up to Jerusalem, and Jesus was leading the way; and the disciples were filled with awe, while those who followed behind were afraid. Once again he took the Twelve aside and began to tell them what was to happen to him. ³³ 'We are now going up to Jerusalem,' he said, 'and the Son of Man will be handed over to the chief priests and the scribes; they will condemn him to death and hand him over to the Gentiles. ³⁴ He will be mocked and spat upon, and flogged and killed; and three days afterwards, he will rise again.'

³⁵ James and John, the sons of Zebedee, approached him and said, 'Teacher, we should like you to do us a favour.' ³⁶ 'What is it you want me to do for you?' he asked. ³⁷ They answered, 'Allow us to sit with you in your glory, one at your right hand and the other at your left.' ³⁸ Jesus said to them, 'You do not understand what you are asking. Can you drink the cup that I drink, or be baptized with the baptism I am baptized with?' ³⁹ 'We can,' they answered. Jesus said, 'The cup that I drink you shall drink, and the baptism I am baptized with shall be your baptism; ⁴⁰ but to sit on my right or on my left is not for me to grant; that honour is for those to whom it has already been assigned.'

⁴¹ When the other ten heard this, they were indignant with James and John. ⁴² Jesus called them to him and said, 'You know that among the Gentiles the recognized rulers lord it over their subjects, and the great make their authority felt. ⁴³ It shall not be so with you; among you, whoever wants to be great must be your servant, ⁴⁴ and whoever wants to be first must be the slave of all. ⁴⁵ For the Son of Man did not come to be served but to serve, and to give his life as a ransom for many.'

10:24 **how hard it is:** *some witnesses add* for those who trust in riches.

⁴⁶ They came to Jericho; and as he was leaving the town, with his disciples and a large crowd, Bartimaeus (that is, son of Timaeus), a blind beggar, was seated at the roadside. ⁴⁷ Hearing that it was Jesus of Nazareth, he began to shout, 'Son of David, Jesus, have pity on me!' ⁴⁸ Many of the people told him to hold his tongue; but he shouted all the more, 'Son of David, have pity on me.' ⁴⁹ Jesus stopped and said, 'Call him'; so they called the blind man: 'Take heart,' they said. 'Get up; he is calling you.' ⁵⁰ At that he threw off his cloak, jumped to his feet, and came to Jesus. ⁵¹ Jesus said to him, 'What do you want me to do for you?' 'Rabbi,' the blind man answered, 'I want my sight back.' ⁵² Jesus said to him, 'Go; your faith has healed you.' And at once he recovered his sight and followed him on the road.

The challenge to Jerusalem

11 THEY were now approaching Jerusalem, and when they reached Bethphage and Bethany, close by the mount of Olives, he sent off two of his disciples. ² 'Go into the village opposite,' he told them, 'and just as you enter you will find tethered there a colt which no one has yet ridden. Untie it and bring it here. ³ If anyone asks why you are doing this, say, "The Master needs it, and will send it back here without delay."' ⁴ So they went off, and found the colt outside in the street, tethered beside a door. As they were untying it, ⁵ some of the by-standers asked, 'What are you doing, untying that colt?' ⁶ They answered as Jesus had told them, and were then allowed to take it. ⁷ So they brought the colt to Jesus, and when they had spread their cloaks on it he mounted it. ⁸ Many people carpeted the road with their cloaks, while others spread greenery which they had cut in the fields; ⁹ and those in front and those behind shouted, 'Hosanna! Blessed is he who comes in the name of the Lord! ¹⁰ Blessed is the kingdom of our father David which is coming! Hosanna in the heavens!'

¹¹ He entered Jerusalem and went into the temple. He looked round at everything; then, as it was already late, he went out to Bethany with the Twelve.

¹² On the following day, as they left Bethany, he felt hungry, ¹³ and, noticing in the distance a fig tree in leaf, he went to see if he could find anything on it. But when he reached it he found nothing but leaves; for it was not the season for figs. ¹⁴ He said to the tree, 'May no one ever again eat fruit from you!' And his disciples were listening.

¹⁵ So they came to Jerusalem, and he went into the temple and began to drive out those who bought and sold there. He upset the tables of the money-changers and the seats of the dealers in pigeons; ¹⁶ and he would not allow anyone to carry goods through the temple court. ¹⁷ Then he began to teach them, and said, 'Does not scripture say, "My house shall be called a house of prayer for all nations"? But you have made it a robbers' cave.' ¹⁸ The chief priests and the scribes heard of this and looked for a way to bring about his death; for they were afraid of him, because the whole crowd was spellbound by his teaching. ¹⁹ And when evening came they went out of the city.

²⁰ Early next morning, as they passed by, they saw that the fig tree had withered from the roots up; ²¹ and Peter, recalling what had happened, said to him, 'Rabbi, look, the fig tree which you cursed has withered.' ²² Jesus answered them, 'Have faith in God. ²³ Truly I tell you: if anyone says to this mountain, "Be lifted from your place and hurled into the sea," and has no inward doubts, but believes that what he says will happen, it will be done for him. ²⁴ I tell you, then, whatever you ask for in prayer, believe that you have received it and it will be yours.

²⁵ 'And when you stand praying, if you have a grievance against anyone, forgive him, so that your Father in heaven may forgive you the wrongs you have done.'

²⁷ THEY came once more to Jerusalem. And as he was walking in the temple court the chief priests, scribes, and elders came to him ²⁸ and said, 'By what authority are you acting like this? Who gave you authority to act in this way?' ²⁹ Jesus said to them, 'I also have a question for you, and if you give me an answer, I will tell you by what authority I act. ³⁰ The

---

11:3 **The Master:** *or* Its owner.　　11:25 **wrongs you have done:** *some witnesses add* ²⁶ But if you do not forgive others, then the wrongs you have done will not be forgiven by your Father in heaven.

baptism of John: was it from God, or from men? Answer me.' ³¹ This set them arguing among themselves: 'What shall we say? If we say, "From God," he will say, "Then why did you not believe him?" ³² Shall we say, "From men"?'— but they were afraid of the people, for all held that John was in fact a prophet. ³³ So they answered, 'We do not know.' And Jesus said to them, 'Then I will not tell you either by what authority I act.'

12 He went on to speak to them in parables: 'A man planted a vineyard and put a wall round it, hewed out a winepress, and built a watch-tower; then he let it out to vine-growers and went abroad. ² When the season came, he sent a servant to the tenants to collect from them his share of the produce. ³ But they seized him, thrashed him, and sent him away empty-handed. ⁴ Again, he sent them another servant, whom they beat about the head and treated outrageously. ⁵ and then another, whom they killed. He sent many others and they thrashed some and killed the rest. ⁶ He had now no one left to send except his beloved son, and in the end he sent him. "They will respect my son," he said; ⁷ but the tenants said to one another, "This is the heir; come on, let us kill him, and the inheritance will be ours." ⁸ So they seized him and killed him, and flung his body out of the vineyard. ⁹ What will the owner of the vineyard do? He will come and put the tenants to death and give the vineyard to others. ¹⁰ 'Have you never read this text: "The stone which the builders rejected has become the main corner-stone. ¹¹ This is the Lord's doing, and it is wonderful in our eyes"?'

¹² They saw that the parable was aimed at them and wanted to arrest him; but they were afraid of the people, so they left him alone and went away.

¹³ A NUMBER of Pharisees and men of Herod's party were sent to trap him with a question. ¹⁴ They came and said, 'Teacher, we know you are a sincere man and court no one's favour, whoever he may be; you teach in all sincerity the way of life that God requires. Are we or are we not permitted to pay taxes to the Roman emperor? ¹⁵ Shall we pay or not?' He saw through their duplicity, and said, 'Why are you trying to catch me out? Fetch me a silver piece, and let me look at it.' ¹⁶ They brought one, and he asked them, 'Whose head is this, and whose inscription?' 'Caesar's,' they replied. ¹⁷ Then Jesus said, 'Pay Caesar what belongs to Caesar, and God what belongs to God.' His reply left them completely taken aback.

¹⁸ Next Sadducees, who maintain that there is no resurrection, came to him and asked: ¹⁹ 'Teacher, Moses laid it down for us that if there are brothers, and one dies leaving a wife but no child, then the next should marry the widow and provide an heir for his brother. ²⁰ Now there were seven brothers. The first took a wife and died without issue. ²¹ Then the second married her, and he too died without issue; so did the third; ²² none of the seven left any issue. Finally the woman died. ²³ At the resurrection, when they rise from the dead, whose wife will she be, since all seven had married her?' ²⁴ Jesus said to them, 'How far you are from the truth! You know neither the scriptures nor the power of God. ²⁵ When they rise from the dead, men and women do not marry; they are like angels in heaven.

²⁶ 'As for the resurrection of the dead, have you not read in the book of Moses, in the story of the burning bush, how God spoke to him and said, "I am the God of Abraham, the God of Isaac, the God of Jacob"? ²⁷ He is not God of the dead but of the living. You are very far from the truth.'

²⁸ Then one of the scribes, who had been listening to these discussions and had observed how well Jesus answered, came forward and asked him, 'Which is the first of all the commandments?' ²⁹ He answered, 'The first is, "Hear, O Israel: the Lord our God is the one Lord, ³⁰ and you must love the Lord your God with all your heart, with all your soul, with all your mind, and with all your strength." ³¹ The second is this: "You must love your neighbour as yourself." No other commandment is greater than these.' ³² The scribe said to him, 'Well said, Teacher. You are right in saying that God is one and beside him there is no other. ³³ And to love him with all your heart, all your

---

12:6 **his beloved son:** *or* his only son.

understanding, and all your strength, and to love your neighbour as yourself—that means far more than any whole-offerings and sacrifices.' ³⁴ When Jesus saw how thoughtfully he answered, he said to him, 'You are not far from the kingdom of God.' After that nobody dared put any more questions to him.

³⁵ As he taught in the temple, Jesus went on to say, 'How can the scribes maintain that the Messiah is a son of David? ³⁶ It was David himself who said, when inspired by the Holy Spirit, "The Lord said to my Lord, 'Sit at my right hand until I put your enemies under your feet.'" ³⁷ David himself calls him "Lord"; how can he be David's son?'

There was a large crowd listening eagerly. ³⁸ As he taught them, he said, 'Beware of the scribes, who love to walk up and down in long robes and be greeted respectfully in the street, ³⁹ to have the chief seats in synagogues and places of honour at feasts. ⁴⁰ Those who eat up the property of widows, while for appearance' sake they say long prayers, will receive a sentence all the more severe.'

⁴¹ As he was sitting opposite the temple treasury, he watched the people dropping their money into the chest. Many rich people were putting in large amounts. ⁴² Presently there came a poor widow who dropped in two tiny coins, together worth a penny. ⁴³ He called his disciples to him and said, 'Truly I tell you: this poor widow has given more than all those giving to the treasury; ⁴⁴ for the others who have given had more than enough, but she, with less than enough, has given all that she had to live on.'

Warnings about the end

13 As HE was leaving the temple, one of his disciples exclaimed, 'Look, Teacher, what huge stones! What fine buildings!' ² Jesus said to him, 'You see these great buildings? Not one stone will be left upon another; they will all be thrown down.'

³ As he sat on the mount of Olives opposite the temple he was questioned privately by Peter, James, John, and Andrew. ⁴ 'Tell us,' they said, 'when will this happen? What will be the sign that all these things are about to be fulfilled?'

⁵ Jesus began: 'Be on your guard; let no one mislead you. ⁶ Many will come claim-ing my name, and saying, "I am he"; and many will be misled by them. ⁷ When you hear of wars and rumours of wars, do not be alarmed. Such things are bound to happen; but the end is still to come. ⁸ For nation will go to war against nation, kingdom against kingdom; there will be earthquakes in many places; there will be famines. These are the first birth-pangs of the new age.

⁹ 'As for you, be on your guard. You will be handed over to the courts; you will be beaten in synagogues; you will be summoned to appear before governors and kings on my account to testify in their presence. ¹⁰ Before the end the gospel must be proclaimed to all nations. ¹¹ So when you are arrested and put on trial do not worry beforehand about what you will say, but when the time comes say whatever is given you to say, for it is not you who will be speaking, but the Holy Spirit. ¹² Brother will hand over brother to death, and a father his child; children will turn against their parents and send them to their death. ¹³ Everyone will hate you for your allegiance to me, but whoever endures to the end will be saved.

¹⁴ 'But when you see "the abomination of desolation" usurping a place which is not his (let the reader understand), then those who are in Judaea must take to the hills. ¹⁵ If anyone is on the roof, he must not go down into the house to fetch anything out; ¹⁶ if anyone is in the field, he must not turn back for his coat. ¹⁷ Alas for women with child in those days, and for those who have children at the breast! ¹⁸ Pray that it may not come in winter. ¹⁹ For those days will bring distress such as there has never been before since the beginning of the world which God created, and will never be again. ²⁰ If the Lord had not cut short that time of troubles, no living thing could survive. However, for the sake of his own, whom he has chosen, he has cut short the time.

²¹ 'If anyone says to you then, "Look, here is the Messiah," or, "Look, there he is," do not believe it. ²² Impostors will come claiming to be messiahs or prophets, and they will produce signs and wonders to mislead, if possible, God's chosen. ²³ Be on your guard; I have forewarned you of it all.

[24] 'But in those days, after that distress,

the sun will be darkened,
the moon will not give her light;
[25] the stars will come falling from the
sky,
the celestial powers will be shaken.

[26] 'Then they will see the Son of Man coming in the clouds with great power and glory, [27] and he will send out the angels and gather his chosen from the four winds, from the farthest bounds of earth to the farthest bounds of heaven.

[28] 'Learn a lesson from the fig tree. When its tender shoots appear and are breaking into leaf, you know that summer is near. [29] In the same way, when you see all this happening, you may know that the end is near, at the very door. [30] Truly I tell you: the present generation will live to see it all. [31] Heaven and earth will pass away, but my words will never pass away.

[32] 'Yet about that day or hour no one knows, not even the angels in heaven, not even the Son; no one but the Father.

[33] 'Be on your guard, keep watch. You do not know when the moment is coming. [34] It is like a man away from home: he has left his house and put his servants in charge, each with his own work to do, and he has ordered the door-keeper to stay awake. [35] Keep awake, then, for you do not know when the master of the house will come. Evening or midnight, cock-crow or early dawn—[36] if he comes suddenly, do not let him find you asleep. [37] And what I say to you, I say to everyone: Keep awake.'

The trial and crucifixion of Jesus

14 IT was two days before the festival of Passover and Unleavened Bread, and the chief priests and the scribes were trying to devise some scheme to seize him and put him to death. [2] 'It must not be during the festival,' they said, 'or we should have rioting among the people.'

[3] Jesus was at Bethany, in the house of Simon the leper. As he sat at table, a woman came in carrying a bottle of very costly perfume, pure oil of nard. She broke it open and poured the oil over his head.

[4] Some of those present said indignantly to one another, 'Why this waste? [5] The perfume might have been sold for more than three hundred denarii and the money given to the poor'; and they began to scold her. [6] But Jesus said, 'Leave her alone. Why make trouble for her? It is a fine thing she has done for me. [7] You have the poor among you always, and you can help them whenever you like; but you will not always have me. [8] She has done what lay in her power; she has anointed my body in anticipation of my burial. [9] Truly I tell you: wherever the gospel is proclaimed throughout the world, what she has done will be told as her memorial.'

[10] Then Judas Iscariot, one of the Twelve, went to the chief priests to betray him to them. [11] When they heard what he had come for, they were glad and promised him money; and he began to look for an opportunity to betray him.

[12] Now ON the first day of Unleavened Bread, when the Passover lambs were being slaughtered, his disciples said to him, 'Where would you like us to go and prepare the Passover for you?' [13] So he sent off two of his disciples with these instructions: 'Go into the city, and a man will meet you carrying a jar of water. Follow him, [14] and when he enters a house give this message to the householder: "The Teacher says, 'Where is the room in which I am to eat the Passover with my disciples?'" [15] He will show you a large upstairs room, set out in readiness. Make the preparations for us there.' [16] Then the disciples went off, and when they came into the city they found everything just as he had told them. So they prepared the Passover.

[17] In the evening he came to the house with the Twelve. [18] As they sat at supper Jesus said, 'Truly I tell you: one of you will betray me—one who is eating with me.' [19] At this they were distressed; and one by one they said to him, 'Surely you do not mean me?' [20] 'It is one of the Twelve', he said, 'who is dipping into the bowl with me. [21] The Son of Man is going the way appointed for him in the scriptures; but alas for that man by whom the Son of Man is betrayed! It would be better for that man if he had never been born.'

13:29 **the end is near:** *or* he is near.   13:33 **keep watch:** *some witnesses add* and pray.
14:5 **denari:** *see p. xi.*

²² During supper he took bread, and having said the blessing he broke it and gave it to them, with the words: 'Take this; this is my body.' ²³ Then he took a cup, and having offered thanks to God he gave it to them; and they all drank from it. ²⁴ And he said to them, 'This is my blood, the blood of the covenant, shed for many. ²⁵ Truly I tell you: never again shall I drink from the fruit of the vine until that day when I drink it new in the kingdom of God.'

²⁶ After singing the Passover hymn, they went out to the mount of Olives. ²⁷ And Jesus said to them, 'You will all lose faith; for it is written: "I will strike the shepherd and the sheep will be scattered." ²⁸ Nevertheless, after I am raised I shall go ahead of you into Galilee.' ²⁹ Peter answered, 'Everyone else may lose faith, but I will not.' ³⁰ Jesus said to him, 'Truly I tell you: today, this very night, before the cock crows twice, you yourself will disown me three times.' ³¹ But Peter insisted: 'Even if I have to die with you, I will never disown you.' And they all said the same.

³² WHEN they reached a place called Gethsemane, he said to his disciples, 'Sit here while I pray.' ³³ And he took Peter and James and John with him. Horror and anguish overwhelmed him, ³⁴ and he said to them, 'My heart is ready to break with grief; stop here, and stay awake.' ³⁵ Then he went on a little farther, threw himself on the ground, and prayed that if it were possible this hour might pass him by. ³⁶ 'Abba, Father,' he said, 'all things are possible to you; take this cup from me. Yet not my will but yours.'

³⁷ He came back and found them asleep; and he said to Peter, 'Asleep, Simon? Could you not stay awake for one hour? ³⁸ Stay awake, all of you; and pray that you may be spared the test. The spirit is willing, but the flesh is weak.' ³⁹ Once more he went away and prayed. ⁴⁰ On his return he found them asleep again, for their eyes were heavy; and they did not know how to answer him. ⁴¹ He came a third time and said to them, 'Still asleep? Still resting? Enough! The hour has come. The Son of Man is betrayed into the hands of sinners. ⁴² Up, let us go! The traitor is upon us.'

⁴³ He was still speaking when Judas, one of the Twelve, appeared, and with him a crowd armed with swords and cudgels, sent by the chief priests, scribes, and elders. ⁴⁴ Now the traitor had agreed with them on a signal: 'The one I kiss is your man; seize him and get him safely away.' ⁴⁵ When he reached the spot, he went straight up to him and said, 'Rabbi,' and kissed him. ⁴⁶ Then they seized him and held him fast.

⁴⁷ One of the bystanders drew his sword, and struck the high priest's servant, cutting off his ear. ⁴⁸ Then Jesus spoke: 'Do you take me for a robber, that you have come out with swords and cudgels to arrest me? ⁴⁹ Day after day I have been among you teaching in the temple, and you did not lay hands on me. But let the scriptures be fulfilled.' ⁵⁰ Then the disciples all deserted him and ran away.

⁵¹ Among those who had followed Jesus was a young man with nothing on but a linen cloth. They tried to seize him; ⁵² but he slipped out of the linen cloth and ran away naked.

⁵³ THEN they led Jesus away to the high priest's house, where the chief priests, elders, and scribes were all assembling. ⁵⁴ Peter followed him at a distance right into the high priest's courtyard; and there he remained, sitting among the attendants and warming himself at the fire.

⁵⁵ The chief priests and the whole Council tried to find evidence against Jesus that would warrant a death sentence, but failed to find any. ⁵⁶ Many gave false evidence against him, but their statements did not tally. ⁵⁷ Some stood up and gave false evidence against him to this effect: ⁵⁸ 'We heard him say, "I will pull down this temple, made with human hands, and in three days I will build another, not made with hands."' ⁵⁹ But even on this point their evidence did not agree.

⁶⁰ Then the high priest rose to his feet and questioned Jesus: 'Have you no answer to the accusations that these

14:39 **prayed**: *some witnesses add* using the same words.   14:41 **Enough**: *the meaning of the Greek cannot be confidently decided.*

witnesses bring against you?' ⁶¹ But he remained silent and made no reply.

Again the high priest questioned him: 'Are you the Messiah, the Son of the Blessed One?' ⁶² 'I am,' said Jesus; 'and you will see the Son of Man seated at the right hand of the Almighty and coming with the clouds of heaven.' ⁶³ Then the high priest tore his robes and said, 'Do we need further witnesses? ⁶⁴ You have heard the blasphemy. What is your decision?' Their judgement was unanimous: that he was guilty and should be put to death.

⁶⁵ Some began to spit at him; they blindfolded him and struck him with their fists, crying out, 'Prophesy!' And the attendants slapped him in the face.

⁶⁶ Meanwhile Peter was still below in the courtyard. One of the high priest's servant-girls came by ⁶⁷ and saw him there warming himself. She looked closely at him and said, 'You were with this man from Nazareth, this Jesus.' ⁶⁸ But he denied it: 'I know nothing,' he said; 'I have no idea what you are talking about,' and he went out into the forecourt. ⁶⁹ The servant-girl saw him there and began to say again to the bystanders, 'He is one of them'; ⁷⁰ and again he denied it.

Again, a little later, the bystanders said to Peter, 'You must be one of them; you are a Galilean.' ⁷¹ At this he started to curse, and declared with an oath, 'I do not know this man you are talking about.' ⁷² At that moment the cock crowed for the second time; and Peter remembered how Jesus had said to him, 'Before the cock crows twice, you will disown me three times.' And he burst into tears.

15 As soon as morning came, the whole Council, chief priests, elders, and scribes, made their plans. They bound Jesus and led him away to hand him over to Pilate. ² 'Are you the king of the Jews?' Pilate asked him. 'The words are yours,' he replied. ³ And the chief priests brought many charges against him. ⁴ Pilate questioned him again: 'Have you nothing to say in your defence? You see how many charges they are bringing against you.' ⁵ But, to Pilate's astonishment, Jesus made no further reply.

⁶ At the festival season the governor used to release one prisoner requested by the people. ⁷ As it happened, a man known as Barabbas was then in custody with the rebels who had committed murder in the rising. ⁸ When the crowd appeared and began asking for the usual favour, ⁹ Pilate replied, 'Would you like me to release the king of the Jews?' ¹⁰ For he knew it was out of malice that Jesus had been handed over to him. ¹¹ But the chief priests incited the crowd to ask instead for the release of Barabbas. ¹² Pilate spoke to them again: 'Then what shall I do with the man you call king of the Jews?' ¹³ They shouted back, 'Crucify him!' ¹⁴ 'Why, what wrong has he done?' Pilate asked; but they shouted all the louder, 'Crucify him!' ¹⁵ So Pilate, in his desire to satisfy the mob, released Barabbas to them; and he had Jesus flogged, and then handed him over to be crucified.

¹⁶ The soldiers took him inside the governor's residence, the Praetorium, and called the whole company together. ¹⁷ They dressed him in purple and, plaiting a crown of thorns, placed it on his head. ¹⁸ Then they began to salute him: 'Hail, king of the Jews!' ¹⁹ They beat him about the head with a stick and spat at him, and then knelt and paid homage to him. ²⁰ When they had finished their mockery, they stripped off the purple robe and dressed him in his own clothes.

THEN they led him out to crucify him. ²¹ A man called Simon, from Cyrene, the father of Alexander and Rufus, was passing by on his way in from the country, and they pressed him into service to carry his cross. ²² They brought Jesus to the place called Golgotha, which means 'Place of a Skull', ²³ and they offered him drugged wine, but he did not take it. ²⁴ Then they fastened him to the cross. They shared out his clothes, casting lots to decide what each should have.

²⁵ It was nine in the morning when they crucified him; ²⁶ and the inscription giving the charge against him read, 'The King of the Jews'. ²⁷ Two robbers were crucified with him, one on his right and the other on his left.

14:65 **Prophesy:** *some witnesses add* Who hit you? *as in Matthew and Luke.*   14:68 **into the forecourt:** *some witnesses add* and a cock crowed.   15:2 **The words are yours:** *or* It is as you say.   15:8 **appeared:** *some witnesses read* shouted.   15:27 **on his left:** *some witnesses add* ²⁸ So was fulfilled the text of scripture which says, 'He was reckoned among criminals.'

²⁹ The passers-by wagged their heads and jeered at him: 'Bravo!' they cried, 'So you are the man who was to pull down the temple, and rebuild it in three days! ³⁰ Save yourself and come down from the cross.' ³¹ The chief priests and scribes joined in, jesting with one another: 'He saved others,' they said, 'but he cannot save himself. ³² Let the Messiah, the king of Israel, come down now from the cross. If we see that, we shall believe.' Even those who were crucified with him taunted him.

³³ At midday a darkness fell over the whole land, which lasted till three in the afternoon; ³⁴ and at three Jesus cried aloud, 'Eloï, Eloï, lema sabachthani?' which means, 'My God, my God, why have you forsaken me?' ³⁵ Hearing this, some of the bystanders said, 'Listen! He is calling Elijah.' ³⁶ Someone ran and soaked a sponge in sour wine and held it to his lips on the end of a stick. 'Let us see', he said, 'if Elijah will come to take him down.' ³⁷ Then Jesus gave a loud cry and died; ³⁸ and the curtain of the temple was torn in two from top to bottom. ³⁹ When the centurion who was standing opposite him saw how he died, he said, 'This man must have been a son of God.'

⁴⁰ A NUMBER of women were also present, watching from a distance. Among them were Mary of Magdala, Mary the mother of James the younger and of Joses, and Salome, ⁴¹ who had all followed him and looked after him when he was in Galilee, and there were many others who had come up to Jerusalem with him.

⁴² By this time evening had come; and as it was the day of preparation (that is, the day before the sabbath), ⁴³ Joseph of Arimathaea, a respected member of the Council, a man who looked forward to the kingdom of God, bravely went in to Pilate and asked for the body of Jesus. ⁴⁴ Pilate was surprised to hear that he had died so soon, and sent for the centurion to make sure that he was already dead. ⁴⁵ And when he heard the centurion's report, he gave Joseph leave to take the body. ⁴⁶ So Joseph bought a linen sheet, took him down from the cross, and wrapped him in the sheet. Then he laid him in a tomb cut out of the rock, and rolled a stone against the entrance. ⁴⁷ And Mary of Magdala and Mary the mother of Joses were watching and saw where he was laid.

The resurrection of Jesus

16 WHEN the sabbath was over, Mary of Magdala, Mary the mother of James, and Salome bought aromatic oils, intending to go and anoint him; ² and very early on the first day of the week, just after sunrise, they came to the tomb. ³ They were wondering among themselves who would roll away the stone for them from the entrance to the tomb, ⁴ when they looked up and saw that the stone, huge as it was, had been rolled back already. ⁵ They went into the tomb, where they saw a young man sitting on the right-hand side, wearing a white robe; and they were dumbfounded. ⁶ But he said to them, 'Do not be alarmed; you are looking for Jesus of Nazareth, who was crucified. He has been raised; he is not here. Look, there is the place where they laid him. ⁷ But go and say to his disciples and to Peter: "He is going ahead of you into Galilee: there you will see him, as he told you."' ⁸ Then they went out and ran away from the tomb, trembling with amazement. They said nothing to anyone, for they were afraid.

And they delivered all these instructions briefly to Peter and his companions. Afterwards Jesus himself sent out by them, from east to west, the sacred and imperishable message of eternal salvation.

⁹ WHEN he had risen from the dead, early on the first day of the week, he appeared first to Mary of Magdala, from whom he had driven out seven demons. ¹⁰ She went and carried the news to his mourning and sorrowful followers, ¹¹ but when they were told that he was alive and that she had seen him they did not believe it.

¹² Later he appeared in a different form

15:39 a son of God: *or* the Son of God.   16:1 When ... Salome: *some witnesses omit, reading* And they went and bought ...   16:8 afraid: *at this point some of the most ancient witnesses bring the book to a close.* And they delivered ... salvation: *some witnesses add this passage, which in one of them is the conclusion of the book.* 16:9–20 *Some witnesses give these verses either instead of, or in addition to, the passage* And they delivered ... salvation (*here printed before verse 9*), *and so bring the book to a close. Others insert further additional matter.*

to two of them while they were on their way into the country. ¹³ These also went and took the news to the others, but again no one believed them.

¹⁴ Still later he appeared to the eleven while they were at table, and reproached them for their incredulity and dullness, because they had not believed those who had seen him after he was raised from the dead. ¹⁵ Then he said to them: 'Go to every part of the world, and proclaim the gospel to the whole creation. ¹⁶ Those who believe it and receive baptism will be saved; those who do not believe will be condemned. ¹⁷ Faith will bring with it these miracles: believers will drive out demons in my name and speak in strange tongues; ¹⁸ if they handle snakes or drink any deadly poison, they will come to no harm; and the sick on whom they lay their hands will recover.'

¹⁹ So after talking with them the Lord Jesus was taken up into heaven and took his seat at the right hand of God; ²⁰ but they went out to proclaim their message far and wide, and the Lord worked with them and confirmed their words by the miracles that followed.

THE GOSPEL ACCORDING TO
LUKE

1 To Theophilus: Many writers have undertaken to draw up an account of the events that have taken place among us, ² following the traditions handed down to us by the original eyewitnesses and servants of the gospel. ³ So I in my turn, as one who has investigated the whole course of these events in detail, have decided to write an orderly narrative for you, your excellency, ⁴ so as to give you authentic knowledge about the matters of which you have been informed.

The coming of Christ

⁵ In the reign of Herod king of Judaea there was a priest named Zechariah, of the division of the priesthood called after Abijah. His wife, whose name was Elizabeth, was also of priestly descent. ⁶ Both of them were upright and devout, blamelessly observing all the commandments and ordinances of the Lord. ⁷ But they had no children, for Elizabeth was barren, and both were well on in years.

⁸ Once, when it was the turn of his division and he was there to take part in the temple service, ⁹ he was chosen by lot, by priestly custom, to enter the sanctuary of the Lord and offer the incense; ¹⁰ and at the hour of the offering the people were all assembled at prayer outside. ¹¹ There appeared to him an angel of the Lord, standing on the right of the altar of incense. ¹² At this sight, Zechariah was startled and overcome by fear. ¹³ But the angel said to him, 'Do not be afraid, Zechariah; your prayer has been heard: your wife Elizabeth will bear you a son, and you are to name him John. ¹⁴ His birth will fill you with joy and delight, and will bring gladness to many; ¹⁵ for he will be great in the eyes of the Lord. He is never to touch wine or strong drink. From his very birth he will be filled with the Holy Spirit; ¹⁶ and he will bring back many Israelites to the Lord their God. ¹⁷ He will go before him as forerunner, possessed by the spirit and power of Elijah, to reconcile father and child, to convert the rebellious to the ways of the righteous, to prepare a people that shall be fit for the Lord.'

¹⁸ Zechariah said to the angel, 'How can I be sure of this? I am an old man and my wife is well on in years.'

¹⁹ The angel replied, 'I am Gabriel; I stand in attendance on God, and I have been sent to speak to you and bring you this good news. ²⁰ But now, because you have not believed me, you will lose all power of speech and remain silent until the day when these things take place; at their proper time my words will be proved true.'

²¹ Meanwhile the people were waiting for Zechariah, surprised that he was staying so long inside the sanctuary. ²² When

he did come out he could not speak to them, and they realized that he had had a vision. He stood there making signs to them, and remained dumb.

²³ When his period of duty was completed Zechariah returned home. ²⁴ His wife Elizabeth conceived, and for five months she lived in seclusion, thinking, ²⁵ 'This is the Lord's doing; now at last he has shown me favour and taken away from me the disgrace of childlessness.'

²⁶ In the sixth month the angel Gabriel was sent by God to Nazareth, a town in Galilee, ²⁷ with a message for a girl betrothed to a man named Joseph, a descendant of David; the girl's name was Mary. ²⁸ The angel went in and said to her, 'Greetings, most favoured one! The Lord is with you.' ²⁹ But she was deeply troubled by what he said and wondered what this greeting could mean. ³⁰ Then the angel said to her, 'Do not be afraid, Mary, for God has been gracious to you; ³¹ you will conceive and give birth to a son, and you are to give him the name Jesus. ³² He will be great, and will be called Son of the Most High. The Lord God will give him the throne of his ancestor David, ³³ and he will be king over Israel for ever; his reign shall never end.' ³⁴ 'How can this be?' said Mary. 'I am still a virgin.' ³⁵ The angel answered, 'The Holy Spirit will come upon you, and the power of the Most High will overshadow you; for that reason the holy child to be born will be called Son of God. ³⁶ Moreover your kinswoman Elizabeth has herself conceived a son in her old age; and she who is reputed barren is now in her sixth month, ³⁷ for God's promises can never fail.' ³⁸ 'I am the Lord's servant,' said Mary; 'may it be as you have said.' Then the angel left her.

³⁹ Soon afterwards Mary set out and hurried away to a town in the uplands of Judah. ⁴⁰ She went into Zechariah's house and greeted Elizabeth. ⁴¹ And when Elizabeth heard Mary's greeting, the baby stirred in her womb. Then Elizabeth was filled with the Holy Spirit ⁴² and exclaimed in a loud voice, 'God's blessing is on you above all women, and his blessing is on the fruit of your womb. ⁴³ Who am I, that the mother of my Lord should visit me? ⁴⁴ I tell you, when your greeting sounded

in my ears, the baby in my womb leapt for joy. ⁴⁵ Happy is she who has had faith that the Lord's promise to her would be fulfilled!'

⁴⁶ And Mary said:

'My soul tells out the greatness of the Lord,
⁴⁷ my spirit has rejoiced in God my Saviour;
⁴⁸ for he has looked with favour on his servant,
lowly as she is.
From this day forward
all generations will count me blessed,
⁴⁹ for the Mighty God has done great things for me.
His name is holy,
⁵⁰ his mercy sure from generation to generation
toward those who fear him.
⁵¹ He has shown the might of his arm,
he has routed the proud and all their schemes;
⁵² he has brought down monarchs from their thrones,
and raised on high the lowly.
⁵³ He has filled the hungry with good things,
and sent the rich away empty.
⁵⁴⁻⁵⁵ He has come to the help of Israel his servant,
as he promised to our forefathers;
he has not forgotten to show mercy
to Abraham and his children's children for ever.'

⁵⁶ Mary stayed with Elizabeth about three months and then returned home.

⁵⁷ WHEN the time came for Elizabeth's child to be born, she gave birth to a son. ⁵⁸ Her neighbours and relatives heard what great kindness the Lord had shown her, and they shared her delight. ⁵⁹ On the eighth day they came to circumcise the child; and they were going to name him Zechariah after his father, ⁶⁰ but his mother spoke up: 'No!' she said. 'He is to be called John.' ⁶¹ 'But', they said, 'there is nobody in your family who has that name.' ⁶² They enquired of his father by signs what he would like him to be called. ⁶³ He asked for a writing tablet and to everybody's astonishment wrote, 'His

1:33 **Israel:** *lit.* the house of Jacob.   1:35 **the holy child … God:** *or* the child to be born will be called holy, Son of God.   1:37 **for God's … fail:** *some witnesses read* for with God nothing will prove impossible. 1:46 **Mary:** *a few witnesses read* Elizabeth.

name is John.' ⁶⁴Immediately his lips and tongue were freed and he began to speak, praising God. ⁶⁵All the neighbours were overcome with awe, and throughout the uplands of Judaea the whole story became common talk. ⁶⁶All who heard it were deeply impressed and said, 'What will this child become?' For indeed the hand of the Lord was upon him.

⁶⁷And Zechariah his father was filled with the Holy Spirit and uttered this prophecy:

⁶⁸ 'Praise to the Lord, the God of Israel!
    For he has turned to his people and
        set them free.
⁶⁹ He has raised for us a strong
        deliverer
    from the house of his servant David.

⁷⁰ 'So he promised: age after age he
        proclaimed
    by the lips of his holy prophets,
⁷¹ that he would deliver us from our
        enemies,
    out of the hands of all who hate us;
⁷² that, calling to mind his solemn
        covenant,
    he would deal mercifully with our
        fathers.

⁷³ 'This was the oath he swore to our
        father Abraham,
⁷⁴ to rescue us from enemy hands and
        set us free from fear,
    so that we might worship ⁷⁵in his
        presence
    in holiness and righteousness our
        whole life long.

⁷⁶ 'And you, my child, will be called
        Prophet of the Most High,
    for you will be the Lord's forerunner,
        to prepare his way
⁷⁷ and lead his people to a knowledge of
        salvation
    through the forgiveness of their sins:
⁷⁸ for in the tender compassion of our
        God
    the dawn from heaven will break
        upon us,
⁷⁹ to shine on those who live in
        darkness, under the shadow of
        death,
    and to guide our feet into the way of
        peace.'

⁸⁰As the child grew up he became strong in spirit; he lived out in the wilderness until the day when he appeared publicly before Israel.

2 IN those days a decree was issued by the emperor Augustus for a census to be taken throughout the Roman world. ²This was the first registration of its kind; it took place when Quirinius was governor of Syria. ³Everyone made his way to his own town to be registered. ⁴⁻⁵Joseph went up to Judaea from the town of Nazareth in Galilee, to register in the city of David called Bethlehem, because he was of the house of David by descent; and with him went Mary, his betrothed, who was expecting her child. ⁶While they were there the time came for her to have her baby, ⁷and she gave birth to a son, her firstborn. She wrapped him in swaddling clothes, and laid him in a manger, because there was no room for them at the inn.

⁸Now in this same district there were shepherds out in the fields, keeping watch through the night over their flock. ⁹Suddenly an angel of the Lord appeared to them, and the glory of the Lord shone round them. They were terrified, ¹⁰but the angel said, 'Do not be afraid; I bring you good news, news of great joy for the whole nation. ¹¹Today there has been born to you in the city of David a deliverer—the Messiah, the Lord. ¹²This will be the sign for you: you will find a baby wrapped in swaddling clothes, and lying in a manger.' ¹³All at once there was with the angel a great company of the heavenly host, singing praise to God:

¹⁴ 'Glory to God in highest heaven,
    and on earth peace to all in whom
        he delights.'

¹⁵After the angels had left them and returned to heaven the shepherds said to one another, 'Come, let us go straight to Bethlehem and see this thing that has happened, which the Lord has made known to us.' ¹⁶They hurried off and found Mary and Joseph, and the baby lying in the manger. ¹⁷When they saw the child, they related what they had been told about him; ¹⁸and all who heard were astonished at what the shepherds said.

2:2 **registration** ... **Quirinius:** *or* registration carried out while Quirinius.   2:7 **no** ... **inn:** *or* no other space in their lodging.   2:11 **the Messiah, the Lord:** *some witnesses read* the Lord's Messiah.

¹⁹ But Mary treasured up all these things and pondered over them. ²⁰ The shepherds returned glorifying and praising God for what they had heard and seen; it had all happened as they had been told.

²¹ Eight days later the time came to circumcise him, and he was given the name Jesus, the name given by the angel before he was conceived.

²² Then, after the purification had been completed in accordance with the law of Moses, they brought him up to Jerusalem to present him to the Lord ²³ (as prescribed in the law of the Lord: 'Every firstborn male shall be deemed to belong to the Lord'), ²⁴ and also to make the offering as stated in the law: 'a pair of turtle-doves or two young pigeons'.

²⁵ There was at that time in Jerusalem a man called Simeon. This man was upright and devout, one who watched and waited for the restoration of Israel, and the Holy Spirit was upon him. ²⁶ It had been revealed to him by the Holy Spirit that he would not see death until he had seen the Lord's Messiah. ²⁷ Guided by the Spirit he came into the temple; and when the parents brought in the child Jesus to do for him what the law required, ²⁸ he took him in his arms, praised God, and said:

²⁹ 'Now, Lord, you are releasing your
    servant in peace,
    according to your promise.
³⁰ For I have seen with my own eyes
    the deliverance ³¹ you have made
    ready in full view of all nations:
³² a light that will bring revelation to
    the Gentiles
    and glory to your people Israel.'

³³ The child's father and mother were full of wonder at what was being said about him. ³⁴⁻³⁵ Simeon blessed them and said to Mary his mother, 'This child is destined to be a sign that will be rejected; and you too will be pierced to the heart. Many in Israel will stand or fall because of him; and so the secret thoughts of many will be laid bare.'

³⁶ There was also a prophetess, Anna the daughter of Phanuel, of the tribe of Asher. She was a very old woman, who had lived seven years with her husband after she was first married, ³⁷ and then alone as a widow to the age of eighty-four. She never left the temple, but worshipped night and day with fasting and prayer. ³⁸ Coming up at that very moment, she gave thanks to God; and she talked about the child to all who were looking for the liberation of Jerusalem.

³⁹ When they had done everything prescribed in the law of the Lord, they returned to Galilee to their own town of Nazareth. ⁴⁰ The child grew big and strong and full of wisdom; and God's favour was upon him.

⁴¹ Now it was the practice of his parents to go to Jerusalem every year for the Passover festival; ⁴² and when he was twelve, they made the pilgrimage as usual. ⁴³ When the festive season was over and they set off for home, the boy Jesus stayed behind in Jerusalem. His parents did not know of this; ⁴⁴ but supposing that he was with the party they travelled for a whole day, and only then did they begin looking for him among their friends and relations. ⁴⁵ When they could not find him they returned to Jerusalem to look for him; ⁴⁶ and after three days they found him sitting in the temple surrounded by the teachers, listening to them and putting questions; ⁴⁷ and all who heard him were amazed at his intelligence and the answers he gave. ⁴⁸ His parents were astonished to see him there, and his mother said to him, 'My son, why have you treated us like this? Your father and I have been anxiously searching for you.' ⁴⁹ 'Why did you search for me?' he said. 'Did you not know that I was bound to be in my Father's house?' ⁵⁰ But they did not understand what he meant. ⁵¹ Then he went back with them to Nazareth, and continued to be under their authority; his mother treasured up all these things in her heart. ⁵² As Jesus grew he advanced in wisdom and in favour with God and men.

John the Baptist and Jesus

3 IN the fifteenth year of the emperor Tiberius, when Pontius Pilate was governor of Judaea, when Herod was tetrarch of Galilee, his brother Philip prince of Ituraea and Trachonitis, and Lysanias prince of Abilene, ² during the high-priesthood of Annas and Caiaphas,

2:49 in ... house: *or* about my Father's business.

the word of God came to John son of Zechariah in the wilderness. ³And he went all over the Jordan valley proclaiming a baptism in token of repentance for the forgiveness of sins, ⁴as it is written in the book of the prophecies of Isaiah:

A voice cries in the wilderness,
'Prepare the way for the Lord;
clear a straight path for him.
⁵ Every ravine shall be filled in,
and every mountain and hill levelled;
winding paths shall be straightened,
and rough ways made smooth;
⁶ and all mankind shall see God's
deliverance.'

⁷ Crowds of people came out to be baptized by him, and he said to them: 'Vipers' brood! Who warned you to escape from the wrath that is to come? ⁸ Prove your repentance by the fruit you bear; and do not begin saying to yourselves, "We have Abraham for our father." I tell you that God can make children for Abraham out of these stones. ⁹ Already the axe is laid to the roots of the trees; and every tree that fails to produce good fruit is cut down and thrown on the fire.'

¹⁰ The people asked him, 'Then what are we to do?' ¹¹ He replied, 'Whoever has two shirts must share with him who has none, and whoever has food must do the same.' ¹² Among those who came to be baptized were tax-collectors, and they said to him, 'Teacher, what are we to do?' ¹³ He told them, 'Exact no more than the assessment.' ¹⁴ Some soldiers also asked him, 'And what of us?' To them he said, 'No bullying; no blackmail; make do with your pay!'

¹⁵ The people were all agog, wondering about John, whether perhaps he was the Messiah, ¹⁶ but he spoke out and said to them all: 'I baptize you with water; but there is one coming who is mightier than I am. I am not worthy to unfasten the straps of his sandals. He will baptize you with the Holy Spirit and with fire. ¹⁷ His winnowing-shovel is ready in his hand, to clear his threshing-floor and gather the wheat into his granary; but the chaff he will burn on a fire that can never be put out.'

¹⁸ In this and many other ways he made his appeal to the people and announced the good news. ¹⁹ But Herod the tetrarch, when he was rebuked by him over the affair of his brother's wife Herodias and all his other misdeeds, ²⁰ crowned them all by shutting John up in prison.

The ancestry of the Messiah

²¹ DURING a general baptism of the people, when Jesus too had been baptized and was praying, heaven opened ²² and the Holy Spirit descended on him in bodily form like a dove, and there came a voice from heaven, 'You are my beloved Son; in you I delight.'

²³ When Jesus began his work he was about thirty years old, the son, as people thought, of Joseph son of Heli, ²⁴ son of Matthat, son of Levi, son of Melchi, son of Jannai, son of Joseph, ²⁵ son of Mattathias, son of Amos, son of Nahum, son of Esli, son of Naggai, ²⁶ son of Maath, son of Mattathias, son of Semein, son of Josech, son of Joda, ²⁷ son of Johanan, son of Rhesa, son of Zerubbabel, son of Shealtiel, son of Neri, ²⁸ son of Melchi, son of Addi, son of Cosam, son of Elmadam, son of Er, ²⁹ son of Joshua, son of Eliezer, son of Jorim, son of Matthat, son of Levi, ³⁰ son of Symeon, son of Judah, son of Joseph, son of Jonam, son of Eliakim, ³¹ son of Melea, son of Menna, son of Mattatha, son of Nathan, son of David, ³² son of Jesse, son of Obed, son of Boaz, son of Salma, son of Nahshon, ³³ son of Amminadab, son of Arni, son of Hezron, son of Perez, son of Judah, ³⁴ son of Jacob, son of Isaac, son of Abraham, son of Terah, son of Nahor, ³⁵ son of Serug, son of Reu, son of Peleg, son of Eber, son of Shelah, ³⁶ son of Cainan, son of Arphaxad, son of Shem, son of Noah, son of Lamech, ³⁷ son of Methuselah, son of Enoch, son of Jared, son of Mahalaleel, son of Cainan, ³⁸ son of Enosh, son of Seth, son of Adam, son of God.

The temptation of Jesus

4 ¹⁻² FULL of the Holy Spirit, Jesus returned from the Jordan, and for forty days he wandered in the wilderness, led by the Spirit and tempted by the devil.

During that time he ate nothing, and at the end of it he was famished. ³ The devil

---

3:22 You are ... Son: *or* You are my only Son. You are ... delight: *some witnesses read* You are my Son; this day I have begotten you.   3:33 Amminadab: *some witnesses add* son of Admin.

said to him, 'If you are the Son of God, tell this stone to become bread.' ⁴ Jesus answered, 'Scripture says, "Man is not to live on bread alone."'

⁵ Next the devil led him to a height and showed him in a flash all the kingdoms of the world. ⁶ 'All this dominion will I give to you,' he said, 'and the glory that goes with it; for it has been put in my hands and I can give it to anyone I choose. ⁷ You have only to do homage to me and it will all be yours.' ⁸ Jesus answered him, 'Scripture says, "You shall do homage to the Lord your God and worship him alone."'

⁹ The devil took him to Jerusalem and set him on the parapet of the temple. 'If you are the Son of God,' he said, 'throw yourself down from here; ¹⁰ for scripture says, "He will put his angels in charge of you," ¹¹ and again, "They will support you in their arms for fear you should strike your foot against a stone."' ¹² Jesus answered him, 'It has been said, "You are not to put the Lord your God to the test."'

¹³ So, having come to the end of all these temptations, the devil departed, biding his time.

Jesus in Galilee

¹⁴ THEN Jesus, armed with the power of the Spirit, returned to Galilee; and reports about him spread through the whole countryside. ¹⁵ He taught in their synagogues and everyone sang his praises.

¹⁶ He came to Nazareth, where he had been brought up, and went to the synagogue on the sabbath day as he regularly did. He stood up to read the lesson ¹⁷ and was handed the scroll of the prophet Isaiah. He opened the scroll and found the passage which says,

¹⁸ 'The spirit of the Lord is upon me
  because he has anointed me;
 he has sent me to announce good
    news to the poor,
  to proclaim release for prisoners
 and recovery of sight for the blind;
  to let the broken victims go free,
¹⁹ to proclaim the year of the Lord's
    favour.'

²⁰ He rolled up the scroll, gave it back to the attendant, and sat down; and all eyes in the synagogue were fixed on him.

²¹ He began to address them: 'Today', he said, 'in your hearing this text has come true.' ²² There was general approval; they were astonished that words of such grace should fall from his lips. 'Is not this Joseph's son?' they asked. ²³ Then Jesus said, 'No doubt you will quote to me the proverb, "Physician, heal yourself!" and say, "We have heard of all your doings at Capernaum; do the same here in your own home town." ²⁴ Truly I tell you,' he went on: 'no prophet is recognized in his own country. ²⁵ There were indeed many widows in Israel in Elijah's time, when for three and a half years the skies never opened, and famine lay hard over the whole country; ²⁶ yet it was to none of these that Elijah was sent, but to a widow at Sarepta in the territory of Sidon. ²⁷ Again, in the time of the prophet Elisha there were many lepers in Israel, and not one of them was healed, but only Naaman, the Syrian.' ²⁸ These words roused the whole congregation to fury; ²⁹ they leapt up, drove him out of the town, and took him to the brow of the hill on which it was built, meaning to hurl him over the edge. ³⁰ But he walked straight through the whole crowd, and went away.

³¹ Coming down to Capernaum, a town in Galilee, he taught the people on the sabbath, ³² and they were amazed at his teaching, for what he said had the note of authority. ³³ Now there was a man in the synagogue possessed by a demon, an unclean spirit. He shrieked at the top of his voice, ³⁴ 'What do you want with us, Jesus of Nazareth? Have you come to destroy us? I know who you are—the Holy One of God.' ³⁵ Jesus rebuked him: 'Be silent', he said, 'and come out of him.' Then the demon, after throwing the man down in front of the people, left him without doing him any injury. ³⁶ Amazement fell on them all and they said to one another: 'What is there in this man's words? He gives orders to the unclean spirits with authority and power, and they go.' ³⁷ So the news spread, and he was the talk of the whole district.

³⁸ On leaving the synagogue he went to Simon's house. Simon's mother-in-law was in the grip of a high fever; and they asked him to help her. ³⁹ He stood over her

4:34 **Have you:** *or* You have.

and rebuked the fever. It left her, and she got up at once and attended to their needs.

40 At sunset all who had friends ill with diseases of one kind or another brought them to him; and he laid his hands on them one by one and healed them. **41** Demons also came out of many of them, shouting, 'You are the Son of God.' But he rebuked them and forbade them to speak, because they knew he was the Messiah.

42 When day broke he went out and made his way to a remote spot. But the crowds went in search of him, and when they came to where he was they pressed him not to leave them. **43** But he said, 'I must give the good news of the kingdom of God to the other towns also, for that is what I was sent to do.' **44** So he proclaimed the gospel in the synagogues of Judaea.

5 One day as he stood by the lake of Gennesaret, with people crowding in on him to listen to the word of God, **2** he noticed two boats lying at the water's edge; the fishermen had come ashore and were washing their nets. **3** He got into one of the boats, which belonged to Simon, and asked him to put out a little way from the shore; then he went on teaching the crowds as he sat in the boat. **4** When he had finished speaking, he said to Simon, 'Put out into deep water and let down your nets for a catch.' **5** Simon answered, 'Master, we were hard at work all night and caught nothing; but if you say so, I will let down the nets.' **6** They did so and made such a huge catch of fish that their nets began to split. **7** So they signalled to their partners in the other boat to come and help them. They came, and loaded both boats to the point of sinking. **8** When Simon saw what had happened he fell at Jesus's knees and said, 'Go, Lord, leave me, sinner that I am!' **9** For he and all his companions were amazed at the catch they had made; **10** so too were his partners James and John, Zebedee's sons. 'Do not be afraid,' said Jesus to Simon; 'from now on you will be catching people.' **11** As soon as they had brought the boats to land, they left everything and followed him.

12 He was once in a certain town where there was a man covered with leprosy; when he saw Jesus, he threw himself to the ground and begged his help. 'Sir,' he said, 'if only you will, you can make me clean.' **13** Jesus stretched out his hand and touched him, saying, 'I will; be clean.' The leprosy left him immediately. **14** Jesus then instructed him not to tell anybody. 'But go,' he said, 'show yourself to the priest, and make the offering laid down by Moses for your cleansing; that will certify the cure.' **15** But the talk about him spread ever wider, so that great crowds kept gathering to hear him and to be cured of their ailments. **16** And from time to time he would withdraw to remote places for prayer.

17 One day as he was teaching, Pharisees and teachers of the law were sitting round him. People had come from every village in Galilee and from Judaea and Jerusalem, and the power of the Lord was with him to heal the sick. **18** Some men appeared carrying a paralysed man on a bed, and tried to bring him in and set him down in front of Jesus. **19** Finding no way to do so because of the crowd, they went up onto the roof and let him down through the tiling, bed and all, into the middle of the company in front of Jesus. **20** When Jesus saw their faith, he said to the man, 'Your sins are forgiven you.'

21 The scribes and Pharisees began asking among themselves, 'Who is this fellow with his blasphemous talk? Who but God alone can forgive sins?' **22** But Jesus knew what they were thinking and answered them: 'Why do you harbour these thoughts? **23** Is it easier to say, "Your sins are forgiven you," or to say, "Stand up and walk"? **24** But to convince you that the Son of Man has the right on earth to forgive sins'—he turned to the paralysed man—'I say to you, stand up, take your bed, and go home.' **25** At once the man rose to his feet before their eyes, took up the bed he had been lying on, and went home praising God. **26** They were all lost in amazement and praised God; filled with awe they said, 'The things we have seen today are beyond belief!'

27 Later, when he went out, he saw a tax-collector, Levi by name, at his seat in the custom-house, and said to him, 'Follow me.' **28** Leaving everything, he got up and followed him.

29 Afterwards Levi held a big reception

5:17 **Pharisees ... Jerusalem**: *some witnesses read* Pharisees and teachers of the law, who had come from every village in Galilee and from Judaea and Jerusalem, were sitting round him.

in his house for Jesus; among the guests was a large party of tax-collectors and others. ³⁰ The Pharisees, some of whom were scribes, complained to his disciples: 'Why', they said, 'do you eat and drink with tax-collectors and sinners?' ³¹ Jesus answered them: 'It is not the healthy that need a doctor, but the sick; ³² I have not come to call the virtuous but sinners to repentance.'

³³ Then they said to him, 'John's disciples are much given to fasting and the practice of prayer, and so are the disciples of the Pharisees; but yours eat and drink.' ³⁴ Jesus replied, 'Can you make the bridegroom's friends fast while the bridegroom is with them? ³⁵ But the time will come when the bridegroom will be taken away from them; that will be the time for them to fast.'

³⁶ He told them this parable also: 'No one tears a piece from a new garment to patch an old one; if he does, he will have made a hole in the new garment, and the patch taken from the new will not match the old. ³⁷ No one puts new wine into old wineskins; if he does, the new wine will burst the skins, the wine will spill out, and the skins be ruined. ³⁸ New wine goes into fresh skins! ³⁹ And no one after drinking old wine wants new; for he says, "The old wine is good."'

6 One sabbath he was going through the cornfields, and his disciples were plucking the ears of corn, rubbing them in their hands, and eating them. ² Some Pharisees said, 'Why are you doing what is forbidden on the sabbath?' ³ Jesus answered, 'Have you not read what David did when he and his men were hungry? ⁴ He went into the house of God and took the sacred bread to eat and gave it to his men, though only the priests are allowed to eat it.' ⁵ He also said to them, 'The Son of Man is master of the sabbath.'

⁶ On another sabbath he had gone to synagogue and was teaching. There was a man in the congregation whose right arm was withered; ⁷ and the scribes and Pharisees were on the watch to see whether Jesus would heal him on the sabbath, so that they could find a charge to bring against him. ⁸ But he knew what was in their minds and said to the man with the withered arm, 'Stand up and come out here.' So he stood up and came out. ⁹ Then Jesus said to them, 'I put this

question to you: is it permitted to do good or to do evil on the sabbath, to save life or to destroy it?' ¹⁰ He looked round at them all, and then he said to the man, 'Stretch out your arm.' He did so, and his arm was restored. ¹¹ But they totally failed to understand, and began to discuss with one another what they could do to Jesus.

¹² During this time he went out one day into the hill-country to pray, and spent the night in prayer to God. ¹³ When day broke he called his disciples to him, and from among them he chose twelve and named them apostles: ¹⁴ Simon, to whom he gave the name Peter, and Andrew his brother, James and John, Philip and Bartholomew, ¹⁵ Matthew and Thomas, James son of Alphaeus, and Simon who was called the Zealot, ¹⁶ Judas son of James, and Judas Iscariot who turned traitor.

¹⁷ He came down the hill with them and stopped on some level ground where a large crowd of his disciples had gathered, and with them great numbers of people from Jerusalem and all Judaea and from the coastal region of Tyre and Sidon, who had come to listen to him, and to be cured of their diseases. ¹⁸ Those who were troubled with unclean spirits were healed; ¹⁹ and everyone in the crowd was trying to touch him, because power went out from him and cured them all.

Jesus's sermon to the disciples
²⁰ TURNING to his disciples he began to speak:

'Blessed are you who are in need;
    the kingdom of God is yours.
²¹ Blessed are you who now go hungry;
    you will be satisfied.
Blessed are you who weep now;
    you will laugh.

²² 'Blessed are you when people hate you and ostracize you, when they insult you and slander your very name, because of the Son of Man. ²³ On that day exult and dance for joy, for you have a rich reward in heaven; that is how their fathers treated the prophets.

²⁴ 'But alas for you who are rich;
    you have had your time of happiness.
²⁵ Alas for you who are well fed now;
    you will go hungry.
Alas for you who laugh now;
    you will mourn and weep.

²⁶ Alas for you when all speak well of you;

that is how their fathers treated the false prophets.

²⁷ 'But to you who are listening I say: Love your enemies; do good to those who hate you; ²⁸ bless those who curse you; pray for those who treat you spitefully. ²⁹ If anyone hits you on the cheek, offer the other also; if anyone takes your coat, let him have your shirt as well. ³⁰ Give to everyone who asks you; if anyone takes what is yours, do not demand it back.

³¹ 'Treat others as you would like them to treat you. ³² If you love only those who love you, what credit is that to you? Even sinners love those who love them. ³³ Again, if you do good only to those who do good to you, what credit is there in that? Even sinners do as much. ³⁴ And if you lend only where you expect to be repaid, what credit is there in that? Even sinners lend to each other to be repaid in full. ³⁵ But you must love your enemies and do good, and lend without expecting any return; and you will have a rich reward: you will be sons of the Most High, because he himself is kind to the ungrateful and the wicked. ³⁶ Be compassionate, as your Father is compassionate.

³⁷ 'Do not judge, and you will not be judged; do not condemn, and you will not be condemned; pardon, and you will be pardoned; ³⁸ give, and gifts will be given you. Good measure, pressed and shaken down and running over, will be poured into your lap; for whatever measure you deal out to others will be dealt to you in turn.'

³⁹ He also spoke to them in a parable: 'Can one blind man guide another? Will not both fall into the ditch? ⁴⁰ No pupil ranks above his teacher; fully trained he can but reach his teacher's level.

⁴¹ 'Why do you look at the speck in your brother's eye, with never a thought for the plank in your own? ⁴² How can you say to your brother, "Brother, let me take the speck out of your eye," when you are blind to the plank in your own? You hypocrite! First take the plank out of your own eye, and then you will see clearly to take the speck out of your brother's.

⁴³ 'There is no such thing as a good tree producing bad fruit, nor yet a bad tree producing good fruit. ⁴⁴ Each tree is known by its own fruit: you do not gather figs from brambles or pick grapes from thistles. ⁴⁵ Good people produce good from the store of good within themselves; and evil people produce evil from the evil within them. For the words that the mouth utters come from the overflowing of the heart.

⁴⁶ 'Why do you call me "Lord, Lord" — and never do what I tell you? ⁴⁷ Everyone who comes to me and hears my words and acts on them—I will show you what he is like. ⁴⁸ He is like a man building a house, who dug deep and laid the foundations on rock. When the river was in flood, it burst upon that house, but could not shift it, because it had been soundly built. ⁴⁹ But he who hears and does not act is like a man who built his house on the soil without foundations. As soon as the river burst upon it, the house collapsed, and fell with a great crash.'

Miracles and parables

7 WHEN he had finished addressing the people, he entered Capernaum. ² A centurion there had a servant whom he valued highly, but the servant was ill and near to death. ³ Hearing about Jesus, he sent some Jewish elders to ask him to come and save his servant's life. ⁴ They approached Jesus and made an urgent appeal to him: 'He deserves this favour from you,' they said, ⁵ 'for he is a friend of our nation and it is he who built us our synagogue.' ⁶ Jesus went with them; but when he was not far from the house, the centurion sent friends with this message: 'Do not trouble further, sir; I am not worthy to have you come under my roof, ⁷ and that is why I did not presume to approach you in person. But say the word and my servant will be cured. ⁸ I know, for I am myself under orders, with soldiers under me. I say to one, "Go," and he goes; to another, "Come here," and he comes; and to my servant, "Do this," and he does it.' ⁹ When Jesus heard this, he was astonished, and, turning to the crowd that was following him, he said, 'I tell you, not even in Israel have I found such faith.' ¹⁰ When the messengers returned to the house, they found the servant in good health.

¹¹ Afterwards Jesus went to a town called Nain, accompanied by his disciples and a large crowd. ¹² As he approached

the gate of the town he met a funeral. The dead man was the only son of his widowed mother; and many of the townspeople were there with her. [13] When the Lord saw her his heart went out to her, and he said, 'Do not weep.' [14] He stepped forward and laid his hand on the bier; and the bearers halted. Then he spoke: 'Young man, I tell you to get up.' [15] The dead man sat up and began to speak; and Jesus restored him to his mother. [16] Everyone was filled with awe and praised God. 'A great prophet has arisen among us,' they said; 'God has shown his care for his people.' [17] The story of what he had done spread through the whole of Judaea and all the region around.

[18] When John was informed of all this by his disciples, [19] he summoned two of them and sent them to the Lord with this question: 'Are you the one who is to come, or are we to expect someone else?' [20] The men made their way to Jesus and said, 'John the Baptist has sent us to ask you, "Are you the one who is to come, or are we to expect someone else?"' [21] There and then he healed many sufferers from diseases, plagues, and evil spirits; and on many blind people he bestowed sight. [22] Then he gave them this answer: 'Go and tell John what you have seen and heard: the blind regain their sight, the lame walk, lepers are made clean, the deaf hear, the dead are raised to life, the poor are brought good news— [23] and happy is he who does not find me an obstacle to faith.'

[24] After John's messengers had left, Jesus began to speak about him to the crowds: 'What did you go out into the wilderness to see? A reed swaying in the wind? [25] No? Then what did you go out to see? A man dressed in finery? Grand clothes and luxury are to be found in palaces. [26] But what did you go out to see? A prophet? Yes indeed, and far more than a prophet. [27] He is the man of whom scripture says,

Here is my herald, whom I send
    ahead of you,
and he will prepare your way before
    you.

[28] 'I tell you, among all who have been born, no one has been greater than John; yet the least in the kingdom of God is greater than he is.'

[29] When they heard him, all the people, including the tax-collectors, acknowledged the goodness of God, for they had accepted John's baptism; [30] but the Pharisees and lawyers, who had refused his baptism, rejected God's purpose for themselves.

[31] 'How can I describe the people of this generation? What are they like? [32] They are like children sitting in the marketplace and calling to each other,

We piped for you and you would not
    dance.
We lamented, and you would not
    mourn.

[33] 'For John the Baptist came, neither eating bread nor drinking wine, and you say, "He is possessed." [34] The Son of Man came, eating and drinking, and you say, "Look at him! A glutton and a drinker, a friend of tax-collectors and sinners!" [35] And yet God's wisdom is proved right by all who are her children.'

[36] One of the Pharisees invited Jesus to a meal; he went to the Pharisee's house and took his place at table. [37] A woman who was living an immoral life in the town had learned that Jesus was a guest in the Pharisee's house and had brought oil of myrrh in a small flask. [38] She took her place behind him, by his feet, weeping. His feet were wet with her tears and she wiped them with her hair, kissing them and anointing them with the myrrh. [39] When his host the Pharisee saw this he said to himself, 'If this man were a real prophet, he would know who this woman is who is touching him, and what a bad character she is.' [40] Jesus took him up: 'Simon,' he said, 'I have something to say to you.' 'What is it, Teacher?' he asked. [41] 'Two men were in debt to a moneylender: one owed him five hundred silver pieces, the other fifty. [42] As they did not have the means to pay he cancelled both debts. Now, which will love him more?' [43] Simon replied, 'I should think the one that was let off more.' 'You are right,' said Jesus. [44] Then turning to the woman, he said to Simon, 'You see this woman? I came to your house: you provided no water for my feet; but this woman has made my feet wet with her tears and wiped them with her hair. [45] You gave me no kiss; but she has been kissing my feet ever since I came in. [46] You

did not anoint my head with oil; but she has anointed my feet with myrrh. [47] So, I tell you, her great love proves that her many sins have been forgiven; where little has been forgiven, little love is shown.' [48] Then he said to her, 'Your sins are forgiven.' [49] The other guests began to ask themselves, 'Who is this, that he can forgive sins?' [50] But he said to the woman, 'Your faith has saved you; go in peace.'

8 AFTER this he went journeying from town to town and village to village, proclaiming the good news of the kingdom of God. With him were the Twelve [2] and a number of women who had been set free from evil spirits and infirmities: Mary, known as Mary of Magdala, from whom seven demons had come out, [3] Joanna, the wife of Chuza a steward of Herod's, Susanna, and many others. These women provided for them out of their own resources.

[4] People were now gathering in large numbers, and as they made their way to him from one town after another, he said in a parable: [5] 'A sower went out to sow his seed. And as he sowed, some of the seed fell along the footpath, where it was trampled on, and the birds ate it up. [6] Some fell on rock and, after coming up, it withered for lack of moisture. [7] Some fell among thistles, and the thistles grew up with it and choked it. [8] And some of the seed fell into good soil, and grew, and yielded a hundredfold.' As he said this he called out, 'If you have ears to hear, then hear.'

[9] His disciples asked him what this parable meant, [10] and he replied, 'It has been granted to you to know the secrets of the kingdom of God; but the others have only parables, so that they may look but see nothing, hear but understand nothing.

[11] 'This is what the parable means. The seed is the word of God. [12] The seed along the footpath stands for those who hear it, and then the devil comes and carries off the word from their hearts for fear they should believe and be saved. [13] The seed sown on rock stands for those who receive the word with joy when they hear it, but have no root; they are believers for a

while, but in the time of testing they give up. [14] That which fell among thistles represents those who hear, but their growth is choked by cares and wealth and the pleasures of life, and they bring nothing to maturity. [15] But the seed in good soil represents those who bring a good and honest heart to the hearing of the word, hold it fast, and by their perseverance yield a harvest.

[16] 'Nobody lights a lamp and then covers it with a basin or puts it under the bed. You put it on a lampstand so that those who come in may see the light. [17] For there is nothing hidden that will not be disclosed, nothing concealed that will not be made known and brought into the open.

[18] 'Take care, then, how you listen; for those who have will be given more, and those who have not will forfeit even what they think they have.'

[19] His mother and his brothers arrived but could not get to him for the crowd. [20] He was told, 'Your mother and brothers are standing outside, and want to see you.' [21] He replied, 'My mother and my brothers are those who hear the word of God and act upon it.'

[22] One day he got into a boat with his disciples and said to them, 'Let us cross over to the other side of the lake.' So they put out; [23] and as they sailed along he fell asleep. Then a heavy squall struck the lake; they began to ship water and were in grave danger. [24] They came and roused him: 'Master, Master, we are sinking!' they cried. He awoke, and rebuked the wind and the turbulent waters. The storm subsided and there was calm. [25] 'Where is your faith?' he asked. In fear and astonishment they said to one another, 'Who can this be? He gives his orders to the wind and the waves, and they obey him.'

[26] So they landed in the country of the Gerasenes, which is opposite Galilee. [27] As he stepped ashore he was met by a man from the town who was possessed by demons. For a long time he had neither worn clothes nor lived in a house, but stayed among the tombs. [28] When he saw Jesus he cried out, and fell at his feet. 'What do you want with me, Jesus, Son of the Most High God?' he shouted. 'I

7:47 **her great ... have been forgiven**: *or* her sins, which are many, have been forgiven because she has loved much.   8:26 **Gerasenes**: *some witnesses read* Gergesenes; *others read* Gadarenes.

implore you, do not torment me.' [29] For Jesus was already ordering the unclean spirit to come out of the man. Many a time it had seized him, and then, for safety's sake, they would secure him with chains and fetters; but each time he broke loose and was driven by the demon out into the wilds.

[30] Jesus asked him, 'What is your name?' 'Legion,' he replied. This was because so many demons had taken possession of him. [31] And they begged him not to banish them to the abyss.

[32] There was a large herd of pigs nearby, feeding on the hillside; and the demons begged him to let them go into these pigs. He gave them leave; [33] the demons came out of the man and went into the pigs, and the herd rushed over the edge into the lake and were drowned.

[34] When the men in charge of them saw what had happened, they took to their heels and carried the news to the town and countryside; [35] and the people came out to see what had happened. When they came to Jesus, and found the man from whom the demons had gone out sitting at his feet clothed and in his right mind, they were afraid. [36] Eyewitnesses told them how the madman had been cured. [37] Then the whole population of the Gerasene district was overcome by fear and asked Jesus to go away. So he got into the boat and went away. [38] The man from whom the demons had gone out begged to go with him; but Jesus sent him away: [39] 'Go back home,' he said, 'and tell them what God has done for you.' The man went all over the town proclaiming what Jesus had done for him.

[40] When Jesus returned, the people welcomed him, for they were all expecting him. [41] Then a man appeared—Jairus was his name and he was president of the synagogue. Throwing himself down at Jesus's feet he begged him to come to his house, [42] because his only daughter, who was about twelve years old, was dying.

While Jesus was on his way he could hardly breathe for the crowds. [43] Among them was a woman who had suffered from haemorrhages for twelve years; and nobody had been able to cure her. [44] She came up from behind and touched the edge of his cloak, and at once her haemorrhage stopped. [45] Jesus said, 'Who was it who touched me?' All disclaimed it, and Peter said, 'Master, the crowds are hemming you in and pressing upon you!' [46] But Jesus said, 'Someone did touch me, for I felt that power had gone out from me.' [47] Then the woman, seeing that she was detected, came trembling and fell at his feet. Before all the people she explained why she had touched him and how she had been cured instantly. [48] He said to her, 'Daughter, your faith has healed you. Go in peace.'

[49] While he was still speaking, a man came from the president's house with the message, 'Your daughter is dead; do not trouble the teacher any more.' [50] But Jesus heard, and said, 'Do not be afraid; simply have faith and she will be well again.' [51] When he arrived at the house he allowed no one to go in with him except Peter, John, and James, and the child's father and mother. [52] Everyone was weeping and lamenting for her. He said, 'Stop your weeping; she is not dead: she is asleep'; [53] and they laughed at him, well knowing that she was dead. [54] But Jesus took hold of her hand and called to her: 'Get up, my child.' [55] Her spirit returned, she stood up immediately, and he told them to give her something to eat. [56] Her parents were astounded; but he forbade them to tell anyone what had happened.

Jesus and the Twelve

9 CALLING the Twelve together he gave them power and authority to overcome all demons and to cure diseases, [2] and sent them out to proclaim the kingdom of God and to heal the sick. [3] 'Take nothing for the journey,' he told them, 'neither stick nor pack, neither bread nor money; nor are you to have a second coat. [4] When you enter a house, stay there until you leave that place. [5] As for those who will not receive you, when you leave their town shake the dust off your feet as a warning to them.' [6] So they set out and travelled from village to village, and everywhere they announced the good news and healed the sick.

[7] Now Herod the tetrarch heard of all that was happening, and did not know

---

8:37 **Gerasene**: *some witnesses read* Gergesene; *others read* Gadarene.   8:43 **years; and**: *some witnesses add* though she had spent all she had on doctors.   8:44 **edge**: *or* tassel.

what to make of it; for some were saying that John had been raised from the dead, [8] others that Elijah had appeared, others again that one of the prophets of old had come back to life. [9] Herod said, 'As for John, I beheaded him; but who is this I hear so much about?' And he was anxious to see him.

[10] On their return the apostles gave Jesus an account of all they had done. Then he took them with him and withdrew privately to a town called Bethsaida, [11] but the crowds found out and followed. He welcomed them, and spoke to them about the kingdom of God, and cured those who were in need of healing. [12] When evening was drawing on, the Twelve came to him and said, 'Send the people off, so that they can go into the villages and farms round about to find food and lodging, for this is a remote place we are in.' [13] 'Give them something to eat yourselves,' he replied. But they said, 'All we have is five loaves and two fish, nothing more—or do you intend us to go and buy food for all these people?' [14] For there were about five thousand men. Then he said to his disciples, 'Make them sit down in groups of about fifty.' [15] They did so and got them all seated. [16] Then, taking the five loaves and the two fish, he looked up to heaven, said the blessing over them, broke them, and gave them to the disciples to distribute to the people. [17] They all ate and were satisfied; and the scraps they left were picked up and filled twelve baskets.

[18] One day, when he had been praying by himself in the company of his disciples, he asked them, 'Who do the people say I am?' [19] They answered, 'Some say John the Baptist, others Elijah, others that one of the prophets of old has come back to life.' [20] 'And you,' he said, 'who do you say I am?' Peter answered, 'God's Messiah.' [21] Then he gave them strict orders not to tell this to anyone. [22] And he said, 'The Son of Man has to endure great sufferings, and to be rejected by the elders, chief priests, and scribes, to be put to death, and to be raised again on the third day.'

[23] To everybody he said, 'Anyone who wants to be a follower of mine must renounce self; day after day he must take up his cross, and follow me. [24] Whoever wants to save his life will lose it, but whoever loses his life for my sake will save it. [25] What does anyone gain by winning the whole world at the cost of destroying himself? [26] If anyone is ashamed of me and my words, the Son of Man will be ashamed of him, when he comes in his glory and the glory of the Father and the holy angels. [27] In truth I tell you: there are some of those standing here who will not taste death before they have seen the kingdom of God.'

[28] About a week after this he took Peter, John, and James and went up a mountain to pray. [29] And while he was praying the appearance of his face changed and his clothes became dazzling white. [30] Suddenly there were two men talking with him—Moses and Elijah—[31] who appeared in glory and spoke of his departure, the destiny he was to fulfil in Jerusalem. [32] Peter and his companions had been overcome by sleep; but when they awoke, they saw his glory and the two men who stood beside him. [33] As these two were moving away from Jesus, Peter said to him, 'Master, it is good that we are here. Shall we make three shelters, one for you, one for Moses, and one for Elijah?' but he spoke without knowing what he was saying. [34] As he spoke there came a cloud which cast its shadow over them; they were afraid as they entered the cloud, [35] and from it a voice spoke: 'This is my Son, my Chosen; listen to him.' [36] After the voice had spoken, Jesus was seen to be alone. The disciples kept silence and did not at that time say a word to anyone of what they had seen.

[37] Next day when they came down from the mountain a large crowd came to meet him. [38] A man in the crowd called out: 'Teacher, I implore you to look at my son, my only child. [39] From time to time a spirit seizes him and with a sudden scream throws him into convulsions so that he foams at the mouth; it keeps on tormenting him and can hardly be made to let him go. [40] I begged your disciples to drive it out, but they could not.' [41] Jesus answered, 'What an unbelieving and perverse generation! How long shall I be with you and endure you? Bring your son here.' [42] But before the boy could reach

9:26 **me and my words:** *some witnesses read* me and mine.   9:31 **departure:** *lit.* exodus.

him the demon dashed him to the ground and threw him into convulsions. Jesus spoke sternly to the unclean spirit, cured the boy, and gave him back to his father. [43] And they were all struck with awe at the greatness of God.

Amid the general astonishment at all he was doing, Jesus said to his disciples, [44] 'Listen to what I have to tell you. The Son of Man is to be given up into the power of men.' [45] But they did not understand what he said; its meaning had been hidden from them, so that they could not grasp it, and they were afraid to ask him about it.

[46] An argument started among them as to which of them was the greatest. [47] Jesus, who knew what was going on in their minds, took a child, stood him by his side, [48] and said, 'Whoever receives this child in my name receives me; and whoever receives me receives the one who sent me. For the least among you all is the greatest.'

[49] 'Master,' said John, 'we saw someone driving out demons in your name, but as he is not one of us we tried to stop him.' [50] Jesus said to him, 'Do not stop him, for he who is not against you is on your side.'

The journey to Jerusalem

[51] As the time approached when he was to be taken up to heaven, he set his face resolutely towards Jerusalem, [52] and sent messengers ahead. They set out and went into a Samaritan village to make arrangements for him; [53] but the villagers would not receive him because he was on his way to Jerusalem. [54] When the disciples James and John saw this they said, 'Lord, do you want us to call down fire from heaven to consume them?' [55] But he turned and rebuked them, [56] and they went on to another village.

[57] As they were going along the road a man said to him, 'I will follow you wherever you go.' [58] Jesus answered, 'Foxes have their holes and birds their roosts; but the Son of Man has nowhere to lay his head.' [59] To another he said, 'Follow me,' but the man replied, 'Let me first go and bury my father.' [60] Jesus said, 'Leave the dead to bury their dead; you

must go and announce the kingdom of God.' [61] Yet another said, 'I will follow you, sir; but let me first say goodbye to my people at home.' [62] To him Jesus said, 'No one who sets his hand to the plough and then looks back is fit for the kingdom of God.'

10 After this the Lord appointed a further seventy-two and sent them on ahead in pairs to every town and place he himself intended to visit. [2] He said to them: 'The crop is heavy, but the labourers are few. Ask the owner therefore to send labourers to bring in the harvest. [3] Be on your way; I am sending you like lambs among wolves. [4] Carry no purse or pack, and travel barefoot. Exchange no greetings on the road. [5] When you go into a house, let your first words be, "Peace to this house." [6] If there is a man of peace there, your peace will rest on him; if not, it will return to you. [7] Stay in that house, sharing their food and drink; for the worker deserves his pay. Do not move around from house to house. [8] When you enter a town and you are made welcome, eat the food provided for you; [9] heal the sick there, and say, "The kingdom of God has come upon you." [10] But when you enter a town and you are not made welcome, go out into its streets and say, [11] "The very dust of your town that clings to our feet we wipe off to your shame. Only take note of this: the kingdom of God has come." [12] I tell you, on the day of judgement the fate of Sodom will be more bearable than the fate of that town.

[13] 'Alas for you, Chorazin! Alas for you, Bethsaida! If the miracles performed in you had taken place in Tyre and Sidon, they would have repented long ago, sitting in sackcloth and ashes. [14] But it will be more bearable for Tyre and Sidon at the judgement than for you. [15] As for you, Capernaum, will you be exalted to heaven? No, you will be brought down to Hades!

[16] 'Whoever listens to you listens to me; whoever rejects you rejects me. And whoever rejects me rejects the One who sent me.'

[17] The seventy-two came back jubilant. 'In your name, Lord,' they said, 'even the

---

9:54 **consume them:** *some witnesses add* as Elijah did.   9:55 **rebuked them:** *some witnesses add* 'You do not know', he said, 'to what spirit you belong; (56) for the Son of Man did not come to destroy men's lives but to save them.'   10:1 **seventy-two:** *some witnesses read* seventy.   10:9 **come upon you:** *or* come close to you. 10:11 **has come:** *or* has come close.   10:17 **seventy-two:** *some witnesses read* seventy.

demons submit to us.' [18] He replied, 'I saw Satan fall, like lightning, from heaven. [19] And I have given you the power to tread underfoot snakes and scorpions and all the forces of the enemy. Nothing will ever harm you. [20] Nevertheless, do not rejoice that the spirits submit to you, but that your names are enrolled in heaven.'

[21] At that moment Jesus exulted in the Holy Spirit and said, 'I thank you, Father, Lord of heaven and earth, for hiding these things from the learned and wise, and revealing them to the simple. Yes, Father, such was your choice. [22] Everything is entrusted to me by my Father; no one knows who the Son is but the Father, or who the Father is but the Son, and those to whom the Son chooses to reveal him.'

[23] When he was alone with his disciples he turned to them and said, 'Happy the eyes that see what you are seeing! [24] I tell you, many prophets and kings wished to see what you now see, yet never saw it; to hear what you hear, yet never heard it.'

[25] A LAWYER once came forward to test him by asking: 'Teacher, what must I do to inherit eternal life?' [26] Jesus said, 'What is written in the law? What is your reading of it?' [27] He replied, 'Love the Lord your God with all your heart, and with all your soul, with all your strength, and with all your mind; and your neighbour as yourself.' [28] 'That is the right answer,' said Jesus; 'do that and you will have life.'

[29] Wanting to justify his question, he asked, 'But who is my neighbour?' [30] Jesus replied, 'A man was on his way from Jerusalem down to Jericho when he was set upon by robbers, who stripped and beat him, and went off leaving him half dead. [31] It so happened that a priest was going down by the same road, and when he saw him, he went past on the other side. [32] So too a Levite came to the place, and when he saw him went past on the other side. [33] But a Samaritan who was going that way came upon him, and when he saw him he was moved to pity. [34] He went up and bandaged his wounds, bathing them with oil and wine. Then he lifted him on to his own beast, brought him to an inn, and looked after him. [35] Next day he produced two silver pieces and gave them to the innkeeper, and said, "Look after him; and if you spend more, I will repay you on my way back." [36] Which of these three do you think was neighbour to the man who fell into the hands of the robbers?' [37] He answered, 'The one who showed him kindness.' Jesus said to him, 'Go and do as he did.'

[38] While they were on their way Jesus came to a village where a woman named Martha made him welcome. [39] She had a sister, Mary, who seated herself at the Lord's feet and stayed there listening to his words. [40] Now Martha was distracted by her many tasks, so she came to him and said, 'Lord, do you not care that my sister has left me to get on with the work by myself? Tell her to come and give me a hand.' [41] But the Lord answered, 'Martha, Martha, you are fretting and fussing about so many things; [42] only one thing is necessary. Mary has chosen what is best; it shall not be taken away from her.'

11 At one place after Jesus had been praying, one of his disciples said, 'Lord, teach us to pray, as John taught his disciples.' [2] He answered, 'When you pray, say,

Father, may your name be hallowed; your kingdom come.
[3] Give us each day our daily bread.
[4] And forgive us our sins,
for we too forgive all who have done us wrong.
And do not put us to the test.'

[5] Then he said to them, 'Suppose one of you has a friend who comes to him in the middle of the night and says, "My friend, lend me three loaves, [6] for a friend of mine on a journey has turned up at my house, and I have nothing to offer him"; [7] and he replies from inside, "Do not bother me. The door is shut for the night; my children and I have gone to bed; and I cannot get up and give you what you want." [8] I tell you that even if he will not get up and provide for him out of friendship, his very

---

10:21 **Holy Spirit:** *some witnesses omit* Holy. **Yes ... such:** *or* Yes, I thank you, Father, that such.

10:42 **only ... necessary:** *some witnesses read* only few things are necessary, or rather, one alone.

11:2 **Father:** *some witnesses read* Our Father in heaven. **your kingdom come:** *one witness reads* your kingdom come upon us; *some others have* your Holy Spirit come upon us and cleanse us; *some add* your will be done, on earth as in heaven.   11:3 **daily bread:** *or* bread for the morrow.   11:4 **to the test:** *some witnesses add* but save us from the evil one (*or* from evil).

persistence will make the man get up and give him all he needs. ⁹ So I say to you, ask, and you will receive; seek, and you will find; knock, and the door will be opened to you. ¹⁰ For everyone who asks receives, those who seek find, and to those who knock, the door will be opened.

¹¹ 'Would any father among you offer his son a snake when he asks for a fish, ¹² or a scorpion when he asks for an egg? ¹³ If you, bad as you are, know how to give good things to your children, how much more will the heavenly Father give the Holy Spirit to those who ask him!'

Opposition and questioning

¹⁴ HE was driving out a demon which was dumb; and when the demon had come out, the dumb man began to speak. The people were astonished, ¹⁵ but some of them said, 'It is by Beelzebul prince of demons that he drives the demons out.' ¹⁶ Others, by way of a test, demanded of him a sign from heaven. ¹⁷ But he knew what was in their minds, and said, 'Every kingdom divided against itself is laid waste, and a divided household falls. ¹⁸ And if Satan is divided against himself, how can his kingdom stand—since, as you claim, I drive out the demons by Beelzebul? ¹⁹ If it is by Beelzebul that I drive out demons, by whom do your own people drive them out? If this is your argument, they themselves will refute you. ²⁰ But if it is by the finger of God that I drive out the demons, then be sure the kingdom of God has already come upon you.

²¹ 'When a strong man fully armed is on guard over his palace, his possessions are safe. ²² But when someone stronger attacks and overpowers him, he carries off the arms and armour on which the man had relied and distributes the spoil.

²³ 'He who is not with me is against me, and he who does not gather with me scatters.

²⁴ 'When an unclean spirit comes out of someone it wanders over the desert sands seeking a resting-place; and if it finds none, it says, "I will go back to the home I left." ²⁵ So it returns and finds the house swept clean and tidy. ²⁶ It goes off and collects seven other spirits more wicked than itself, and they all come in and settle there; and in the end that person's plight is worse than before.'

²⁷ While he was speaking thus, a woman in the crowd called out, 'Happy the womb that carried you and the breasts that suckled you!' ²⁸ He rejoined, 'No, happy are those who hear the word of God and keep it.'

²⁹ With the crowds swarming round him he went on to say: 'This is a wicked generation. It demands a sign, and the only sign that will be given it is the sign of Jonah. ³⁰ For just as Jonah was a sign to the Ninevites, so will the Son of Man be to this generation. ³¹ The queen of the south will appear in court when the men of this generation are on trial, and ensure their condemnation; for she came from the ends of the earth to listen to the wisdom of Solomon, and what is here is greater than Solomon. ³² The men of Nineveh will appear in court when this generation is on trial, and ensure its condemnation; for they repented at the preaching of Jonah; and what is here is greater than Jonah.

³³ 'No one lights a lamp and puts it in a cellar, but on the lampstand so that those who come in may see the light. ³⁴ The lamp of your body is the eye. When your eyes are sound, you have light for your whole body; but when they are bad, your body is in darkness. ³⁵ See to it then that the light you have is not darkness. ³⁶ If you have light for your whole body with no trace of darkness, it will all be full of light, as when the light of a lamp shines on you.'

³⁷ WHEN he had finished speaking, a Pharisee invited him to a meal, and he came in and sat down. ³⁸ The Pharisee noticed with surprise that he had not begun by washing before the meal. ³⁹ But the Lord said to him, 'You Pharisees clean the outside of cup and plate; but inside you are full of greed and wickedness. ⁴⁰ You fools! Did not he who made the outside make the inside too? ⁴¹ But let what is inside be given in charity, and all is clean.

⁴² 'Alas for you Pharisees! You pay

11:11 *offer his son*: *some witnesses add* a stone when he asks for bread, or.   11:31 *will appear ... trial*: *or* will be raised to life at the judgement together with the men of this generation.   11:32 *The men ... ensure*: *or* At the judgement the men of Nineveh will rise again together with this generation and will ensure.
11:33 *in a cellar*: *some witnesses add* or under the measuring bowl.

tithes of mint and rue and every garden herb, but neglect justice and the love of God. It is these you should have practised, without overlooking the others.

⁴³ 'Alas for you Pharisees! You love to have the chief seats in synagogues, and to be greeted respectfully in the street.

⁴⁴ 'Alas, alas, you are like unmarked graves which people walk over unawares.'

⁴⁵ At this one of the lawyers said, 'Teacher, when you say things like this you are insulting us too.' ⁴⁶ Jesus rejoined: 'Alas for you lawyers also! You load men with intolerable burdens, and will not lift a finger to lighten the load.

⁴⁷ 'Alas, you build monuments to the prophets whom your fathers murdered, ⁴⁸ and so testify that you approve of the deeds your fathers did; they committed the murders and you provide the monuments.

⁴⁹ 'This is why the Wisdom of God said, "I will send them prophets and messengers; and some of these they will persecute and kill"; ⁵⁰ so that this generation will have to answer for the blood of all the prophets shed since the foundation of the world; ⁵¹ from the blood of Abel to the blood of Zechariah who met his death between the altar and the sanctuary. I tell you, this generation will have to answer for it all.

⁵² 'Alas for you lawyers! You have taken away the key of knowledge. You did not go in yourselves, and those who were trying to go in, you prevented.'

⁵³ After he had left the house, the scribes and Pharisees began to assail him fiercely and to ply him with a host of questions, ⁵⁴ laying snares to catch him with his own words.

12 MEANWHILE, when a crowd of many thousands had gathered, packed so close that they were trampling on one another, he began to speak first to his disciples: 'Be on your guard against the leaven of the Pharisees—I mean their hypocrisy. ² There is nothing covered up that will not be uncovered, nothing hidden that will not be made known. ³ Therefore everything you have said in the dark will be heard in broad daylight, and what you have whispered behind closed doors will be shouted from the housetops.

⁴ 'To you who are my friends I say: do not fear those who kill the body and after that have nothing more they can do. ⁵ I will show you whom to fear: fear him who, after he has killed, has authority to cast into hell. Believe me, he is the one to fear.

⁶ 'Are not five sparrows sold for twopence? Yet not one of them is overlooked by God. ⁷ More than that, even the hairs of your head have all been counted. Do not be afraid; you are worth more than any number of sparrows.

⁸ 'I tell you this: whoever acknowledges me before others, the Son of Man will acknowledge before the angels of God; ⁹ but whoever disowns me before others will be disowned before the angels of God.

¹⁰ 'Anyone who speaks a word against the Son of Man will be forgiven; but for him who slanders the Holy Spirit there will be no forgiveness.

¹¹ 'When you are brought before synagogues and state authorities, do not worry about how you will conduct your defence or what you will say. ¹² When the time comes the Holy Spirit will instruct you what to say.'

¹³ Someone in the crowd said to him, 'Teacher, tell my brother to divide the family property with me.' ¹⁴ He said to the man, 'Who set me over you to judge or arbitrate?' ¹⁵ Then to the people he said, 'Beware! Be on your guard against greed of every kind, for even when someone has more than enough, his possessions do not give him life.' ¹⁶ And he told them this parable: 'There was a rich man whose land yielded a good harvest. ¹⁷ He debated with himself: "What am I to do? I have not the space to store my produce. ¹⁸ This is what I will do," said he: "I will pull down my barns and build them bigger. I will collect in them all my grain and other goods, ¹⁹ and I will say to myself, 'You have plenty of good things laid by, enough for many years to come: take life easy, eat, drink, and enjoy yourself.'" ²⁰ But God said to him, "You fool, this very night you must surrender your life; and the money you have made, who will get it now?" ²¹ That is how it is with the man who piles up treasure for himself and remains a pauper in the sight of God.'

²² To his disciples he said, 'This is why I tell you not to worry about food to keep you alive or clothes to cover your body.

23 Life is more than food, the body more than clothes. 24 Think of the ravens: they neither sow nor reap; they have no storehouse or barn; yet God feeds them. You are worth far more than the birds! 25 Can anxious thought add a day to your life? 26 If, then, you cannot do even a very little thing, why worry about the rest?

27 'Think of the lilies: they neither spin nor weave; yet I tell you, even Solomon in all his splendour was not attired like one of them. 28 If that is how God clothes the grass, which is growing in the field today, and tomorrow is thrown on the stove, how much more will he clothe you! How little faith you have! 29 Do not set your minds on what you are to eat or drink; do not be anxious. 30 These are all things that occupy the minds of the Gentiles; but your Father knows that you need them. 31 No, set your minds on his kingdom, and the rest will come to you as well.

32 'Have no fear, little flock; for your Father has chosen to give you the kingdom. 33 Sell your possessions and give to charity. Provide for yourselves purses that do not wear out, and never-failing treasure in heaven, where no thief can get near it, no moth destroy it. 34 For where your treasure is, there will your heart be also.

35 'Be ready for action, with your robes hitched up and your lamps alight. 36 Be like people who wait for their master's return from a wedding party, ready to let him in the moment he arrives and knocks. 37 Happy are those servants whom the master finds awake when he comes. Truly I tell you: he will hitch up his robe, seat them at table, and come and wait on them. 38 If it is the middle of the night or before dawn when he comes and he still finds them awake, then are they happy indeed. 39 Remember, if the householder had known at what time the burglar was coming he would not have let his house be broken into. 40 So hold yourselves in readiness, because the Son of Man will come at the time you least expect him.'

41 Peter said, 'Lord, do you intend this parable specially for us or is it for everyone?' 42 The Lord said, 'Who is the trusty and sensible man whom his master will appoint as his steward, to manage his servants and issue their rations at the proper time? 43 Happy that servant if his master comes home and finds him at work! 44 I tell you this: he will be put in charge of all his master's property. 45 But if that servant says to himself, "The master is a long time coming," and begins to bully the menservants and maids, and to eat and drink and get drunk, 46 then the master will arrive on a day when the servant does not expect him, at a time he has not been told. He will cut him in pieces and assign him a place among the faithless.

47 'The servant who knew his master's wishes, yet made no attempt to carry them out, will be flogged severely. 48 But one who did not know them and earned a beating will be flogged less severely. Where someone has been given much, much will be expected of him; and the more he has had entrusted to him the more will be demanded of him.

49 'I have come to set fire to the earth, and how I wish it were already kindled! 50 I have a baptism to undergo, and what constraint I am under until it is over! 51 Do you suppose I came to establish peace on the earth? No indeed, I have come to bring dissension. 52 From now on, a family of five will be divided, three against two and two against three; 53 father against son and son against father, mother against daughter and daughter against mother, mother-in-law against daughter-in-law and daughter-in-law against mother-in-law.'

54 He also said to the people, 'When you see clouds gathering in the west, you say at once, "It is going to rain," and rain it does. 55 And when the wind is from the south, you say, "It will be hot," and it is. 56 What hypocrites you are! You know how to interpret the appearance of earth and sky, but cannot interpret this fateful hour.

57 'Why can you not judge for yourselves what is right? 58 When you are going with your opponent to court, make an effort to reach a settlement with him while you are still on the way; otherwise he may drag you before the judge, and the judge hand you over to the officer, and the officer throw you into jail. 59 I tell you, you will not be let out until you have paid the very last penny.'

12:25 **a day** ... **life:** *or* a foot to your height.

65

13 AT that time some people came and told him about the Galileans whose blood Pilate had mixed with their sacrifices. ² He answered them: 'Do you suppose that, because these Galileans suffered this fate, they must have been greater sinners than anyone else in Galilee? ³ No, I tell you; but unless you repent, you will all of you come to the same end. ⁴ Or the eighteen people who were killed when the tower fell on them at Siloam—do you imagine they must have been more guilty than all the other people living in Jerusalem? ⁵ No, I tell you; but unless you repent, you will all come to an end like theirs.'

⁶ He told them this parable: 'A man had a fig tree growing in his vineyard; and he came looking for fruit on it, but found none. ⁷ So he said to the vine-dresser, "For the last three years I have come looking for fruit on this fig tree without finding any. Cut it down. Why should it go on taking goodness from the soil?" ⁸ But he replied, "Leave it, sir, for this one year, while I dig round it and manure it. ⁹ And if it bears next season, well and good; if not, you shall have it down."'

¹⁰ He was teaching in one of the synagogues on the sabbath, ¹¹ and there was a woman there possessed by a spirit that had crippled her for eighteen years. She was bent double and quite unable to stand up straight. ¹² When Jesus saw her he called her and said, 'You are rid of your trouble,' ¹³ and he laid his hands on her. Immediately she straightened up and began to praise God. ¹⁴ But the president of the synagogue, indignant with Jesus for healing on the sabbath, intervened and said to the congregation, 'There are six working days: come and be cured on one of them, and not on the sabbath.' ¹⁵ The Lord gave him this answer: 'What hypocrites you are!' he said. 'Is there a single one of you who does not loose his ox or his donkey from its stall and take it out to water on the sabbath? ¹⁶ And here is this woman, a daughter of Abraham, who has been bound by Satan for eighteen long years: was it not right for her to be loosed from her bonds on the sabbath?' ¹⁷ At these words all his opponents were covered with confusion, while the mass of the people were delighted at all the wonderful things he was doing.

¹⁸ 'What is the kingdom of God like?' he continued. 'To what shall I compare it? ¹⁹ It is like a mustard seed which a man took and sowed in his garden; and it grew to be a tree and the birds came to roost among its branches.'

²⁰ Again he said, 'To what shall I compare the kingdom of God? ²¹ It is like yeast which a woman took and mixed with three measures of flour till it was all leavened.'

²² HE continued his journey through towns and villages, teaching as he made his way towards Jerusalem. ²³ Someone asked him, 'Sir, are only a few to be saved?' His answer was: ²⁴ 'Make every effort to enter through the narrow door; for I tell you that many will try to enter but will not succeed.

²⁵ 'When once the master of the house has got up and locked the door, you may stand outside and knock, and say, "Sir, let us in!" but he will only answer, "I do not know where you come from." ²⁶ Then you will protest, "We used to eat and drink with you, and you taught in our streets." ²⁷ But he will repeat, "I tell you, I do not know where you come from. Out of my sight, all of you, you and your wicked ways!" ²⁸ There will be wailing and grinding of teeth there, when you see Abraham, Isaac, Jacob, and all the prophets, in the kingdom of God, and you yourselves are driven away. ²⁹ From east and west, from north and south, people will come and take their places at the banquet in the kingdom of God. ³⁰ Yes, and some who are now last will be first, and some who are first will be last.'

³¹ At that time a number of Pharisees came and warned him, 'Leave this place and be on your way; Herod wants to kill you.' ³² He replied, 'Go and tell that fox, "Listen: today and tomorrow I shall be driving out demons and working cures; on the third day I reach my goal." ³³ However, I must go on my way today and tomorrow and the next day, because it is unthinkable for a prophet to meet his death anywhere but in Jerusalem.

³⁴ 'O Jerusalem, Jerusalem, city that murders the prophets and stones the messengers sent to her! How often have I longed to gather your children, as a hen gathers her brood under her wings; but you would not let me. ³⁵ Look! There is

your temple, forsaken by God. I tell you, you will not see me until the time comes when you say, "Blessings on him who comes in the name of the Lord!"'

14 ONE sabbath he went to have a meal in the house of one of the leading Pharisees; and they were watching him closely. ² There, in front of him, was a man suffering from dropsy, ³ and Jesus asked the lawyers and the Pharisees: 'Is it permitted to heal people on the sabbath or not?' ⁴ They said nothing. So he took the man, cured him, and sent him away. ⁵ Then he turned to them and said, 'If one of you has a son or an ox that falls into a well, will he hesitate to pull him out on the sabbath day?' ⁶ To this they could find no reply.

⁷ When he noticed how the guests were trying to secure the places of honour, he spoke to them in a parable: ⁸ 'When somebody asks you to a wedding feast, do not sit down in the place of honour. It may be that some person more distinguished than yourself has been invited; ⁹ and the host will come to say to you, "Give this man your seat." Then you will look foolish as you go to take the lowest place. ¹⁰ No, when you receive an invitation, go and sit down in the lowest place, so that when your host comes he will say, "Come up higher, my friend." Then all your fellow-guests will see the respect in which you are held. ¹¹ For everyone who exalts himself will be humbled; and whoever humbles himself will be exalted.'

¹² Then he said to his host, 'When you are having guests for lunch or supper, do not invite your friends, your brothers or other relations, or your rich neighbours; they will only ask you back again and so you will be repaid. ¹³ But when you give a party, ask the poor, the crippled, the lame, and the blind. ¹⁴ That is the way to find happiness, because they have no means of repaying you. You will be repaid on the day when the righteous rise from the dead.'

¹⁵ Hearing this one of the company said to him, 'Happy are those who will sit at the feast in the kingdom of God!' ¹⁶ Jesus answered, 'A man was giving a big dinner party and had sent out many invitations. ¹⁷ At dinner-time he sent his servant to tell

his guests, "Come please, everything is now ready." ¹⁸ One after another they all sent excuses. The first said, "I have bought a piece of land, and I must go and inspect it; please accept my apologies." ¹⁹ The second said, "I have bought five yoke of oxen, and I am on my way to try them out; please accept my apologies." ²⁰ The next said, "I cannot come; I have just got married." ²¹ When the servant came back he reported this to his master. The master of the house was furious and said to him, "Go out quickly into the streets and alleys of the town, and bring in the poor, the crippled, the blind, and the lame." ²² When the servant informed him that his orders had been carried out and there was still room, ²³ his master replied, "Go out on the highways and along the hedgerows and compel them to come in; I want my house full. ²⁴ I tell you, not one of those who were invited shall taste my banquet."'

²⁵ Once when great crowds were accompanying him, he turned to them and said: ²⁶ 'If anyone comes to me and does not hate his father and mother, wife and children, brothers and sisters, even his own life, he cannot be a disciple of mine. ²⁷ No one who does not carry his cross and come with me can be a disciple of mine. ²⁸ Would any of you think of building a tower without first sitting down and calculating the cost, to see whether he could afford to finish it? ²⁹ Otherwise, if he has laid its foundation and then is unable to complete it, everyone who sees it will laugh at him. ³⁰ "There goes the man", they will say, "who started to build and could not finish." ³¹ Or what king will march to battle against another king, without first sitting down to consider whether with ten thousand men he can face an enemy coming to meet him with twenty thousand? ³² If he cannot, then, long before the enemy approaches, he sends envoys and asks for terms. ³³ So also, if you are not prepared to leave all your possessions behind, you cannot be my disciples.

³⁴ 'Salt is good; but if salt itself becomes tasteless, how will it be seasoned? ³⁵ It is useless either on the land or on the dungheap; it can only be thrown away. If you have ears to hear, then hear.'

14: 5 son: *some witnesses read* donkey.

Finding the lost

15 ANOTHER time, the tax-collectors and sinners were all crowding in to listen to him; [2] and the Pharisees and scribes began murmuring their disapproval: 'This fellow', they said, 'welcomes sinners and eats with them.' [3] He answered them with this parable: [4] 'If one of you has a hundred sheep and loses one of them, does he not leave the ninety-nine in the wilderness and go after the one that is missing until he finds it? [5] And when he does, he lifts it joyfully on to his shoulders, [6] and goes home to call his friends and neighbours together. "Rejoice with me!" he cries. "I have found my lost sheep." [7] In the same way, I tell you, there will be greater joy in heaven over one sinner who repents than over ninety-nine righteous people who do not need to repent.

[8] 'Or again, if a woman has ten silver coins and loses one of them, does she not light the lamp, sweep out the house, and look in every corner till she finds it? [9] And when she does, she calls her friends and neighbours together, and says, "Rejoice with me! I have found the coin that I lost." [10] In the same way, I tell you, there is joy among the angels of God over one sinner who repents.'

[11] Again he said: 'There was once a man who had two sons; [12] and the younger said to his father, "Father, give me my share of the property." So he divided his estate between them. [13] A few days later the younger son turned the whole of his share into cash and left home for a distant country, where he squandered it in dissolute living. [14] He had spent it all, when a severe famine fell upon that country and he began to be in need. [15] So he went and attached himself to one of the local landowners, who sent him on to his farm to mind the pigs. [16] He would have been glad to fill his belly with the pods that the pigs were eating, but no one gave him anything. [17] Then he came to his senses: "How many of my father's hired servants have more food than they can eat," he said, "and here am I, starving to death! [18] I will go at once to my father, and say to him, 'Father, I have sinned against God and against you; [19] I am no longer fit to be called your son; treat me as one of your hired servants.'" [20] So he set out for his father's house. But while he was still a long way off his father saw him, and his

heart went out to him; he ran to meet him, flung his arms round him, and kissed him. [21] The son said, "Father, I have sinned against God and against you; I am no longer fit to be called your son." [22] But the father said to his servants, "Quick! Fetch a robe, the best we have, and put it on him; put a ring on his finger and sandals on his feet. [23] Bring the fatted calf and kill it, and let us celebrate with a feast. [24] For this son of mine was dead and has come back to life; he was lost and is found." And the festivities began.

[25] 'Now the elder son had been out on the farm; and on his way back, as he approached the house, he heard music and dancing. [26] He called one of the servants and asked what it meant. [27] The servant told him, "Your brother has come home, and your father has killed the fatted calf because he has him back safe and sound." [28] But he was angry and refused to go in. His father came out and pleaded with him; [29] but he retorted, "You know how I have slaved for you all these years; I never once disobeyed your orders; yet you never gave me so much as a kid, to celebrate with my friends. [30] But now that this son of yours turns up, after running through your money with his women, you kill the fatted calf for him." [31] "My boy," said the father, "you are always with me, and everything I have is yours. [32] How could we fail to celebrate this happy day? Your brother here was dead and has come back to life; he was lost and has been found."'

Instructing the disciples

16 HE said to his disciples, 'There was a rich man who had a steward, and he received complaints that this man was squandering the property. [2] So he sent for him, and said, "What is this that I hear about you? Produce your accounts, for you cannot be steward any longer." [3] The steward said to himself, "What am I to do now that my master is going to dismiss me from my post? I am not strong enough to dig, and I am too proud to beg. [4] I know what I must do, to make sure that, when I am dismissed, there will be people who will take me into their homes." [5] He summoned his master's debtors one by one. To the first he said, "How much do you owe my master?" [6] He replied, "A hundred jars of olive oil." He said, "Here is your account. Sit down and make it fifty, and be quick about it." ⁷ Then he said to another, "And you, how much do you owe?" He said, "A hundred measures of wheat," and was told, "Here is your account; make it eighty." ⁸ And the master applauded the dishonest steward for acting so astutely. For in dealing with their own kind the children of this world are more astute than the children of light.

⁹ 'So I say to you, use your worldly wealth to win friends for yourselves, so that when money is a thing of the past you may be received into an eternal home.

¹⁰ 'Anyone who can be trusted in small matters can be trusted also in great; and anyone who is dishonest in small matters is dishonest also in great. ¹¹ If, then, you have not proved trustworthy with the wealth of this world, who will trust you with the wealth that is real? ¹² And if you have proved untrustworthy with what belongs to another, who will give you anything of your own?

¹³ 'No slave can serve two masters; for either he will hate the first and love the second, or he will be devoted to the first and despise the second. You cannot serve God and Money.'

¹⁴ The Pharisees, who loved money, heard all this and scoffed at him. ¹⁵ He said to them, 'You are the people who impress others with your righteousness; but God sees through you; for what is considered admirable in human eyes is detestable in the sight of God.

¹⁶ 'The law and the prophets were until John: since then, the good news of the kingdom of God is proclaimed, and everyone forces a way in.

¹⁷ 'It is easier for heaven and earth to come to an end than for one letter of the law to lose its force.

¹⁸ 'A man who divorces his wife and marries another commits adultery; and anyone who marries a woman divorced from her husband commits adultery.

¹⁹ 'There was once a rich man, who used to dress in purple and the finest linen, and feasted sumptuously every day. ²⁰ At his gate lay a poor man named Lazarus, who was covered with sores. ²¹ He would have been glad to satisfy his hunger with the scraps from the rich man's table. Dogs used to come and lick his sores. ²² One day the poor man died

and was carried away by the angels to be with Abraham. The rich man also died and was buried. ²³ In Hades, where he was in torment, he looked up and there, far away, was Abraham with Lazarus close beside him. ²⁴ "Abraham, my father," he called out, "take pity on me! Send Lazarus to dip the tip of his finger in water, to cool my tongue, for I am in agony in this fire." ²⁵ But Abraham said, "My child, remember that the good things fell to you in your lifetime, and the bad to Lazarus. Now he has his consolation here and it is you who are in agony. ²⁶ But that is not all: there is a great gulf fixed between us; no one can cross it from our side to reach you, and none may pass from your side to us." ²⁷ "Then, father," he replied, "will you send him to my father's house, ²⁸ where I have five brothers, to warn them, so that they may not come to this place of torment?" ²⁹ But Abraham said, "They have Moses and the prophets; let them listen to them." ³⁰ "No, father Abraham," he replied, "but if someone from the dead visits them, they will repent." ³¹ Abraham answered, "If they do not listen to Moses and the prophets they will pay no heed even if someone should rise from the dead."'

17 He said to his disciples, 'There are bound to be causes of stumbling; but woe betide the person through whom they come. ² It would be better for him to be thrown into the sea with a millstone round his neck than to cause the downfall of one of these little ones. ³ So be on your guard.

'If your brother does wrong, reprove him; and if he repents, forgive him. ⁴ Even if he wrongs you seven times in a day and comes back to you seven times saying, "I am sorry," you are to forgive him.'

⁵ The apostles said to the Lord, 'Increase our faith'; ⁶ and the Lord replied, 'If you had faith no bigger than a mustard seed, you could say to this mulberry tree, "Be rooted up and planted in the sea"; and it would obey you.

⁷ 'Suppose one of you has a servant ploughing or minding sheep. When he comes in from the fields, will the master say, "Come and sit down straight away"? ⁸ Will he not rather say, "Prepare my supper; hitch up your robe, and wait on me while I have my meal. You can have

yours afterwards"? ⁹ Is he grateful to the servant for carrying out his orders? ¹⁰ So with you: when you have carried out all you have been ordered to do, you should say, "We are servants and deserve no credit; we have only done our duty."'

¹¹ In the course of his journey to Jerusalem he was travelling through the borderlands of Samaria and Galilee. ¹²As he was entering a village he was met by ten men with leprosy. They stood some way off ¹³ and called out to him, 'Jesus, Master, take pity on us.' ¹⁴ When he saw them he said, 'Go and show yourselves to the priests'; and while they were on their way, they were made clean. ¹⁵ One of them, finding himself cured, turned back with shouts of praise to God. ¹⁶ He threw himself down at Jesus's feet and thanked him. And he was a Samaritan. ¹⁷At this Jesus said: 'Were not all ten made clean? The other nine, where are they? ¹⁸ Was no one found returning to give praise to God except this foreigner?' ¹⁹And he said to the man, 'Stand up and go on your way; your faith has cured you.'

²⁰ THE Pharisees asked him, 'When will the kingdom of God come?' He answered, 'You cannot tell by observation when the kingdom of God comes. ²¹ You cannot say, "Look, here it is," or "There it is!" For the kingdom of God is among you!'

²² He said to the disciples, 'The time will come when you will long to see one of the days of the Son of Man and will not see it. ²³ They will say to you, "Look! There!" and "Look! Here!" Do not go running off in pursuit. ²⁴ For like a lightning-flash, that lights up the earth from end to end, will the Son of Man be in his day. ²⁵ But first he must endure much suffering and be rejected by this generation.

²⁶ 'As it was in the days of Noah, so will it be in the days of the Son of Man. ²⁷ They ate and drank and married, until the day that Noah went into the ark and the flood came and made an end of them all. ²⁸ So too in the days of Lot, they ate and drank, they bought and sold, they planted and built; ²⁹ but on the day that Lot left Sodom, fire and sulphur rained from the sky and made an end of them all. ³⁰ It will

be like that on the day when the Son of Man is revealed.

³¹ 'On that day if anyone is on the roof while his belongings are in the house, he must not go down to fetch them; and if anyone is in the field, he must not turn back. ³² Remember Lot's wife. ³³ Whoever seeks to preserve his life will lose it; and whoever loses his life will gain it.

³⁴ 'I tell you, on that night there will be two people in one bed: one will be taken, the other left. ³⁵ There will be two women together grinding corn: one will be taken, the other left.' ³⁷ When they heard this they asked, 'Where, Lord?' He said, 'Where the carcass is, there will the vultures gather.'

18 HE told them a parable to show that they should keep on praying and never lose heart: ² 'In a certain city there was a judge who had no fear of God or respect for man, ³ and in the same city there was a widow who kept coming before him to demand justice against her opponent. ⁴ For a time he refused; but in the end he said to himself, "Although I have no fear of God or respect for man, ⁵ yet this widow is so great a nuisance that I will give her justice before she wears me out with her persistence."' ⁶ The Lord said, 'You hear what the unjust judge says. ⁷ Then will not God give justice to his chosen, to whom he listens patiently while they cry out to him day and night? ⁸ I tell you, he will give them justice soon enough. But when the Son of Man comes, will he find faith on earth?'

⁹ Here is another parable that he told; it was aimed at those who were sure of their own goodness and looked down on everyone else. ¹⁰ 'Two men went up to the temple to pray, one a Pharisee and the other a tax-collector. ¹¹ The Pharisee stood up and prayed this prayer: "I thank you, God, that I am not like the rest of mankind—greedy, dishonest, adulterous—or, for that matter, like this tax-collector. ¹² I fast twice a week; I pay tithes on all that I get." ¹³ But the other kept his distance and would not even raise his eyes to heaven, but beat upon his breast, saying, "God, have mercy on me,

17:21 For ... among you!: *or* For the kingdom of God is within you! *or* For the kingdom of God is within your grasp! *or* For suddenly the kingdom of God will be among you.   17:35 the other left: *some witnesses add* ³⁶ 'There will be two men in the fields: one will be taken, the other left.'

sinner that I am." [14] It was this man, I tell you, and not the other, who went home acquitted of his sins. For everyone who exalts himself will be humbled; and whoever humbles himself will be exalted.'

[15] They brought babies for him to touch, and when the disciples saw them they rebuked them. [16] But Jesus called for the children and said, 'Let the children come to me; do not try to stop them; for the kingdom of God belongs to such as these. [17] Truly I tell you: whoever does not accept the kingdom of God like a child will never enter it.'

[18] One of the rulers put this question to him: 'Good Teacher, what must I do to win eternal life?' [19] Jesus said to him, 'Why do you call me good? No one is good except God alone. [20] You know the commandments: "Do not commit adultery; do not murder; do not steal; do not give false evidence; honour your father and mother."' [21] The man answered, 'I have kept all these since I was a boy.' [22] On hearing this Jesus said, 'There is still one thing you lack: sell everything you have and give to the poor, and you will have treasure in heaven; then come and follow me.' [23] When he heard this his heart sank, for he was a very rich man. [24] When Jesus saw it he said, 'How hard it is for the wealthy to enter the kingdom of God! [25] It is easier for a camel to go through the eye of a needle than for a rich man to enter the kingdom of God.' [26] Those who heard asked, 'Then who can be saved?' [27] He answered, 'What is impossible for men is possible for God.'

[28] Peter said, 'What about us? We left all we had to follow you.' [29] Jesus said to them, 'Truly I tell you: there is no one who has given up home, or wife, brothers, parents, or children, for the sake of the kingdom of God, [30] who will not be repaid many times over in this age, and in the age to come have eternal life.'

Jesus's challenge to Jerusalem

[31] HE took the Twelve aside and said, 'We are now going up to Jerusalem; and everything that was written by the prophets will find its fulfilment in the Son of Man. [32] He will be handed over to the Gentiles. He will be mocked, maltreated, and spat upon; [33] they will flog him and kill him; and on the third day he will rise again.' [34] But they did not understand this

at all or grasp what he was talking about; its meaning was concealed from them.

[35] As he approached Jericho a blind man sat at the roadside begging. [36] Hearing a crowd going past, he asked what was happening, [37] and was told that Jesus of Nazareth was passing by. [38] Then he called out, 'Jesus, Son of David, have pity on me.' [39] The people in front told him to hold his tongue; but he shouted all the more, 'Son of David, have pity on me.' [40] Jesus stopped and ordered the man to be brought to him. When he came up Jesus asked him, [41] 'What do you want me to do for you?' 'Sir, I want my sight back,' he answered. [42] Jesus said to him, 'Have back your sight; your faith has healed you.' [43] He recovered his sight instantly and followed Jesus, praising God. And all the people gave praise to God for what they had seen.

19 Entering Jericho he made his way through the city. [2] There was a man there named Zacchaeus; he was superintendent of taxes and very rich. [3] He was eager to see what Jesus looked like; but, being a little man, he could not see him for the crowd. [4] So he ran on ahead and climbed a sycomore tree in order to see him, for he was to pass that way. [5] When Jesus came to the place, he looked up and said, 'Zacchaeus, be quick and come down, for I must stay at your house today.' [6] He climbed down as quickly as he could and welcomed him gladly. [7] At this there was a general murmur of disapproval. 'He has gone in to be the guest of a sinner,' they said. [8] But Zacchaeus stood there and said to the Lord, 'Here and now, sir, I give half my possessions to charity; and if I have defrauded anyone, I will repay him four times over.' [9] Jesus said to him, 'Today salvation has come to this house—for this man too is a son of Abraham. [10] The Son of Man has come to seek and to save what is lost.'

[11] While they were listening to this, he went on to tell them a parable, because he was now close to Jerusalem and they thought the kingdom of God might dawn at any moment. [12] He said, 'A man of noble birth went on a long journey abroad, to have himself appointed king and then return. [13] But first he called ten of his servants and gave them each a sum of money, saying, "Trade with this while I

am away." ¹⁴His fellow-citizens hated him and sent a delegation after him to say, "We do not want this man as our king." ¹⁵He returned however as king, and sent for the servants to whom he had given the money, to find out what profit each had made. ¹⁶The first came and said, "Your money, sir, has increased tenfold." ¹⁷"Well done," he replied; "you are a good servant. Because you have shown yourself trustworthy in a very small matter, you shall have charge of ten cities." ¹⁸The second came and said, "Your money, sir, has increased fivefold"; ¹⁹and he was told, "You shall be in charge of five cities." ²⁰The third came and said, "Here is your money, sir; I kept it wrapped up in a handkerchief. ²¹I was afraid of you, because you are a hard man: you draw out what you did not put in and reap what you did not sow." ²²"You scoundrel!" he replied. "I will condemn you out of your own mouth. You knew me to be a hard man, did you, drawing out what I never put in, and reaping what I did not sow? ²³Then why did you not put my money on deposit, and I could have claimed it with interest when I came back?" ²⁴Turning to his attendants he said, "Take the money from him and give it to the man with the most." ²⁵"But, sir," they replied, "he has ten times as much already." ²⁶"I tell you," he said, "everyone who has will be given more; but whoever has nothing will forfeit even what he has. ²⁷But as for those enemies of mine who did not want me for their king, bring them here and slaughter them in my presence."'

²⁸WITH that Jesus set out on the ascent to Jerusalem. ²⁹As he approached Bethphage and Bethany at the hill called Olivet, he sent off two of the disciples, ³⁰telling them: 'Go into the village opposite; as you enter it you will find tethered there a colt which no one has yet ridden. Untie it and bring it here. ³¹If anyone asks why you are untying it, say, "The Master needs it."' ³²The two went on their errand and found everything just as he had told them. ³³As they were untying the colt, its owners asked, 'Why are you untying that colt?' ³⁴They answered, 'The Master needs it.' ³⁵So they brought the colt to Jesus, and threw their cloaks on it for Jesus to

mount. ³⁶As he went along people laid their cloaks on the road. ³⁷And when he reached the descent from the mount of Olives, the whole company of his disciples in their joy began to sing aloud the praises of God for all the great things they had seen:

³⁸'Blessed is he who comes as king in the name of the Lord!
Peace in heaven, glory in highest heaven!'

³⁹Some Pharisees in the crowd said to him, 'Teacher, restrain your disciples.' ⁴⁰He answered, 'I tell you, if my disciples are silent the stones will shout aloud.'

⁴¹When he came in sight of the city, he wept over it ⁴²and said, 'If only you had known this day the way that leads to peace! But no; it is hidden from your sight. ⁴³For a time will come upon you, when your enemies will set up siege-works against you; they will encircle you and hem you in at every point; ⁴⁴they will bring you to the ground, you and your children within your walls, and not leave you one stone standing on another, because you did not recognize the time of God's visitation.'

⁴⁵Then he went into the temple and began driving out the traders, ⁴⁶with these words: 'Scripture says, "My house shall be a house of prayer"; but you have made it a bandits' cave.'

⁴⁷Day by day he taught in the temple. The chief priests and scribes, with the support of the leading citizens, wanted to bring about his death, ⁴⁸but found they were helpless, because the people all hung on his words.

20 ONE day, as he was teaching the people in the temple and telling them the good news, the chief priests and scribes, accompanied by the elders, confronted him. ²'Tell us', they said, 'by what authority you are acting like this; who gave you this authority?' ³He answered them, 'I also have a question for you: tell me, ⁴was the baptism of John from God or from man?' ⁵This set them arguing among themselves: 'If we say, "From God," he will say, "Why did you not believe him?" ⁶And if we say, "From man," the people will all stone us, for they are convinced that John was a prophet.' ⁷So they answered that they could not

tell. [8] And Jesus said to them, 'Then neither will I tell you by what authority I act.'

[9] He went on to tell the people this parable: 'A man planted a vineyard, let it out to vine-growers, and went abroad for a long time. [10] When the season came, he sent a servant to the tenants to collect from them his share of the produce; but the tenants thrashed him and sent him away empty-handed. [11] He tried again and sent a second servant; but they thrashed him too, treated him outrageously, and sent him away empty-handed. [12] He tried once more and sent a third; him too they wounded and flung out. [13] Then the owner of the vineyard said, "What am I to do? I will send my beloved son; perhaps they will respect him." [14] But when the tenants saw him they discussed what they should do. "This is the heir," they said; "let us kill him so that the inheritance may come to us." [15] So they flung him out of the vineyard and killed him. What, therefore, will the owner of the vineyard do to them? [16] He will come and put those tenants to death and give the vineyard to others.'

When they heard this, they said, 'God forbid!' [17] But he looked straight at them and said, 'Then what does this text of scripture mean: "The stone which the builders rejected has become the main corner-stone"? [18] Everyone who falls on that stone will be dashed to pieces; anyone on whom it falls will be crushed.'

[19] The scribes and chief priests wanted to seize him there and then, for they saw that this parable was aimed at them; but they were afraid of the people. [20] So they watched their opportunity and sent agents in the guise of honest men, to seize on some word of his that they could use as a pretext for handing him over to the authority and jurisdiction of the governor. [21] They put a question to him: 'Teacher,' they said, 'we know that what you speak and teach is sound; you pay deference to no one, but teach in all sincerity the way of life that God requires. [22] Are we or are we not permitted to pay taxes to the Roman emperor?' [23] He saw through their trick and said, [24] 'Show me a silver piece. Whose head does it bear, and whose inscription?' 'Caesar's,' they replied. [25] 'Very well then,' he said, 'pay to Caesar what belongs to Caesar, and to God what belongs to God.' [26] Thus their attempt to catch him out in public failed, and, taken aback by his reply, they fell silent.

[27] Then some Sadducees, who deny that there is a resurrection, came forward and asked: [28] 'Teacher, Moses laid it down for us that if there are brothers, and one dies leaving a wife but no child, then the next should marry the widow and provide an heir for his brother. [29] Now, there were seven brothers: the first took a wife and died childless; [30] then the second married her, [31] then the third. In this way the seven of them died leaving no children. [32] Last of all the woman also died. [33] At the resurrection, therefore, whose wife is she to be, since all seven had married her?' [34] Jesus said to them, 'The men and women of this world marry; [35] but those who have been judged worthy of a place in the other world, and of the resurrection from the dead, do not marry, [36] for they are no longer subject to death. They are like angels; they are children of God, because they share in the resurrection. [37] That the dead are raised to life again is shown by Moses himself in the story of the burning bush, when he calls the Lord "the God of Abraham, the God of Isaac, the God of Jacob". [38] God is not God of the dead but of the living; in his sight all are alive.'

[39] At this some of the scribes said, 'Well spoken, Teacher.' [40] And nobody dared put any further question to him.

[41] He said to them, 'How can they say that the Messiah is David's son? [42] For David himself says in the book of Psalms: "The Lord said to my Lord, 'Sit at my right hand [43] until I make your enemies your footstool.'" [44] Thus David calls him "Lord"; how then can he be David's son?'

[45] In the hearing of all the people Jesus said to his disciples: [46] 'Beware of the scribes, who like to walk up and down in long robes, and love to be greeted respectfully in the street, to have the chief seats in synagogues and places of honour at feasts. [47] These are the men who eat up the property of widows, while for appearance' sake they say long prayers; the

20:13 **my beloved son:** *or* my only son.

sentence they receive will be all the more severe.'

Warnings about the end

21 As JESUS looked up and saw rich people dropping their gifts into the chest of the temple treasury, ² he noticed a poor widow putting in two tiny coins. ³ 'I tell you this,' he said: 'this poor widow has given more than any of them; ⁴ for those others who have given had more than enough, but she, with less than enough, has given all she had to live on.'

⁵ SOME people were talking about the temple and the beauty of its fine stones and ornaments. He said, ⁶ 'These things you are gazing at—the time will come when not one stone will be left upon another; they will all be thrown down.' ⁷ 'Teacher,' they asked, 'when will that be? What will be the sign that these things are about to happen?'

⁸ He said, 'Take care that you are not misled. For many will come claiming my name and saying, "I am he," and, "The time has come." Do not follow them. ⁹ And when you hear of wars and insurrections, do not panic. These things are bound to happen first; but the end does not follow at once.' ¹⁰ Then he added, 'Nation will go to war against nation, kingdom against kingdom; ¹¹ there will be severe earthquakes, famines and plagues in many places, and in the sky terrors and great portents.

¹² 'But before all this happens they will seize you and persecute you. You will be handed over to synagogues and put in prison; you will be haled before kings and governors for your allegiance to me. ¹³ This will be your opportunity to testify. ¹⁴ So resolve not to prepare your defence beforehand, ¹⁵ because I myself will give you such words and wisdom as no opponent can resist or refute. ¹⁶ Even your parents and brothers, your relations and friends, will betray you. Some of you will be put to death; ¹⁷ and everyone will hate you for your allegiance to me. ¹⁸ But not a hair of your head will be lost. ¹⁹ By standing firm you will win yourselves life.

²⁰ 'But when you see Jerusalem encircled by armies, then you may be sure that her devastation is near. ²¹ Then those who are in Judaea must take to the hills; those who are in the city itself must leave it, and those who are out in the country must not return; ²² because this is the time of retribution, when all that stands written is to be fulfilled. ²³ Alas for women with child in those days, and for those who have children at the breast! There will be great distress in the land and a terrible judgement on this people. ²⁴ They will fall by the sword; they will be carried captive into all countries; and Jerusalem will be trampled underfoot by Gentiles until the day of the Gentiles has run its course.

²⁵ 'Portents will appear in sun and moon and stars. On earth nations will stand helpless, not knowing which way to turn from the roar and surge of the sea. ²⁶ People will faint with terror at the thought of all that is coming upon the world; for the celestial powers will be shaken. ²⁷ Then they will see the Son of Man coming in a cloud with power and great glory. ²⁸ When all this begins to happen, stand upright and hold your heads high, because your liberation is near.'

²⁹ He told them a parable: 'Look at the fig tree, or at any other tree. ³⁰ As soon as it buds, you can see for yourselves that summer is near. ³¹ In the same way, when you see all this happening, you may know that the kingdom of God is near.

³² 'Truly I tell you: the present generation will live to see it all. ³³ Heaven and earth will pass away, but my words will never pass away.

³⁴ 'Be on your guard; do not let your minds be dulled by dissipation and drunkenness and worldly cares so that the great day catches you suddenly ³⁵ like a trap; for that day will come on everyone, the whole world over. ³⁶ Be on the alert, praying at all times for strength to pass safely through all that is coming and to stand in the presence of the Son of Man.'

³⁷ His days were given to teaching in the temple; every evening he would leave the city and spend the night on the hill called Olivet. ³⁸ And in the early morning the people flocked to listen to him in the temple.

The last supper

22 THE festival of Unleavened Bread, known as Passover, was approaching, ² and the chief priests and the

---

21:38 **in the temple:** *some witnesses here insert the passage printed on p. 102.*

scribes were trying to devise some means of doing away with him; for they were afraid of the people.

[3] Then Satan entered into Judas, who was called Iscariot, one of the Twelve; [4] and he went to the chief priests and temple guards to discuss ways of betraying Jesus to them. [5] They were glad and undertook to pay him a sum of money. [6] He agreed, and began to look for an opportunity to betray him to them without collecting a crowd.

[7] Then came the day of Unleavened Bread, on which the Passover lambs had to be slaughtered, [8] and Jesus sent off Peter and John, saying, 'Go and prepare the Passover supper for us.' [9] 'Where would you like us to make the preparations?' they asked. [10] He replied, 'As soon as you set foot in the city a man will meet you carrying a jar of water. Follow him into the house that he enters [11] and give this message to the householder: "The Teacher says, 'Where is the room in which I am to eat the Passover with my disciples?'" [12] He will show you a large room upstairs all set out: make the preparations there.' [13] They went and found everything as he had said. So they prepared for Passover.

[14] When the hour came he took his place at table, and the apostles with him; [15] and he said to them, 'How I have longed to eat this Passover with you before my death! [16] For I tell you, never again shall I eat it until the time when it finds its fulfilment in the kingdom of God.'

[17] Then he took a cup, and after giving thanks he said, 'Take this and share it among yourselves; [18] for I tell you, from this moment I shall not drink the fruit of the vine until the time when the kingdom of God comes.' [19] Then he took bread, and after giving thanks he broke it, and gave it to them with the words: 'This is my body.'

[21] 'Even now my betrayer is here, his hand with mine on the table. [22] For the Son of Man is going his appointed way; but alas for that man by whom he is betrayed!' [23] At that they began to ask among themselves which of them it could possibly be who was to do this.

[24] Then a dispute began as to which of them should be considered the greatest. [25] But he said, 'Among the Gentiles, kings lord it over their subjects; and those in authority are given the title Benefactor. [26] Not so with you: on the contrary, the greatest among you must bear himself like the youngest, the one who rules like one who serves. [27] For who is greater— the one who sits at table or the servant who waits on him? Surely the one who sits at table. Yet I am among you like a servant.

[28] 'You have stood firmly by me in my times of trial; [29] and I now entrust to you the kingdom which my Father entrusted to me; [30] in my kingdom you shall eat and drink at my table and sit on thrones as judges of the twelve tribes of Israel.

[31] 'Simon, Simon, take heed: Satan has been given leave to sift all of you like wheat; [32] but I have prayed for you, Simon, that your faith may not fail; and when you are restored, give strength to your brothers.' [33] 'Lord,' he replied, 'I am ready to go with you to prison and to death.' [34] Jesus said, 'I tell you, Peter, the cock will not crow tonight until you have denied three times over that you know me.'

[35] He said to them, 'When I sent you out barefoot without purse or pack, were you ever short of anything?' 'No,' they answered. [36] 'It is different now,' he said; 'whoever has a purse had better take it with him, and his pack too; and if he has no sword, let him sell his cloak to buy one. [37] For scripture says, "And he was reckoned among transgressors"; and this, I tell you, must be fulfilled in me; indeed, all that is written of me is reaching its fulfilment.' [38] 'Lord,' they said, 'we have two swords here.' 'Enough!' he replied.

[39] THEN he went out and made his way as usual to the mount of Olives, accompanied by the disciples. [40] When he reached the place he said to them, 'Pray that you may be spared the test.' [41] He himself withdrew from them about a stone's throw, knelt down, and began to pray: [42] 'Father, if it be your will, take this cup

---

22:16 For ... shall I: *some witnesses read* But I tell you, I shall not.　　22:19 my body: *some witnesses add, in whole or in part, and with various arrangements, the following:* 'which is given for you; do this as a memorial of me.' [20] In the same way he took the cup after supper, and said, 'This cup, poured out for you, is the new covenant sealed by my blood.'　　22:29-30 and I now ... and sit: *or* and as my Father gave me the right to reign, so I give you the right to eat and to drink at my table in my kingdom and to sit.

from me. Yet not my will but yours be done.'

⁴³ And now there appeared to him an angel from heaven bringing him strength, ⁴⁴ and in anguish of spirit he prayed the more urgently; and his sweat was like drops of blood falling to the ground. ⁴⁵ When he rose from prayer and came to the disciples he found them asleep, worn out by grief. ⁴⁶ 'Why are you sleeping?' he said. 'Rise and pray that you may be spared the test.'

The trial and crucifixion of Jesus

⁴⁷ WHILE he was still speaking a crowd appeared with the man called Judas, one of the Twelve, at their head. He came up to Jesus to kiss him; ⁴⁸ but Jesus said, 'Judas, would you betray the Son of Man with a kiss?'

⁴⁹ When his followers saw what was coming, they said, 'Lord, shall we use our swords?' ⁵⁰ And one of them struck at the high priest's servant, cutting off his right ear. ⁵¹ But Jesus answered, 'Stop! No more of that!' Then he touched the man's ear and healed him.

⁵² Turning to the chief priests, the temple guards, and the elders, who had come to seize him, he said, 'Do you take me for a robber, that you have come out with swords and cudgels? ⁵³ Day after day, I have been with you in the temple, and you did not raise a hand against me. But this is your hour—when darkness reigns.'

⁵⁴ Then they arrested him and led him away. They brought him to the high priest's house, and Peter followed at a distance. ⁵⁵ They lit a fire in the middle of the courtyard and sat round it, and Peter sat among them. ⁵⁶ A serving-maid who saw him sitting in the firelight stared at him and said, 'This man was with him too.' ⁵⁷ But he denied it: 'I do not know him,' he said. ⁵⁸ A little later a man noticed him and said, 'You also are one of them.' But Peter said to him, 'No, I am not.' ⁵⁹ About an hour passed and someone else spoke more strongly still: 'Of course he was with him. He must have been; he is a Galilean.' ⁶⁰ But Peter said, 'I do not know what you are talking about.' At that moment, while he was still speaking, a cock crowed; ⁶¹ and the Lord turned

and looked at Peter. Peter remembered the Lord's words, 'Tonight before the cock crows you will disown me three times.' ⁶² And he went outside, and wept bitterly.

⁶³ The men who were guarding Jesus mocked him. They beat him, ⁶⁴ they blindfolded him, and kept asking him, 'If you are a prophet, tell us who hit you.' ⁶⁵ And so they went on heaping insults upon him.

⁶⁶ AS SOON as it was day, the elders of the people, chief priests, and scribes assembled, and he was brought before their Council. ⁶⁷ 'Tell us,' they said, 'are you the Messiah?' 'If I tell you,' he replied, 'you will not believe me; ⁶⁸ and if I ask questions, you will not answer. ⁶⁹ But from now on, the Son of Man will be seated at the right hand of Almighty God.' ⁷⁰ 'You are the Son of God, then?' they all said, and he replied, 'It is you who say I am.' ⁷¹ At that they said, 'What further evidence do we need? We have heard this ourselves from his own lips.'

23 With that the whole assembly rose and brought him before Pilate. ² They opened the case against him by saying, 'We found this man subverting our nation, opposing the payment of taxes to Caesar, and claiming to be Messiah, a king.' ³ Pilate asked him, 'Are you the king of the Jews?' He replied, 'The words are yours.' ⁴ Pilate then said to the chief priests and the crowd, 'I find no case for this man to answer.' ⁵ But they insisted: 'His teaching is causing unrest among the people all over Judaea. It started from Galilee and now has spread here.'

⁶ When Pilate heard this, he asked if the man was a Galilean, ⁷ and on learning that he belonged to Herod's jurisdiction he remitted the case to him, for Herod was also in Jerusalem at that time. ⁸ When Herod saw Jesus he was greatly pleased; he had heard about him and had long been wanting to see him in the hope of witnessing some miracle performed by him. ⁹ He questioned him at some length without getting any reply; ¹⁰ but the chief priests and scribes appeared and pressed the case against him vigorously. ¹¹ Then Herod and his troops treated him with

---

22:43–44 *Some witnesses omit* And now ... ground. way.   22:69 **of Almighty God:** *lit.* of the Power of God. 23:3 **The words are yours:** *or* It is as you say.

22:51 **Stop! No more of that:** *or* Let them have their way.   22:70 **It is ... I am:** *or* You are right, for I am.

contempt and ridicule, and sent him back to Pilate dressed in a gorgeous robe. [12] That same day Herod and Pilate became friends; till then there had been a feud between them.

[13] Pilate now summoned the chief priests, councillors, and people, [14] and said to them, 'You brought this man before me on a charge of subversion. But, as you see, I have myself examined him in your presence and found nothing in him to support your charges. [15] No more did Herod, for he has referred him back to us. Clearly he has done nothing to deserve death. [16] I therefore propose to flog him and let him go.' [18] But there was a general outcry. 'Away with him! Set Barabbas free!' [19] (Now Barabbas had been put in prison for his part in a rising in the city and for murder.) [20] Pilate addressed them again, in his desire to release Jesus, [21] but they shouted back, 'Crucify him, crucify him!' [22] For the third time he spoke to them: 'Why, what wrong has he done? I have not found him guilty of any capital offence. I will therefore flog him and let him go.' [23] But they persisted with their demand, shouting that Jesus should be crucified. Their shouts prevailed, [24] and Pilate decided that they should have their way. [25] He released the man they asked for, the man who had been put in prison for insurrection and murder, and gave Jesus over to their will.

[26] As THEY led him away to execution they took hold of a man called Simon, from Cyrene, on his way in from the country; putting the cross on his back they made him carry it behind Jesus. [27] Great numbers of people followed, among them many women who mourned and lamented over him. [28] Jesus turned to them and said, 'Daughters of Jerusalem, do not weep for me; weep for yourselves and your children. [29] For the days are surely coming when people will say, "Happy are the barren, the wombs that never bore a child, the breasts that never fed one." [30] Then they will begin to say to the mountains, "Fall on us," and to the hills, "Cover us." [31] For if these things are done when the wood is green, what will happen when it is dry?'

[32] There were two others with him, criminals who were being led out to execution; [33] and when they reached the place called The Skull, they crucified him there, and the criminals with him, one on his right and the other on his left. [34] Jesus said, 'Father, forgive them; they do not know what they are doing.'

They shared out his clothes by casting lots. [35] The people stood looking on, and their rulers jeered at him: 'He saved others: now let him save himself, if this is God's Messiah, his Chosen.' [36] The soldiers joined in the mockery and came forward offering him sour wine. [37] 'If you are the king of the Jews,' they said, 'save yourself.' [38] There was an inscription above his head which ran: 'This is the king of the Jews.'

[39] One of the criminals hanging there taunted him: 'Are not you the Messiah? Save yourself, and us.' [40] But the other rebuked him: 'Have you no fear of God? You are under the same sentence as he is. [41] In our case it is plain justice; we are paying the price for our misdeeds. But this man has done nothing wrong.' [42] And he said, 'Jesus, remember me when you come to your throne.' [43] Jesus answered, 'Truly I tell you: today you will be with me in Paradise.'

[44] By now it was about midday and a darkness fell over the whole land, which lasted until three in the afternoon: [45] the sun's light failed. And the curtain of the temple was torn in two. [46] Then Jesus uttered a loud cry and said, 'Father, into your hands I commit my spirit'; and with these words he died. [47] When the centurion saw what had happened, he gave praise to God. 'Beyond all doubt', he said, 'this man was innocent.'

[48] The crowd who had assembled for the spectacle, when they saw what had happened, went home beating their breasts.

[49] His friends had all been standing at a distance; the women who had accompanied him from Galilee stood with them and watched it all.

[50] Now there was a man called Joseph, a member of the Council, a good and upright man, [51] who had dissented from

---

23:18 **But there was**: *some witnesses read* [17]At festival time he was obliged to release one person for them; [18]and now there was.   23:34 *Some witnesses omit* Jesus said, 'Father ... doing.'

their policy and the action they had taken. He came from the Judaean town of Arimathaea, and he was one who looked forward to the kingdom of God. ⁵² This man now approached Pilate and asked for the body of Jesus. ⁵³ Taking it down from the cross, he wrapped it in a linen sheet, and laid it in a tomb cut out of the rock, in which no one had been laid before. ⁵⁴ It was the day of preparation, and the sabbath was about to begin.

⁵⁵ The women who had accompanied Jesus from Galilee followed; they took note of the tomb and saw his body laid in it. ⁵⁶ Then they went home and prepared spices and perfumes; and on the sabbath they rested in obedience to the commandment.

The resurrection

24 BUT very early on the first day of the week they came to the tomb bringing the spices they had prepared. ² They found that the stone had been rolled away from the tomb, ³ but when they went inside, they did not find the body of the Lord Jesus. ⁴ While they stood utterly at a loss, suddenly two men in dazzling garments were at their side. ⁵ They were terrified, and stood with eyes cast down, but the men said, 'Why search among the dead for one who is alive? ⁶ Remember how he told you, while he was still in Galilee, ⁷ that the Son of Man must be given into the power of sinful men and be crucified, and must rise again on the third day.' ⁸ Then they recalled his words ⁹ and, returning from the tomb, they reported everything to the eleven and all the others.

¹⁰ The women were Mary of Magdala, Joanna, and Mary the mother of James, and they, with the other women, told these things to the apostles. ¹¹ But the story appeared to them to be nonsense, and they would not believe them.

¹³ THAT same day two of them were on their way to a village called Emmaus, about seven miles from Jerusalem, ¹⁴ talking together about all that had happened. ¹⁵ As they talked and argued, Jesus himself came up and walked with them; ¹⁶ but something prevented them from recognizing him. ¹⁷ He asked them, 'What is it you are debating as you walk?' They stood still, their faces full of sadness, ¹⁸ and one, called Cleopas, answered, 'Are you the only person staying in Jerusalem not to have heard the news of what has happened there in the last few days?' ¹⁹ 'What news?' he said. 'About Jesus of Nazareth,' they replied, 'who, by deeds and words of power, proved himself a prophet in the sight of God and the whole people; ²⁰ and how our chief priests and rulers handed him over to be sentenced to death, and crucified him. ²¹ But we had been hoping that he was to be the liberator of Israel. What is more, this is the third day since it happened, ²² and now some women of our company have astounded us: they went early to the tomb, ²³ but failed to find his body, and returned with a story that they had seen a vision of angels who told them he was alive. ²⁴ Then some of our people went to the tomb and found things just as the women had said; but him they did not see.'

²⁵ 'How dull you are!' he answered. 'How slow to believe all that the prophets said! ²⁶ Was not the Messiah bound to suffer in this way before entering upon his glory?' ²⁷ Then, starting from Moses and all the prophets, he explained to them in the whole of scripture the things that referred to himself.

²⁸ By this time they had reached the village to which they were going, and he made as if to continue his journey. ²⁹ But they pressed him: 'Stay with us, for evening approaches, and the day is almost over.' So he went in to stay with them. ³⁰ And when he had sat down with them at table, he took bread and said the blessing; he broke the bread, and offered it to them. ³¹ Then their eyes were opened, and they recognized him; but he vanished from their sight. ³² They said to one another, 'Were not our hearts on fire as he talked with us on the road and explained the scriptures to us?'

³³ Without a moment's delay they set out and returned to Jerusalem. There they found that the eleven and the rest of the company had assembled, ³⁴ and were saying, 'It is true: the Lord has risen; he has appeared to Simon.' ³⁵ Then they

24:5 who is alive: *some witnesses add* He is not here: he has been raised.   24:11 believe them: *some witnesses add* ¹² Peter, however, got up and ran to the tomb, and, peering in, saw the wrappings and nothing more; and he went home amazed at what had happened.

described what had happened on their journey and told how he had made himself known to them in the breaking of the bread.

³⁶ As they were talking about all this, there he was, standing among them. ³⁷ Startled and terrified, they thought they were seeing a ghost. ³⁸ But he said, 'Why are you so perturbed? Why do doubts arise in your minds? ³⁹ Look at my hands and feet. It is I myself. Touch me and see; no ghost has flesh and bones as you can see that I have.' ⁴¹ They were still incredulous, still astounded, for it seemed too good to be true. So he asked them, 'Have you anything here to eat?' ⁴² They offered him a piece of fish they had cooked, ⁴³ which he took and ate before their eyes.

⁴⁴ And he said to them, 'This is what I meant by saying, while I was still with you, that everything written about me in the law of Moses and in the prophets and psalms was bound to be fulfilled.' ⁴⁵ Then he opened their minds to understand the scriptures. ⁴⁶ 'So you see', he said, 'that scripture foretells the sufferings of the Messiah and his rising from the dead on the third day, ⁴⁷ and declares that in his name repentance bringing the forgiveness of sins is to be proclaimed to all nations beginning from Jerusalem. ⁴⁸ You are to be witnesses to it all. ⁴⁹ I am sending on you the gift promised by my Father; wait here in this city until you are armed with power from above.'

⁵⁰ Then he led them out as far as Bethany, and blessed them with uplifted hands; ⁵¹ and in the act of blessing he parted from them. ⁵² And they returned to Jerusalem full of joy, ⁵³ and spent all their time in the temple praising God.

24:36 **among them:** *some witnesses add* And he said to them, 'Peace be with you!'   24:39 **I have:** *some witnesses add* ⁴⁰ After saying this he showed them his hands and feet.   24:51 **parted from them:** *some witnesses add* and was carried up into heaven.   24:52 **And they:** *some witnesses add* worshipped him and.

THE GOSPEL ACCORDING TO
JOHN

The coming of Christ

1 In the beginning the Word already was. The Word was in God's presence, and what God was, the Word was. ² He was with God at the beginning, ³ and through him all things came to be; without him no created thing came into being. ⁴ In him was life, and that life was the light of mankind. ⁵ The light shines in the darkness, and the darkness has never mastered it.

⁶ There appeared a man named John. He was sent from God, ⁷ and came as a witness to testify to the light, so that through him all might become believers. ⁸ He was not himself the light; he came to bear witness to the light. ⁹ The true light which gives light to everyone was even then coming into the world.

¹⁰ He was in the world; but the world, though it owed its being to him, did not recognize him. ¹¹ He came to his own, and his own people would not accept him. ¹² But to all who did accept him, to those who put their trust in him, he gave the right to become children of God, ¹³ born not of human stock, by the physical desire of a human father, but of God. ¹⁴ So the Word became flesh; he made his home among us, and we saw his glory, such glory as befits the Father's only Son, full of grace and truth.

¹⁵ John bore witness to him and proclaimed: 'This is the man of whom I said, "He comes after me, but ranks ahead of me"; before I was born, he already was.'

¹⁶ From his full store we have all received grace upon grace; ¹⁷ for the law

1:3–4 **through him ... was life:** *or* without him no single thing was created. All that came to be was alive with his life.   1:9 **The true ... world:** *or* The true light was in being, which gives light to everyone entering the world.

was given through Moses, but grace and truth came through Jesus Christ. [18] No one has ever seen God; God's only Son, he who is nearest to the Father's heart, has made him known.

Testimony of the Baptist and the first disciples

[19] THIS is the testimony John gave when the Jews of Jerusalem sent a deputation of priests and Levites to ask him who he was. [20] He readily acknowledged, 'I am not the Messiah.' [21] 'What then? Are you Elijah?' 'I am not,' he replied. 'Are you the Prophet?' 'No,' he said. [22] 'Then who are you?' they asked. 'We must give an answer to those who sent us. What account do you give of yourself?' [23] He answered in the words of the prophet Isaiah: 'I am a voice crying in the wilderness, "Make straight the way for the Lord."'

[24] Some Pharisees who were in the deputation [25] asked him, 'If you are not the Messiah, nor Elijah, nor the Prophet, then why are you baptizing?' [26] 'I baptize in water,' John replied, 'but among you, though you do not know him, stands the one [27] who is to come after me. I am not worthy to unfasten the strap of his sandal.' [28] This took place at Bethany beyond Jordan, where John was baptizing.

[29] The next day he saw Jesus coming towards him. 'There is the Lamb of God,' he said, 'who takes away the sin of the world. [30] He it is of whom I said, "After me there comes a man who ranks ahead of me"; before I was born, he already was. [31] I did not know who he was; but the reason why I came, baptizing in water, was that he might be revealed to Israel.'

[32] John testified again: 'I saw the Spirit come down from heaven like a dove and come to rest on him. [33] I did not know him; but he who sent me to baptize in water had told me, "The man on whom you see the Spirit come down and rest is the one who is to baptize in Holy Spirit." [34] I have seen it and have borne witness: this is God's Chosen One.'

[35] The next day again, John was standing with two of his disciples [36] when Jesus passed by. John looked towards him and said, 'There is the Lamb of God!' [37] When the two disciples heard what he said, they followed Jesus. [38] He turned and saw them following; 'What are you looking for?' he asked. They said, 'Rabbi,' (which means 'Teacher') 'where are you staying?' [39] 'Come and see,' he replied. So they went and saw where he was staying, and spent the rest of the day with him. It was about four in the afternoon.

[40] One of the two who followed Jesus after hearing what John said was Andrew, Simon Peter's brother. [41] The first thing he did was to find his brother Simon and say to him, 'We have found the Messiah' (which is the Hebrew for Christ). [42] He brought Simon to Jesus, who looked at him and said, 'You are Simon son of John; you shall be called Cephas' (that is, Peter, 'the Rock').

[43-44] The next day Jesus decided to leave for Galilee. He met Philip, who, like Andrew and Peter, came from Bethsaida, and said to him, 'Follow me.' [45] Philip went to find Nathanael and told him, 'We have found the man of whom Moses wrote in the law, the man foretold by the prophets: it is Jesus son of Joseph, from Nazareth.' [46] 'Nazareth!' Nathanael exclaimed. 'Can anything good come from Nazareth?' Philip said, 'Come and see.' [47] When Jesus saw Nathanael coming towards him, he said, 'Here is an Israelite worthy of the name; there is nothing false in him.' [48] Nathanael asked him, 'How is it you know me?' Jesus replied, 'I saw you under the fig tree before Philip spoke to you.' [49] 'Rabbi,' said Nathanael, 'you are the Son of God; you are king of Israel.' [50] Jesus answered, 'Do you believe this because I told you I saw you under the fig tree? You will see greater things than that.' [51] Then he added, 'In very truth I tell you all: you will see heaven wide open and God's angels ascending and descending upon the Son of Man.'

Signs and discourses

2 TWO DAYS later there was a wedding at Cana-in-Galilee. The mother of Jesus was there, [2] and Jesus and his disciples were also among the guests. [3] The wine gave out, so Jesus's mother said to him, 'They have no wine left.' [4] He answered, 'That is no concern of mine.

---

1 : 18 **God's only Son**: *some witnesses read* the only begotten God.   1 : 34 **this ... One**: *some witnesses read* this is the Son of God.

My hour has not yet come.' [5] His mother said to the servants, 'Do whatever he tells you.' [6] There were six stone water-jars standing near, of the kind used for Jewish rites of purification; each held from twenty to thirty gallons. [7] Jesus said to the servants, 'Fill the jars with water,' and they filled them to the brim. [8] 'Now draw some off,' he ordered, 'and take it to the master of the feast'; and they did so. [9] The master tasted the water now turned into wine, not knowing its source, though the servants who had drawn the water knew. He hailed the bridegroom [10] and said, 'Everyone else serves the best wine first, and the poorer only when the guests have drunk freely; but you have kept the best wine till now.'

[11] So Jesus performed at Cana-in-Galilee the first of the signs which revealed his glory and led his disciples to believe in him.

[12] AFTER this he went down to Capernaum with his mother, his brothers, and his disciples, and they stayed there a few days. [13] As it was near the time of the Jewish Passover, Jesus went up to Jerusalem. [14] In the temple precincts he found the dealers in cattle, sheep, and pigeons, and the money-changers seated at their tables. [15] He made a whip of cords and drove them out of the temple, sheep, cattle, and all. He upset the tables of the money-changers, scattering their coins. [16] Then he turned on the dealers in pigeons: 'Take them out of here,' he said; 'do not turn my Father's house into a market.' [17] His disciples recalled the words of scripture: 'Zeal for your house will consume me.' [18] The Jews challenged Jesus: 'What sign can you show to justify your action?' [19] 'Destroy this temple,' Jesus replied, 'and in three days I will raise it up again.' [20] The Jews said, 'It has taken forty-six years to build this temple. Are you going to raise it up again in three days?' [21] But the temple he was speaking of was his body. [22] After his resurrection his disciples recalled what he had said, and they believed the scripture and the words that Jesus had spoken.

[23] WHILE he was in Jerusalem for Passover many put their trust in him when they saw the signs that he performed. [24] But Jesus for his part would not trust himself to them. He knew them all, [25] and had no need of evidence from others about anyone, for he himself could tell what was in people.

3 ONE of the Pharisees, called Nicodemus, a member of the Jewish Council, [2] came to Jesus by night. 'Rabbi,' he said, 'we know that you are a teacher sent by God; no one could perform these signs of yours unless God were with him.' [3] Jesus answered, 'In very truth I tell you, no one can see the kingdom of God unless he has been born again.' [4] 'But how can someone be born when he is old?' asked Nicodemus. 'Can he enter his mother's womb a second time and be born?' [5] Jesus answered, 'In very truth I tell you, no one can enter the kingdom of God without being born from water and spirit. [6] Flesh can give birth only to flesh; it is spirit that gives birth to spirit. [7] You ought not to be astonished when I say, "You must all be born again." [8] The wind blows where it wills; you hear the sound of it, but you do not know where it comes from or where it is going. So it is with everyone who is born from the Spirit.'

[9] 'How is this possible?' asked Nicodemus. [10] 'You a teacher of Israel and ignorant of such things!' said Jesus. [11] 'In very truth I tell you, we speak of what we know, and testify to what we have seen, and yet you all reject our testimony. [12] If you do not believe me when I talk to you about earthly things, how are you to believe if I should talk about the things of heaven?

[13] 'No one has gone up into heaven except the one who came down from heaven, the Son of Man who is in heaven. [14] Just as Moses lifted up the serpent in the wilderness, so the Son of Man must be lifted up, [15] in order that everyone who has faith may in him have eternal life.

[16] 'God so loved the world that he gave his only Son, that everyone who has faith in him may not perish but have eternal life. [17] It was not to judge the world that God sent his Son into the world, but that through him the world might be saved. [18] 'No one who puts his faith in him comes under judgement; but the

3:8 *wind and* spirit *are translations of the same Greek word, which has both meanings.*   3:13 *Some witnesses omit* who is in heaven.

unbeliever has already been judged because he has not put his trust in God's only Son. [19] This is the judgement: the light has come into the world, but people preferred darkness to light because their deeds were evil. [20] Wrongdoers hate the light and avoid it, for fear their misdeeds should be exposed. [21] Those who live by the truth come to the light so that it may be clearly seen that God is in all they do.'

[22] AFTER this Jesus went with his disciples into Judaea; he remained there with them and baptized. [23] John too was baptizing at Aenon, near Salim, because water was plentiful in that region; and all the time people were coming for baptism. [24] This was before John's imprisonment.

[25] John's disciples were engaged in a debate with some Jews about purification; [26] so they came to John and said, 'Rabbi, there was a man with you on the other side of the Jordan, to whom you bore your witness. Now he is baptizing, and everyone is flocking to him.' [27] John replied: 'One can have only what is given one from Heaven. [28] You yourselves can testify that I said, "I am not the Messiah; I have been sent as his forerunner." [29] It is the bridegroom who marries the bride. The bridegroom's friend, who stands by and listens to him, is overjoyed at hearing the bridegroom's voice. This is my joy and now it is complete. [30] He must grow greater; I must become less.'

[31] He who comes from above is above all others; he who is from the earth belongs to the earth and uses earthly speech. He who comes from heaven [32] bears witness to what he has seen and heard, even though no one accepts his witness. [33] To accept his witness is to affirm that God speaks the truth; [34] for he whom God sent utters the words of God, so measureless is God's gift of the Spirit. [35] The Father loves the Son and has entrusted him with complete authority. [36] Whoever puts his faith in the Son has eternal life. Whoever disobeys the Son will not see that life; God's wrath rests upon him.

4 [1-2] NEWS now reached the Pharisees that Jesus was winning and baptizing more disciples than John; although, in fact, it was his disciples who were baptizing, not Jesus himself. When Jesus heard this, [3] he left Judaea and set out once more for Galilee. [4] He had to pass through Samaria, [5] and on his way came to a Samaritan town called Sychar, near the plot of ground which Jacob gave to his son Joseph; [6] Jacob's well was there. It was about noon, and Jesus, tired after his journey, was sitting by the well.

[8] His disciples had gone into the town to buy food. [7] Meanwhile a Samaritan woman came to draw water, and Jesus said to her, 'Give me a drink.' [9] The woman said, 'What! You, a Jew, ask for a drink from a Samaritan woman?' (Jews do not share drinking vessels with Samaritans.) [10] Jesus replied, 'If only you knew what God gives, and who it is that is asking you for a drink, you would have asked him and he would have given you living water.' [11] 'Sir,' the woman said, 'you have no bucket and the well is deep, so where can you get "living water"? [12] Are you greater than Jacob our ancestor who gave us the well and drank from it himself, he and his sons and his cattle too?' [13] Jesus answered, 'Everyone who drinks this water will be thirsty again; [14] but whoever drinks the water I shall give will never again be thirsty. The water that I shall give will be a spring of water within him, welling up and bringing eternal life.' [15] 'Sir,' said the woman, 'give me this water, and then I shall not be thirsty, nor have to come all this way to draw water.'

[16] 'Go and call your husband,' said Jesus, 'and come back here.' [17] She answered, 'I have no husband.' Jesus said, 'You are right in saying that you have no husband, [18] for though you have had five husbands, the man you are living with now is not your husband. You have spoken the truth!' [19] 'Sir,' replied the woman, 'I can see you are a prophet. [20] Our fathers worshipped on this mountain, but you Jews say that the place where God must be worshipped is in Jerusalem.' [21] 'Believe me,' said Jesus, 'the time is coming when you will worship the Father neither on this mountain nor in Jerusalem. [22] You Samaritans worship you know not what; we worship what we

3:25 *some Jews: some witnesses read* a Jew.   3:31 *from heaven: some witnesses add* is above all and.
4:9 *Jews … Samaritans: some witnesses omit these words.*

82

know. It is from the Jews that salvation comes. [23] But the time is coming, indeed it is already here, when true worshippers will worship the Father in spirit and in truth. These are the worshippers the Father wants. [24] God is spirit, and those who worship him must worship in spirit and in truth.' [25] The woman answered, 'I know that Messiah' (that is, Christ) 'is coming. When he comes he will make everything clear to us.' [26] Jesus said to her, 'I am he, I who am speaking to you.'

[27] At that moment his disciples returned, and were astonished to find him talking with a woman; but none of them said, 'What do you want?' or, 'Why are you talking with her?' [28] The woman left her water-jar and went off to the town, where she said to the people, [29] 'Come and see a man who has told me everything I ever did. Could this be the Messiah?' [30] They left the town and made their way towards him.

[31] MEANWHILE the disciples were urging him, 'Rabbi, have something to eat.' [32] But he said, 'I have food to eat of which you know nothing.' [33] At this the disciples said to one another, 'Can someone have brought him food?' [34] But Jesus said, 'For me it is meat and drink to do the will of him who sent me until I have finished his work.

[35] 'Do you not say, "Four months more and then comes harvest"? But look, I tell you, look around at the fields: they are already white, ripe for harvesting. [36] The reaper is drawing his pay and harvesting a crop for eternal life, so that sower and reaper may rejoice together. [37] That is how the saying comes true: "One sows, another reaps." [38] I sent you to reap a crop for which you have not laboured. Others laboured and you have come in for the harvest of their labour.'

[39] Many Samaritans of that town came to believe in him because of the woman's testimony: 'He told me everything I ever did.' [40] So when these Samaritans came to him they pressed him to stay with them; and he stayed there two days. [41] Many more became believers because of what they heard from his own lips. [42] They told the woman, 'It is no longer because of

what you said that we believe, for we have heard him ourselves; and we are convinced that he is the Saviour of the world.'

Jesus the giver of life

[43] WHEN the two days were over Jesus left for Galilee; [44] for he himself had declared that a prophet is without honour in his own country. [45] On his arrival the Galileans made him welcome, because they had seen all he did at the festival in Jerusalem; they had been at the festival themselves.

[46] Once again he visited Cana-in-Galilee, where he had turned the water into wine. An officer in the royal service was there, whose son was lying ill at Capernaum. [47] When he heard that Jesus had come from Judaea into Galilee, he went to him and begged him to go down and cure his son, who was at the point of death. [48] Jesus said to him, 'Will none of you ever believe without seeing signs and portents?' [49] The officer pleaded with him, 'Sir, come down before my boy dies.' [50] 'Return home,' said Jesus; 'your son will live.' The man believed what Jesus said and started for home. [51] While he was on his way down his servants met him with the news that his child was going to live. [52] So he asked them at what time he had begun to recover, and they told him, 'It was at one o'clock yesterday afternoon that the fever left him.' [53] The father realized that this was the time at which Jesus had said to him, 'Your son will live,' and he and all his household became believers.

[54] This was the second sign which Jesus performed after coming from Judaea into Galilee.

5 SOME time later, Jesus went up to Jerusalem for one of the Jewish festivals. [2] Now at the Sheep Gate in Jerusalem there is a pool whose Hebrew name is Bethesda. It has five colonnades [3] and in them lay a great number of sick people, blind, lame, and paralysed. [5] Among them was a man who had been crippled for thirty-eight years. [6] Jesus saw him lying there, and knowing that he had been ill a long time he asked him, 'Do you want to

---

5: 3 **paralysed**: *some witnesses add* waiting for the disturbance of the water; *some also add* [4] for from time to time an angel came down into the pool and stirred up the water. The first to plunge in after this disturbance recovered from whatever disease had afflicted him.

get well?' [7] 'Sir,' he replied, 'I have no one to put me in the pool when the water is disturbed; while I am getting there, someone else steps into the pool before me.' [8] Jesus answered, 'Stand up, take your bed and walk.' [9] The man recovered instantly; he took up his bed, and began to walk.

That day was a sabbath. [10] So the Jews said to the man who had been cured, 'It is the sabbath. It is against the law for you to carry your bed.' [11] He answered, 'The man who cured me, he told me, "Take up your bed and walk."' [12] They asked him, 'Who is this man who told you to take it up and walk?' [13] But the man who had been cured did not know who it was; for the place was crowded and Jesus had slipped away. [14] A little later Jesus found him in the temple and said to him, 'Now that you are well, give up your sinful ways, or something worse may happen to you.' [15] The man went off and told the Jews that it was Jesus who had cured him.

[16] It was for doing such things on the sabbath that the Jews began to take action against Jesus. [17] He defended himself by saying, 'My Father continues to work, and I must work too.' [18] This made the Jews all the more determined to kill him, because not only was he breaking the sabbath but, by calling God his own Father, he was claiming equality with God.

[19] To this charge Jesus replied, 'In very truth I tell you, the Son can do nothing by himself; he does only what he sees the Father doing: whatever the Father does, the Son does. [20] For the Father loves the Son and shows him all that he himself is doing, and will show him even greater deeds, to fill you with wonder. [21] As the Father raises the dead and gives them life, so the Son gives life as he chooses. [22] Again, the Father does not judge anyone, but has given full jurisdiction to the Son; [23] it is his will that all should pay the same honour to the Son as to the Father. To deny honour to the Son is to deny it to the Father who sent him.

[24] 'In very truth I tell you, whoever heeds what I say and puts his trust in him who sent me has eternal life; he does not come to judgement, but has already passed from death to life. [25] In very truth I tell you, the time is coming, indeed it is already here, when the dead shall hear the voice of the Son of God, and those who hear shall come to life. [26] For as the Father has life in himself, so by his gift the Son also has life in himself.

[27] 'As Son of Man he has also been given authority to pass judgement. [28] Do not be surprised at this, because the time is coming when all who are in the grave shall hear his voice [29] and come out: those who have done right will rise to life; those who have done wrong will rise to judgement. [30] I cannot act by myself; I judge as I am bidden, and my sentence is just, because I seek to do not my own will, but the will of him who sent me.

[31] 'If I testify on my own behalf, that testimony is not valid. [32] There is another who bears witness for me, and I know that his testimony about me is valid. [33] You sent messengers to John, and he has testified to the truth. [34] Not that I rely on human testimony, but I remind you of it for your own salvation. [35] John was a brightly burning lamp, and for a time you were ready to exult in his light. [36] But I rely on a testimony higher than John's: the work my Father has given me to do and to finish, the very work I have in hand, testifies that the Father has sent me. [37] And the Father who has sent me has borne witness on my behalf. His voice you have never heard, his form you have never seen; [38] his word has found no home in you, because you do not believe the one whom he sent. [39] You study the scriptures diligently, supposing that in having them you have eternal life; their testimony points to me, [40] yet you refuse to come to me to receive that life.

[41] 'I do not look to men for honour. [42] But I know that with you it is different, for you have no love of God in you. [43] I have come accredited by my Father, and you have no welcome for me; but let someone self-accredited come, and you will give him a welcome. [44] How can you believe when you accept honour from one another, and care nothing for the honour that comes from him who alone is God? [45] Do not imagine that I shall be your accuser at the Father's tribunal. Your accuser is Moses, the very Moses on whom you have set your hope. [46] If you believed him you would believe me, for it was of me that he wrote. [47] But if you do not believe what he wrote, how are you to believe what I say?'

Bread from heaven

6 SOME time later Jesus withdrew to the farther shore of the sea of Galilee (or Tiberias), ² and a large crowd of people followed him because they had seen the signs he performed in healing the sick. ³ Jesus went up the hillside and sat down with his disciples. ⁴ It was near the time of Passover, the great Jewish festival. ⁵ Looking up and seeing a large crowd coming towards him, Jesus said to Philip, 'Where are we to buy bread to feed these people?' ⁶ He said this to test him; Jesus himself knew what he meant to do. ⁷ Philip replied, 'We would need two hundred denarii to buy enough bread for each of them to have a little.' ⁸ One of his disciples, Andrew, the brother of Simon Peter, said to him, ⁹ 'There is a boy here who has five barley loaves and two fish; but what is that among so many?' ¹⁰ Jesus said, 'Make the people sit down.' There was plenty of grass there, so the men sat down, about five thousand of them. ¹¹ Then Jesus took the loaves, gave thanks, and distributed them to the people as they sat there. He did the same with the fish, and they had as much as they wanted. ¹² When everyone had had enough, he said to his disciples, 'Gather up the pieces left over, so that nothing is wasted.' ¹³ They gathered them up, and filled twelve baskets with the pieces of the five barley loaves that were left uneaten.

¹⁴ When the people saw the sign Jesus had performed, the word went round, 'Surely this must be the Prophet who was to come into the world.' ¹⁵ Jesus, realizing that they meant to come and seize him to proclaim him king, withdrew again to the hills by himself.

¹⁶ At nightfall his disciples went down to the sea, ¹⁷ and set off by boat to cross to Capernaum. Though darkness had fallen, Jesus had not yet joined them; ¹⁸ a strong wind was blowing and the sea grew rough. ¹⁹ When they had rowed about three or four miles they saw Jesus walking on the sea and approaching the boat. They were terrified, ²⁰ but he called out, 'It is I; do not be afraid.' ²¹ With that they were ready to take him on board, and immediately the boat reached the land they were making for.

²² NEXT morning the crowd was still on the opposite shore. They had seen only one boat there, and Jesus, they knew, had not embarked with his disciples, who had set off by themselves. ²³ Boats from Tiberias, however, had come ashore near the place where the people had eaten the bread over which the Lord gave thanks. ²⁴ When the crowd saw that Jesus had gone as well as his disciples, they went on board these boats and made for Capernaum in search of him. ²⁵ They found him on the other side. 'Rabbi,' they asked, 'when did you come here?' ²⁶ Jesus replied, 'In very truth I tell you, it is not because you saw signs that you came looking for me, but because you ate the bread and your hunger was satisfied. ²⁷ You should work, not for this perishable food, but for the food that lasts, the food of eternal life.

'This food the Son of Man will give you, for on him God the Father has set the seal of his authority.' ²⁸ 'Then what must we do', they asked him, 'if our work is to be the work of God?' ²⁹ Jesus replied, 'This is the work that God requires: to believe in the one whom he has sent.'

³⁰ They asked, 'What sign can you give us, so that we may see it and believe you? What is the work you are doing? ³¹ Our ancestors had manna to eat in the desert; as scripture says, "He gave them bread from heaven to eat."' ³² Jesus answered, 'In very truth I tell you, it was not Moses who gave you the bread from heaven; it is my Father who gives you the true bread from heaven. ³³ The bread that God gives comes down from heaven and brings life to the world.' ³⁴ 'Sir,' they said to him, 'give us this bread now and always.' ³⁵ Jesus said to them, 'I am the bread of life. Whoever comes to me will never be hungry, and whoever believes in me will never be thirsty. ³⁶ But you, as I said, have seen and yet you do not believe. ³⁷ All that the Father gives me will come to me, and anyone who comes to me I will never turn away. ³⁸ I have come down from heaven, to do not my own will, but the will of him who sent me. ³⁹ It is his will that I should not lose even one of those he has given me, but should raise them all up on the last day. ⁴⁰ For it is my Father's will that

---

6:7 **denarii:** *see p. xi.*   6:23 *Some witnesses omit* over which the Lord gave thanks.   6:36 you ... have seen: *some witnesses add* me.

Bread from heaven

everyone who sees the Son and has faith in him should have eternal life; and I will raise them up on the last day.'

⁴¹ At this the Jews began to grumble because he said, 'I am the bread which came down from heaven.' ⁴² They said, 'Surely this is Jesus, Joseph's son! We know his father and mother. How can he say, "I have come down from heaven"?' ⁴³ 'Stop complaining among yourselves,' Jesus told them. ⁴⁴ 'No one can come to me unless he is drawn by the Father who sent me; and I will raise him up on the last day. ⁴⁵ It is written in the prophets: "They will all be taught by God." Everyone who has listened to the Father and learned from him comes to me.

⁴⁶ 'I do not mean that anyone has seen the Father; he who has come from God has seen the Father, and he alone. ⁴⁷ In very truth I tell you, whoever believes has eternal life. ⁴⁸ I am the bread of life. ⁴⁹ Your ancestors ate manna in the wilderness, yet they are dead. ⁵⁰ I am speaking of the bread that comes down from heaven; whoever eats it will never die. ⁵¹ I am the living bread that has come down from heaven; if anyone eats this bread, he will live for ever. The bread which I shall give is my own flesh, given for the life of the world.'

⁵² This led to a fierce dispute among the Jews. 'How can this man give us his flesh to eat?' they protested. ⁵³ Jesus answered them, 'In very truth I tell you, unless you eat the flesh of the Son of Man and drink his blood you can have no life in you. ⁵⁴ Whoever eats my flesh and drinks my blood has eternal life, and I will raise him up on the last day. ⁵⁵ My flesh is real food; my blood is real drink. ⁵⁶ Whoever eats my flesh and drinks my blood dwells in me and I in him. ⁵⁷ As the living Father sent me, and I live because of the Father, so whoever eats me will live because of me. ⁵⁸ This is the bread which came down from heaven; it is not like the bread which our fathers ate; they are dead, but whoever eats this bread will live for ever.'

⁵⁹ JESUS said these things in the synagogue as he taught in Capernaum. ⁶⁰ On hearing them, many of his disciples exclaimed, 'This is more than we can stand! How can anyone listen to such talk?'

⁶¹ Jesus was aware that his disciples were grumbling about it and asked them, 'Does this shock you? ⁶² Then what if you see the Son of Man ascending to where he was before? ⁶³ It is the spirit that gives life; the flesh can achieve nothing; the words I have spoken to you are both spirit and life. ⁶⁴ Yet there are some of you who have no faith.' For Jesus knew from the outset who were without faith and who was to betray him. ⁶⁵ So he said, 'This is why I told you that no one can come to me unless it has been granted to him by the Father.'

⁶⁶ From that moment many of his disciples drew back and no longer went about with him. ⁶⁷ So Jesus asked the Twelve, 'Do you also want to leave?' ⁶⁸ Simon Peter answered him, 'Lord, to whom shall we go? Your words are words of eternal life. ⁶⁹ We believe and know that you are God's Holy One.' ⁷⁰ Jesus answered, 'Have I not chosen the twelve of you? Yet one of you is a devil.' ⁷¹ He meant Judas son of Simon Iscariot. It was he who would betray him, and he was one of the Twelve.

The great controversy

7 AFTER that Jesus travelled around within Galilee; he decided to avoid Judaea because the Jews were looking for a chance to kill him. ² But when the Jewish feast of Tabernacles was close at hand, ³ his brothers said to him, 'You should leave here and go into Judaea, so that your disciples may see the great things you are doing. ⁴ No one can hope for recognition if he works in obscurity. If you can really do such things as these, show yourself to the world.' ⁵ For even his brothers had no faith in him. ⁶ Jesus answered: 'The right time for me has not yet come, but any time is right for you. ⁷ The world cannot hate you; but it hates me for exposing the wickedness of its ways. ⁸ Go up to the festival yourselves. I am not going to this festival, because the right time for me has not yet come.' ⁹ So saying he stayed behind in Galilee.

¹⁰ Later, when his brothers had gone to the festival, he went up too, not openly, but in secret. ¹¹ At the festival the Jews were looking for him and asking where he was, ¹² and there was much murmuring about him in the crowds. 'He is a good

7:8 *not going:* some witnesses read not yet going.

man,' said some. 'No,' said others, 'he is leading the people astray.' [13] No one talked freely about him, however, for fear of the Jews.

[14] WHEN the festival was already half over, Jesus went up to the temple and began to teach. [15] The Jews were astonished: 'How is it', they said, 'that this untrained man has such learning?' [16] Jesus replied, 'My teaching is not my own but his who sent me. [17] Whoever chooses to do the will of God will know whether my teaching comes from him or is merely my own. [18] Anyone whose teaching is merely his own seeks his own glory; but if anyone seeks the glory of him who sent him, he is sincere and there is nothing false in him.

[19] 'Did not Moses give you the law? Yet not one of you keeps it. Why are you trying to kill me?' [20] The crowd answered, 'You are possessed! Who wants to kill you?' [21] Jesus replied, 'I did one good deed, and you are all taken aback. [22] But consider: Moses gave you the law of circumcision (not that it originated with Moses, but with the patriarchs) and you circumcise even on the sabbath. [23] Well then, if someone can be circumcised on the sabbath to avoid breaking the law of Moses, why are you indignant with me for making someone's whole body well on the sabbath? [24] Stop judging by appearances; be just in your judgements.'

[25] This prompted some of the people of Jerusalem to say, 'Is not this the man they want to put to death? [26] Yet here he is, speaking in public, and they say not one word to him. Can it be that our rulers have decided that this is the Messiah? [27] Yet we know where this man comes from; when the Messiah appears no one is to know where he comes from.' [28] Jesus responded to this as he taught in the temple: 'Certainly you know me,' he declared, 'and you know where I come from. Yet I have not come of my own accord; I was sent by one who is true, and him you do not know. [29] I know him because I come from him, and he it is who sent me.' [30] At this they tried to seize him, but no one could lay hands on him because his appointed hour had not yet

come. [31] Among the people many believed in him. 'When the Messiah comes,' they said, 'is it likely that he will perform more signs than this man?'

[32] The Pharisees overheard these mutterings about him among the people, so the chief priests and the Pharisees sent temple police to arrest him. [33] Then Jesus said, 'For a little longer I shall be with you; then I am going away to him who sent me. [34] You will look for me, but you will not find me; and where I am, you cannot come.' [35] So the Jews said to one another, 'Where does he intend to go, that we should not be able to find him? Will he go to the Dispersion among the Gentiles, and teach Gentiles? [36] What does he mean by saying, "You will look for me, but you will not find me; and where I am, you cannot come"?'

[37] ON the last and greatest day of the festival Jesus stood and declared, 'If anyone is thirsty, let him come to me and drink. [38] Whoever believes in me, as scripture says, "Streams of living water shall flow from within him."' [39] He was speaking of the Spirit which believers in him would later receive; for the Spirit had not yet been given, because Jesus had not yet been glorified.

[40] On hearing his words some of the crowd said, 'This must certainly be the Prophet.' [41] Others said, 'This is the Messiah.' But others argued, 'Surely the Messiah is not to come from Galilee? [42] Does not scripture say that the Messiah is to be of the family of David, from David's village of Bethlehem?' [43] Thus he was the cause of a division among the people. [44] Some were for arresting him, but no one laid hands on him.

[45] The temple police went back to the chief priests and Pharisees, who asked them, 'Why have you not brought him?' [46] 'No one ever spoke as this man speaks,' they replied. [47] The Pharisees retorted, 'Have you too been misled? [48] Has a single one of our rulers believed in him, or any of the Pharisees? [49] As for this rabble, which cares nothing for the law, a curse is on them.' [50] Then one of their number, Nicodemus (the man who once visited Jesus), intervened. [51] 'Does our law', he asked

7:28 **Certainly ... come from:** *or* Do you know me? And do you know where I come from? 7:37–38 **If anyone ... within him:** *or* If anyone is thirsty, let him come to me; whoever believes in me, let him drink. As scripture says, "Streams of living water shall flow from within him."

them, 'permit us to pass judgement on someone without first giving him a hearing and learning the facts?' ⁵² 'Are you a Galilean too?' they retorted. 'Study the scriptures and you will find that the Prophet does not come from Galilee.'

8 ¹² ONCE again Jesus addressed the people: 'I am the light of the world. No follower of mine shall walk in darkness; he shall have the light of life.' ¹³ The Pharisees said to him, 'You are witness in your own cause; your testimony is not valid.' ¹⁴ Jesus replied, 'My testimony is valid, even though I do testify on my own behalf; because I know where I come from, and where I am going. But you know neither where I come from nor where I am going. ¹⁵ You judge by worldly standards; I pass judgement on no one. ¹⁶ If I do judge, my judgement is valid because it is not I alone who judge, but I and he who sent me. ¹⁷ In your own law it is written that the testimony of two witnesses is valid. ¹⁸ I am a witness in my own cause, and my other witness is the Father who sent me.' ¹⁹ 'Where is your father?' they asked him. Jesus replied, 'You do not know me or my Father; if you knew me you would know my Father too.' ²⁰ Jesus was teaching near the treasury in the temple when he said this; but no one arrested him, because his hour had not yet come.

²¹ Again he said to them, 'I am going away. You will look for me, but you will die in your sin; where I am going, you cannot come.' ²² At this the Jews said, 'Perhaps he will kill himself: is that what he means when he says, "Where I am going, you cannot come"?' ²³ Jesus continued, 'You belong to this world below, I to the world above. Your home is in this world, mine is not. ²⁴ That is why I told you that you would die in your sins; and you will die in your sins unless you believe that I am what I am.' ²⁵ 'And who are you?' they asked him. Jesus answered, 'What I have told you all along. ²⁶ I have much to say about you—and in judgement. But he who sent me speaks the truth, and what I heard from him I report to the world.' ²⁷ They did not understand that he was

speaking to them about the Father. ²⁸ So Jesus said to them, 'When you have lifted up the Son of Man you will know that I am what I am. I do nothing on my own authority, but in all I say, I have been taught by my Father. ²⁹ He who sent me is present with me, and has not left me on my own; for I always do what is pleasing to him.' ³⁰ As he said this, many put their faith in him.

³¹ Turning to the Jews who had believed him, Jesus said, 'If you stand by my teaching, you are truly my disciples; ³² you will know the truth, and the truth will set you free.' ³³ 'We are Abraham's descendants,' they replied; 'we have never been in slavery to anyone. What do you mean by saying, "You will become free"?' ³⁴ 'In very truth I tell you', said Jesus, 'that everyone who commits sin is a slave. ³⁵ The slave has no permanent standing in the household, but the son belongs to it for ever. ³⁶ If then the Son sets you free, you will indeed be free.

³⁷ 'I know that you are descended from Abraham, yet you are bent on killing me because my teaching makes no headway with you. ³⁸ I tell what I have seen in my Father's presence; you do what you have learned from your father.' ³⁹ They retorted, 'Abraham is our father.' 'If you were Abraham's children', Jesus replied, 'you would do as Abraham did. ⁴⁰ As it is, you are bent on killing me, because I have told you the truth, which I heard from God. That is not how Abraham acted. ⁴¹ You are doing your own father's work.'

They said, 'We are not illegitimate; God is our father, and God alone.' ⁴² Jesus said to them, 'If God were your father, you would love me, for God is the source of my being, and from him I come. I have not come of my own accord; he sent me. ⁴³ Why do you not understand what I am saying? It is because my teaching is beyond your grasp. ⁴⁴ Your father is the devil and you choose to carry out your father's desires. He was a murderer from the beginning, and is not rooted in the truth; there is no truth in him. When he tells a lie he is speaking his own language, for he is a liar and the father of lies. ⁴⁵ But because I speak the truth, you do not believe me. ⁴⁶ Which of you can convict

---

7:52 **the Prophet does not:** *most witnesses read* the prophets do not. **Galilee:** *some witnesses here insert the passage* 7:53—8:11, *which is printed on p. 102.*   8:25 **What ... along:** *or* Why should I speak to you at all?

me of sin? If what I say is true, why do you not believe me? [47] He who has God for his father listens to the words of God. You are not God's children, and that is why you do not listen.'

[48] The Jews answered, 'Are we not right in saying that you are a Samaritan, and that you are possessed?' [49] 'I am not possessed,' said Jesus; 'I am honouring my Father, but you dishonour me. [50] I do not care about my own glory; there is one who does care, and he is judge. [51] In very truth I tell you, if anyone obeys my teaching he will never see death.'

[52] The Jews said, 'Now we are certain that you are possessed. Abraham is dead and so are the prophets; yet you say, "If anyone obeys my teaching he will never taste death." [53] Are you greater than our father Abraham? He is dead and the prophets too are dead. Who do you claim to be?'

[54] Jesus replied, 'If I glorify myself, that glory of mine is worthless. It is the Father who glorifies me, he of whom you say, "He is our God," [55] though you do not know him. But I know him; if I were to say that I did not know him I should be a liar like you. I do know him and I obey his word. [56] Your father Abraham was overjoyed to see my day; he saw it and was glad.' [57] The Jews protested, 'You are not yet fifty years old. How can you have seen Abraham?' [58] Jesus said, 'In very truth I tell you, before Abraham was born, I am.' [59] They took up stones to throw at him, but he was not to be seen; and he left the temple.

Seeing and believing

9 As HE went on his way Jesus saw a man who had been blind from birth. [2] His disciples asked him, 'Rabbi, why was this man born blind? Who sinned, this man or his parents?' [3] 'It is not that he or his parents sinned,' Jesus answered; 'he was born blind so that God's power might be displayed in curing him. [4] While daylight lasts we must carry on the work of him who sent me; night is coming, when no one can work. [5] While I am in the world I am the light of the world.' [6] With these words he spat on the ground and made a paste with the spittle; he spread it on the man's eyes, [7] and said

to him, 'Go and wash in the pool of Siloam.' (The name means 'Sent'.) The man went off and washed, and came back able to see.

[8] His neighbours and those who were accustomed to see him begging said, 'Is not this the man who used to sit and beg?' [9] Some said, 'Yes, it is.' Others said, 'No, but it is someone like him.' He himself said, 'I am the man.' [10] They asked him, 'How were your eyes opened?' [11] He replied, 'The man called Jesus made a paste and smeared my eyes with it, and told me to go to Siloam and wash. So I went and washed, and found I could see.' [12] 'Where is he?' they asked. 'I do not know,' he said.

[13] The man who had been blind was brought before the Pharisees. [14] As it was a sabbath day when Jesus made the paste and opened his eyes, [15] the Pharisees too asked him how he had gained his sight. The man told them, 'He spread a paste on my eyes; then I washed, and now I can see.' [16] Some of the Pharisees said, 'This man cannot be from God; he does not keep the sabbath.' Others said, 'How could such signs come from a sinful man?' So they took different sides. [17] Then they continued to question him: 'What have you to say about him? It was your eyes he opened.' He answered, 'He is a prophet.'

[18] The Jews would not believe that the man had been blind and had gained his sight, until they had summoned his parents [19] and questioned them: 'Is this your son? Do you say that he was born blind? How is it that he can see now?' [20] The parents replied, 'We know that he is our son, and that he was born blind. [21] But how it is that he can now see, or who opened his eyes, we do not know. Ask him; he is of age; let him speak for himself.' [22] His parents gave this answer because they were afraid of the Jews; for the Jewish authorities had already agreed that anyone who acknowledged Jesus as Messiah should be banned from the synagogue. [23] That is why the parents said, 'He is of age; ask him.'

[24] So for the second time they summoned the man who had been blind, and said, 'Speak the truth before God. We know that this man is a sinner.'

9:4 we: *some witnesses read* I.

²⁵ 'Whether or not he is a sinner, I do not know,' the man replied. 'All I know is this: I was blind and now I can see.' ²⁶ 'What did he do to you?' they asked. 'How did he open your eyes?' ²⁷ 'I have told you already,' he retorted, 'but you took no notice. Why do you want to hear it again? Do you also want to become his disciples?' ²⁸ Then they became abusive. 'You are that man's disciple,' they said, 'but we are disciples of Moses. ²⁹ We know that God spoke to Moses, but as for this man, we do not know where he comes from.'

³⁰ The man replied, 'How extraordinary! Here is a man who has opened my eyes, yet you do not know where he comes from! ³¹ We know that God does not listen to sinners; he listens to anyone who is devout and obeys his will. ³² To open the eyes of a man born blind—that is unheard of since time began. ³³ If this man was not from God he could do nothing.' ³⁴ 'Who are you to lecture us?' they retorted. 'You were born and bred in sin.' Then they turned him out.

³⁵ Hearing that they had turned him out, Jesus found him and asked, 'Have you faith in the Son of Man?' ³⁶ The man answered, 'Tell me who he is, sir, that I may put my faith in him.' ³⁷ 'You have seen him,' said Jesus; 'indeed, it is he who is speaking to you.' ³⁸ 'Lord, I believe,' he said, and fell on his knees before him.

³⁹ Jesus said, 'It is for judgement that I have come into this world—to give sight to the sightless and to make blind those who see.' ⁴⁰ Some Pharisees who were present asked, 'Do you mean that we are blind?' ⁴¹ 'If you were blind,' said Jesus, 'you would not be guilty, but because you claim to see, your guilt remains.'

Victory over death

10 'IN very truth I tell you, the man who does not enter the sheepfold by the door, but climbs in some other way, is nothing but a thief and a robber. ² He who enters by the door is the shepherd in charge of the sheep. ³ The doorkeeper admits him, and the sheep hear his voice; he calls his own sheep by name, and leads them out. ⁴ When he has brought them all out, he goes ahead of them and the sheep follow, because they

know his voice. ⁵ They will not follow a stranger; they will run away from him, because they do not recognize the voice of strangers.'

⁶ This was a parable that Jesus told them, but they did not understand what he meant by it.

⁷ So Jesus spoke again: 'In very truth I tell you, I am the door of the sheepfold. ⁸ The sheep paid no heed to any who came before me, for they were all thieves and robbers. ⁹ I am the door; anyone who comes into the fold through me will be safe. He will go in and out and find pasture.

¹⁰ 'A thief comes only to steal, kill, and destroy; I have come that they may have life, and may have it in all its fullness. ¹¹ I am the good shepherd; the good shepherd lays down his life for the sheep. ¹² The hired man, when he sees the wolf coming, abandons the sheep and runs away, because he is not the shepherd and the sheep are not his. Then the wolf harries the flock and scatters the sheep. ¹³ The man runs away because he is a hired man and cares nothing for the sheep.

¹⁴ 'I am the good shepherd; I know my own and my own know me, ¹⁵ as the Father knows me and I know the Father; and I lay down my life for the sheep. ¹⁶ But there are other sheep of mine, not belonging to this fold; I must lead them as well, and they too will listen to my voice. There will then be one flock, one shepherd. ¹⁷ The Father loves me because I lay down my life, to receive it back again. ¹⁸ No one takes it away from me; I am laying it down of my own free will. I have the right to lay it down, and I have the right to receive it back again; this charge I have received from my Father.'

¹⁹ These words once again caused a division among the Jews. ²⁰ Many of them said, 'He is possessed, he is out of his mind. Why listen to him?' ²¹ Others said, 'No one possessed by a demon could speak like this. Could a demon open the eyes of the blind?'

²² IT was winter, and the festival of the Dedication was being held in Jerusalem. ²³ As Jesus was walking in the temple precincts, in Solomon's Portico, ²⁴ the Jews gathered round him and asked:

9:35 **Son of Man:** *some witnesses read* Son of God.

'How long are you going to keep us in suspense? Tell us plainly: are you the Messiah?' [25] 'I have told you,' said Jesus, 'and you do not believe. My deeds done in my Father's name are my credentials, [26] but because you are not sheep of my flock you do not believe. [27] My own sheep listen to my voice; I know them and they follow me. [28] I give them eternal life and they will never perish; no one will snatch them from my care. [29] My Father who has given them to me is greater than all, and no one can snatch them out of the Father's care. [30] The Father and I are one.'

[31] Once again the Jews picked up stones to stone him. [32] At this Jesus said to them, 'By the Father's power I have done many good deeds before your eyes; for which of these are you stoning me?' [33] 'We are not stoning you for any good deed,' the Jews replied, 'but for blasphemy: you, a man, are claiming to be God.' [34] Jesus answered, 'Is it not written in your law, "I said: You are gods"? [35] It is those to whom God's word came who are called gods—and scripture cannot be set aside. [36] Then why do you charge me with blasphemy for saying, "I am God's son," I whom the Father consecrated and sent into the world?

[37] 'If my deeds are not the deeds of my Father, do not believe me. [38] But if they are, then even if you do not believe me, believe the deeds, so that you may recognize and know that the Father is in me, and I in the Father.'

[39] This provoked them to make another attempt to seize him, but he escaped from their clutches.

[40] JESUS withdrew again across the Jordan, to the place where John had been baptizing earlier, and stayed there [41] while crowds came to him. 'John gave us no miraculous sign,' they said, 'but all that he told us about this man was true.' [42] And many came to believe in him there.

11 There was a man named Lazarus who had fallen ill. His home was at Bethany, the village of Mary and her sister Martha. [2] This Mary, whose brother Lazarus had fallen ill, was the woman who anointed the Lord with ointment and wiped his feet with her hair. [3] The sisters sent a message to him: 'Sir, you should know that your friend lies ill.' [4] When Jesus heard this he said, 'This illness is not to end in death; through it God's glory is to be revealed and the Son of God glorified.' [5] Therefore, though he loved Martha and her sister and Lazarus, [6] he stayed where he was for two days after hearing of Lazarus's illness.

[7] He then said to his disciples, 'Let us go back to Judaea.' [8] 'Rabbi,' his disciples said, 'it is not long since the Jews there were wanting to stone you. Are you going there again?' [9] Jesus replied, 'Are there not twelve hours of daylight? Anyone can walk in the daytime without stumbling, because he has this world's light to see by. [10] But if he walks after nightfall he stumbles, because the light fails him.'

[11] After saying this he added, 'Our friend Lazarus has fallen asleep, but I shall go and wake him.' [12] The disciples said, 'Master, if he is sleeping he will recover.' [13] Jesus had been speaking of Lazarus's death, but they thought that he meant natural sleep. [14] Then Jesus told them plainly: 'Lazarus is dead. [15] I am glad for your sake that I was not there; for it will lead you to believe. But let us go to him.' [16] Thomas, called 'the Twin', said to his fellow-disciples, 'Let us also go and die with him.'

[17] ON his arrival Jesus found that Lazarus had already been four days in the tomb. [18] Bethany was just under two miles from Jerusalem, [19] and many of the Jews had come from the city to visit Martha and Mary and condole with them about their brother. [20] As soon as Martha heard that Jesus was on his way, she went to meet him, and left Mary sitting at home.

[21] Martha said to Jesus, 'Lord, if you had been here my brother would not have died. [22] Even now I know that God will grant you whatever you ask of him.' [23] Jesus said, 'Your brother will rise again.' [24] 'I know that he will rise again', said Martha, 'at the resurrection on the last day.' [25] Jesus said, 'I am the resurrection and the life. Whoever has faith in me shall live, even though he dies; [26] and no one who lives and has faith in me shall ever die. Do you believe this?' [27] 'I do,

10: 29 **My Father . . . snatch them:** *some witnesses read* That which my Father has given me is greater than all, and no one can snatch it.   10: 33 **claiming . . . God:** *or* claiming to be a god.   11: 25 *Some witnesses omit* and the life.

Lord,' she answered; 'I believe that you are the Messiah, the Son of God who was to come into the world.'

²⁸ So saying she went to call her sister Mary and, taking her aside, she said, 'The Master is here and is asking for you.' ²⁹ As soon as Mary heard this she rose and went to him. ³⁰ Jesus had not yet entered the village, but was still at the place where Martha had met him. ³¹ When the Jews who were in the house condoling with Mary saw her hurry out, they went after her, assuming that she was going to the tomb to weep there.

³² Mary came to the place where Jesus was, and as soon as she saw him she fell at his feet and said, 'Lord, if you had been here my brother would not have died.' ³³ When Jesus saw her weeping and the Jews who had come with her weeping, he was moved with indignation and deeply distressed. ³⁴ 'Where have you laid him?' he asked. They replied, 'Come and see.' ³⁵ Jesus wept. ³⁶ The Jews said, 'How dearly he must have loved him!' ³⁷ But some of them said, 'Could not this man, who opened the blind man's eyes, have done something to keep Lazarus from dying?'

³⁸ Jesus, again deeply moved, went to the tomb. It was a cave, with a stone placed against it. ³⁹ Jesus said, 'Take away the stone.' Martha, the dead man's sister, said to him, 'Sir, by now there will be a stench; he has been there four days.' ⁴⁰ Jesus said, 'Did I not tell you that if you have faith you will see the glory of God?' ⁴¹ Then they removed the stone.

Jesus looked upwards and said, 'Father, I thank you for hearing me. ⁴² I know that you always hear me, but I have spoken for the sake of the people standing round, that they may believe it was you who sent me.'

⁴³ Then he raised his voice in a great cry: 'Lazarus, come out.' ⁴⁴ The dead man came out, his hands and feet bound with linen bandages, his face wrapped in a cloth. Jesus said, 'Loose him; let him go.'

⁴⁵ MANY of the Jews who had come to visit Mary, and had seen what Jesus did, put their faith in him. ⁴⁶ But some of them went off to the Pharisees and reported what he had done.

⁴⁷ Thereupon the chief priests and the Pharisees convened a meeting of the Council. 'This man is performing many signs,' they said, 'and what action are we taking? ⁴⁸ If we let him go on like this the whole populace will believe in him, and then the Romans will come and sweep away our temple and our nation.' ⁴⁹ But one of them, Caiaphas, who was high priest that year, said, 'You have no grasp of the situation at all; ⁵⁰ you do not realize that it is more to your interest that one man should die for the people, than that the whole nation should be destroyed.' ⁵¹ He did not say this of his own accord, but as the high priest that year he was prophesying that Jesus would die for the nation, ⁵² and not for the nation alone but to gather together the scattered children of God. ⁵³ So from that day on they plotted his death.

⁵⁴ Accordingly Jesus no longer went about openly among the Jews, but withdrew to a town called Ephraim, in the country bordering on the desert, and stayed there with his disciples.

The Passover in Jerusalem

⁵⁵ THE Jewish Passover was now at hand, and many people went up from the country to Jerusalem to purify themselves before the festival. ⁵⁶ They looked out for Jesus, and as they stood in the temple they asked one another, 'What do you think? Perhaps he is not coming to the festival.' ⁵⁷ Now the chief priests and the Pharisees had given orders that anyone who knew where he was must report it, so that they might arrest him.

12 SIX days before the Passover festival Jesus came to Bethany, the home of Lazarus whom he had raised from the dead. ² They gave a supper in his honour, at which Martha served, and Lazarus was among the guests with Jesus. ³ Then Mary brought a pound of very costly perfume, pure oil of nard, and anointed Jesus's feet and wiped them with her hair, till the house was filled with the fragrance. ⁴ At this, Judas Iscariot, one of his disciples—the one who was to betray him—protested, ⁵ 'Could not this perfume have been sold for three hundred denarii and the money given to the poor?' ⁶ He

12:5 denarii: *see p. xi.*

said this, not out of any concern for the poor, but because he was a thief; he had charge of the common purse and used to pilfer the money kept in it. [7] 'Leave her alone,' said Jesus. 'Let her keep it for the day of my burial. [8] The poor you have always among you, but you will not always have me.'

[9] Learning he was there the Jews came in large numbers, not only because of Jesus but also to see Lazarus whom he had raised from the dead. [10] The chief priests then resolved to do away with Lazarus as well, [11] since on his account many Jews were going over to Jesus and putting their faith in him.

[12] THE next day the great crowd of pilgrims who had come for the festival, hearing that Jesus was on the way to Jerusalem, [13] went out to meet him with palm branches in their hands, shouting, 'Hosanna! Blessed is he who comes in the name of the Lord! Blessed is the king of Israel!' [14] Jesus found a donkey and mounted it, in accordance with the words of scripture: [15] 'Fear no more, daughter of Zion; see, your king is coming, mounted on a donkey's colt.' [16] At the time his disciples did not understand this, but after Jesus had been glorified they remembered that this had been written about him, and that it had happened to him.

[17] The people who were present when he called Lazarus out of the tomb and raised him from the dead kept telling what they had seen and heard. [18] That is why the crowd went to meet him: they had heard of this sign that he had performed. [19] The Pharisees said to one another, 'You can see we are getting nowhere; all the world has gone after him!'

[20] AMONG those who went up to worship at the festival were some Gentiles. [21] They approached Philip, who was from Bethsaida in Galilee, and said to him, 'Sir, we should like to see Jesus.' [22] Philip went and told Andrew, and the two of them went to tell Jesus. [23] Jesus replied: 'The hour has come for the Son of Man to be glorified. [24] In very truth I tell you, unless a grain of wheat falls into the ground and dies, it remains that and nothing more; but if it dies, it bears a rich harvest.

[25] Whoever loves himself is lost, but he who hates himself in this world will be kept safe for eternal life. [26] If anyone is to serve me, he must follow me; where I am, there will my servant be. Whoever serves me will be honoured by the Father.

[27] 'Now my soul is in turmoil, and what am I to say? "Father, save me from this hour"? No, it was for this that I came to this hour. [28] Father, glorify your name.' A voice came from heaven: 'I have glorified it, and I will glorify it again.' [29] The crowd standing by said it was thunder they heard, while others said, 'An angel has spoken to him.' [30] Jesus replied, 'This voice spoke for your sake, not mine. [31] Now is the hour of judgement for this world; now shall the prince of this world be driven out. [32] And when I am lifted up from the earth I shall draw everyone to myself.' [33] This he said to indicate the kind of death he was to die.

[34] The people answered, 'Our law teaches us that the Messiah remains for ever. What do you mean by saying that the Son of Man must be lifted up? What Son of Man is this?' [35] Jesus answered them: 'The light is among you still, but not for long. Go on your way while you have the light, so that darkness may not overtake you. He who journeys in the dark does not know where he is going. [36] Trust to the light while you have it, so that you may become children of light.' After these words Jesus went away from them into hiding.

[37] IN spite of the many signs which Jesus had performed in their presence they would not believe in him, [38] for the prophet Isaiah's words had to be fulfilled: 'Lord, who has believed what we reported, and to whom has the power of the Lord been revealed?' [39] And there is another saying of Isaiah which explains why they could not believe: [40] 'He has blinded their eyes and dulled their minds, lest they should see with their eyes, and perceive with their minds, and turn to me to heal them.' [41] Isaiah said this because he saw his glory and spoke about him.

[42] For all that, even among those in authority many believed in him, but would not acknowledge him on account of the Pharisees, for fear of being banned

12:8 *Some witnesses omit* The poor ... have me.

from the synagogue. [43] For they valued human reputation rather than the honour which comes from God.

[44] JESUS proclaimed: 'To believe in me, is not to believe in me but in him who sent me; [45] to see me, is to see him who sent me. [46] I have come into the world as light, so that no one who has faith in me should remain in darkness. [47] But if anyone hears my words and disregards them, I am not his judge; I have not come to judge the world, but to save the world. [48] There is a judge for anyone who rejects me and does not accept my words; the word I have spoken will be his judge on the last day. [49] I do not speak on my own authority, but the Father who sent me has himself commanded me what to say and how to speak. [50] I know that his commands are eternal life. What the Father has said to me, therefore—that is what I speak.'

Farewell discourses

13 IT was before the Passover festival, and Jesus knew that his hour had come and that he must leave this world and go to the Father. He had always loved his own who were in the world, and he loved them to the end.

[2] The devil had already put it into the mind of Judas son of Simon Iscariot to betray him. During supper, [3] Jesus, well aware that the Father had entrusted everything to him, and that he had come from God and was going back to God, [4] rose from the supper table, took off his outer garment and, taking a towel, tied it round him. [5] Then he poured water into a basin, and began to wash his disciples' feet and to wipe them with the towel.

[6] When he came to Simon Peter, Peter said to him, 'You, Lord, washing my feet?' [7] Jesus replied, 'You do not understand now what I am doing, but one day you will.' [8] Peter said, 'I will never let you wash my feet.' 'If I do not wash you,' Jesus replied, 'you have no part with me.' [9] 'Then, Lord,' said Simon Peter, 'not my feet only; wash my hands and head as well!'

[10] Jesus said to him, 'Anyone who has bathed needs no further washing; he is clean all over; and you are clean, though not every one of you.' [11] He added the words 'not every one of you' because he knew who was going to betray him.

[12] After washing their feet he put on his garment and sat down again. 'Do you understand what I have done for you?' he asked. [13] 'You call me Teacher and Lord, and rightly so, for that is what I am. [14] Then if I, your Lord and Teacher, have washed your feet, you also ought to wash one another's feet. [15] I have set you an example: you are to do as I have done for you. [16] In very truth I tell you, a servant is not greater than his master, nor a messenger than the one who sent him. [17] If you know this, happy are you if you act upon it.

[18] 'I am not speaking about all of you; I know whom I have chosen. But there is a text of scripture to be fulfilled: "He who eats bread with me has turned against me." [19] I tell you this now, before the event, so that when it happens you may believe that I am what I am. [20] In very truth I tell you, whoever receives any messenger of mine receives me; and receiving me, he receives the One who sent me.'

[21] After saying this, Jesus exclaimed in deep distress, 'In very truth I tell you, one of you is going to betray me.' [22] The disciples looked at one another in bewilderment: which of them could he mean? [23] One of them, the disciple he loved, was reclining close beside Jesus. [24] Simon Peter signalled to him to find out which one he meant. [25] That disciple leaned back close to Jesus and asked, 'Lord, who is it?' [26] Jesus replied, 'It is the one to whom I give this piece of bread when I have dipped it in the dish.' Then he took it, dipped it in the dish, and gave it to Judas son of Simon Iscariot. [27] As soon as Judas had received it Satan entered him. Jesus said to him, 'Do quickly what you have to do.' [28] No one at the table understood what he meant by this. [29] Some supposed that, as Judas was in charge of the common purse, Jesus was telling him to buy what was needed for the festival, or to make some gift to the poor. [30] As soon as Judas had received the bread he went out. It was night.

[31] WHEN he had gone out, Jesus said, 'Now the Son of Man is glorified, and in

---

13:10 needs ... washing: *some witnesses read* needs only to wash his feet.

him God is glorified. [32] If God is glorified in him, God will also glorify him in himself; and he will glorify him now. [33] My children, I am to be with you for a little longer; then you will look for me, and, as I told the Jews, I tell you now: where I am going you cannot come. [34] I give you a new commandment: love one another; as I have loved you, so you are to love one another. [35] If there is this love among you, then everyone will know that you are my disciples.'

[36] Simon Peter said to him, 'Lord, where are you going?' Jesus replied, 'I am going where you cannot follow me now, but one day you will.' [37] Peter said, 'Lord, why cannot I follow you now? I will lay down my life for you.' [38] Jesus answered, 'Will you really lay down your life for me? In very truth I tell you, before the cock crows you will have denied me three times.

14 'Set your troubled hearts at rest. Trust in God always; trust also in me. [2] There are many dwelling-places in my Father's house; if it were not so I should have told you; for I am going to prepare a place for you. [3] And if I go and prepare a place for you, I shall come again and take you to myself, so that where I am you may be also; [4] and you know the way I am taking.' [5] Thomas said, 'Lord, we do not know where you are going, so how can we know the way?' [6] Jesus replied, 'I am the way, the truth, and the life; no one comes to the Father except by me.

[7] 'If you knew me you would know my Father too. From now on you do know him; you have seen him.' [8] Philip said to him, 'Lord, show us the Father; we ask no more.' [9] Jesus answered, 'Have I been all this time with you, Philip, and still you do not know me? Anyone who has seen me has seen the Father. Then how can you say, "Show us the Father"? [10] Do you not believe that I am in the Father, and the Father in me? I am not myself the source of the words I speak to you: it is the Father who dwells in me doing his own work. [11] Believe me when I say that I am in the Father and the Father in me; or else accept the evidence of the deeds themselves. [12] In very truth I tell you, whoever has faith in me will do what I am doing;

indeed he will do greater things still because I am going to the Father. [13] Anything you ask in my name I will do, so that the Father may be glorified in the Son. [14] If you ask anything in my name I will do it.

[15] 'If you love me you will obey my commands; [16] and I will ask the Father, and he will give you another to be your advocate, who will be with you for ever— [17] the Spirit of truth. The world cannot accept him, because the world neither sees nor knows him; but you know him, because he dwells with you and will be in you. [18] I will not leave you bereft; I am coming back to you. [19] In a little while the world will see me no longer, but you will see me; because I live, you too will live. [20] When that day comes you will know that I am in my Father, and you in me and I in you. [21] Anyone who has received my commands and obeys them—he it is who loves me; and he who loves me will be loved by my Father; and I will love him and disclose myself to him.'

[22] Judas said—the other Judas, not Iscariot—'Lord, how has it come about that you mean to disclose yourself to us and not to the world?' [23] Jesus replied, 'Anyone who loves me will heed what I say; then my Father will love him, and we will come to him and make our dwelling with him; [24] but whoever does not love me does not heed what I say. And the word you hear is not my own: it is the word of the Father who sent me. [25] I have told you these things while I am still with you; [26] but the advocate, the Holy Spirit whom the Father will send in my name, will teach you everything and remind you of all that I have told you.

[27] 'Peace is my parting gift to you, my own peace, such as the world cannot give. Set your troubled hearts at rest, and banish your fears. [28] You heard me say, "I am going away, and I am coming back to you." If you loved me you would be glad that I am going to the Father; for the Father is greater than I am. [29] I have told you now, before it happens, so that when it does happen you may have faith. [30] 'I shall not talk much longer with you, for the prince of this world approaches. He has no rights over me; [31] but the world must be shown that I love the

---

13:32 *Some witnesses omit* If God ... in him.   14:3 **also:** *some witnesses add* you know where I am going. 14:7 **If you ... too:** *some witnesses read* If you know me you will know my Father too.   14:14 **If you ask:** *some witnesses add* me.   14:17 **will be:** *some witnesses read* is.

95

Father and am doing what he commands; come, let us go!

15 'I AM the true vine, and my Father is the gardener. ²Any branch of mine that is barren he cuts away; and any fruiting branch he prunes clean, to make it more fruitful still. ³You are already clean because of the word I have spoken to you. ⁴Dwell in me, as I in you. No branch can bear fruit by itself, but only if it remains united with the vine; no more can you bear fruit, unless you remain united with me.

⁵'I am the vine; you are the branches. Anyone who dwells in me, as I dwell in him, bears much fruit; apart from me you can do nothing. ⁶Anyone who does not dwell in me is thrown away like a withered branch. The withered branches are gathered up, thrown on the fire, and burnt.

⁷'If you dwell in me, and my words dwell in you, ask whatever you want, and you shall have it. ⁸This is how my Father is glorified: you are to bear fruit in plenty and so be my disciples. ⁹As the Father has loved me, so I have loved you. Dwell in my love. ¹⁰If you heed my commands you will dwell in my love, as I have heeded my Father's commands and dwell in his love.

¹¹'I have spoken thus to you, so that my joy may be in you, and your joy complete. ¹²This is my commandment: love one another, as I have loved you. ¹³There is no greater love than this, that someone should lay down his life for his friends. ¹⁴You are my friends, if you do what I command you. ¹⁵No longer do I call you servants, for a servant does not know what his master is about. I have called you friends, because I have disclosed to you everything that I heard from my Father. ¹⁶You did not choose me: I chose you. I appointed you to go on and bear fruit, fruit that will last; so that the Father may give you whatever you ask in my name. ¹⁷This is my commandment to you: love one another.

¹⁸'If the world hates you, it hated me first, as you know well. ¹⁹If you belonged to the world, the world would love its own; but you do not belong to the world, now that I have chosen you out of the world, and for that reason the world hates

you. ²⁰Remember what I said: "A servant is not greater than his master." If they persecuted me, they will also persecute you; if they have followed my teaching, they will follow yours. ²¹All this will they do to you on my account, because they do not know the One who sent me.

²²'If I had not come and spoken to them, they would not be guilty of sin; but now they have no excuse for their sin: ²³whoever hates me, hates my Father also. ²⁴If I had not done such deeds among them as no one else has ever done, they would not be guilty of sin; but now they have seen and hated both me and my Father. ²⁵This text in their law had to come true: "They hated me without reason."

²⁶'When the advocate has come, whom I shall send you from the Father— the Spirit of truth that issues from the Father—he will bear witness to me. ²⁷And you also are my witnesses, because you have been with me from the first.

16 'I have told you all this to guard you against the breakdown of your faith. ²They will ban you from the synagogue; indeed, the time is coming when anyone who kills you will suppose that he is serving God. ³They will do these things because they did not know either the Father or me. ⁴I have told you all this so that when the time comes for it to happen you may remember my warning. I did not tell you this at first, because then I was with you; ⁵but now I am going away to him who sent me. None of you asks me, "Where are you going?" ⁶Yet you are plunged into grief at what I have told you. ⁷Nevertheless I assure you that it is in your interest that I am leaving you. If I do not go, the advocate will not come, whereas if I go, I will send him to you. ⁸When he comes, he will prove the world wrong about sin, justice, and judgement: ⁹about sin, because they refuse to believe in me; ¹⁰about justice, because I go to the Father when I pass from your sight; ¹¹about judgement, because the prince of this world stands condemned.

¹²'There is much more that I could say to you, but the burden would be too great for you now. ¹³However, when the Spirit of truth comes, he will guide you into all the truth; for he will not speak on his own

15:18 **it hated ... well:** *or* bear in mind that it hated me first.

authority, but will speak only what he hears; and he will make known to you what is to come. [14] He will glorify me, for he will take what is mine and make it known to you. [15] All that the Father has is mine, and that is why I said, "He will take what is mine and make it known to you."

[16] 'A LITTLE while, and you see me no more; again a little while, and you will see me.' [17] Some of his disciples said to one another, 'What does he mean by this: "A little while, and you will not see me, and again a little while, and you will see me," and by this: "Because I am going to the Father"?' [18] So they asked, 'What is this "little while" that he is talking about? We do not know what he means.'

[19] Jesus knew that they were wanting to question him, and said, 'Are you discussing that saying of mine: "A little while, and you will not see me, and again a little while, and you will see me"? [20] In very truth I tell you, you will weep and mourn, but the world will be glad. But though you will be plunged in grief, your grief will be turned to joy. [21] A woman in labour is in pain because her time has come; but when her baby is born she forgets the anguish in her joy that a child has been born into the world. [22] So it is with you: for the moment you are sad; but I shall see you again, and then you will be joyful, and no one shall rob you of your joy. [23] When that day comes you will ask me nothing more. In very truth I tell you, if you ask the Father for anything in my name, he will give it you. [24] So far you have asked nothing in my name. Ask and you will receive, that your joy may be complete.

[25] 'Till now I have been using figures of speech; a time is coming when I shall no longer use figures, but tell you of the Father in plain words. [26] When that day comes you will make your request in my name, and I do not say that I shall pray to the Father for you, [27] for the Father loves you himself, because you have loved me and believed that I came from God. [28] I came from the Father and have come into the world; and now I am leaving the world again and going to the Father.'

[29] His disciples said, 'Now you are speaking plainly, not in figures of speech! [30] We are certain now that you know everything, and do not need to be asked; because of this we believe that you have come from God.'

[31] Jesus answered, 'Do you now believe? [32] I warn you, the hour is coming, has indeed already come, when you are to be scattered, each to his own home, leaving me alone. Yet I am not alone, for the Father is with me. [33] I have told you all this so that in me you may find peace. In the world you will have suffering. But take heart! I have conquered the world.'

17 THEN Jesus looked up to heaven and said:

'Father, the hour has come. Glorify your Son, that the Son may glorify you. [2] For you have made him sovereign over all mankind, to give eternal life to all whom you have given him. [3] This is eternal life: to know you the only true God, and Jesus Christ whom you have sent.

[4] 'I have glorified you on earth by finishing the work which you gave me to do; [5] and now, Father, glorify me in your own presence with the glory which I had with you before the world began.

[6] 'I have made your name known to the men whom you gave me out of the world. They were yours and you gave them to me, and they have obeyed your command. [7] Now they know that all you gave me has come from you; [8] for I have taught them what I learned from you, and they have received it: they know with certainty that I came from you, and they have believed that you sent me.

[9] 'I pray for them; I am not praying for the world but for those whom you have given me, because they belong to you. [10] All that is mine is yours, and what is yours is mine; and through them is my glory revealed.

[11] 'I am no longer in the world; they are still in the world, but I am coming to you. Holy Father, protect them by the power of your name, the name you have given me, that they may be one, as we are one. [12] While I was with them, I protected them by the power of your name which

16:23 **if you ask … you**: *some witnesses read* if you ask the Father for anything, he will give it you in my name.
17:11 **protect … given me**: *some witnesses read* protect by the power of your name those whom you have given me. 17:12 **protected … gave me**: *some witnesses read* protected by the power of your name those whom you have given me.

you gave me, and kept them safe. Not one of them is lost except the man doomed to be lost, for scripture has to be fulfilled.

¹³ 'Now I am coming to you; but while I am still in the world I speak these words, so that they may have my joy within them in full measure. ¹⁴ I have delivered your word to them, and the world hates them because they are strangers in the world, as I am. ¹⁵ I do not pray you to take them out of the world, but to keep them from the evil one. ¹⁶ They are strangers in the world, as I am. ¹⁷ Consecrate them by the truth; your word is truth. ¹⁸ As you sent me into the world, I have sent them into the world, ¹⁹ and for their sake I consecrate myself, that they too may be consecrated by the truth.

²⁰ 'It is not for these alone that I pray, but for those also who through their words put their faith in me. ²¹ May they all be one; as you, Father, are in me, and I in you, so also may they be in us, that the world may believe that you sent me. ²² The glory which you gave me I have given to them, that they may be one, as we are one; ²³ I in them and you in me, may they be perfectly one. Then the world will know that you sent me, and that you loved them as you loved me.

²⁴ 'Father, they are your gift to me; and my desire is that they may be with me where I am, so that they may look upon my glory, which you have given me because you loved me before the world began. ²⁵ Righteous Father, although the world does not know you, I know you, and they know that you sent me. ²⁶ I made your name known to them, and will make it known, so that the love you had for me may be in them, and I in them.'

The trial and crucifixion of Jesus

18 AFTER this prayer, Jesus went out with his disciples across the Kedron ravine. There was a garden there, and he and his disciples went into it. ² The place was known to Judas, his betrayer, because Jesus had often met there with his disciples. ³ So Judas made his way there with a detachment of soldiers, and with temple police provided by the chief priests and the Pharisees; they were equipped with lanterns, torches, and weapons. ⁴ Jesus, knowing everything that was to happen to him, stepped forward and asked them, 'Who is it you want?' ⁵ 'Jesus

of Nazareth,' they answered. Jesus said, 'I am he.' And Judas the traitor was standing there with them. ⁶ When Jesus said, 'I am he,' they drew back and fell to the ground. ⁷ Again he asked, 'Who is it you want?' 'Jesus of Nazareth,' they repeated. ⁸ 'I have told you that I am he,' Jesus answered. 'If I am the man you want, let these others go.' ⁹ (This was to make good his words, 'I have not lost one of those you gave me.') ¹⁰ Thereupon Simon Peter drew the sword he was wearing and struck at the high priest's servant, cutting off his right ear. The servant's name was Malchus. ¹¹ Jesus said to Peter, 'Put away your sword. This is the cup the Father has given me; shall I not drink it?'

¹² THE troops with their commander, and the Jewish police, now arrested Jesus and secured him. ¹³ They took him first to Annas, father-in-law of Caiaphas, the high priest for that year—¹⁴ the same Caiaphas who had advised the Jews that it would be to their interest if one man died for the people. ¹⁵ Jesus was followed by Simon Peter and another disciple. This disciple, who was known to the high priest, went with Jesus into the high priest's courtyard, ¹⁶ but Peter stayed outside at the door. So the other disciple, the high priest's acquaintance, went back and spoke to the girl on duty at the door, and brought Peter in. ¹⁷ The girl said to Peter, 'Are you another of this man's disciples?' 'I am not,' he said. ¹⁸ As it was cold, the servants and the police had made a charcoal fire, and were standing round it warming themselves. Peter too was standing with them, sharing the warmth.

¹⁹ The high priest questioned Jesus about his disciples and about his teaching. ²⁰ Jesus replied, 'I have spoken openly for all the world to hear; I have always taught in synagogues or in the temple, where all Jews congregate; I have said nothing in secret. ²¹ Why are you questioning me? Question those who heard me; they know what I said.' ²² When he said this, one of the police standing near him struck him on the face. 'Is that the way to answer the high priest?' he demanded. ²³ Jesus replied, 'If I was wrong to speak what I did, produce evidence to prove it; if I was right, why strike me?' ²⁴ So Annas sent him bound to Caiaphas the high priest.

²⁵ Meanwhile, as Simon Peter stood warming himself, he was asked, 'Are you another of his disciples?' But he denied it: 'I am not,' he said. ²⁶ One of the high priest's servants, a relation of the man whose ear Peter had cut off, insisted, 'Did I not see you with him in the garden?' ²⁷ Once again Peter denied it; and at that moment a cock crowed.

²⁸ FROM Caiaphas Jesus was led into the governor's headquarters. It was now early morning, and the Jews themselves stayed outside the headquarters to avoid defilement, so that they could eat the Passover meal. ²⁹ So Pilate came out to them and asked, 'What charge do you bring against this man?' ³⁰ 'If he were not a criminal', they replied, 'we would not have brought him before you.' ³¹ Pilate said, 'Take him yourselves and try him by your own law.' The Jews answered, 'We are not allowed to put anyone to death.' ³² Thus they ensured the fulfilment of the words by which Jesus had indicated the kind of death he was to die.

³³ Pilate then went back into his headquarters and summoned Jesus. 'So you are the king of the Jews?' he said. ³⁴ Jesus replied, 'Is that your own question, or have others suggested it to you?' ³⁵ 'Am I a Jew?' said Pilate. 'Your own nation and their chief priests have brought you before me. What have you done?' ³⁶ Jesus replied, 'My kingdom does not belong to this world. If it did, my followers would be fighting to save me from the clutches of the Jews. My kingdom belongs elsewhere.' ³⁷ 'You are a king, then?' said Pilate. Jesus answered, '"King" is your word. My task is to bear witness to the truth. For this I was born; for this I came into the world, and all who are not deaf to truth listen to my voice.' ³⁸ Pilate said, 'What is truth?' With those words he went out again to the Jews and said, 'For my part I find no case against him. ³⁹ But you have a custom that I release one prisoner for you at Passover. Would you like me to release the king of the Jews?' ⁴⁰ At this they shouted back: 'Not him; we want Barabbas!' Barabbas was a bandit.

19 Pilate now took Jesus and had him flogged; ² and the soldiers plaited a crown of thorns and placed it on his head, and robed him in a purple cloak. ³ Then one after another they came up to him, crying, 'Hail, king of the Jews!' and struck him on the face.

⁴ Once more Pilate came out and said to the Jews, 'Here he is; I am bringing him out to let you know that I find no case against him'; ⁵ and Jesus came out, wearing the crown of thorns and the purple cloak. 'Here is the man,' said Pilate. ⁶ At the sight of him the chief priests and the temple police shouted, 'Crucify! Crucify!' 'Take him yourselves and crucify him,' said Pilate; 'for my part I find no case against him.' ⁷ The Jews answered, 'We have a law; and according to that law he ought to die, because he has claimed to be God's Son.'

⁸ When Pilate heard that, he was more afraid than ever, ⁹ and going back into his headquarters he asked Jesus, 'Where have you come from?' But Jesus gave him no answer. ¹⁰ 'Do you refuse to speak to me?' said Pilate. 'Surely you know that I have authority to release you, and authority to crucify you?' ¹¹ 'You would have no authority at all over me', Jesus replied, 'if it had not been granted you from above; and therefore the deeper guilt lies with the one who handed me over to you.'

¹² From that moment Pilate tried hard to release him; but the Jews kept shouting, 'If you let this man go, you are no friend to Caesar; anyone who claims to be a king is opposing Caesar.' ¹³ When Pilate heard what they were saying, he brought Jesus out and took his seat on the tribunal at the place known as The Pavement (in Hebrew, 'Gabbatha'). ¹⁴ It was the day of preparation for the Passover, about noon. Pilate said to the Jews, 'Here is your king.' ¹⁵ They shouted, 'Away with him! Away with him! Crucify him!' 'Am I to crucify your king?' said Pilate. 'We have no king but Caesar,' replied the chief priests. ¹⁶ Then at last, to satisfy them, he handed Jesus over to be crucified.

JESUS was taken away, ¹⁷ and went out, carrying the cross himself, to the place called The Skull (in Hebrew, 'Golgotha'); ¹⁸ there they crucified him, and with him two others, one on either side, with Jesus in between.

19:14 It was ... Passover: *or* It was Friday in Passover.

¹⁹ Pilate had an inscription written and fastened to the cross; it read, 'Jesus of Nazareth, King of the Jews'. ²⁰ This inscription, in Hebrew, Latin, and Greek, was read by many Jews, since the place where Jesus was crucified was not far from the city. ²¹ So the Jewish chief priests said to Pilate, 'You should not write "King of the Jews", but rather "He claimed to be king of the Jews".' ²² Pilate replied, 'What I have written, I have written.'

²³ When the soldiers had crucified Jesus they took his clothes and, leaving aside the tunic, divided them into four parts, one for each soldier. The tunic was seamless, woven in one piece throughout; ²⁴ so they said to one another, 'We must not tear this; let us toss for it.' Thus the text of scripture came true: 'They shared my garments among them, and cast lots for my clothing.'

That is what the soldiers did. ²⁵ Meanwhile near the cross on which Jesus hung, his mother was standing with her sister, Mary wife of Clopas, and Mary of Magdala. ²⁶ Seeing his mother, with the disciple whom he loved standing beside her, Jesus said to her, 'Mother, there is your son'; ²⁷ and to the disciple, 'There is your mother'; and from that moment the disciple took her into his home.

²⁸ After this, Jesus, aware that all had now come to its appointed end, said in fulfilment of scripture, 'I am thirsty.' ²⁹ A jar stood there full of sour wine; so they soaked a sponge with the wine, fixed it on hyssop, and held it up to his lips. ³⁰ Having received the wine, he said, 'It is accomplished!' Then he bowed his head and gave up his spirit.

³¹ Because it was the eve of the sabbath, the Jews were anxious that the bodies should not remain on the crosses, since that sabbath was a day of great solemnity; so they requested Pilate to have the legs broken and the bodies taken down. ³² The soldiers accordingly came to the men crucified with Jesus and broke the legs of each in turn, ³³ but when they came to Jesus and found he was already dead, they did not break his legs. ³⁴ But one of the soldiers thrust a lance into his side, and at once there was a flow of blood and water. ³⁵ This is vouched for by an eyewitness, whose evidence is to be trusted. He knows that he speaks the truth, so that you too may believe; ³⁶ for this happened in fulfilment of the text of scripture: 'No bone of his shall be broken.' ³⁷ And another text says, 'They shall look on him whom they pierced.'

³⁸ AFTER that, Joseph of Arimathaea, a disciple of Jesus, but a secret disciple for fear of the Jews, asked Pilate for permission to remove the body of Jesus. He consented; so Joseph came and removed the body. ³⁹ He was joined by Nicodemus (the man who had visited Jesus by night), who brought with him a mixture of myrrh and aloes, more than half a hundredweight. ⁴⁰ They took the body of Jesus and following Jewish burial customs they wrapped it, with the spices, in strips of linen cloth. ⁴¹ Near the place where he had been crucified there was a garden, and in the garden a new tomb, not yet used for burial; ⁴² and there, since it was the eve of the Jewish sabbath and the tomb was near at hand, they laid Jesus.

The resurrection

20 EARLY on the first day of the week, while it was still dark, Mary of Magdala came to the tomb. She saw that the stone had been moved away from the entrance, ² and ran to Simon Peter and the other disciple, the one whom Jesus loved. 'They have taken the Lord out of the tomb,' she said, 'and we do not know where they have laid him.' ³ So Peter and the other disciple set out and made their way to the tomb. ⁴ They ran together, but the other disciple ran faster than Peter and reached the tomb first. ⁵ He peered in and saw the linen wrappings lying there, but he did not enter. ⁶ Then Simon Peter caught up with him and went into the tomb. He saw the linen wrappings lying there, ⁷ and the napkin which had been round his head, not with the wrappings but rolled up in a place by itself. ⁸ Then the disciple who had reached the tomb first also went in, and he saw and believed; ⁹ until then they had not understood the scriptures, which showed that he must rise from the dead.

¹⁰ So the disciples went home again; ¹¹ but Mary stood outside the tomb weep-

19:29 hyssop: *one witness reads* a javelin.

ing. And as she wept, she peered into the tomb, [12] and saw two angels in white sitting there, one at the head, and one at the feet, where the body of Jesus had lain. [13] They asked her, 'Why are you weeping?' She answered, 'They have taken my Lord away, and I do not know where they have laid him.' [14] With these words she turned round and saw Jesus standing there, but she did not recognize him. [15] Jesus asked her, 'Why are you weeping? Who are you looking for?' Thinking it was the gardener, she said, 'If it is you, sir, who removed him, tell me where you have laid him, and I will take him away.' [16] Jesus said, 'Mary!' She turned and said to him, 'Rabbuni!' (which is Hebrew for 'Teacher'). [17] 'Do not cling to me,' said Jesus, 'for I have not yet ascended to the Father. But go to my brothers, and tell them that I am ascending to my Father and your Father, to my God and your God.' [18] Mary of Magdala went to tell the disciples. 'I have seen the Lord!' she said, and gave them his message.

[19] Late that same day, the first day of the week, when the disciples were together behind locked doors for fear of the Jews, Jesus came and stood among them. 'Peace be with you!' he said; [20] then he showed them his hands and his side. On seeing the Lord the disciples were overjoyed. [21] Jesus said again, 'Peace be with you! As the Father sent me, so I send you.' [22] Then he breathed on them, saying, 'Receive the Holy Spirit! [23] If you forgive anyone's sins, they are forgiven; if you pronounce them unforgiven, unforgiven they remain.'

[24] One of the Twelve, Thomas the Twin, was not with the rest when Jesus came. [25] So the others kept telling him, 'We have seen the Lord.' But he said, 'Unless I see the mark of the nails on his hands, unless I put my finger into the place where the nails were, and my hand into his side, I will never believe it.'

[26] A week later his disciples were once again in the room, and Thomas was with them. Although the doors were locked, Jesus came and stood among them, saying, 'Peace be with you!' [27] Then he said to Thomas, 'Reach your finger here; look at my hands. Reach your hand here and put it into my side. Be unbelieving no

longer, but believe.' [28] Thomas said, 'My Lord and my God!' [29] Jesus said to him, 'Because you have seen me you have found faith. Happy are they who find faith without seeing me.'

[30] There were indeed many other signs that Jesus performed in the presence of his disciples, which are not recorded in this book. [31] Those written here have been recorded in order that you may believe that Jesus is the Christ, the Son of God, and that through this faith you may have life by his name.

21 SOME time later, Jesus showed himself to his disciples once again, by the sea of Tiberias. This is how it happened. [2] Simon Peter was with Thomas the Twin, Nathanael from Cana-in-Galilee, the sons of Zebedee, and two other disciples. [3] 'I am going out fishing,' said Simon Peter. 'We will go with you,' said the others. So they set off and got into the boat; but that night they caught nothing.

[4] Morning came, and Jesus was standing on the beach, but the disciples did not know that it was Jesus. [5] He called out to them, 'Friends, have you caught anything?' 'No,' they answered. [6] He said, 'Throw out the net to starboard, and you will make a catch.' They did so, and found they could not haul the net on board, there were so many fish in it. [7] Then the disciple whom Jesus loved said to Peter, 'It is the Lord!' As soon as Simon Peter heard him say, 'It is the Lord,' he fastened his coat about him (for he had stripped) and plunged into the sea. [8] The rest of them came on in the boat, towing the net full of fish. They were only about a hundred yards from land.

[9] When they came ashore, they saw a charcoal fire there with fish laid on it, and some bread. [10] Jesus said, 'Bring some of the fish you have caught.' [11] Simon Peter went on board and hauled the net to land; it was full of big fish, a hundred and fifty-three in all; and yet, many as they were, the net was not torn. [12] Jesus said, 'Come and have breakfast.' None of the disciples dared to ask 'Who are you?' They knew it was the Lord. [13] Jesus came, took the bread and gave it to them, and the fish in the same way. [14] This makes

20: 31 **believe:** *witnesses read different tenses, some implying* continue to believe, *others* come to believe.

the third time that Jesus appeared to his disciples after his resurrection from the dead.

[15] After breakfast Jesus said to Simon Peter, 'Simon son of John, do you love me more than these others?' 'Yes, Lord,' he answered, 'you know that I love you.' 'Then feed my lambs,' he said. [16] A second time he asked, 'Simon son of John, do you love me?' 'Yes, Lord, you know I love you.' 'Then tend my sheep.' [17] A third time he said, 'Simon son of John, do you love me?' Peter was hurt that he asked him a third time, 'Do you love me?' 'Lord,' he said, 'you know everything; you know I love you.' Jesus said, 'Then feed my sheep.

[18] 'In very truth I tell you: when you were young you fastened your belt about you and walked where you chose; but when you are old you will stretch out your arms, and a stranger will bind you fast, and carry you where you have no wish to go.' [19] He said this to indicate the manner of death by which Peter was to glorify God. Then he added, 'Follow me.'

[20] Peter looked round, and saw the disciple whom Jesus loved following—the one who at supper had leaned back close to him to ask the question, 'Lord, who is it that will betray you?' [21] When he saw him, Peter asked, 'Lord, what about him?' [22] Jesus said, 'If it should be my will that he stay until I come, what is it to you? Follow me.'

[23] That saying of Jesus became current among his followers, and was taken to mean that that disciple would not die. But in fact Jesus did not say he would not die; he only said, 'If it should be my will that he stay until I come, what is it to you?'

[24] It is this same disciple who vouches for what has been written here. He it is who wrote it, and we know that his testimony is true.

[25] There is much else that Jesus did. If it were all to be recorded in detail, I suppose the world could not hold the books that would be written.

21:24 is true: *some witnesses here insert the passage printed below.*

An incident in the temple*

8 [53] AND they all went home, [1] while Jesus went to the mount of Olives. [2] At daybreak he appeared again in the temple, and all the people gathered round him. He had taken his seat and was engaged in teaching them [3] when the scribes and the Pharisees brought in a woman caught committing adultery. Making her stand in the middle [4] they said to him, 'Teacher, this woman was caught in the very act of adultery. [5] In the law Moses has laid down that such women are to be stoned. What do you say about it?' [6] They put the question as a test, hoping to frame a charge against him.

Jesus bent down and wrote with his finger on the ground. [7] When they continued to press their question he sat up straight and said, 'Let whichever of you is free from sin throw the first stone at her.' [8] Then once again he bent down and wrote on the ground. [9] When they heard what he said, one by one they went away, the eldest first; and Jesus was left alone, with the woman still standing there. [10] Jesus again sat up and said to the woman, 'Where are they? Has no one condemned you?' [11] She answered, 'No one, sir.' 'Neither do I condemn you,' Jesus said. 'Go; do not sin again.'

*This passage, which in most editions of the New Testament is printed in the text of John, 7:53—8:11, has no fixed place in our witnesses. Some of them do not contain it at all. Some place it after Luke 21:38, others after John 7:36, or 7:52, or 21:24.   8:9 they went away: *some witnesses add* convicted by their conscience.

ACTS OF THE APOSTLES

1 IN the first part of my work, Theophilus, I gave an account of all that Jesus did and taught from the beginning [2] until the day when he was taken up to heaven, after giving instructions through the Holy Spirit to the apostles whom he had chosen. [3] To these men he showed himself after his death and gave ample proof that he was alive: he was seen by them over a period of forty days and spoke to them about the kingdom of God. [4] While he was in their company he directed them not to leave Jerusalem. 'You must wait', he said, 'for the gift promised by the Father, of which I told you; [5] John, as you know, baptized with water, but within the next few days you will be baptized with the Holy Spirit.'

[6] When they were all together, they asked him, 'Lord, is this the time at which you are to restore sovereignty to Israel?' [7] He answered, 'It is not for you to know about dates or times which the Father has set within his own control. [8] But you will receive power when the Holy Spirit comes upon you; and you will bear witness for me in Jerusalem, and throughout all Judaea and Samaria, and even in the farthest corners of the earth.'

[9] After he had said this, he was lifted up before their very eyes, and a cloud took him from their sight. [10] They were gazing intently into the sky as he went, and all at once there stood beside them two men robed in white, [11] who said, 'Men of Galilee, why stand there looking up into the sky? This Jesus who has been taken from you up to heaven will come in the same way as you have seen him go.'

The church in Jerusalem

[12] THEY then returned to Jerusalem from the hill called Olivet, which is near the city, no farther than a sabbath day's journey. [13] On their arrival they went to the upstairs room where they were lodging: Peter and John and James and Andrew, Philip and Thomas, Bartholomew and Matthew, James son of Alphaeus, Simon the Zealot, and Judas son of James. [14] All these with one accord were constantly at prayer, together with a group of women, and Mary the mother of Jesus, and his brothers.

[15] It was during this time that Peter stood up before the assembled brotherhood, about one hundred and twenty in all, and said: [16] 'My friends, the prophecy in scripture, which the Holy Spirit uttered concerning Judas through the mouth of David, was bound to come true; Judas acted as guide to those who arrested Jesus—[17] he was one of our number and had his place in this ministry.' [18] (After buying a plot of land with the price of his villainy, this man fell headlong and burst open so that all his entrails spilled out; [19] everyone in Jerusalem came to hear of this, and in their own language they named the plot Akeldama, which means 'Blood Acre'.) [20] 'The words I have in mind', Peter continued, 'are in the book of Psalms: "Let his homestead fall desolate; let there be none to inhabit it." And again, "Let his charge be given to another." [21] Therefore one of those who bore us company all the while the Lord Jesus was going about among us, [22] from his baptism by John until the day when he was taken up from us—one of those must now join us as a witness to his resurrection.'

[23] Two names were put forward: Joseph, who was known as Barsabbas and bore the added name of Justus, and Matthias. [24] Then they prayed and said, 'You know the hearts of everyone, Lord; declare which of these two you have chosen [25] to receive this office of ministry and apostleship which Judas abandoned to go where he belonged.' [26] They drew lots, and the lot fell to Matthias; so he was elected to be an apostle with the other eleven.

2 THE day of Pentecost had come, and they were all together in one place. [2] Suddenly there came from the sky what sounded like a strong, driving wind, a noise which filled the whole house where they were sitting. [3] And there appeared to them flames like tongues of fire distributed among them and coming to rest on each one. [4] They were all filled with the Holy

Spirit and began to talk in other tongues, as the Spirit gave them power of utterance.

5 Now there were staying in Jerusalem devout Jews drawn from every nation under heaven. 6 At this sound a crowd of them gathered, and were bewildered because each one heard his own language spoken; 7 they were amazed and in astonishment exclaimed, 'Surely these people who are speaking are all Galileans! 8 How is it that each of us can hear them in his own native language? 9 Parthians, Medes, Elamites; inhabitants of Mesopotamia, of Judaea and Cappadocia, of Pontus and Asia, 10 of Phrygia and Pamphylia, of Egypt and the districts of Libya around Cyrene; visitors from Rome, both Jews and proselytes; 11 Cretans and Arabs—all of us hear them telling in our own tongues the great things God has done.' 12 They were all amazed and perplexed, saying to one another, 'What can this mean?' 13 Others said contemptuously, 'They have been drinking!'

14 But Peter stood up with the eleven, and in a loud voice addressed the crowd: 'Fellow-Jews, and all who live in Jerusalem, listen and take note of what I say. 15 These people are not drunk, as you suppose; it is only nine in the morning! 16 No, this is what the prophet Joel spoke of: 17 "In the last days, says God, I will pour out my Spirit on all mankind; and your sons and daughters shall prophesy; your young men shall see visions, and your old men shall dream dreams. 18 Yes, on my servants and my handmaids I will pour out my Spirit in those days, and they shall prophesy. 19 I will show portents in the sky above, and signs on the earth below—blood and fire and a pall of smoke. 20 The sun shall be turned to darkness, and the moon to blood, before that great, resplendent day, the day of the Lord, shall come. 21 Everyone who calls on the name of the Lord on that day shall be saved."

22 'Men of Israel, hear me: I am speaking of Jesus of Nazareth, singled out by God and made known to you through miracles, portents, and signs, which God worked among you through him, as you well know. 23 By the deliberate will and plan of God he was given into your power,

and you killed him, using heathen men to crucify him. 24 But God raised him to life again, setting him free from the pangs of death, because it could not be that death should keep him in its grip.

25 'For David says of him:

I foresaw that the Lord would be
  with me for ever,
with him at my right hand I cannot
  be shaken;
26 therefore my heart is glad
  and my tongue rejoices;
moreover, my flesh shall dwell in
  hope,
27 for you will not abandon me to
  death,
nor let your faithful servant suffer
  corruption.
28 You have shown me the paths of life;
  your presence will fill me with joy.

29 'My friends, nobody can deny that the patriarch David died and was buried; we have his tomb here to this very day. 30 It is clear therefore that he spoke as a prophet who knew that God had sworn to him that one of his own direct descendants should sit on his throne; 31 and when he said he was not abandoned to death, and his flesh never saw corruption, he spoke with foreknowledge of the resurrection of the Messiah. 32 Now Jesus has been raised by God, and of this we are all witnesses. 33 Exalted at God's right hand he received from the Father the promised Holy Spirit, and all that you now see and hear flows from him. 34 For it was not David who went up to heaven; his own words are: "The Lord said to my Lord, 'Sit at my right hand 35 until I make your enemies your footstool.'" 36 Let all Israel then accept as certain that God has made this same Jesus, whom you crucified, both Lord and Messiah.'

37 When they heard this they were cut to the heart, and said to Peter and the other apostles, 'Friends, what are we to do?' 38 'Repent', said Peter, 'and be baptized, every one of you, in the name of Jesus the Messiah; then your sins will be forgiven and you will receive the gift of the Holy Spirit. 39 The promise is to you and to your children and to all who are far away, to everyone whom the Lord our God may call.'

2:33 at: *or* by.

⁴⁰ He pressed his case with many other arguments and pleaded with them: 'Save yourselves from this crooked age.' ⁴¹ Those who accepted what he said were baptized, and some three thousand were added to the number of believers that day. ⁴² They met constantly to hear the apostles teach and to share the common life, to break bread, and to pray.

⁴³ A sense of awe was felt by everyone, and many portents and signs were brought about through the apostles. ⁴⁴ All the believers agreed to hold everything in common: ⁴⁵ they began to sell their property and possessions and distribute to everyone according to his need. ⁴⁶ One and all they kept up their daily attendance at the temple, and, breaking bread in their homes, they shared their meals with unaffected joy, ⁴⁷ as they praised God and enjoyed the favour of the whole people. And day by day the Lord added new converts to their number.

3 ONE day at three in the afternoon, the hour of prayer, Peter and John were on their way up to the temple. ² Now a man who had been a cripple from birth used to be carried there and laid every day by the temple gate called Beautiful to beg from people as they went in. ³ When he saw Peter and John on their way into the temple, he asked for alms. ⁴ They both fixed their eyes on him, and Peter said, 'Look at us.' ⁵ Expecting a gift from them, the man was all attention. ⁶ Peter said, 'I have no silver or gold; but what I have I give you: in the name of Jesus Christ of Nazareth, get up and walk.' ⁷ Then, grasping him by the right hand he helped him up; and at once his feet and ankles grew strong; ⁸ he sprang to his feet, and started to walk. He entered the temple with them, leaping and praising God as he went. ⁹ Everyone saw him walking and praising God, ¹⁰ and when they recognized him as the man who used to sit begging at Beautiful Gate they were filled with wonder and amazement at what had happened to him.

¹¹ While he still clung to Peter and John all the people came running in astonishment towards them in Solomon's Portico, as it is called. ¹² Peter saw them coming and met them with these words: 'Men of Israel, why be surprised at this? Why stare at us as if we had made this man walk by some power or godliness of our own? ¹³⁻¹⁴ The God of Abraham, Isaac, and Jacob, the God of our fathers, has given the highest honour to his servant Jesus, whom you handed over for trial and disowned in Pilate's court—disowned the holy and righteous one when Pilate had decided to release him. You asked for the reprieve of a murderer, ¹⁵ and killed the Prince of life. But God raised him from the dead; of that we are witnesses. ¹⁶ The name of Jesus, by awakening faith, has given strength to this man whom you see and know, and this faith has made him completely well as you can all see.

¹⁷ 'Now, my friends, I know quite well that you acted in ignorance, as did your rulers; ¹⁸ but this is how God fulfilled what he had foretold through all the prophets: that his Messiah would suffer. ¹⁹ Repent, therefore, and turn to God, so that your sins may be wiped out. Then the Lord may grant you a time of recovery ²⁰ and send the Messiah appointed for you, that is, Jesus. ²¹ He must be received into heaven until the time comes for the universal restoration of which God has spoken through his holy prophets from the beginning. ²² Moses said, "The Lord God will raise up for you a prophet like me from among yourselves. Listen to everything he says to you, ²³ for anyone who refuses to listen to that prophet must be cut off from the people." ²⁴ From Samuel onwards, every prophet who spoke predicted this present time.

²⁵ 'You are the heirs of the prophets, and of that covenant which God made with your fathers when he said to Abraham, "And in your offspring all the families on earth shall find blessing." ²⁶ When God raised up his servant, he sent him to you first, to bring you blessing by turning every one of you from your wicked ways.'

4 They were still addressing the people when the chief priests, together with the controller of the temple and the Sadducees, broke in on them, ² annoyed because they were proclaiming the resurrection from the dead by teaching the people about Jesus. ³ They were arrested

3:22 **a prophet like me:** *or* a prophet as he raised up me. 4:1 **the chief priests:** *some witnesses omit* chief.

and, as it was already evening, put in prison for the night. ⁴But many of those who had heard the message became believers, bringing the number of men to about five thousand.

⁵Next day the Jewish rulers, elders, and scribes met in Jerusalem. ⁶There were present Annas the high priest, Caiaphas, John, Alexander, and all who were of the high-priestly family. ⁷They brought the apostles before the court and began to interrogate them. 'By what power', they asked, 'or by what name have such men as you done this?' ⁸Then Peter, filled with the Holy Spirit, answered, 'Rulers of the people and elders, ⁹if it is about help given to a sick man that we are being questioned today, and the means by which he was cured, ¹⁰this is our answer to all of you and to all the people of Israel: it was by the name of Jesus Christ of Nazareth, whom you crucified, and whom God raised from the dead; through him this man stands here before you fit and well. ¹¹This Jesus is the stone, rejected by you the builders, which has become the corner-stone. ¹²There is no salvation through anyone else; in all the world no other name has been granted to mankind by which we can be saved.'

¹³Observing that Peter and John were uneducated laymen, they were astonished at their boldness and took note that they had been companions of Jesus; ¹⁴but with the man who had been cured standing in full view beside them, they had nothing to say in reply. ¹⁵So they ordered them to leave the court, and then conferred among themselves. 'What are we to do with these men?' they said. 'It is common knowledge in Jerusalem that a notable miracle has come about through them; and we cannot deny it. ¹⁷But to stop this from spreading farther among the people, we had better caution them never again to speak to anyone in this name.' ¹⁸They then called them in and ordered them to refrain from all public speaking and teaching in the name of Jesus.

¹⁹But Peter and John replied: 'Is it right in the eyes of God for us to obey you rather than him? Judge for yourselves. ²⁰We cannot possibly give up speaking about what we have seen and heard.'

²¹With a repeated caution the court discharged them. They could not see how they were to punish them, because the people were all giving glory to God for what had happened. ²²The man upon whom this miracle of healing had been performed was over forty years old.

²³As soon as they were discharged the apostles went back to their friends and told them everything that the chief priests and elders had said. ²⁴When they heard it, they raised their voices with one accord and called upon God.

'Sovereign Lord, Maker of heaven and earth and sea and of everything in them, ²⁵you said by the Holy Spirit, through the mouth of David your servant,

Why did the Gentiles rage
and the peoples hatch their futile
    plots?
²⁶The kings of the earth took their
    stand
and the rulers made common cause
against the Lord and against his
    Messiah.

²⁷'They did indeed make common cause in this very city against your holy servant Jesus whom you anointed as Messiah. Herod and Pontius Pilate conspired with the Gentiles and with the peoples of Israel ²⁸to do all the things which, under your hand and by your decree, were foreordained. ²⁹And now, O Lord, mark their threats, and enable those who serve you to speak your word with all boldness. ³⁰Stretch out your hand to heal and cause signs and portents to be done through the name of your holy servant Jesus.'

³¹When they had ended their prayer, the building where they were assembled rocked, and all were filled with the Holy Spirit and spoke God's word with boldness.

³²THE whole company of believers was united in heart and soul. Not one of them claimed any of his possessions as his own; everything was held in common. ³³With great power the apostles bore witness to the resurrection of the Lord Jesus, and all were held in high esteem. ³⁴There was never a needy person among them, because those who had property in land or houses would sell it, bring the proceeds of

---

4:6 **John:** *some witnesses read* Jonathan.   4:33 **all ... esteem:** *or* grace was strongly at work in them all.

the sale, ³⁵ and lay them at the feet of the apostles, to be distributed to any who were in need. ³⁶ For instance Joseph, surnamed by the apostles Barnabas (which means 'Son of Encouragement'), a Levite and by birth a Cypriot, ³⁷ sold an estate which he owned; he brought the money and laid it at the apostles' feet.

5 But a man called Ananias sold a property, ² and with the connivance of his wife Sapphira kept back some of the proceeds, and brought part only to lay at the apostles' feet. ³ Peter said, 'Ananias, how was it that Satan so possessed your mind that you lied to the Holy Spirit by keeping back part of the price of the land? ⁴ While it remained unsold, did it not remain yours? Even after it was turned into money, was it not still at your own disposal? What made you think of doing this? You have lied not to men but to God.' ⁵ When Ananias heard these words he dropped dead; and all who heard were awestruck. ⁶ The younger men rose and covered his body, then carried him out and buried him.

⁷ About three hours passed, and his wife came in, unaware of what had happened. ⁸ Peter asked her, 'Tell me, were you paid such and such a price for the land?' 'Yes,' she replied, 'that was the price.' ⁹ Peter said, 'Why did the two of you conspire to put the Spirit of the Lord to the test? Those who buried your husband are there at the door, and they will carry you away.' ¹⁰ At once she dropped dead at his feet. When the young men came in, they found her dead; and they carried her out and buried her beside her husband.

¹¹ Great awe fell on the whole church and on all who heard of this. ¹² Many signs and wonders were done among the people by the apostles. All the believers used to meet by common consent in Solomon's Portico; ¹³ no one from outside their number ventured to join them, yet people in general spoke highly of them. ¹⁴ An ever-increasing number of men and women who believed in the Lord were added to their ranks. ¹⁵ As a result the sick were carried out into the streets and laid there on beds and stretchers, so that at least Peter's shadow might fall on one or another as he passed by; ¹⁶ and the people from the towns round Jerusalem flocked

in, bringing those who were ill or harassed by unclean spirits, and all were cured.

¹⁷ Then the high priest and his colleagues, the Sadducean party, were goaded by jealousy ¹⁸ to arrest the apostles and put them in official custody. ¹⁹ But during the night, an angel of the Lord opened the prison doors, led them out, and said, ²⁰ 'Go, stand in the temple and tell the people all about this new life.' ²¹ Accordingly they entered the temple at daybreak and went on with their teaching.

When the high priest arrived with his colleagues they summoned the Sanhedrin, the full Council of the Israelite nation, and sent to the jail for the prisoners. ²² The officers who went to the prison failed to find them there, so they returned and reported, ²³ 'We found the jail securely locked at every point, with the warders at their posts by the doors, but on opening them we found no one inside.' ²⁴ When they heard this, the controller of the temple and the chief priests were at a loss to know what could have become of them, ²⁵ until someone came and reported: 'The men you put in prison are standing in the temple teaching the people.' ²⁶ Then the controller went off with the officers and fetched them, but without use of force, for fear of being stoned by the people.

²⁷ When they had been brought in and made to stand before the Council, the high priest began his examination. ²⁸ 'We gave you explicit orders', he said, 'to stop teaching in that name; and what has happened? You have filled Jerusalem with your teaching, and you are trying to hold us responsible for that man's death.' ²⁹ Peter replied for the apostles: 'We must obey God rather than men. ³⁰ The God of our fathers raised up Jesus; after you had put him to death by hanging him on a gibbet, ³¹ God exalted him at his right hand as leader and saviour, to grant Israel repentance and forgiveness of sins. ³² And we are witnesses to all this, as is the Holy Spirit who is given by God to those obedient to him.'

³³ This touched them on the raw, and they wanted to put them to death. ³⁴ But a member of the Council rose to his feet, a Pharisee called Gamaliel, a teacher of the

5:31 **at his right hand:** *or* with his right hand.

law held in high regard by all the people. He had the men put outside for a while, [35] and then said, 'Men of Israel, be very careful in deciding what to do with these men. [36] Some time ago Theudas came forward, making claims for himself, and a number of our people, about four hundred, joined him. But he was killed and his whole movement was destroyed and came to nothing. [37] After him came Judas the Galilean at the time of the census; he induced some people to revolt under his leadership, but he too perished and his whole movement was broken up. [38] Now, my advice to you is this: keep clear of these men; let them alone. For if what is being planned and done is human in origin, it will collapse; [39] but if it is from God, you will never be able to stamp it out, and you risk finding yourselves at war with God.'

[40] Convinced by this, they sent for the apostles and had them flogged; then they ordered them to give up speaking in the name of Jesus, and discharged them. [41] The apostles went out from the Council rejoicing that they had been found worthy to suffer humiliation for the sake of the name. [42] And every day they went steadily on with their teaching in the temple and in private houses, telling the good news of Jesus the Messiah.

The church moves outwards

6 DURING this period, when disciples were growing in number, a grievance arose on the part of those who spoke Greek, against those who spoke the language of the Jews; they complained that their widows were being overlooked in the daily distribution. [2] The Twelve called the whole company of disciples together and said, 'It would not be fitting for us to neglect the word of God in order to assist in the distribution. [3] Therefore, friends, pick seven men of good repute from your number, men full of the Spirit and of wisdom, and we will appoint them for this duty; [4] then we can devote ourselves to prayer and to the ministry of the word.' [5] This proposal proved acceptable to the whole company. They elected Stephen, a man full of faith and of the Holy Spirit, along with Philip, Prochorus, Nicanor, Timon, Parmenas, and Nicolas

of Antioch, who had been a convert to Judaism, [6] and presented them to the apostles, who prayed and laid their hands on them.

[7] The word of God spread more and more widely; the number of disciples in Jerusalem was increasing rapidly, and very many of the priests adhered to the faith.

[8] Stephen, full of grace and power, began to do great wonders and signs among the people. [9] Some members of the synagogue called the Synagogue of Freedmen, comprising Cyrenians and Alexandrians and people from Cilicia and Asia, came forward and argued with Stephen, [10] but could not hold their own against the inspired wisdom with which he spoke. [11] They then put up men to allege that they had heard him make blasphemous statements against Moses and against God. [12] They stirred up the people and the elders and scribes, set upon him and seized him, and brought him before the Council. [13] They produced false witnesses who said, 'This fellow is for ever saying things against this holy place and against the law. [14] For we have heard him say this Jesus of Nazareth will destroy this place and alter the customs handed down to us by Moses.' [15] All who were sitting in the Council fixed their eyes on him, and his face seemed to them like the face of an angel.

7 Then the high priest asked him, 'Is this true?' [2] He replied, 'My brothers, fathers of this nation, listen to me. The God of glory appeared to Abraham our ancestor while he was in Mesopotamia, before he had settled in Harran, [3] and said: "Leave your country and your kinsfolk, and come away to a land that I will show you." [4] Thereupon he left the land of the Chaldaeans and settled in Harran. From there, after his father's death, God led him to migrate to this land where you now live. [5] He gave him no foothold in it, nothing to call his own, but promised to give it as a possession for ever to him and to his descendants after him, though he was then childless. [6] This is what God said: "Abraham's descendants shall live as aliens in a foreign land, held in slavery and oppression for four hundred years. [7] And I will pass judgement", he said, "on

6:1 *those who spoke Greek*: *lit.* the Hellenists. *those who spoke the language of the Jews*: *lit.* the Hebrews.

the nation whose slaves they are; and after that they shall escape and worship me in this place." [8] God gave Abraham the covenant of circumcision, and so, when his son Isaac was born, he circumcised him on the eighth day; and Isaac was the father of Jacob, and Jacob of the twelve patriarchs.

[9] 'The patriarchs out of jealousy sold Joseph into slavery in Egypt, but God was with him [10] and rescued him from all his troubles. He gave him wisdom which so commended him to Pharaoh king of Egypt that he appointed him governor of Egypt and of the whole royal household.

[11] 'When famine struck all Egypt and Canaan, causing great distress, and our ancestors could find nothing to eat, [12] Jacob heard that there was food in Egypt and sent our fathers there. This was their first visit. [13] On the second visit Joseph made himself known to his brothers, and his ancestry was disclosed to Pharaoh. [14] Joseph sent for his father Jacob and the whole family, seventy-five persons in all; [15] and Jacob went down into Egypt. There he and our fathers ended their days. [16] Their remains were later removed to Shechem and buried in the tomb for which Abraham paid a sum of money to the sons of Hamor at Shechem.

[17] 'Now as the time approached for God to fulfil the promise he had made to Abraham, our people in Egypt grew and increased in numbers. [18] At length another king, who knew nothing of Joseph, ascended the throne of Egypt. [19] He employed cunning to harm our race, and forced our ancestors to expose their children so that they should not survive. [20] It was at this time that Moses was born. He was a fine child, and pleasing to God. For three months he was nursed in his father's house; [21] then when he was exposed, Pharaoh's daughter adopted him and brought him up as her own son. [22] So Moses was trained in all the wisdom of the Egyptians, a powerful speaker and a man of action.

[23] 'He was approaching the age of forty, when it occurred to him to visit his fellow-countrymen the Israelites. [24] Seeing one of them being ill-treated, he went to his aid, and avenged the victim by striking down the Egyptian. [25] He thought his countrymen would understand that God was offering them deliverance through him, but they did not understand. [26] The next day he came upon two of them fighting, and tried to persuade them to make up their quarrel. "Men, you are brothers!" he said. "Why are you ill-treating one another?" [27] But the man who was at fault pushed him away. "Who made you ruler and judge over us?" he said. [28] "Are you going to kill me as you killed the Egyptian yesterday?" [29] At this Moses fled the country and settled in Midianite territory. There two sons were born to him.

[30] 'After forty years had passed, an angel appeared to him in the flame of a burning bush in the desert near Mount Sinai. [31] Moses was amazed at the sight, and as he approached to look more closely, the voice of the Lord came to him: [32] "I am the God of your fathers, the God of Abraham, Isaac, and Jacob." Moses was terrified and did not dare to look. [33] Then the Lord said to him, "Take off your sandals; the place where you are standing is holy ground. [34] I have indeed seen how my people are oppressed in Egypt and have heard their groans; and I have come down to rescue them. Come now, I will send you to Egypt."

[35] 'This Moses, whom they had rejected with the words, "Who made you ruler and judge?"—this very man was commissioned as ruler and liberator by God himself, speaking through the angel who appeared to him in the bush. [36] It was Moses who led them out, doing signs and wonders in Egypt, at the Red Sea, and for forty years in the desert. [37] It was he who said to the Israelites, "God will raise up for you from among yourselves a prophet like me." [38] It was he again who, in the assembly in the desert, kept company with the angel, who spoke to him on Mount Sinai, and with our forefathers, and received the living utterances of God to pass on to us.

[39] 'Our forefathers would not accept his leadership but thrust him aside. They wished themselves back in Egypt, [40] and said to Aaron, "Make us gods to go before us. As for this fellow Moses, who brought us out of Egypt, we do not know what has become of him." [41] That was when they

7:37 **like me:** *or* as he raised up me.

made the bull-calf and offered sacrifice to the idol, and held festivities in honour of what their hands had made. ⁴²So God turned away from them and gave them over to the worship of the host of heaven, as it stands written in the book of the prophets: "Did you bring me victims and offerings those forty years in the desert, you people of Israel? ⁴³No, you carried aloft the shrine of Moloch and the star of the god Rephan, the images which you had made for your adoration. I will banish you beyond Babylon."

⁴⁴'Our forefathers had the Tent of the Testimony in the desert, as God commanded when he told Moses to make it after the pattern which he had seen. ⁴⁵In the next generation, our fathers under Joshua brought it with them when they dispossessed the nations whom God drove out before them, and so it was until the time of David. ⁴⁶David found favour with God and begged leave to provide a dwelling-place for the God of Jacob; ⁴⁷but it was Solomon who built him a house. ⁴⁸However, the Most High does not live in houses made by men; as the prophet says: ⁴⁹"Heaven is my throne and earth my footstool. What kind of house will you build for me, says the Lord; where shall my resting-place be? ⁵⁰Are not all these things of my own making?"

⁵¹'How stubborn you are, heathen still at heart and deaf to the truth! You always resist the Holy Spirit. You are just like your fathers! ⁵²Was there ever a prophet your fathers did not persecute? They killed those who foretold the coming of the righteous one, and now you have betrayed him and murdered him. ⁵³You received the law given by God's angels and yet you have not kept it.'

⁵⁴This touched them on the raw, and they ground their teeth with fury. ⁵⁵But Stephen, filled with the Holy Spirit, and gazing intently up to heaven, saw the glory of God, and Jesus standing at God's right hand. ⁵⁶'Look!' he said. 'I see the heavens opened and the Son of Man standing at the right hand of God.' ⁵⁷At this they gave a great shout, and stopped their ears; they made a concerted rush at him, ⁵⁸threw him out of the city, and set about stoning him. The witnesses laid their coats at the feet of a young man

named Saul. ⁵⁹As they stoned him Stephen called out, 'Lord Jesus, receive my spirit.' ⁶⁰He fell on his knees and cried aloud, 'Lord, do not hold this sin against them,' and with that he died. ¹ Saul **8** was among those who approved of his execution.

The church in Judaea and Samaria

THAT day was the beginning of a time of violent persecution for the church in Jerusalem; and all except the apostles were scattered over the country districts of Judaea and Samaria. ²Stephen was given burial by devout men, who made a great lamentation for him. ³Saul, meanwhile, was harrying the church; he entered house after house, seizing men and women and sending them to prison.

⁴As for those who had been scattered, they went through the country preaching the word. ⁵Philip came down to a city in Samaria and began proclaiming the Messiah there. ⁶As the crowds heard Philip and saw the signs he performed, everyone paid close attention to what he had to say. ⁷In many cases of possession the unclean spirits came out with a loud cry, and many paralysed and crippled folk were cured; ⁸and there was great rejoicing in that city.

⁹A man named Simon had been in the city for some time and had captivated the Samaritans with his magical arts, making large claims for himself. ¹⁰Everybody, high and low, listened intently to him. 'This man', they said, 'is that power of God which is called "The Great Power".' ¹¹They listened because they had for so long been captivated by his magic. ¹²But when they came to believe Philip, with his good news about the kingdom of God and the name of Jesus Christ, men and women alike were baptized. ¹³Even Simon himself believed, and after his baptism was constantly in Philip's company. He was captivated when he saw the powerful signs and miracles that were taking place.

¹⁴When the apostles in Jerusalem heard that Samaria had accepted the word of God, they sent off Peter and John, ¹⁵who went down there and prayed for the converts, asking that they might receive the Holy Spirit. ¹⁶Until then the Spirit had not come upon any of them;

7:46 **for ... Jacob**: *some witnesses read* for the house of Jacob.

they had been baptized into the name of the Lord Jesus, that and nothing more. [17] So Peter and John laid their hands on them, and they received the Holy Spirit.

[18] When Simon observed that the Spirit was bestowed through the laying on of the apostles' hands, he offered them money [19] and said, 'Give me too the same power, so that anyone I lay my hands on will receive the Holy Spirit.' [20] Peter replied, 'You thought God's gift was for sale? Your money can go with you to damnation! [21] You have neither part nor share in this, for you are corrupt in the eyes of God. [22] Repent of this wickedness of yours and pray the Lord to forgive you for harbouring such a thought. [23] I see that bitter gall and the chains of sin will be your fate.' [24] Simon said to them, 'Pray to the Lord for me, and ask that none of the things you have spoken of may befall me.'

[25] After giving their testimony and speaking the word of the Lord, they took the road back to Jerusalem, bringing the good news to many Samaritan villages on the way.

[26] Then the angel of the Lord said to Philip, 'Start out and go south to the road that leads down from Jerusalem to Gaza.' (This is the desert road.) [27] He set out and was on his way when he caught sight of an Ethiopian. This man was a eunuch, a high official of the Kandake, or queen, of Ethiopia, in charge of all her treasure; he had been to Jerusalem on a pilgrimage [28] and was now returning home, sitting in his carriage and reading aloud from the prophet Isaiah. [29] The Spirit said to Philip, 'Go and meet the carriage.' [30] When Philip ran up he heard him reading from the prophet Isaiah and asked, 'Do you understand what you are reading?' [31] He said, 'How can I without someone to guide me?' and invited Philip to get in and sit beside him.

[32] The passage he was reading was this: 'He was led like a sheep to the slaughter; like a lamb that is dumb before the shearer, he does not open his mouth. [33] He has been humiliated and has no redress. Who will be able to speak of his posterity? For he is cut off from the world of the living.'

[34] 'Please tell me', said the eunuch to Philip, 'who it is that the prophet is speaking about here: himself or someone else?' [35] Then Philip began and, starting from this passage, he told him the good news of Jesus. [36] As they were going along the road, they came to some water. 'Look,' said the eunuch, 'here is water: what is to prevent my being baptized?' [38] and he ordered the carriage to stop. Then they both went down into the water, Philip and the eunuch, and he baptized him. [39] When they came up from the water the Spirit snatched Philip away; the eunuch did not see him again, but went on his way rejoicing. [40] Philip appeared at Azotus, and toured the country, preaching in all the towns till he reached Caesarea.

9 SAUL, still breathing murderous threats against the Lord's disciples, went to the high priest [2] and applied for letters to the synagogues at Damascus authorizing him to arrest any followers of the new way whom he found, men or women, and bring them to Jerusalem. [3] While he was still on the road and nearing Damascus, suddenly a light from the sky flashed all around him. [4] He fell to the ground and heard a voice saying, 'Saul, Saul, why are you persecuting me?' [5] 'Tell me, Lord,' he said, 'who you are.' The voice answered, 'I am Jesus, whom you are persecuting. [6] But now get up and go into the city, and you will be told what you have to do.' [7] Meanwhile the men who were travelling with him stood speechless; they heard the voice but could see no one. [8] Saul got up from the ground, but when he opened his eyes he could not see; they led him by the hand and brought him into Damascus. [9] He was blind for three days, and took no food or drink.

[10] There was in Damascus a disciple named Ananias. He had a vision in which he heard the Lord say: 'Ananias!' 'Here I am, Lord,' he answered. [11] The Lord said to him, 'Go to Straight Street, to the house of Judas, and ask for a man from Tarsus named Saul. You will find him at prayer; [12] he has had a vision of a man named Ananias coming in and laying hands on him to restore his sight.' [13] Ananias

---

8 : 36 **baptized**: *some witnesses add* [37] Philip said, 'If you wholeheartedly believe, it is permitted.' He replied, 'I believe that Jesus Christ is the Son of God.'

answered, 'Lord, I have often heard about this man and all the harm he has done your people in Jerusalem. [14] Now he is here with authority from the chief priests to arrest all who invoke your name.' [15] But the Lord replied, 'You must go, for this man is my chosen instrument to bring my name before the nations and their kings, and before the people of Israel. [16] I myself will show him all that he must go through for my name's sake.'

[17] So Ananias went and, on entering the house, laid his hands on him and said, 'Saul, my brother, the Lord Jesus, who appeared to you on your way here, has sent me to you so that you may recover your sight and be filled with the Holy Spirit.' [18] Immediately it was as if scales had fallen from his eyes, and he regained his sight. He got up and was baptized, [19] and when he had eaten his strength returned.

He stayed some time with the disciples in Damascus. [20] Without delay he proclaimed Jesus publicly in the synagogues, declaring him to be the Son of God. [21] All who heard were astounded. 'Is not this the man', they said, 'who was in Jerusalem hunting down those who invoke this name? Did he not come here for the sole purpose of arresting them and taking them before the chief priests?' [22] But Saul went from strength to strength, and confounded the Jews of Damascus with his cogent proofs that Jesus was the Messiah.

[23] When some time had passed, the Jews hatched a plot against his life; [24] but their plans became known to Saul. They kept watch on the city gates day and night so that they might murder him; [25] but one night some disciples took him and, lowering him in a basket, let him down over the wall.

[26] On reaching Jerusalem he tried to join the disciples, but they were all afraid of him, because they did not believe that he really was a disciple. [27] Barnabas, however, took him and introduced him to the apostles; he described to them how on his journey Saul had seen the Lord and heard his voice, and how at Damascus he had spoken out boldly in the name of Jesus. [28] Saul now stayed with them, moving about freely in Jerusalem. [29] He spoke out boldly and openly in the name of the Lord, talking and debating with the Greek-speaking Jews. But they planned to murder him, [30] and when the brethren discovered this they escorted him down to Caesarea and sent him away to Tarsus.

[31] MEANWHILE the church, throughout Judaea, Galilee, and Samaria, was left in peace to build up its strength, and to live in the fear of the Lord. Encouraged by the Holy Spirit, it grew in numbers.

[32] In the course of a tour Peter was making throughout the region he went down to visit God's people at Lydda. [33] There he found a man named Aeneas who had been bedridden with paralysis for eight years. [34] Peter said to him, 'Aeneas, Jesus Christ cures you; get up and make your bed!' and immediately he stood up. [35] All who lived in Lydda and Sharon saw him; and they turned to the Lord.

[36] In Joppa there was a disciple named Tabitha (in Greek, Dorcas, meaning 'Gazelle'), who filled her days with acts of kindness and charity. [37] At that time she fell ill and died; and they washed her body and laid it in a room upstairs. [38] As Lydda was near Joppa, the disciples, who had heard that Peter was there, sent two men to him with the urgent request, 'Please come over to us without delay.' [39] At once Peter went off with them. When he arrived he was taken up to the room, and all the widows came and stood round him in tears, showing him the shirts and coats that Dorcas used to make while she was with them. [40] Peter sent them all outside, and knelt down and prayed; then, turning towards the body, he said, 'Tabitha, get up.' She opened her eyes, saw Peter, and sat up. [41] He gave her his hand and helped her to her feet. Then he called together the members of the church and the widows and showed her to them alive. [42] News of it spread all over Joppa, and many came to believe in the Lord. [43] Peter stayed on in Joppa for some time at the house of a tanner named Simon.

10 At Caesarea there was a man named Cornelius, a centurion in the Italian Cohort, as it was called. [2] He was a devout man, and he and his whole family joined in the worship of God; he gave generously to help the Jewish

---

9:29 **Greek-speaking Jews**: *lit.* Hellenists.

people, and was regular in his prayers to God. ³One day about three in the afternoon he had a vision in which he clearly saw an angel of God come into his room and say, 'Cornelius!' ⁴Cornelius stared at him in terror. 'What is it, my lord?' he asked. The angel said, 'Your prayers and acts of charity have gone up to heaven to speak for you before God. ⁵Now send to Joppa for a man named Simon, also called Peter: ⁶he is lodging with another Simon, a tanner, whose house is by the sea.' ⁷When the angel who spoke to him had gone, he summoned two of his servants and a military orderly who was a religious man, ⁸told them the whole story, and ordered them to Joppa.

⁹Next day about noon, while they were still on their way and approaching the city, Peter went up on the roof to pray. ¹⁰He grew hungry and wanted something to eat, but while they were getting it ready, he fell into a trance. ¹¹He saw heaven opened, and something coming down that looked like a great sheet of sailcloth; it was slung by the four corners and was being lowered to the earth, ¹²and in it he saw creatures of every kind, four-footed beasts, reptiles, and birds. ¹³There came a voice which said to him, 'Get up, Peter, kill and eat.' ¹⁴But Peter answered, 'No, Lord! I have never eaten anything profane or unclean.' ¹⁵The voice came again, a second time: 'It is not for you to call profane what God counts clean.' ¹⁶This happened three times, and then the thing was taken up into heaven.

¹⁷While Peter was still puzzling over the meaning of the vision he had seen, the messengers from Cornelius had been asking the way to Simon's house, and now arrived at the entrance. ¹⁸They called out and asked if Simon Peter was lodging there. ¹⁹Peter was thinking over the vision, when the Spirit said to him, 'Some men are here looking for you; ²⁰get up and go downstairs. You may go with them without any misgiving, for it was I who sent them.' ²¹Peter came down to the men and said, 'You are looking for me? Here I am. What brings you here?' ²²'We are from the centurion Cornelius,' they replied, 'a good and religious man, acknowledged as such by the whole Jewish nation. He was directed by a holy angel to send for you to his house and hear what you have to say.' ²³So Peter

asked them in and gave them a night's lodging.

Next day he set out with them, accompanied by some members of the congregation at Joppa, ²⁴and on the following day arrived at Caesarea. Cornelius was expecting them and had called together his relatives and close friends. ²⁵When Peter arrived, Cornelius came to meet him, and bowed to the ground in deep reverence. ²⁶But Peter raised him to his feet and said, 'Stand up; I am only a man like you.' ²⁷Still talking with him he went in and found a large gathering. ²⁸He said to them, 'I need not tell you that a Jew is forbidden by his religion to visit or associate with anyone of another race. Yet God has shown me clearly that I must not call anyone profane or unclean; ²⁹that is why I came here without demur when you sent for me. May I ask what was your reason for doing so?'

³⁰Cornelius said, 'Three days ago, just about this time, I was in the house here saying the afternoon prayers, when suddenly a man in shining robes stood before me. ³¹He said: "Cornelius, your prayer has been heard and your acts of charity have spoken for you before God. ³²Send to Simon Peter at Joppa, and ask him to come; he is lodging in the house of Simon the tanner, by the sea." ³³I sent to you there and then, and you have been good enough to come. So now we are all met here before God, to listen to everything that the Lord has instructed you to say.'

³⁴Peter began: 'I now understand how true it is that God has no favourites, ³⁵but that in every nation those who are god-fearing and do what is right are acceptable to him. ³⁶He sent his word to the Israelites and gave the good news of peace through Jesus Christ, who is Lord of all. ³⁷I need not tell you what has happened lately all over the land of the Jews, starting from Galilee after the baptism proclaimed by John. ³⁸You know how God anointed Jesus of Nazareth with the Holy Spirit and with power. Because God was with him he went about doing good and healing all who were oppressed by the devil. ³⁹And we can bear witness to all that he did in the Jewish countryside and in Jerusalem. They put him to death, hanging him on a gibbet; ⁴⁰but God raised him to life on the third day, and allowed him to be clearly seen, ⁴¹not by

the whole people, but by witnesses whom God had chosen in advance—by us, who ate and drank with him after he rose from the dead. [42] He commanded us to proclaim him to the people, and affirm that he is the one designated by God as judge of the living and the dead. [43] It is to him that all the prophets testify, declaring that everyone who trusts in him receives forgiveness of sins through his name.'

[44] Peter was still speaking when the Holy Spirit came upon all who were listening to the message. [45] The believers who had come with Peter, men of Jewish birth, were amazed that the gift of the Holy Spirit should have been poured out even on Gentiles, [46] for they could hear them speaking in tongues of ecstasy and acclaiming the greatness of God. Then Peter spoke: [47] 'Is anyone prepared to withhold the water of baptism from these persons, who have received the Holy Spirit just as we did?' [48] Then he ordered them to be baptized in the name of Jesus Christ. After that they asked him to stay on with them for a time.

11 News came to the apostles and the members of the church in Judaea that Gentiles too had accepted the word of God; [2] and when Peter came up to Jerusalem those who were of Jewish birth took issue with him. [3] 'You have been visiting men who are uncircumcised,' they said, 'and sitting at table with them!' [4] Peter began by laying before them the facts as they had happened.

[5] 'I was at prayer in the city of Joppa,' he said, 'and while in a trance I had a vision: I saw something coming down that looked like a great sheet of sailcloth, slung by the four corners and lowered from heaven till it reached me. [6] I looked intently to make out what was in it and I saw four-footed beasts, wild animals, reptiles, and birds. [7] Then I heard a voice saying to me, "Get up, Peter, kill and eat." [8] But I said, "No, Lord! Nothing profane or unclean has ever entered my mouth." [9] A voice from heaven came a second time: "It is not for you to call profane what God counts clean." [10] This happened three times, and then they were all drawn up again into heaven. [11] At that very moment three men who had been

sent to me from Caesarea arrived at the house where I was staying; [12] and the Spirit told me to go with them. My six companions here came with me and we went into the man's house. [13] He told us how he had seen an angel standing in his house who said, "Send to Joppa for Simon Peter. [14] He will speak words that will bring salvation to you and all your household." [15] Hardly had I begun speaking, when the Holy Spirit came upon them, just as upon us at the beginning, [16] and I recalled what the Lord had said: "John baptized with water, but you will be baptized with the Holy Spirit." [17] God gave them no less a gift than he gave us when we came to believe in the Lord Jesus Christ. How could I stand in God's way?'

[18] When they heard this their doubts were silenced, and they gave praise to God. 'This means', they said, 'that God has granted life-giving repentance to the Gentiles also.'

[19] MEANWHILE those who had been scattered after the persecution that arose over Stephen made their way to Phoenicia, Cyprus, and Antioch, bringing the message to Jews only and to no others. [20] But there were some natives of Cyprus and Cyrene among them, and these, when they arrived at Antioch, began to speak to Gentiles as well, telling them the good news of the Lord Jesus. [21] The power of the Lord was with them, and a great many became believers and turned to the Lord.

[22] The news reached the ears of the church in Jerusalem; and they sent Barnabas to Antioch. [23] When he arrived and saw the divine grace at work, he rejoiced and encouraged them all to hold fast to the Lord with resolute hearts, [24] for he was a good man, full of the Holy Spirit and of faith. And large numbers were won over to the Lord.

[25] He then went off to Tarsus to look for Saul; [26] and when he had found him, he brought him to Antioch. For a whole year the two of them lived in fellowship with the church there, and gave instruction to large numbers. It was in Antioch that the disciples first got the name of Christians.

[27] During this period some prophets came down from Jerusalem to Antioch,

11:11 I was: *some witnesses read* we were.   11:12 with them: *some witnesses add* making no distinctions; *others add* without any misgiving, *as in* 10:20.

²⁸ and one of them, Agabus by name, was inspired to stand up and predict a severe and world-wide famine, which in fact occurred in the reign of Claudius. ²⁹ So the disciples agreed to make a contribution, each according to his means, for the relief of their fellow-Christians in Judaea. ³⁰ This they did, and sent it off to the elders, entrusting it to Barnabas and Saul.

12 It was about this time that King Herod launched an attack on certain members of the church. ² He beheaded James, the brother of John, ³ and, when he saw that the Jews approved, proceeded to arrest Peter also. This happened during the festival of Unleavened Bread. ⁴ Having secured him, he put him in prison under a military guard, four squads of four men each, meaning to produce him in public after Passover. ⁵ So, while Peter was held in prison, the church kept praying fervently to God for him.

⁶ On the very night before Herod had planned to produce him, Peter was asleep between two soldiers, secured by two chains, while outside the doors sentries kept guard over the prison. ⁷ All at once an angel of the Lord stood there, and the cell was ablaze with light. He tapped Peter on the shoulder to wake him. 'Quick! Get up!' he said, and the chains fell away from Peter's wrists. ⁸ The angel said, 'Do up your belt and put on your sandals.' He did so. 'Now wrap your cloak round you and follow me.' ⁹ Peter followed him out, with no idea that the angel's intervention was real: he thought it was just a vision. ¹⁰ They passed the first guard-post, then the second, and reached the iron gate leading out into the city. This opened for them of its own accord; they came out and had walked the length of one street when suddenly the angel left him.

¹¹ Then Peter came to himself. 'Now I know it is true,' he said: 'the Lord has sent his angel and rescued me from Herod's clutches and from all that the Jewish people were expecting.' ¹² Once he had realized this, he made for the house of Mary, the mother of John Mark, where a large company was at prayer. ¹³ He knocked at the outer door and a maidservant called Rhoda came to answer it. ¹⁴ She recognized Peter's voice and was so

overjoyed that instead of opening the door she ran in and announced that Peter was standing outside. ¹⁵ 'You are crazy,' they told her; but she insisted that it was so. Then they said, 'It must be his angel.'

¹⁶ Peter went on knocking, and when they opened the door and saw him, they were astounded. ¹⁷ He motioned to them with his hand to keep quiet, and described to them how the Lord had brought him out of prison. 'Tell James and the members of the church,' he said. Then he left the house and went off elsewhere.

¹⁸ When morning came, there was consternation among the soldiers: what could have become of Peter? ¹⁹ Herod made careful search, but failed to find him, so he interrogated the guards and ordered their execution.

Afterwards Herod left Judaea to reside for a while at Caesarea. ²⁰ He had for some time been very angry with the people of Tyre and Sidon, who now by common agreement presented themselves at his court. There they won over Blastus the royal chamberlain, and sued for peace, because their country drew its supplies from the king's territory. ²¹ On an appointed day Herod, attired in his royal robes and seated on the rostrum, addressed the populace; ²² they responded, 'It is a god speaking, not a man!' ²³ Instantly an angel of the Lord struck him down, because he had usurped the honour due to God; he was eaten up with worms and so died.

²⁴ Meanwhile the word of God continued to grow and spread; ²⁵ and Barnabas and Saul, their task fulfilled, returned from Jerusalem, taking John Mark with them.

Paul's work among the Gentiles

13 There were in the church at Antioch certain prophets and teachers: Barnabas, Simeon called Niger, Lucius of Cyrene, Manaen, a close friend of Prince Herod, and Saul. ² While they were offering worship to the Lord and fasting, the Holy Spirit said, 'Set Barnabas and Saul apart for me, to do the work to which I have called them.' ³ Then, after further fasting and prayer, they laid their hands on them and sent them on their way.

12:25 from Jerusalem: *some witnesses read* to Jerusalem.

⁴ These two, sent out on their mission by the Holy Spirit, came down to Seleucia, and from there sailed to Cyprus. ⁵ Arriving at Salamis, they declared the word of God in the Jewish synagogues; they had John with them as their assistant. ⁶ They went through the whole island as far as Paphos, and there they came upon a sorcerer, a Jew who posed as a prophet, Barjesus by name. ⁷ He was in the retinue of the governor, Sergius Paulus, a learned man, who had sent for Barnabas and Saul and wanted to hear the word of God. ⁸ This Elymas the sorcerer (so his name may be translated) opposed them, trying to turn the governor away from the faith. ⁹ But Saul, also known as Paul, filled with the Holy Spirit, fixed his eyes on him ¹⁰ and said, 'You are a swindler, an out-and-out fraud! You son of the devil and enemy of all goodness, will you never stop perverting the straight ways of the Lord? ¹¹ Look now, the hand of the Lord strikes: you shall be blind, and for a time you shall not see the light of the sun.' At once mist and darkness came over his eyes, and he groped about for someone to lead him by the hand. ¹² When the governor saw what had happened he became a believer, deeply impressed by what he learnt about the Lord.

¹³ Sailing from Paphos, Paul and his companions went to Perga in Pamphylia; John, however, left them and returned to Jerusalem. ¹⁴ From Perga they continued their journey as far as Pisidian Antioch. On the sabbath they went to synagogue and took their seats; ¹⁵ and after the readings from the law and the prophets, the officials of the synagogue sent this message to them: 'Friends, if you have anything to say to the people by way of exhortation, let us hear it.' ¹⁶ Paul stood up, raised his hand for silence, and began.

'Listen, men of Israel and you others who worship God! ¹⁷ The God of this people, Israel, chose our forefathers. When they were still living as aliens in Egypt, he made them into a great people and, with arm outstretched, brought them out of that country. ¹⁸ For some forty years he bore with their conduct in the desert. ¹⁹ Then in the Canaanite country, after overthrowing seven nations,

whose lands he gave them to be their heritage ²⁰ for some four hundred and fifty years, he appointed judges for them until the time of the prophet Samuel.

²¹ 'It was then that they asked for a king, and God gave them Saul son of Kish, a man of the tribe of Benjamin. He reigned for forty years ²² before God removed him and appointed David as their king, with this commendation: "I have found David the son of Jesse to be a man after my own heart; he will carry out all my purposes." ²³ This is the man from whose descendants God, as he promised, has brought Israel a saviour, Jesus. ²⁴ John had made ready for his coming by proclaiming a baptism in token of repentance to the whole people of Israel; ²⁵ and, nearing the end of his earthly course, John said, "I am not the one you think I am. No, after me comes one whose sandals I am not worthy to unfasten."

²⁶ 'My brothers, who come of Abraham's stock, and others among you who worship God, we are the people to whom this message of salvation has been sent. ²⁷ The people of Jerusalem and their rulers did not recognize Jesus, or understand the words of the prophets which are read sabbath by sabbath; indeed, they fulfilled them by condemning him. ²⁸ Though they failed to find grounds for the sentence of death, they asked Pilate to have him executed. ²⁹ When they had carried out all that the scriptures said about him, they took him down from the gibbet and laid him in a tomb. ³⁰ But God raised him from the dead; ³¹ and over a period of many days he appeared to those who had come up with him from Galilee to Jerusalem, and they are now his witnesses before our people.

³² 'We are here to give you the good news that God, who made the promise to the fathers, ³³ has fulfilled it for the children by raising Jesus from the dead, as indeed it stands written in the second Psalm: "You are my son; this day I have begotten you." ³⁴ Again, that he raised him from the dead, never to be subjected to corruption, he declares in these words: "I will give you the blessings promised to David, holy and sure." ³⁵ This is borne out by another passage: "You will not let

---

13:18 he ... conduct: *some witnesses read* he sustained them. *for our children; others read* for us their children.   13:33 **for the children:** *some witnesses read*

your faithful servant suffer corruption."
[36] As for David, when he had served the purpose of God in his own generation, he died and was gathered to his fathers, and suffered corruption; [37] but the one whom God raised up did not suffer corruption. [38] You must understand, my brothers, it is through him that forgiveness of sins is now being proclaimed to you. [39] It is through him that everyone who has faith is acquitted of everything for which there was no acquittal under the law of Moses. [40] Beware, then, lest you bring down upon yourselves the doom proclaimed by the prophets: [41] "See this, you scoffers, marvel, and begone; for I am doing a deed in your days, a deed which you will never believe when you are told of it."'

[42] As they were leaving the synagogue they were asked to come again and speak on these subjects next sabbath; [43] and after the congregation had dispersed, many Jews and gentile worshippers went with Paul and Barnabas, who spoke to them and urged them to hold fast to the grace of God.

[44] On the following sabbath almost the whole city gathered to hear the word of God. [45] When the Jews saw the crowds, they were filled with jealous resentment, and contradicted what Paul had said with violent abuse. [46] But Paul and Barnabas were outspoken in their reply. 'It was necessary', they said, 'that the word of God should be declared to you first. But since you reject it and judge yourselves unworthy of eternal life, we now turn to the Gentiles. [47] For these are our instructions from the Lord: "I have appointed you to be a light for the Gentiles, and a means of salvation to earth's farthest bounds."' [48] When the Gentiles heard this, they were overjoyed and thankfully acclaimed the word of the Lord, and those who were marked out for eternal life became believers. [49] Thus the word of the Lord spread throughout the region. [50] But the Jews stirred up feeling among those worshippers who were women of standing, and among the leading men of the city; a campaign of persecution was started against Paul and Barnabas, and they were expelled from the district. [51] They shook the dust off their feet in protest against them and went to Iconium. [52] And the disciples were filled with joy and with the Holy Spirit.

14 At Iconium they went together into the Jewish synagogue and spoke to such purpose that Jews and Greeks in large numbers became believers. [2] But the unconverted Jews stirred up the Gentiles and poisoned their minds against the Christians. [3] So Paul and Barnabas stayed on for some time, and spoke boldly and openly in reliance on the Lord, who confirmed the message of his grace by enabling them to work signs and miracles. [4] The populace was divided, some siding with the Jews, others with the apostles. [5] A move was made by Gentiles and Jews together, with the connivance of the city authorities, to maltreat them and stone them, [6] and when they became aware of this, they made their escape to the Lycaonian cities of Lystra and Derbe and the surrounding country. [7] There they continued to spread the good news.

[8] At Lystra a cripple, lame from birth, who had never walked in his life, [9] sat listening to Paul as he spoke. Paul fixed his eyes on him and, seeing that he had the faith to be cured, [10] said in a loud voice, 'Stand up straight on your feet'; and he sprang up and began to walk. [11] When the crowds saw what Paul had done, they shouted, in their native Lycaonian, 'The gods have come down to us in human form!' [12] They called Barnabas Zeus, and Paul they called Hermes, because he was the spokesman. [13] The priest of Zeus, whose temple was just outside the city, brought oxen and garlands to the gates, and he and the people were about to offer sacrifice.

[14] But when the apostles Barnabas and Paul heard of it, they tore their clothes and rushed into the crowd shouting, [15] 'Men, why are you doing this? We are human beings, just like you. The good news we bring tells you to turn from these follies to the living God, who made heaven and earth and sea and everything in them. [16] In past ages he has allowed all nations to go their own way; [17] and yet he has not left you without some clue to his nature, in the benefits he bestows: he sends you rain from heaven and the crops in their seasons, and gives you food in plenty and keeps you in good heart.' [18] Even with these words they barely managed to prevent the crowd from offering sacrifice to them.

[19] Then Jews from Antioch and Iconium

came on the scene and won over the crowds. They stoned Paul, and dragged him out of the city, thinking him dead. [20] The disciples formed a ring round him, and he got to his feet and went into the city. Next day he left with Barnabas for Derbe.

[21] After bringing the good news to that town and gaining many converts, they returned to Lystra, then to Iconium, then to Antioch, [22] strengthening the disciples and encouraging them to be true to the faith. They warned them that to enter the kingdom of God we must undergo many hardships. [23] They also appointed for them elders in each congregation, and with prayer and fasting committed them to the Lord in whom they had put their trust.

[24] They passed through Pisidia and came into Pamphylia. [25] When they had delivered the message at Perga, they went down to Attalia, [26] and from there sailed to Antioch, where they had originally been commended to the grace of God for the task which they had now completed. [27] On arrival there, they called the congregation together and reported all that God had accomplished through them, and how he had thrown open the gates of faith to the Gentiles. [28] And they stayed for some time with the disciples there.

15 SOME people who had come down from Judaea began to teach the brotherhood that those who were not circumcised in accordance with Mosaic practice could not be saved. [2] That brought them into fierce dissension and controversy with Paul and Barnabas, and it was arranged that these two and some others from Antioch should go up to Jerusalem to see the apostles and elders about this question.

[3] They were sent on their way by the church, and travelled through Phoenicia and Samaria, telling the full story of the conversion of the Gentiles, and causing great rejoicing among all the Christians. [4] When they reached Jerusalem they were welcomed by the church and the apostles and elders, and they reported all that God had accomplished through them. [5] But some of the Pharisaic party

who had become believers came forward and declared, 'Those Gentiles must be circumcised and told to keep the law of Moses.'

[6] The apostles and elders met to look into this matter, [7] and, after a long debate, Peter rose to address them. 'My friends,' he said, 'in the early days, as you yourselves know, God made his choice among you: from my lips the Gentiles were to hear and believe the message of the gospel. [8] And God, who can read human hearts, showed his approval by giving the Holy Spirit to them as he did to us. [9] He made no difference between them and us; for he purified their hearts by faith. [10] Then why do you now try God's patience by laying on the shoulders of these converts a yoke which neither we nor our forefathers were able to bear? [11] For our belief is that we are saved in the same way as they are: by the grace of the Lord Jesus.'

[12] At that the whole company fell silent and listened to Barnabas and Paul as they described all the signs and portents that God had worked among the Gentiles through them.

[13] When they had finished speaking, James summed up: 'My friends,' he said, 'listen to me. [14] Simon has described how it first happened that God, in his providence, chose from among the Gentiles a people to bear his name. [15] This agrees with the words of the prophets: as scripture has it,

[16] Thereafter I will return and
  rebuild the fallen house of David;
I will rebuild its ruins and set it up
  again,
[17] that the rest of mankind may seek
  the Lord,
all the Gentiles whom I have claimed
  for my own.
Thus says the Lord, who is doing this
[18] as he made known long ago.

[19] 'In my judgement, therefore, we should impose no irksome restrictions on those of the Gentiles who are turning to God; [20] instead we should instruct them by letter to abstain from things polluted by contact with idols, from fornication, from anything that has been strangled,

15:14 Simon: *Gk* Simeon.   15:20 from fornication ... blood: *some witnesses omit* from fornication; *others omit* from anything that has been strangled; *some add (after* blood) and to refrain from doing to others what they would not like done to themselves.

and from blood. ²¹ Moses, after all, has never lacked spokesmen in every town for generations past; he is read in the synagogues sabbath by sabbath.'

²² Then, with the agreement of the whole church, the apostles and elders resolved to choose representatives and send them to Antioch with Paul and Barnabas. They chose two leading men in the community, Judas Barsabbas and Silas, ²³ and gave them this letter to deliver:

From the apostles and elders to our brothers of gentile origin in Antioch, Syria, and Cilicia. Greetings!

²⁴ We have heard that some of our number, without any instructions from us, have disturbed you with their talk and unsettled your minds. ²⁵ In consequence, we have resolved unanimously to send to you our chosen representatives with our well-beloved Barnabas and Paul, ²⁶ who have given up their lives to the cause of our Lord Jesus Christ; ²⁷ so we are sending Judas and Silas, who will, by word of mouth, confirm what is written in this letter. ²⁸ It is the decision of the Holy Spirit, and our decision, to lay no further burden upon you beyond these essentials: ²⁹ you are to abstain from meat that has been offered to idols, from blood, from anything that has been strangled, and from fornication. If you keep yourselves free from these things you will be doing well. Farewell.

³⁰ So they took their leave and travelled down to Antioch, where they called the congregation together and delivered the letter. ³¹ When it was read, all rejoiced at the encouragement it brought, ³² and Judas and Silas, who were themselves prophets, said much to encourage and strengthen the members. ³³ After spending some time there, they took their leave with the good wishes of the brethren, to return to those who had sent them. ³⁵ But Paul and Barnabas stayed on at Antioch, where, along with many others, they taught and preached the word of the Lord.

³⁶ AFTER a while Paul said to Barnabas, 'Let us go back and see how our brothers are getting on in the various towns where we proclaimed the word of the Lord.' ³⁷ Barnabas wanted to take John Mark with them; ³⁸ but Paul insisted that the man who had deserted them in Pamphylia and had not gone on to share in their work was not the man to take with them now. ³⁹ The dispute was so sharp that they parted company. Barnabas took Mark with him and sailed for Cyprus. ⁴⁰ Paul chose Silas and started on his journey, commended by the brothers to the grace of the Lord. ⁴¹ He travelled through Syria and Cilicia bringing new strength to the churches.

16 He went on to Derbe and then to Lystra, where he found a disciple named Timothy, the son of a Jewish Christian mother and a gentile father, ² well spoken of by the Christians at Lystra and Iconium. ³ Paul wanted to take him with him when he left, so he had him circumcised out of consideration for the Jews who lived in those parts, for they all knew that his father was a Gentile. ⁴ As they made their way from town to town they handed on the decisions taken by the apostles and elders in Jerusalem and enjoined their observance. ⁵ So, day by day, the churches grew stronger in faith and increased in numbers.

⁶ They travelled through the Phrygian and Galatian region, prevented by the Holy Spirit from delivering the message in the province of Asia. ⁷ When they approached the Mysian border they tried to enter Bithynia, but, as the Spirit of Jesus would not allow them, ⁸ they passed through Mysia and reached the coast at Troas. ⁹ During the night a vision came to Paul: a Macedonian stood there appealing to him, 'Cross over to Macedonia and help us.' ¹⁰ As soon as he had seen this vision, we set about getting a passage to Macedonia, convinced that God had called us to take the good news there.

¹¹ We sailed from Troas and made a straight run to Samothrace, the next day to Neapolis, ¹² and from there to Philippi, a leading city in that district of Macedonia and a Roman colony. Here we stayed for

---

15:29 **from anything** ... **fornication:** *some witnesses omit* from anything that has been strangled; *some omit* and from fornication; *and some witnesses add* and refrain from doing to others what you would not like done to yourselves.   15:33 **sent them:** *some witnesses add* ³⁴ But Silas decided to remain there.   16:6 **through** ... **region:** *or* through Phrygia and the Galatian region.

some days, [13] and on the sabbath we went outside the city gate by the riverside, where we thought there would be a place of prayer; we sat down and talked to the women who had gathered there. [14] One of those listening was called Lydia, a dealer in purple fabric, who came from the city of Thyatira; she was a worshipper of God, and the Lord opened her heart to respond to what Paul said. [15] She was baptized, and her household with her, and then she urged us, 'Now that you have accepted me as a believer in the Lord, come and stay at my house.' And she insisted on our going.

[16] Once, on our way to the place of prayer, we met a slave-girl who was possessed by a spirit of divination and brought large profits to her owners by telling fortunes. [17] She followed Paul and the rest of us, shouting, 'These men are servants of the Most High God, and are declaring to you a way of salvation.' [18] She did this day after day, until, in exasperation, Paul rounded on the spirit. 'I command you in the name of Jesus Christ to come out of her,' he said, and it came out instantly.

[19] When the girl's owners saw that their hope of profit had gone, they seized Paul and Silas and dragged them to the city authorities in the main square; [20] bringing them before the magistrates, they alleged, 'These men are causing a disturbance in our city; they are Jews, [21] and they are advocating practices which it is illegal for us Romans to adopt and follow.' [22] The mob joined in the attack; and the magistrates had the prisoners stripped and gave orders for them to be flogged. [23] After a severe beating they were flung into prison and the jailer was ordered to keep them under close guard. [24] In view of these orders, he put them into the inner prison and secured their feet in the stocks.

[25] About midnight Paul and Silas, at their prayers, were singing praises to God, and the other prisoners were listening, [26] when suddenly there was such a violent earthquake that the foundations of the jail were shaken; the doors burst open and all the prisoners found their fetters unfastened. [27] The jailer woke up to see the prison doors wide open and, assuming that the prisoners had escaped, drew his sword intending to kill himself. [28] But Paul shouted, 'Do yourself no harm; we are all here.' [29] The jailer called for lights, rushed in, and threw himself down before Paul and Silas, trembling with fear. [30] He then escorted them out and said, 'Sirs, what must I do to be saved?' [31] They answered, 'Put your trust in the Lord Jesus, and you will be saved, you and your household,' [32] and they imparted the word of the Lord to him and to everyone in his house. [33] At that late hour of the night the jailer took them and washed their wounds, and there and then he and his whole family were baptized. [34] He brought them up into his house, set out a meal, and rejoiced with his whole household in his new-found faith in God.

[35] When daylight came, the magistrates sent their officers with the order, 'Release those men.' [36] The jailer reported these instructions to Paul: 'The magistrates have sent an order for your release. Now you are free to go in peace.' [37] But Paul said to the officers: 'We are Roman citizens! They gave us a public flogging and threw us into prison without trial. Are they now going to smuggle us out by stealth? No indeed! Let them come in person and escort us out.' [38] The officers reported his words to the magistrates. Alarmed to hear that they were Roman citizens, [39] they came and apologized to them, and then escorted them out and requested them to go away from the city. [40] On leaving the prison, they went to Lydia's house, where they met their fellow-Christians and spoke words of encouragement to them, and then they took their departure.

17 THEY now travelled by way of Amphipolis and Apollonia and came to Thessalonica, where there was a Jewish synagogue. [2] Following his usual practice Paul went to their meetings; and for the next three sabbaths he argued with them, quoting texts of scripture [3] which he expounded and applied to show that the Messiah had to suffer and rise from the dead. 'And this Jesus', he said, 'whom I am proclaiming to you is the Messiah.' [4] Some of them were convinced and joined Paul and Silas, as did a

16:13 where ... prayer: *some witnesses read* where there was a recognized place of prayer.

great number of godfearing Gentiles and a good many influential women.
⁵The Jews in their jealousy recruited some ruffians from the dregs of society to gather a mob. They put the city in an uproar, and made for Jason's house with the intention of bringing Paul and Silas before the town assembly. ⁶Failing to find them, they dragged Jason himself and some members of the congregation before the magistrates, shouting, 'The men who have made trouble the whole world over have now come here, ⁷and Jason has harboured them. All of them flout the emperor's laws, and assert there is a rival king, Jesus.' ⁸These words alarmed the mob and the magistrates also, ⁹who took security from Jason and the others before letting them go.
¹⁰As soon as darkness fell, the members of the congregation sent Paul and Silas off to Beroea; and, on arrival, they made their way to the synagogue. ¹¹The Jews here were more fair-minded than those at Thessalonica: they received the message with great eagerness, studying the scriptures every day to see whether it was true. ¹²Many of them therefore became believers, and so did a fair number of Gentiles, women of standing as well as men. ¹³But when the Thessalonian Jews learnt that the word of God had now been proclaimed by Paul in Beroea, they followed him there to stir up trouble and rouse the rabble. ¹⁴At once the members of the congregation sent Paul down to the coast, while Silas and Timothy both stayed behind. ¹⁵Paul's escort brought him as far as Athens, and came away with instructions for Silas and Timothy to rejoin him with all speed.
¹⁶While Paul was waiting for them at Athens, he was outraged to see the city so full of idols. ¹⁷He argued in the synagogue with the Jews and gentile worshippers, and also in the city square every day with casual passers-by. ¹⁸Moreover, some of the Epicurean and Stoic philosophers joined issue with him. Some said, 'What can this charlatan be trying to say?' and others, 'He would appear to be a propagandist for foreign deities'—this because he was preaching about Jesus and the Resurrection. ¹⁹They brought him to

the Council of the Areopagus and asked, 'May we know what this new doctrine is that you propound? ²⁰You are introducing ideas that sound strange to us, and we should like to know what they mean.' ²¹Now, all the Athenians and the resident foreigners had time for nothing except talking or hearing about the latest novelty.
²²Paul stood up before the Council of the Areopagus and began: 'Men of Athens, I see that in everything that concerns religion you are uncommonly scrupulous. ²³As I was going round looking at the objects of your worship, I noticed among other things an altar bearing the inscription "To an Unknown God". What you worship but do not know—this is what I now proclaim.
²⁴'The God who created the world and everything in it, and who is Lord of heaven and earth, does not live in shrines made by human hands. ²⁵It is not because he lacks anything that he accepts service at our hands, for he is himself the universal giver of life and breath—indeed of everything. ²⁶He created from one stock every nation of men to inhabit the whole earth's surface. He determined their eras in history and the limits of their territory. ²⁷They were to seek God in the hope that, groping after him, they might find him; though indeed he is not far from each one of us, ²⁸for in him we live and move, in him we exist; as some of your own poets have said, "We are also his offspring." ²⁹Being God's offspring, then, we ought not to suppose that the deity is like an image in gold or silver or stone, shaped by human craftsmanship and design. ³⁰God has overlooked the age of ignorance; but now he commands men and women everywhere to repent, ³¹because he has fixed the day on which he will have the world judged, and justly judged, by a man whom he has designated; of this he has given assurance to all by raising him from the dead.'
³²When they heard about the raising of the dead, some scoffed; others said, 'We will hear you on this subject some other time.' ³³So Paul left the assembly. ³⁴Some men joined him and became believers, including Dionysius, a member of the

17:19 to ... **Areopagus:** *or* to Mars' Hill.   17:22 before ... **Areopagus:** *or* in the middle of Mars' Hill.
17:26 **determined ... history:** *or* fixed the ordered seasons.

Council of the Areopagus; and also a woman named Damaris, with others besides.

18 After this he left Athens and went to Corinth. [2] There he met a Jew named Aquila, a native of Pontus, and his wife Priscilla; they had recently arrived from Italy because Claudius had issued an edict that all Jews should leave Rome. Paul approached them [3] and, because he was of the same trade, he made his home with them; they were tentmakers and Paul worked with them. [4] He also held discussions in the synagogue sabbath by sabbath, trying to convince both Jews and Gentiles.

[5] Then Silas and Timothy came down from Macedonia, and Paul devoted himself entirely to preaching, maintaining before the Jews that the Messiah is Jesus. [6] When, however, they opposed him and resorted to abuse, he shook out the folds of his cloak and declared, 'Your blood be on your own heads! My conscience is clear! From now on I shall go to the Gentiles.' [7] With that he left, and went to the house of a worshipper of God named Titius Justus, who lived next door to the synagogue. [8] Crispus, the president of the synagogue, became a believer in the Lord, as did all his household; and a number of Corinthians who heard him believed and were baptized. [9] One night in a vision the Lord said to Paul, 'Have no fear: go on with your preaching and do not be silenced. [10] I am with you, and no attack shall harm you, for I have many in this city who are my people.' [11] So he settled there for eighteen months, teaching the word of God among them.

[12] But when Gallio was proconsul of Achaia, the Jews made a concerted attack on Paul and brought him before the court. [13] 'This man', they said, 'is inducing people to worship God in ways that are against the law.' [14] Paul was just about to speak when Gallio declared, 'If it had been a question of crime or grave misdemeanour, I should, of course, have given you Jews a patient hearing, [15] but if it is some bickering about words and names and your Jewish law, you may settle it yourselves. I do not intend to be a judge of these matters.' [16] And he dismissed them from the court. [17] Then they all attacked Sosthenes, the president of the synagogue, and beat him up in full view of the tribunal. But all this left Gallio quite unconcerned.

[18] Paul stayed on at Corinth for some time, and then took leave of the congregation. Accompanied by Priscilla and Aquila, he sailed for Syria, having had his hair cut off at Cenchreae in fulfilment of a vow. [19] They put in at Ephesus, where he parted from his companions; he himself went into the synagogue and held a discussion with the Jews. [20] He was asked to stay longer, but he declined [21] and set sail from Ephesus, promising, as he took leave of them, 'I shall come back to you if it is God's will.' [22] On landing at Caesarea, he went up and greeted the church; and then went down to Antioch. [23] After some time there he set out again on a journey through the Galatian country and then through Phrygia, bringing new strength to all the disciples.

[24] THERE arrived at Ephesus a Jew named Apollos, an Alexandrian by birth, an eloquent man, powerful in his use of the scriptures. [25] He had been instructed in the way of the Lord and was full of spiritual fervour; and in his discourses he taught accurately the facts about Jesus, though the only baptism he knew was John's. [26] He now began to speak boldly in the synagogue, where Priscilla and Aquila heard him; they took him in hand and expounded the way to him in greater detail. [27] Finding that he wanted to go across to Achaia, the congregation gave him their support, and wrote to the disciples there to make him welcome. From the time of his arrival, he was very helpful to those who had by God's grace become believers, [28] for he strenuously confuted the Jews, demonstrating publicly from the scriptures that the Messiah is Jesus.

19 While Apollos was at Corinth, Paul travelled through the inland regions till he came to Ephesus, where he found a number of disciples. [2] When he asked them, 'Did you receive the Holy Spirit when you became believers?' they replied, 'No, we were not even told that there is a Holy Spirit.' [3] He asked, 'Then what baptism were you given?' 'John's

---

18:24 **an eloquent man:** *or* a learned man.   18:26 **the way:** *some witnesses read* the way of God.

baptism,' they answered. [4] Paul said, 'The baptism that John gave was a baptism in token of repentance, and he told the people to put their trust in one who was to come after him, that is, in Jesus.' [5] On hearing this they were baptized into the name of the Lord Jesus; [6] and when Paul had laid his hands on them, the Holy Spirit came upon them and they spoke in tongues of ecstasy and prophesied. [7] There were about a dozen men in all.

[8] During the next three months he attended the synagogue and with persuasive argument spoke boldly about the kingdom of God. [9] When some proved obdurate and would not believe, speaking evil of the new way before the congregation, he withdrew from them, taking the disciples with him, and continued to hold discussions daily in the lecture hall of Tyrannus. [10] This went on for two years, with the result that the whole population of the province of Asia, both Jews and Gentiles, heard the word of the Lord. [11] God worked extraordinary miracles through Paul: [12] when handkerchiefs and scarves which had been in contact with his skin were carried to the sick, they were cured of their diseases, and the evil spirits came out of them.

[13] Some itinerant Jewish exorcists tried their hand at using the name of the Lord Jesus on those possessed by evil spirits; they would say, 'I adjure you by Jesus whom Paul proclaims.' [14] There were seven sons of Sceva, a Jewish chief priest, who were doing this, [15] when the evil spirit responded, 'Jesus I recognize, Paul I know, but who are you?' [16] The man with the evil spirit flew at them, overpowered them all, and handled them with such violence that they ran out of the house battered and naked. [17] Everybody in Ephesus, Jew and Gentile alike, got to know of it, and all were awestruck, while the name of the Lord Jesus gained in honour. [18] Moreover many of those who had become believers came and openly confessed that they had been using magical spells. [19] A good many of those who formerly practised magic collected their books and burnt them publicly, and when the total value was reckoned up it came to fifty thousand pieces of silver. [20] In such ways the word of the Lord showed its power, spreading more and more widely and effectively.

[21] When matters had reached this stage, Paul made up his mind to visit Macedonia and Achaia and then go on to Jerusalem. 'After I have been there,' he said, 'I must see Rome also.' [22] He sent two of his assistants, Timothy and Erastus, to Macedonia, while he himself stayed some time longer in the province of Asia.

[23] It was about this time that the Christian movement gave rise to a serious disturbance. [24] There was a man named Demetrius, a silversmith who made silver shrines of Artemis, and provided considerable employment for the craftsmen. [25] He called a meeting of them and of the workers in allied trades, and addressed them: 'As you men know, our prosperity depends on this industry. [26] But this fellow Paul, as you can see and hear for yourselves, has perverted crowds of people with his propaganda, not only at Ephesus but also in practically the whole of the province of Asia; he tells them that gods made by human hands are not gods at all. [27] There is danger for us here; it is not only that our line of business will be discredited, but also that the sanctuary of the great goddess Artemis will cease to command respect; and then it will not be long before she who is worshipped by all Asia and the civilized world is brought down from her divine pre-eminence.'

[28] On hearing this, they were enraged, and began to shout, 'Great is Artemis of the Ephesians!' [29] The whole city was in an uproar; they made a concerted rush into the theatre, hustling along with them Paul's travelling companions, the Macedonians Gaius and Aristarchus. [30] Paul wanted to appear before the assembly but the other Christians would not let him. [31] Even some of the dignitaries of the province, who were friendly towards him, sent a message urging him not to venture into the theatre. [32] Meanwhile some were shouting one thing, some another, for the assembly was in an uproar and most of them did not know what they had all come for. [33] Some of the crowd explained the trouble to Alexander, whom the Jews had pushed to the front, and he, motioning for silence, attempted to make a defence before the assembly. [34] But when they recognized that he was a Jew, one shout arose from them all: 'Great is Artemis of the Ephesians!' and they kept it up for about two hours.

³⁵The town clerk, however, quietened the crowd. 'Citizens of Ephesus,' he said, 'all the world knows that our city of Ephesus is temple warden of the great Artemis and of that image of her which fell from heaven. ³⁶Since these facts are beyond dispute, your proper course is to keep calm and do nothing rash. ³⁷These men whom you have brought here as offenders have committed no sacrilege and uttered no blasphemy against our goddess. ³⁸If, therefore, Demetrius and his craftsmen have a case against anyone, there are assizes and there are proconsuls; let the parties bring their charges and countercharges. ³⁹But if it is a larger question you are raising, it will be dealt with in the statutory assembly. ⁴⁰We certainly run the risk of being charged with riot for this day's work. There is no justification for it, and it would be impossible for us to give any explanation of this turmoil.' ⁴¹With that he dismissed the assembly.

20 WHEN the disturbance was over, Paul sent for the disciples and, after encouraging them, said goodbye and set out on his journey to Macedonia. ²He travelled through that region, constantly giving encouragement to the Christians, and finally reached Greece. ³When he had spent three months there and was on the point of embarking for Syria, a plot was laid against him by the Jews, so he decided to return by way of Macedonia. ⁴He was accompanied by Sopater son of Pyrrhus from Beroea, Aristarchus and Secundus from Thessalonica, Gaius of Derbe, and Timothy, and from Asia Tychicus and Trophimus. ⁵These went ahead and waited for us at Troas; ⁶we ourselves sailed from Philippi after the Passover season, and five days later rejoined them at Troas, where we spent a week.

⁷On the Saturday night, when we gathered for the breaking of bread, Paul, who was to leave next day, addressed the congregation and went on speaking until midnight. ⁸Now there were many lamps in the upstairs room where we were assembled, ⁹and a young man named Eutychus, who was sitting on the window-ledge, grew more and more drowsy as Paul went on talking, until, completely overcome by sleep, he fell from the third storey to the ground, and was picked up dead. ¹⁰Paul went down, threw himself upon him, and clasped him in his arms. 'Do not distress yourselves,' he said to them; 'he is alive.' ¹¹He then went upstairs, broke bread and ate, and after much conversation, which lasted until dawn, he departed. ¹²And they took the boy home, greatly relieved that he was alive.

¹³We went on ahead to the ship and embarked for Assos, where we were to take Paul aboard; this was the arrangement he had made, since he was going to travel by road. ¹⁴When he met us at Assos, we took him aboard and proceeded to Mitylene. ¹⁵We sailed from there and next day arrived off Chios. On the second day we made Samos, and the following day we reached Miletus. ¹⁶Paul had decided to bypass Ephesus and so avoid having to spend time in the province of Asia; he was eager to be in Jerusalem on the day of Pentecost, if that were possible. ¹⁷He did, however, send from Miletus to Ephesus and summon the elders of the church. ¹⁸When they joined him, he spoke to them as follows.

'You know how, from the day that I first set foot in the province of Asia, I spent my whole time with you, ¹⁹serving the Lord in all humility amid the sorrows and trials that came upon me through the intrigues of the Jews. ²⁰You know that I kept back nothing that was for your good: I delivered the message to you, and taught you, in public and in your homes; ²¹with Jews and Gentiles alike I insisted on repentance before God and faith in our Lord Jesus. ²²Now, as you see, I am constrained by the Spirit to go to Jerusalem. I do not know what will befall me there, ²³except that in city after city the Holy Spirit assures me that imprisonment and hardships await me. ²⁴For myself, I set no store by life; all I want is to finish the race, and complete the task which the Lord Jesus assigned to me, that of bearing my testimony to the gospel of God's grace.

²⁵'One thing more: I have gone about among you proclaiming the kingdom, but now I know that none of you will ever see my face again. ²⁶That being so, I here and

20: 6 **after ... season:** *lit.* after the days of Unleavened Bread.

now declare that no one's fate can be laid at my door; I have kept back nothing; ²⁷ I have disclosed to you the whole purpose of God. ²⁸ Keep guard over yourselves and over all the flock of which the Holy Spirit has given you charge, as shepherds of the church of the Lord, which he won for himself by his own blood. ²⁹ I know that when I am gone, savage wolves will come in among you and will not spare the flock. ³⁰ Even from your own number men will arise who will distort the truth in order to get the disciples to break away and follow them. ³¹ So be on the alert; remember how with tears I never ceased to warn each one of you night and day for three years.

³² 'And now I commend you to God and to the word of his grace, which has power to build you up and give you your heritage among all those whom God has made his own. ³³ I have not wanted anyone's money or clothes for myself; ³⁴ you all know that these hands of mine earned enough for the needs of myself and my companions. ³⁵ All along I showed you that it is our duty to help the weak in this way, by hard work, and that we should keep in mind the words of the Lord Jesus, who himself said, "Happiness lies more in giving than in receiving."'

³⁶ As he finished speaking, he knelt down with them all and prayed. ³⁷ There were loud cries of sorrow from them all, as they folded Paul in their arms and kissed him; ³⁸ what distressed them most was his saying that they would never see his face again. Then they escorted him to the ship.

21 We tore ourselves away from them and, putting to sea, made a straight run and came to Cos; next day to Rhodes, and thence to Patara. ² There we found a ship bound for Phoenicia, so we went aboard and sailed in her. ³ We came in sight of Cyprus, and leaving it to port, we continued our voyage to Syria and put in at Tyre, where the ship was to unload her cargo. ⁴ We sought out the disciples and stayed there a week. Warned by the Spirit, they urged Paul to abandon his visit to Jerusalem. ⁵ But when our time ashore was ended, we left and continued our journey; and they and their wives and children all escorted us out of the city.

We knelt down on the beach and prayed, ⁶ and then bade each other goodbye; we went on board, and they returned home.

⁷ We made the passage from Tyre and reached Ptolemais, where we greeted the brotherhood and spent a day with them. ⁸ Next day we left and came to Caesarea, where we went to the home of Philip the evangelist, who was one of the Seven, and stayed with him. ⁹ He had four unmarried daughters, who possessed the gift of prophecy. ¹⁰ When we had been there several days, a prophet named Agabus arrived from Judaea. ¹¹ He came to us, took Paul's belt, bound his own feet and hands with it, and said, 'These are the words of the Holy Spirit: Thus will the Jews in Jerusalem bind the man to whom this belt belongs, and hand him over to the Gentiles.' ¹² When we heard this, we and the local people begged and implored Paul to abandon his visit to Jerusalem. ¹³ Then Paul gave his answer: 'Why all these tears? Why are you trying to weaken my resolution? I am ready, not merely to be bound, but even to die at Jerusalem for the name of the Lord Jesus.' ¹⁴ So, as he would not be dissuaded, we gave up and said, 'The Lord's will be done.'

¹⁵ At the end of our stay we packed our baggage and took the road up to Jerusalem. ¹⁶ Some of the disciples from Caesarea came along with us, to direct us to a Cypriot named Mnason, a Christian from the early days, with whom we were to spend the night. ¹⁷ On our arrival at Jerusalem, the congregation welcomed us gladly.

¹⁸ Next day Paul paid a visit to James; we accompanied him, and all the elders were present. ¹⁹ After greeting them, he described in detail all that God had done among the Gentiles by means of his ministry. ²⁰ When they heard this, they gave praise to God. Then they said to Paul: 'You observe, brother, how many thousands of converts we have among the Jews, all of them staunch upholders of the law. ²¹ Now they have been given certain information about you: it is said that you teach all the Jews in the gentile world to turn their backs on Moses, and tell them not to circumcise their children or follow our way of life. ²² What is to be done,

20: 28 **of the Lord ... blood:** *some witnesses read* of God, which he won for himself by the blood of his Own.

then? They are sure to hear that you have arrived. [23] Our proposal is this: we have four men here who are under a vow; [24] take them with you and go through the ritual of purification together, and pay their expenses, so that they may have their heads shaved; then everyone will know that there is nothing in the reports they have heard about you, but that you are yourself a practising Jew and observe the law. [25] As for the gentile converts, we sent them our decision that they should abstain from meat that has been offered to idols, from blood, from anything that has been strangled, and from fornication.' [26] So Paul took the men, and next day, after going through the ritual of purification with them, he went into the temple to give notice of the date when the period of purification would end and the offering be made for each of them.

Paul's work in Jerusalem

[27] But just before the seven days were up, the Jews from the province of Asia saw him in the temple. They stirred up all the crowd and seized him, [28] shouting, 'Help us, men of Israel! This is the fellow who attacks our people, our law, and this sanctuary, and spreads his teaching the whole world over. What is more, he has brought Gentiles into the temple and profaned this holy place.' [29] They had previously seen Trophimus the Ephesian with him in the city, and assumed that Paul had brought him into the temple.

[30] The whole city was in a turmoil, and people came running from all directions. They seized Paul and dragged him out of the temple, and at once the doors were shut. [31] They were bent on killing him, but word came to the officer commanding the cohort that all Jerusalem was in an uproar. [32] He immediately took a force of soldiers with their centurions and came down at the double to deal with the riot. When the crowd saw the commandant and his troops, they stopped beating Paul. [33] As soon as the commandant could reach Paul, he arrested him and ordered him to be shackled with two chains; he enquired who he was and what he had been doing. [34] Some in the crowd shouted one thing, some another, and as the commandant could not get at the truth

because of the hubbub, he ordered him to be taken to the barracks. [35] When Paul reached the steps, he found himself carried up by the soldiers because of the violence of the mob; [36] for the whole crowd was at their heels yelling, 'Kill him!'

[37] Just before he was taken into the barracks Paul said to the commandant, 'May I have a word with you?' The commandant said, 'So you speak Greek? [38] Then you are not the Egyptian who started a revolt some time ago and led a force of four thousand terrorists out into the desert?' [39] Paul replied, 'I am a Jew from Tarsus in Cilicia, a citizen of no mean city. May I have your permission to speak to the people?' [40] When this was given, Paul stood on the steps and raised his hand to call for the attention of the people. As soon as quiet was restored, he addressed them in the Jewish language:

22 'Brothers and fathers, give me a hearing while I put my case to you.' [2] When they heard him speaking to them in their own language, they listened more quietly. [3] 'I am a true-born Jew,' he began, 'a native of Tarsus in Cilicia. I was brought up in this city, and as a pupil of Gamaliel I was thoroughly trained in every point of our ancestral law. I have always been ardent in God's service, as you all are today. [4] And so I persecuted this movement to the death, arresting its followers, men and women alike, and committing them to prison, [5] as the high priest and the whole Council of Elders can testify. It was they who gave me letters to our fellow-Jews at Damascus, and I was on my way to make arrests there also and bring the prisoners to Jerusalem for punishment. [6] What happened to me on my journey was this: when I was nearing Damascus, about midday, a great light suddenly flashed from the sky all around me. [7] I fell to the ground, and heard a voice saying: "Saul, Saul, why do you persecute me?" [8] I answered, "Tell me, Lord, who you are." "I am Jesus of Nazareth, whom you are persecuting," he said. [9] My companions saw the light, but did not hear the voice that spoke to me. [10] "What shall I do, Lord?" I asked, and he replied, "Get up, and go on to Damascus; there you will be told all that

21:25 from anything ... strangled: *some witnesses omit.*

you are appointed to do." [11] As I had been blinded by the brilliance of that light, my companions led me by the hand, and so I came to Damascus.

[12] 'There a man called Ananias, a devout observer of the law and well spoken of by all the Jews who lived there, [13] came and stood beside me, and said, "Saul, my brother, receive your sight again!" Instantly I recovered my sight and saw him. [14] He went on: "The God of our fathers appointed you to know his will and to see the Righteous One and to hear him speak, [15] because you are to be his witness to tell the world what you have seen and heard. [16] Do not delay. Be baptized at once and wash away your sins, calling on his name."

[17] 'After my return to Jerusalem, as I was praying in the temple I fell into a trance [18] and saw him there, speaking to me. "Make haste", he said, "and leave Jerusalem quickly, for they will not accept your testimony about me." [19] "But surely, Lord," I answered, "they know that I imprisoned those who believe in you and flogged them in every synagogue; [20] when the blood of Stephen your witness was shed I stood by, approving, and I looked after the clothes of those who killed him." [21] He said to me, "Go, for I mean to send you far away to the Gentiles."'

[22] Up to this point the crowd had given him a hearing; but now they began to shout, 'Down with the scoundrel! He is not fit to be alive!' [23] And as they were yelling and waving their cloaks and flinging dust in the air, [24] the commandant ordered him to be brought into the barracks, and gave instructions that he should be examined under the lash, to find out what reason there was for such an outcry against him. [25] But when they tied him up for the flogging, Paul said to the centurion who was standing there, 'Does the law allow you to flog a Roman citizen, and an unconvicted one at that?' [26] When the centurion heard this, he went and reported to the commandant: 'What are you about? This man is a Roman citizen.' [27] The commandant came to Paul and asked, 'Tell me, are you a Roman citizen?' 'Yes,' said he. [28] The commandant rejoined, 'Citizenship cost me a large sum of money.' Paul said, 'It was mine by birth.' [29] Then those who were about to examine him promptly withdrew; and the commandant himself was alarmed when he realized that Paul was a Roman citizen and that he had put him in irons.

Paul's trials

[30] THE following day, wishing to be quite sure what charge the Jews were bringing against Paul, he released him and ordered the chief priests and the entire Council to assemble. He then brought Paul down to stand before them.

23 With his eyes steadily fixed on the Council, Paul said, 'My brothers, all my life to this day I have lived with a perfectly clear conscience before God.' [2] At this the high priest Ananias ordered his attendants to strike him on the mouth. [3] Paul retorted, 'God will strike you, you whitewashed wall! You sit there to judge me in accordance with the law; then, in defiance of the law, you order me to be struck!' [4] The attendants said, 'Would you insult God's high priest?' [5] 'Brothers,' said Paul, 'I had no idea he was high priest; scripture, I know, says: "You shall not abuse the ruler of your people."'

[6] Well aware that one section of them were Sadducees and the other Pharisees, Paul called out in the Council, 'My brothers, I am a Pharisee, a Pharisee born and bred; and the issue in this trial is our hope of the resurrection of the dead.' [7] At these words the Pharisees and Sadducees fell out among themselves, and the assembly was divided. [8] (The Sadducees deny that there is any resurrection or angel or spirit, but the Pharisees believe in all three.) [9] A great uproar ensued; and some of the scribes belonging to the Pharisaic party openly took sides and declared, 'We find no fault with this man; perhaps an angel or spirit has spoken to him.' [10] In the mounting dissension, the commandant was afraid that Paul would be torn to pieces, so he ordered the troops to go down, pull him out of the crowd, and bring him into the barracks.

[11] The following night the Lord appeared to him and said, 'Keep up your courage! You have affirmed the truth about me in Jerusalem, and you must do the same in Rome.'

[12] When day broke, the Jews banded together and took an oath not to eat or drink until they had killed Paul. [13] There were more than forty in the conspiracy;

[14] they went to the chief priests and elders and said, 'We have bound ourselves by a solemn oath not to taste food until we have killed Paul. [15] It is now up to you and the rest of the Council to apply to the commandant to have him brought down to you on the pretext of a closer investigation of his case; we have arranged to make away with him before he reaches you.'

[16] The son of Paul's sister, however, learnt of the plot and, going to the barracks, obtained entry, and reported it to Paul, [17] who called one of the centurions and said, 'Take this young man to the commandant; he has something to report.' [18] The centurion brought him to the commandant and explained, 'The prisoner Paul sent for me and asked me to bring this young man to you; he has something to tell you.' [19] The commandant took him by the arm, drew him aside, and asked him, 'What is it you have to report?' [20] He replied, 'The Jews have agreed on a plan: they will request you to bring Paul down to the Council tomorrow on the pretext of obtaining more precise information about him. [21] Do not listen to them; for a party more than forty strong are lying in wait for him, and they have sworn not to eat or drink until they have done away with him. They are now ready, waiting only for your consent.' [22] The commandant dismissed the young man, with orders not to let anyone know that he had given him this information.

[23] He then summoned two of his centurions and gave them these orders: 'Have two hundred infantry ready to proceed to Caesarea, together with seventy cavalrymen and two hundred light-armed troops; parade them three hours after sunset, [24] and provide mounts for Paul so that he may be conducted under safe escort to Felix the governor.' [25] And he wrote a letter to this effect:

[26] From Claudius Lysias to His Excellency the Governor Felix. Greeting.
[27] This man was seized by the Jews and was on the point of being murdered when I intervened with the troops, and, on discovering that he was a Roman citizen, I removed him to safety. [28] As I wished to ascertain the ground of their charge against him, I brought him down to their Council. [29] I found that their case had to do with controversial matters of their law, but there was no charge against him which merited death or imprisonment. [30] Information, however, has now been brought to my notice of an attempt to be made on the man's life, so I am sending him to you without delay, and have instructed his accusers to state their case against him before you.

[31] Acting on their orders, the infantry took custody of Paul and brought him by night to Antipatris. [32] Next day they returned to their barracks, leaving the cavalry to escort him the rest of the way. [33] When the cavalry reached Caesarea, they delivered the letter to the governor, and handed Paul over to him. [34] He read the letter, and asked him what province he was from; and learning that he was from Cilicia [35] he said, 'I will hear your case when your accusers arrive.' He ordered him to be held in custody at his headquarters in Herod's palace.

24 [1] FIVE days later the high priest Ananias came down, accompanied by some of the elders and an advocate named Tertullus, to lay before the governor their charge against Paul. [2–3] When the prisoner was called, Tertullus opened the case.

'Your excellency,' he said to Felix, 'we owe it to you that we enjoy unbroken peace, and it is due to your provident care that, in all kinds of ways and in all sorts of places, improvements are being made for the good of this nation. We appreciate this, and are most grateful to you. [4] And now, not to take up too much of your time, I crave your indulgence for a brief statement of our case. [5] We have found this man to be a pest, a fomenter of discord among the Jews all over the world, a ringleader of the sect of the Nazarenes. [6] He made an attempt to profane the temple and we arrested him. [8] If you examine him yourself you can ascertain the truth of all the charges we bring against him.' [9] The Jews supported the

---

24:6 *arrested him: some witnesses add* It was our intention to try him under our law; [7] but Lysias the commandant intervened and forcibly removed him out of our hands, [(8)] ordering his accusers to come before you.

charge, alleging that the facts were as he stated.

[10] The governor then motioned to Paul to speak, and he replied as follows: 'Knowing as I do that for many years you have administered justice to this nation, I make my defence with confidence. [11] As you can ascertain for yourself, it is not more than twelve days since I went up to Jerusalem on a pilgrimage. [12] They did not find me in the temple arguing with anyone or collecting a crowd, or in the synagogues or anywhere else in the city; [13] and they cannot make good the charges they now bring against me. [14] But this much I will admit: I am a follower of the new way (the "sect" they speak of), and it is in that manner that I worship the God of our fathers; for I believe all that is written in the law and the prophets, [15] and in reliance on God I hold the hope, which my accusers too accept, that there is to be a resurrection of good and wicked alike. [16] Accordingly I, no less than they, train myself to keep at all times a clear conscience before God and man.

[17] 'After an absence of several years I came to bring charitable gifts to my nation and to offer sacrifices. [18] I was ritually purified and engaged in this service when they found me in the temple; I had no crowd with me, and there was no disturbance. But some Jews from the province of Asia were there, [19] and if they had any charge against me, it is they who ought to have been in court to state it. [20] Failing that, it is for these persons here present to say what crime they discovered when I was brought before the Council, [21] apart from this one declaration which I made as I stood there: "The issue in my trial before you today is the resurrection of the dead."'

[22] Then Felix, who was well informed about the new way, adjourned the hearing. 'I will decide your case when Lysias the commanding officer comes down,' he said. [23] He gave orders to the centurion to keep Paul under open arrest and not to prevent any of his friends from making themselves useful to him.

[24] Some days later Felix came with his wife Drusilla, who was a Jewess, and sent for Paul. He let him talk to him about faith in Christ Jesus, [25] but when the discourse turned to questions of morals, self-control, and the coming judgement, Felix became alarmed and exclaimed, 'Enough for now! When I find it convenient I will send for you again.' [26] He also had hopes of a bribe from Paul, so he sent for him frequently and talked with him. [27] When two years had passed, Felix was succeeded by Porcius Festus. Wishing to curry favour with the Jews, Felix left Paul in custody.

25 THREE days after taking up his appointment, Festus went up from Caesarea to Jerusalem, [2] where the chief priests and the Jewish leaders laid before him their charge against Paul. [3] They urged Festus to support them in their case and have Paul sent to Jerusalem, for they were plotting to kill him on the way. [4] Festus, however, replied, 'Paul is in safe custody at Caesarea, and I shall be leaving Jerusalem shortly myself; [5] so let your leading men come down with me, and if the man is at fault in any way, let them prosecute him.'

[6] After spending eight or ten days at most in Jerusalem, he went down to Caesarea, and next day he took his seat in court and ordered Paul to be brought before him. [7] When he appeared, the Jews who had come down from Jerusalem stood round bringing many grave charges, which they were unable to prove. [8] Paul protested: 'I have committed no offence against the Jewish law, or against the temple, or against the emperor.' [9] Festus, anxious to ingratiate himself with the Jews, turned to Paul and asked, 'Are you willing to go up to Jerusalem and stand trial on these charges before me there?' [10] But Paul said, 'I am now standing before the emperor's tribunal; that is where I ought to be tried. I have committed no offence against the Jews, as you very well know. [11] If I am guilty of any capital crime, I do not ask to escape the death penalty; if, however, there is no substance in the charges which these men bring against me, it is not open to anyone to hand me over to them. I appeal to Caesar!' [12] Then Festus, after conferring with his advisers, replied, 'You have appealed to Caesar: to Caesar you shall go!'

[13] Some days later King Agrippa and Bernice arrived at Caesarea on a courtesy visit to Festus. [14] They spent some time there, and during their stay Festus raised

Paul's case with the king. 'There is a man here', he said, 'left in custody by Felix; [15] and when I was in Jerusalem the chief priests and elders of the Jews brought a charge against him, demanding his condemnation. [16] I replied that it was not Roman practice to hand a man over before he had been confronted with his accusers and given an opportunity of answering the charge. [17] So when they had come here with me I lost no time, but took my seat in court the very next day and ordered the man to be brought before me. [18] When his accusers rose to speak, they brought none of the charges I was expecting; [19] they merely had certain points of disagreement with him about their religion, and about someone called Jesus, a dead man whom Paul alleged to be alive. [20] Finding myself out of my depth in such discussions, I asked if he was willing to go to Jerusalem and stand trial there on these issues. [21] But Paul appealed to be remanded in custody for his imperial majesty's decision, and I ordered him to be detained until I could send him to the emperor.' [22] Agrippa said to Festus, 'I should rather like to hear the man myself.' 'You shall hear him tomorrow,' he answered.

[23] Next day Agrippa and Bernice came in full state and entered the audience-chamber accompanied by high-ranking officers and prominent citizens; and on the orders of Festus, Paul was brought in. [24] Then Festus said, 'King Agrippa, and all you who are in attendance, you see this man: the whole body of the Jews approached me both in Jerusalem and here, loudly insisting that he had no right to remain alive. [25] It was clear to me, however, that he had committed no capital crime, and when he himself appealed to his imperial majesty, I decided to send him. [26] As I have nothing definite about him to put in writing for our sovereign, I have brought him before you all and particularly before you, King Agrippa, so that as a result of this preliminary enquiry I may have something to report. [27] There is no sense, it seems to me, in sending on a prisoner without indicating the charges against him.'

26 Agrippa said to Paul: 'You have our permission to give an account of yourself.' Then Paul stretched out his hand and began his defence.

[2] 'I consider myself fortunate, King Agrippa, that it is before you I am to make my defence today on all the charges brought against me by the Jews, [3] particularly as you are expert in all our Jewish customs and controversies. I beg you therefore to give me a patient hearing.

[4] 'My life from my youth up, a life spent from the first among my nation and in Jerusalem, is familiar to all Jews. [5] Indeed they have known me long enough to testify, if they would, that I belonged to the strictest group in our religion: I was a Pharisee. [6] It is the hope based on the promise God made to our forefathers that has led to my being on trial today. [7] Our twelve tribes worship with intense devotion night and day in the hope of seeing the fulfilment of that promise; and for this very hope I am accused, your majesty, and accused by Jews. [8] Why should Jews find it incredible that God should raise the dead?

[9] 'I myself once thought it my duty to work actively against the name of Jesus of Nazareth; [10] and I did so in Jerusalem. By authority obtained from the chief priests, I sent many of God's people to prison, and when they were condemned to death, my vote was cast against them. [11] In all the synagogues I tried by repeated punishment to make them commit blasphemy; indeed my fury rose to such a pitch that I extended my persecution to foreign cities.

[12] 'On one such occasion I was travelling to Damascus with authority and commission from the chief priests; [13] and as I was on my way, your majesty, at midday I saw a light from the sky, more brilliant than the sun, shining all around me and my companions. [14] We all fell to the ground, and I heard a voice saying to me in the Jewish language, "Saul, Saul, why do you persecute me? It hurts to kick like this against the goad." [15] I said, "Tell me, Lord, who you are," and the Lord replied, "I am Jesus, whom you are persecuting. [16] But now, get to your feet. I have appeared to you for a purpose: to appoint you my servant and witness, to tell what you have seen and what you shall yet see of me. [17] I will rescue you from your own people and from the Gentiles to whom I am sending you. [18] You are to open their eyes and to turn them from darkness to light, from the dominion of Satan to God, so that they

may obtain forgiveness of sins and a place among those whom God has made his own through faith in me."

[19] 'So, King Agrippa, I did not disobey the heavenly vision. [20] I preached first to the inhabitants of Damascus, and then to Jerusalem and all the country of Judaea, and to the Gentiles, calling on them to repent and turn to God, and to prove their repentance by their deeds. [21] That is why the Jews seized me in the temple and tried to do away with me. [22] But I have had God's help to this very day, and here I stand bearing witness to the great and to the lowly. I assert nothing beyond what was foretold by the prophets and by Moses: [23] that the Messiah would suffer and that, as the first to rise from the dead, he would announce the dawn both to the Jewish people and to the Gentiles.'

[24] While Paul was thus making his defence, Festus shouted at the top of his voice, 'Paul, you are raving; too much study is driving you mad.' [25] 'I am not mad, your excellency,' said Paul; 'what I am asserting is sober truth. [26] The king is well versed in these matters, and I can speak freely to him. I do not believe that he can be unaware of any of these facts, for this has been no hole-and-corner business. [27] King Agrippa, do you believe the prophets? I know you do.' [28] Agrippa said to Paul, 'With a little more of your persuasion you will make a Christian of me.' [29] 'Little or much,' said Paul, 'I wish to God that not only you, but all those who are listening to me today, might become what I am—apart from these chains!'

[30] With that the king rose, and with him the governor, Bernice, and the rest of the company, [31] and after they had withdrawn they talked it over. 'This man', they agreed, 'is doing nothing that deserves death or imprisonment.' [32] Agrippa said to Festus, 'The fellow could have been discharged, if he had not appealed to the emperor.'

Paul's journey to Rome

27 WHEN it was decided that we should sail for Italy, Paul and some other prisoners were handed over to a centurion named Julius, of the Augustan Cohort. [2] We embarked in a ship of Adramyttium, bound for ports in the province of Asia, and put out to sea. Aristarchus, a Macedonian from Thessalonica, came with us. [3] Next day we landed at Sidon, and Julius very considerately allowed Paul to go to his friends to be cared for. [4] Leaving Sidon we sailed under the lee of Cyprus because of the head winds, [5] then across the open sea off the coast of Cilicia and Pamphylia, and so reached Myra in Lycia.

[6] There the centurion found an Alexandrian vessel bound for Italy and put us on board. [7] For a good many days we made little headway, and we were hard put to it to reach Cnidus. Then, as the wind continued against us, off Salmone we began to sail under the lee of Crete, [8] and, hugging the coast, struggled on to a place called Fair Havens, not far from the town of Lasea.

[9] By now much time had been lost, and with the Fast already over, it was dangerous to go on with the voyage. So Paul gave them this warning: [10] 'I can see, gentlemen, that this voyage will be disastrous; it will mean heavy loss, not only of ship and cargo but also of life.' [11] But the centurion paid more attention to the captain and to the owner of the ship than to what Paul said; [12] and as the harbour was unsuitable for wintering, the majority were in favour of putting to sea, hoping, if they could get so far, to winter at Phoenix, a Cretan harbour facing south-west and north-west. [13] When a southerly breeze sprang up, they thought that their purpose was as good as achieved, and, weighing anchor, they sailed along the coast of Crete hugging the land. [14] But before very long a violent wind, the Northeaster as they call it, swept down from the landward side. [15] It caught the ship and, as it was impossible to keep head to wind, we had to give way and run before it. [16] As we passed under the lee of a small island called Cauda, we managed with a struggle to get the ship's boat under control. [17] When they had hoisted it on board, they made use of tackle to brace the ship. Then, afraid of running on to the sandbanks of Syrtis, they put out a sea-anchor and let her drift. [18] Next day, as we were making very heavy weather, they began to lighten the

27:17 put ... sea-anchor: or lowered the mainsail.

131

ship; ¹⁹ and on the third day they jetti-
soned the ship's gear with their own
hands. ²⁰ For days on end there was no
sign of either sun or stars, the storm was
raging unabated, and our last hopes of
coming through alive began to fade.

²¹ When they had gone for a long time
without food, Paul stood up among them
and said, 'You should have taken my
advice, gentlemen, not to put out from
Crete: then you would have avoided this
damage and loss. ²² But now I urge you
not to lose heart; not a single life will be
lost, only the ship. ²³ Last night there
stood by me an angel of the God whose I
am and whom I worship. ²⁴ "Do not be
afraid, Paul," he said; "it is ordained that
you shall appear before Caesar; and, be
assured, God has granted you the lives of
all who are sailing with you." ²⁵ So take
heart, men! I trust God: it will turn out as
I have been told; ²⁶ we are to be cast
ashore on an island.'

²⁷ The fourteenth night came and we
were still drifting in the Adriatic Sea. At
midnight the sailors felt that land was
getting nearer, ²⁸ so they took a sounding
and found twenty fathoms. Sounding
again after a short interval they found
fifteen fathoms; ²⁹ then, fearing that we
might be cast ashore on a rugged coast,
they let go four anchors from the stern
and prayed for daylight to come. ³⁰ The
sailors tried to abandon ship; they had
already lowered the ship's boat, pretend-
ing they were going to lay out anchors
from the bows, ³¹ when Paul said to the
centurion and the soldiers, 'Unless these
men stay on board you cannot reach
safety.' ³² At that the soldiers cut the ropes
of the boat and let it drop away.

³³ Shortly before daybreak Paul urged
them all to take some food. 'For the last
fourteen days', he said, 'you have lived in
suspense and gone hungry; you have
eaten nothing. ³⁴ So have something to
eat, I beg you; your lives depend on it.
Remember, not a hair of your heads will
be lost.' ³⁵ With these words, he took
bread, gave thanks to God in front of them
all, broke it, and began eating. ³⁶ Then
they plucked up courage, and began to
take food themselves. ³⁷ All told there were
on board two hundred and seventy-six of
us. ³⁸ After they had eaten as much as
they wanted, they lightened the ship by
dumping the grain into the sea.

³⁹ When day broke, they did not recognize the land, but they sighted a bay with
a sandy beach, on which they decided, if
possible, to run ashore. ⁴⁰ So they slipped
the anchors and let them go; at the same
time they loosened the lashings of the
steering-paddles, set the foresail to the
wind, and let her drive to the beach. ⁴¹ But
they found themselves caught between
cross-currents and ran the ship aground,
so that the bow stuck fast and remained
immovable, while the stern was being
pounded to pieces by the breakers. ⁴² The
soldiers thought they had better kill the
prisoners for fear that any should swim
away and escape; ⁴³ but the centurion
was determined to bring Paul safely
through, and prevented them from carrying out their plan. He gave orders that
those who could swim should jump over-
board first and get to land; ⁴⁴ the rest were
to follow, some on planks, some on parts
of the ship. And thus it was that all came
safely to land.

28 Once we had made our way to
safety, we identified the island as
Malta. ² The natives treated us with un-
common kindness: because it had started
to rain and was cold they lit a bonfire and
made us all welcome. ³ Paul had got
together an armful of sticks and put them
on the fire, when a viper, driven out by
the heat, fastened on his hand. ⁴ The
natives, seeing the snake hanging on
to his hand, said to one another, 'The
man must be a murderer; he may have
escaped from the sea, but divine justice
would not let him live.' ⁵ Paul, however,
shook off the snake into the fire and was
none the worse. ⁶ They still expected him
to swell up or suddenly drop down dead,
but after waiting a long time without
seeing anything out of the way happen to
him, they changed their minds and said,
'He is a god.'

⁷ In that neighbourhood there were
lands belonging to the chief magistrate of
the island, whose name was Publius. He
took us in and entertained us hospitably
for three days. ⁸ It so happened that this
man's father was in bed suffering from
recurrent bouts of fever and dysentery.
Paul visited him and, after prayer, laid his
hands on him and healed him; ⁹ where-
upon the other sick people on the island
came and were cured. ¹⁰ They honoured
us with many marks of respect, and when

we were leaving they put on board the supplies we needed. [11] Three months had passed when we put to sea in a ship which had wintered in the island; she was the *Castor and Pollux* of Alexandria. [12] We landed at Syracuse and spent three days there; [13] then we sailed up the coast and arrived at Rhegium. Next day a south wind sprang up and we reached Puteoli in two days. [14] There we found fellow-Christians and were invited to stay a week with them. And so to Rome. [15] The Christians there had had news of us and came out to meet us as far as Appii Forum and the Three Taverns, and when Paul saw them, he gave thanks to God and took courage.

[16] WHEN we entered Rome Paul was allowed to lodge privately, with a soldier in charge of him. [17] Three days later he called together the local Jewish leaders, and when they were assembled, he said to them: 'My brothers, I never did anything against our people or against the customs of our forefathers; yet I was arrested in Jerusalem and handed over to the Romans. [18] They examined me and would have liked to release me because there was no capital charge against me; [19] but the Jews objected, and I had no option but to appeal to Caesar; not that I had any accusation to bring against my own people. [20] This is why I have asked to see and talk to you; it is for loyalty to the hope of Israel that I am in these chains.' [21] They replied, 'We have had no communication about you from Judaea, nor has any countryman of ours arrived with any report or gossip to your discredit. [22] We should like to hear from you what your views are; all we know about this sect is that no one has a good word to say for it.'

[23] So they fixed a day, and came in large numbers to his lodging. From dawn to dusk he put his case to them; he spoke urgently of the kingdom of God and sought to convince them about Jesus by appealing to the law of Moses and the prophets. [24] Some were won over by his arguments; others remained unconvinced. [25] Without reaching any agreement among themselves they began to disperse, but not before Paul had spoken this final word: 'How well the Holy Spirit spoke to your fathers through the prophet Isaiah [26] when he said, "Go to this people and say: You may listen and listen, but you will never understand; you may look and look, but you will never see. [27] For this people's mind has become dull; they have stopped their ears and closed their eyes. Otherwise, their eyes might see, their ears hear, and their mind understand, and then they might turn again, and I would heal them." [28] Therefore take note that this salvation of God has been sent to the Gentiles; the Gentiles will listen.'

[30] He stayed there two full years at his own expense, with a welcome for all who came to him; [31] he proclaimed the kingdom of God and taught the facts about the Lord Jesus Christ quite openly and without hindrance.

28:28 **listen:** *some witnesses add* [29] After he had spoken, the Jews went away, arguing vigorously among themselves.

THE LETTER OF PAUL TO THE

ROMANS

The gospel of Christ

1 FROM Paul, servant of Christ Jesus, called by God to be an apostle and set apart for the service of his gospel. ² This gospel God announced beforehand in sacred scriptures through his prophets. ³⁻⁴ It is about his Son: on the human level he was a descendant of David, but on the level of the spirit—the Holy Spirit—he was proclaimed Son of God by an act of power that raised him from the dead: it is about Jesus Christ our Lord. ⁵ Through him I received the privilege of an apostolic commission to bring people of all nations to faith and obedience in his name, ⁶ including you who have heard the call and belong to Jesus Christ.

⁷ I send greetings to all of you in Rome, who are loved by God and called to be his people. Grace and peace to you from God our Father and the Lord Jesus Christ.

⁸ Let me begin by thanking my God, through Jesus Christ, for you all, because the story of your faith is being told all over the world. ⁹ God is my witness, to whom I offer the service of my spirit by preaching the gospel of his Son: God knows that I make mention of you in my prayers continually, ¹⁰ and am always asking that by his will I may, somehow or other, at long last succeed in coming to visit you. ¹¹ For I long to see you; I want to bring you some spiritual gift to make you strong; ¹² or rather, I want us to be encouraged by one another's faith when I am with you, I by yours and you by mine.

¹³ Brothers and sisters, I should like you to know that I have often planned to come, though so far without success, in the hope of achieving something among you, as I have in the rest of the gentile world. ¹⁴ I have an obligation to Greek and non-Greek, to learned and simple; ¹⁵ hence my eagerness to declare the gospel to you in Rome as well. ¹⁶ For I am not ashamed of the gospel. It is the saving power of God for everyone who has faith—the Jew first, but the Greek also—¹⁷ because in it the righteousness of God is seen at work, beginning in faith and ending in faith; as scripture says, 'Whoever is justified through faith shall gain life.'

God's judgement on sin

¹⁸ DIVINE retribution is to be seen at work, falling from heaven on all the impiety and wickedness of men and women who in their wickedness suppress the truth. ¹⁹ For all that can be known of God lies plain before their eyes; indeed God himself has disclosed it to them. ²⁰ Ever since the world began his invisible attributes, that is to say his everlasting power and deity, have been visible to the eye of reason, in the things he has made. Their conduct, therefore, is indefensible; ²¹ knowing God, they have refused to honour him as God, or to render him thanks. Hence all their thinking has ended in futility, and their misguided minds are plunged in darkness. ²² They boast of their wisdom, but they have made fools of themselves, ²³ exchanging the glory of the immortal God for an image shaped like mortal man, even for images like birds, beasts, and reptiles.

²⁴ For this reason God has given them up to their own vile desires, and the consequent degradation of their bodies. ²⁵ They have exchanged the truth of God for a lie, and have offered reverence and worship to created things instead of to the Creator. Blessed is he for ever, Amen. ²⁶ As a result God has given them up to shameful passions. Among them women have exchanged natural intercourse for unnatural, ²⁷ and men too, giving up natural relations with women, burn with lust for one another; males behave indecently with males, and are paid in their own persons the fitting wage of such perversion.

²⁸ Thus, because they have not seen fit

1:3–4 **Son of God . . . dead:** *or* Son of God with full power at his resurrection from the dead.   1:17 **Whoever . . . life:** *or* The righteous shall live by faith.

to acknowledge God, he has given them up to their own depraved way of thinking, and this leads them to break all rules of conduct. [29] They are filled with every kind of wickedness, villainy, greed, and malice; they are one mass of envy, murder, rivalry, treachery, and malevolence; gossips [30] and scandalmongers; and blasphemers, insolent, arrogant, and boastful; they invent new kinds of vice, they show no respect to parents, [31] they are without sense or fidelity, without natural affection or pity. [32] They know well enough the just decree of God, that those who behave like this deserve to die; yet they not only do these things themselves but approve such conduct in others.

2 You have no defence, then, whoever you may be, when you sit in judgement—for in judging others you condemn yourself, since you, the judge, are equally guilty. [2] We all know that God's judgement on those who commit such crimes is just; [3] and do you imagine—you that pass judgement on the guilty while committing the same crimes yourself—do you imagine that you, any more than they, will escape the judgement of God? [4] Or do you despise his wealth of kindness and tolerance and patience, failing to see that God's kindness is meant to lead you to repentance? [5] In the obstinate impenitence of your heart you are laying up for yourself a store of retribution against the day of retribution, when God's just judgement will be revealed, [6] and he will pay everyone for what he has done. [7] To those who pursue glory, honour, and immortality by steady persistence in well-doing, he will give eternal life; [8] but the retribution of his wrath awaits those who are governed by selfish ambition, who refuse obedience to truth and take evil for their guide. [9] There will be affliction and distress for every human being who is a wrongdoer, for the Jew first and for the Greek also; [10] but for everyone who does right there will be glory, honour, and peace, for the Jew first and also for the Greek. [11] God has no favourites.

[12] Those who have sinned outside the pale of the law of Moses will perish outside the law, and all who have sinned under that law will be judged by it. [13] None will be justified before God by hearing the law, but by doing it. [14] When Gentiles who do not possess the law carry out its precepts by the light of nature, then, although they have no law, they are their own law; [15] they show that what the law requires is inscribed on their hearts, and to this their conscience gives supporting witness, since their own thoughts argue the case, sometimes against them, sometimes even for them. [16] So it will be on the day when, according to my gospel, God will judge the secrets of human hearts through Christ Jesus.

The Jews and their law

[17] BUT as for you who bear the name of Jew and rely on the law: you take pride in your God; [18] you know his will; taught by the law, you know what really matters; [19] you are confident that you are a guide to the blind, a light to those in darkness, [20] an instructor of the foolish, and a teacher of the immature, because you possess in the law the embodiment of knowledge and truth. [21] You teach others, then; do you not teach yourself? You proclaim, 'Do not steal'; but are you yourself a thief? [22] You say, 'Do not commit adultery'; but are you an adulterer? You abominate false gods; but do you rob shrines? [23] While you take pride in the law, you dishonour God by breaking it. [24] As scripture says, 'Because of you the name of God is profaned among the Gentiles.'

[25] Circumcision has value, provided you keep the law; but if you break the law, then your circumcision is as if it had never been. [26] Equally, if an uncircumcised man keeps the precepts of the law, will he not count as circumcised? [27] He may be physically uncircumcised, but by fulfilling the law he will pass judgement on you who break it, for all your written code and your circumcision. [28] It is not externals that make a Jew, nor an external mark in the flesh that makes circumcision. [29] The real Jew is one who is inwardly a Jew, and his circumcision is of the heart, spiritual not literal; he receives his commendation not from men but from God.

3 Then what advantage has the Jew? What is the value of circumcision? [2] Great, in every way. In the first place, the Jews were entrusted with the oracles of God. [3] What if some of them were unfaithful? Will their faithlessness cancel the faithfulness of God? [4] Certainly not!

God must be true though all men be proved liars; for we read in scripture, 'When you speak you will be vindicated; when you are accused, you will win the case.'

⁵ Another question: if our injustice serves to confirm God's justice, what are we to say? Is it unjust of God (I speak of him in human terms) to bring retribution upon us? ⁶ Certainly not! If God were unjust, how could he judge the world? ⁷ Again, if the truth of God is displayed to his greater glory through my false-hood, why should I any longer be con-demned as a sinner? ⁸ Why not indeed 'do evil that good may come', as some slan-derously report me as saying? To con-demn such men as these is surely just.

⁹ Well then, are we Jews any better off? No, not at all! For we have already drawn up the indictment that all, Jews and Greeks alike, are under the power of sin. ¹⁰ Scripture says:

There is no one righteous; no, not one;

¹¹ no one who understands, no one who seeks God.

¹² All have swerved aside, all alike have become debased;

there is no one to show kindness: no, not one.

¹³ Their throats are open tombs, they use their tongues for treachery, adders' venom is on their lips,

¹⁴ and their mouths are full of bitter curses.

¹⁵ Their feet hasten to shed blood,

¹⁶ ruin and misery mark their tracks,

¹⁷ they are strangers to the path of peace,

¹⁸ and reverence for God does not enter their thoughts.

¹⁹ Now all the words of the law are addressed, as we know, to those who are under the law, so that no one may have anything to say in self-defence, and the whole world may be exposed to God's judgement. ²⁰ For no human being can be justified in the sight of God by keeping the law: law brings only the consciousness of sin.

²¹ But now, quite independently of law, though with the law and the prophets bearing witness to it, the righteousness of God has been made known; ²² it is effect-ive through faith in Christ for all who have such faith—all, without distinction. ²³ For all alike have sinned, and are deprived of the divine glory; ²⁴ and all are justified by God's free grace alone, through his act of liberation in the person of Christ Jesus. ²⁵ For God designed him to be the means of expiating sin by his death, effective through faith. God meant by this to demonstrate his justice, because in his forbearance he had overlooked the sins of the past—²⁶ to demonstrate his justice now in the present, showing that he is himself just and also justifies anyone who puts his faith in Jesus.

²⁷ What room then is left for human pride? It is excluded. And on what prin-ciple? The keeping of the law would not exclude it, but faith does. ²⁸ For our argu-ment is that people are justified by faith quite apart from any question of keeping the law.

²⁹ Do you suppose God is the God of the Jews alone? Is he not the God of Gentiles also? Certainly, of Gentiles also. ³⁰ For if the Lord is indeed one, he will justify the circumcised by their faith and the un-circumcised through their faith. ³¹ Does this mean that we are using faith to undermine the law? By no means: we are upholding the law.

Abraham's faith

4 WHAT, then, are we to say about Abraham, our ancestor by natural descent? ² If Abraham was justified by anything he did, then he has grounds for pride. But not in the eyes of God! ³ For what does scripture say? 'Abraham put his faith in God, and that faith was counted to him as righteousness.'

⁴ Now if someone does a piece of work, his wages are not 'counted' to be a gift; they are paid as his due. ⁵ But if someone without any work to his credit simply puts his faith in him who acquits the wrong-doer, then his faith is indeed 'counted as righteousness'. ⁶ In the same sense David speaks of the happiness of the man whom God 'counts' as righteous, apart from any good works: ⁷ 'Happy are they', he says, 'whose lawless deeds are forgiven, whose sins are blotted out; ⁸ happy is the man

3:9 **No, not at all:** *or* Not altogether.   3:25 **designed him to be:** *or* set him forth as.

whose sin the Lord does not count against him.'

[9] Is this happiness confined to the circumcised, or is it for the uncircumcised also? We have just been saying: 'Abraham's faith was counted as righteousness.' [10] In what circumstances was it so counted? Was he circumcised at the time, or not? He was not yet circumcised, but uncircumcised; [11] he received circumcision later as the sign and hallmark of that righteousness which faith had given him while he was still uncircumcised. It follows that he is the father of all who have faith when uncircumcised, and so have righteousness 'counted' to them; [12] and at the same time he is the father of the circumcised, provided they are not merely circumcised, but also follow that path of faith which our father Abraham trod while he was still uncircumcised.

[13] It was not through law that Abraham and his descendants were given the promise that the world should be their inheritance, but through righteousness that came from faith. [14] If the heirs are those who hold by the law, then faith becomes pointless and the promise goes for nothing; [15] law can bring only retribution, and where there is no law there can be no breach of law. [16] The promise was made on the ground of faith in order that it might be a matter of sheer grace, and that it might be valid for all Abraham's descendants, not only for those who hold by the law, but also for those who have Abraham's faith. For he is the father of us all, [17] as scripture says: 'I have appointed you to be father of many nations.' In the presence of God, the God who makes the dead live and calls into being things that are not, Abraham had faith. [18] When hope seemed hopeless, his faith was such that he became 'father of many nations', in fulfilment of the promise, 'So shall your descendants be.' [19] His faith did not weaken when he considered his own body, which was as good as dead (for he was about a hundred years old), and the deadness of Sarah's womb; [20] no distrust made him doubt God's promise, but, strong in faith, he gave glory to God, [21] convinced that what he had promised he was able to do. [22] And that is why

Abraham's faith was 'counted to him as righteousness'.

[23] The words 'counted to him' were meant to apply not only to Abraham [24] but to us; our faith too is to be 'counted', the faith in the God who raised Jesus our Lord from the dead; [25] for he was given up to death for our misdeeds, and raised to life for our justification.

Life in Christ

5 THEREFORE, now that we have been justified through faith, we are at peace with God through our Lord Jesus Christ, [2] who has given us access to that grace in which we now live; and we exult in the hope of the divine glory that is to be ours. [3] More than this: we even exult in our present sufferings, because we know that suffering is a source of endurance, [4] endurance of approval, and approval of hope. [5] Such hope is no fantasy; through the Holy Spirit he has given us, God's love has flooded our hearts.

[6] It was while we were still helpless that, at the appointed time, Christ died for the wicked. [7] Even for a just man one of us would hardly die, though perhaps for a good man one might actually brave death; [8] but Christ died for us while we were yet sinners, and that is God's proof of his love towards us. [9] And so, since we have now been justified by Christ's sacrificial death, we shall all the more certainly be saved through him from final retribution. [10] For if, when we were God's enemies, we were reconciled to him through the death of his Son, how much more, now that we have been reconciled, shall we be saved by his life! [11] But that is not all: we also exult in God through our Lord Jesus, through whom we have now been granted reconciliation.

[12] What does this imply? It was through one man that sin entered the world, and through sin death, and thus death pervaded the whole human race, inasmuch as all have sinned. [13] For sin was already in the world before there was law; and although in the absence of law no reckoning is kept of sin, [14] death held sway from Adam to Moses, even over those who had not sinned as Adam did, by disobeying a direct command—and

5:1 **we are at peace:** *some witnesses read* let us continue at peace.　　5:2 **we exult:** *or* let us exult.　　5:3 **we even exult:** *or* let us even exult.

Adam foreshadows the man who was to come. ¹⁵ But God's act of grace is out of all proportion to Adam's wrongdoing. For if the wrongdoing of that one man brought death upon so many, its effect is vastly exceeded by the grace of God and the gift that came to so many by the grace of the one man, Jesus Christ. ¹⁶ And again, the gift of God is not to be compared in its effect with that one man's sin; for the judicial action, following on the one offence, resulted in a verdict of condemnation, but the act of grace, following on so many misdeeds, resulted in a verdict of acquittal. ¹⁷ If, by the wrongdoing of one man, death established its reign through that one man, much more shall those who in far greater measure receive grace and the gift of righteousness live and reign through the one man, Jesus Christ.

¹⁸ It follows, then, that as the result of one misdeed was condemnation for all people, so the result of one righteous act is acquittal and life for all. ¹⁹ For as through the disobedience of one man many were made sinners, so through the obedience of one man many will be made righteous.

²⁰ Law intruded into this process to multiply law-breaking. But where sin was multiplied, grace immeasurably exceeded it, ²¹ in order that, as sin established its reign by way of death, so God's grace might establish its reign in righteousness, and result in eternal life through Jesus Christ our Lord.

Baptism into Christ

6 WHAT are we to say, then? Shall we persist in sin, so that there may be all the more grace? ² Certainly not! We died to sin: how can we live in it any longer? ³ Have you forgotten that when we were baptized into union with Christ Jesus we were baptized into his death? ⁴ By that baptism into his death we were buried with him, in order that, as Christ was raised from the dead by the glorious power of the Father, so also we might set out on a new life.

⁵ For if we have become identified with him in his death, we shall also be identified with him in his resurrection. ⁶ We know that our old humanity has been crucified with Christ, for the destruction of the sinful self, so that we may no longer be slaves to sin, ⁷ because death cancels

the claims of sin. ⁸ But if we thus died with Christ, we believe that we shall also live with him, ⁹ knowing as we do that Christ, once raised from the dead, is never to die again: he is no longer under the dominion of death. ¹⁰ When he died, he died to sin, once for all, and now that he lives, he lives to God. ¹¹ In the same way you must regard yourselves as dead to sin and alive to God, in union with Christ Jesus.

¹² Therefore sin must no longer reign in your mortal body, exacting obedience to the body's desires. ¹³ You must no longer put any part of it at sin's disposal, as an implement for doing wrong. Put yourselves instead at the disposal of God; think of yourselves as raised from death to life, and yield your bodies to God as implements for doing right. ¹⁴ Sin shall no longer be your master, for you are no longer under law, but under grace.

¹⁵ What then? Are we to sin, because we are not under law but under grace? Of course not! ¹⁶ You know well enough that if you bind yourselves to obey a master, you are slaves of the master you obey; and this is true whether the master is sin and the outcome death, or obedience and the outcome righteousness. ¹⁷ Once you were slaves of sin, but now, thank God, you have yielded wholehearted obedience to that pattern of teaching to which you were made subject; ¹⁸ emancipated from sin, you have become slaves of righteousness ¹⁹ (to use language that suits your human weakness). As you once yielded your bodies to the service of impurity and lawlessness, making for moral anarchy, so now you must yield them to the service of righteousness, making for a holy life.

²⁰ When you were slaves of sin, you were free from the control of righteousness. ²¹ And what gain did that bring you? Things that now make you ashamed, for their end is death. ²² But now, freed from the commands of sin and bound to the service of God, you have gains that lead to holiness, and the end is eternal life. ²³ For sin pays a wage, and the wage is death, but God gives freely, and his gift is eternal life in union with Christ Jesus our Lord.

The role of the law

7 YOU must be aware, my friends—I am sure you have some knowledge of law—that a person is subject to the law

6:17 **to which … subject:** *or* which was handed on to you.

only so long as he is alive. [2] For example, a married woman is by law bound to her husband while he lives; but if the husband dies, she is released from the marriage bond. [3] If, therefore, in her husband's lifetime she gives herself to another man, she will be held to be an adulteress; but if the husband dies, she is free of the law and she does not commit adultery by giving herself to another man. [4] So too, my friends, through the body of Christ you died to the law and were set free to give yourselves to another, to him who rose from the dead so that we may bear fruit for God. [5] While we lived on the level of mere human nature, the sinful passions evoked by the law were active in our bodies, and bore fruit for death. [6] But now, having died to that which held us bound, we are released from the law, to serve God in a new way, the way of the spirit in contrast to the old way of a written code.

[7] What follows? Is the law identical with sin? Of course not! Yet had it not been for the law I should never have become acquainted with sin. For example, I should never have known what it was to covet, if the law had not said, 'You shall not covet.' [8] Through that commandment sin found its opportunity, and produced in me all kinds of wrong desires. In the absence of law, sin is devoid of life. [9] There was a time when, in the absence of law, I was fully alive; but when the commandment came, sin sprang to life and I died. [10] The commandment which should have led to life proved in my experience to lead to death, [11] because in the commandment sin found its opportunity to seduce me, and through the commandment killed me. [12] So then, the law in itself is holy and the commandment is holy and just and good.

[13] Are we therefore to say that this good thing caused my death? Of course not! It was sin that killed me, and thereby sin exposed its true character: it used a good thing to bring about my death, and so, through the commandment, sin became more sinful than ever. [14] We know that the law is spiritual; but I am not: I am unspiritual, sold as a slave to sin. [15] I do not even acknowledge my own actions as

mine, for what I do is not what I want to do, but what I detest. [16] But if what I do is against my will, then clearly I agree with the law and hold it to be admirable. [17] This means that it is no longer I who perform the action, but sin that dwells in me. [18] For I know that nothing good dwells in me—my unspiritual self, I mean—for though the will to do good is there, the ability to effect it is not. [19] The good which I want to do, I fail to do; but what I do is the wrong which is against my will; [20] and if what I do is against my will, clearly it is no longer I who am the agent, but sin that has its dwelling in me.

[21] I discover this principle, then: that when I want to do right, only wrong is within my reach. [22] In my inmost self I delight in the law of God, [23] but I perceive in my outward actions a different law, fighting against the law that my mind approves, and making me a prisoner under the law of sin which controls my conduct. [24] Wretched creature that I am, who is there to rescue me from this state of death? [25] Who but God? Thanks be to him through Jesus Christ our Lord! To sum up then: left to myself I serve God's law with my mind, but with my unspiritual nature I serve the law of sin.

Life through the Spirit

8 It follows that there is now no condemnation for those who are united with Christ Jesus. [2] In Christ Jesus the life-giving law of the Spirit has set you free from the law of sin and death. [3] What the law could not do, because human weakness robbed it of all potency, God has done: by sending his own Son in the likeness of our sinful nature and to deal with sin, he has passed judgement against sin within that very nature, [4] so that the commandment of the law may find fulfilment in us, whose conduct is no longer controlled by the old nature, but by the Spirit.

[5-6] Those who live on the level of the old nature have their outlook formed by it, and that spells death; but those who live on the level of the spirit have the spiritual outlook, and that is life and peace. [7] For the outlook of the unspiritual nature is enmity with God; it is not subject to the law of God and indeed it

8:3 *and to deal with sin: or* and as a sacrifice for sin.

cannot be; [8] those who live under its control cannot please God.

[9] But you do not live like that. You live by the spirit, since God's Spirit dwells in you; and anyone who does not possess the Spirit of Christ does not belong to Christ. [10] But if Christ is in you, then although the body is dead because of sin, yet the Spirit is your life because you have been justified. [11] Moreover, if the Spirit of him who raised Jesus from the dead dwells in you, then the God who raised Christ Jesus from the dead will also give new life to your mortal bodies through his indwelling Spirit.

[12] It follows, my friends, that our old nature has no claim on us; we are not obliged to live in that way. [13] If you do so, you must die. But if by the Spirit you put to death the base pursuits of the body, then you will live.

[14] For all who are led by the Spirit of God are sons of God. [15] The Spirit you have received is not a spirit of slavery, leading us back into a life of fear, but a Spirit of adoption, enabling us to cry 'Abba! Father!' [16] The Spirit of God affirms to our spirit that we are God's children; [17] and if children, then heirs, heirs of God and fellow-heirs with Christ; but we must share his sufferings if we are also to share his glory.

[18] For I reckon that the sufferings we now endure bear no comparison with the glory, as yet unrevealed, which is in store for us. [19] The created universe is waiting with eager expectation for God's sons to be revealed. [20] It was made subject to frustration, not of its own choice but by the will of him who subjected it, yet with the hope [21] that the universe itself is to be freed from the shackles of mortality and is to enter upon the glorious liberty of the children of God. [22] Up to the present, as we know, the whole created universe in all its parts groans as if in the pangs of childbirth. [23] What is more, we also, to whom the Spirit is given as the firstfruits of the harvest to come, are groaning inwardly while we look forward eagerly to our adoption, our liberation from mortality. [24] It was with this hope that we were saved. Now to see something is no longer to hope: why hope for what is already seen? [25] But if we hope for something we

do not yet see, then we look forward to it eagerly and with patience.

[26] In the same way the Spirit comes to the aid of our weakness. We do not even know how we ought to pray, but through our inarticulate groans the Spirit himself is pleading for us, [27] and God who searches our inmost being knows what the Spirit means, because he pleads for God's people as God himself wills; [28] and in everything, as we know, he co-operates for good with those who love God and are called according to his purpose. [29] For those whom God knew before ever they were, he also ordained to share the likeness of his Son, so that he might be the eldest among a large family of brothers; [30] and those whom he foreordained, he also called, and those whom he called he also justified, and those whom he justified he also glorified.

[31] With all this in mind, what are we to say? If God is on our side, who is against us? [32] He did not spare his own Son, but gave him up for us all; how can he fail to lavish every other gift upon us? [33] Who will bring a charge against those whom God has chosen? Not God, who acquits! [34] Who will pronounce judgement? Not Christ, who died, or rather rose again; not Christ, who is at God's right hand and pleads our cause! [35] Then what can separate us from the love of Christ? Can affliction or hardship? Can persecution, hunger, nakedness, danger, or sword? [36] 'We are being done to death for your sake all day long,' as scripture says; 'we have been treated like sheep for slaughter' —[37] and yet, throughout it all, overwhelming victory is ours through him who loved us. [38] For I am convinced that there is nothing in death or life, in the realm of spirits or superhuman powers, in the world as it is or the world as it shall be, in the forces of the universe, [39] in heights or depths—nothing in all creation that can separate us from the love of God in Christ Jesus our Lord.

Israel and the Gentiles in God's plan

9 I AM speaking the truth as a Christian; my conscience, enlightened by the Holy Spirit, assures me that I do not lie when I tell you [2] that there is great grief

8:24 **why hope for:** *some witnesses read* why endure.   8:28 **and in everything ... God:** *or* and, as we know, all things work together for good for those who love God; *some witnesses read* and we know God himself co-operates for good with those who love God.

and unceasing sorrow in my heart. [3] I would even pray to be an outcast myself, cut off from Christ, if it would help my brothers, my kinsfolk by natural descent. [4] They are descendants of Israel, chosen to be God's sons; theirs is the glory of the divine presence, theirs the covenants, the law, the temple worship, and the promises. [5] The patriarchs are theirs, and from them by natural descent came the Messiah. May God, supreme above all, be blessed for ever! Amen.

[6] It cannot be that God's word has proved false. Not all the offspring of Israel are truly Israel, [7] nor does being Abraham's descendants make them all his true children; but, in the words of scripture, 'It is through the line of Isaac's descendants that your name will be traced.' [8] That is to say, it is not the children of Abraham by natural descent who are children of God; it is the children born through God's promise who are reckoned as Abraham's descendants. [9] For the promise runs: 'In due season I will come, and Sarah shall have a son.'

[10] And that is not all: Rebecca's children had one and the same father, our ancestor Isaac; [11] yet, even before they were born, when they as yet had done nothing, whether good or ill, in order that the purpose of God, which is a matter of his choice, might stand firm, based not on human deeds but on the call of God, [12] she was told, 'The elder shall be servant to the younger.' [13] That accords with the text of scripture, 'Jacob I loved and Esau I hated.'

[14] What shall we say to that? Is God to be charged with injustice? Certainly not! [15] He says to Moses, 'I will show mercy to whom I will show mercy, and have pity on whom I will have pity.' [16] Thus it does not depend on human will or effort, but on God's mercy. [17] For in scripture Pharaoh is told, 'I have raised you up for this very purpose, to exhibit my power in my dealings with you, and to spread my fame over all the earth.' [18] Thus he not only shows mercy as he chooses, but also makes stubborn as he chooses.

[19] You will say, 'Then why does God find fault, if no one can resist his will?' [20] Who do you think you are to answer God back? Can the pot say to the potter,

'Why did you make me like this?'? [21] Surely the potter can do what he likes with the clay. Is he not free to make two vessels out of the same lump, one to be treasured, the other for common use?

[22] But if it is indeed God's purpose to display his retribution and to make his power known, can it be that he has with great patience tolerated vessels that were objects of retribution due for destruction, [23] precisely in order to make known the full wealth of his glory on vessels that were objects of mercy, prepared from the first for glory?

[24] We are those objects of mercy, whom he has called from among Jews and Gentiles alike, [25] as he says in Hosea: 'Those who were not my people I will call my people, and the unloved I will call beloved. [26] In the very place where they were told, "You are no people of mine," they shall be called sons of the living God.' [27] But about Israel Isaiah makes this proclamation: 'Though the Israelites be countless as the sands of the sea, only a remnant shall be saved, [28] for the Lord's sentence on the land will be summary and final'; [29] as also he said previously, 'If the Lord of Hosts had not left us descendants, we should have become like Sodom, and no better than Gomorrah.'

[30] Then what are we to say? That Gentiles, who made no effort after righteousness, nevertheless achieved it, a righteousness based on faith; [31] whereas Israel made great efforts after a law of righteousness, but never attained to it. [32] Why was this? Because their efforts were not based on faith but, mistakenly, on deeds. They tripped over the 'stone' [33] mentioned in scripture: 'Here I lay in Zion a stone to trip over, a rock to stumble against; but he who has faith in it will not be put to shame.'

10 Friends, my heart's desire and my prayer to God is for their salvation. [2] To their zeal for God I can testify; but it is an ill-informed zeal. [3] For they ignore God's way of righteousness, and try to set up their own, and therefore they have not submitted themselves to God's righteousness; [4] for Christ is the end of the law and brings righteousness for everyone who has faith.

---

9 : 5 **Messiah:** *Gk* Christ. **Messiah ... for ever:** *or* Messiah, who is God, supreme above all and blessed for ever; *or* Messiah, who is supreme above all. Blessed be God for ever!   9 : 7 **all ... children:** *or* all children of God.

⁵ Of righteousness attained through the law Moses writes, 'Anyone who keeps it shall have life by it.' ⁶ But the righteousness that comes by faith says, 'Do not say to yourself, "Who can go up to heaven?"' (that is, to bring Christ down) ⁷ 'or, "Who can go down to the abyss?"' (to bring Christ up from the dead). ⁸ And what does it say next? 'The word is near you: it is on your lips and in your heart'; and that means the word of faith which we proclaim. ⁹ If the confession 'Jesus is Lord' is on your lips, and the faith that God raised him from the dead is in your heart, you will find salvation. ¹⁰ For faith in the heart leads to righteousness, and confession on the lips leads to salvation.

¹¹ Scripture says, 'No one who has faith in him will be put to shame': ¹² there is no distinction between Jew and Greek, because the same Lord is Lord of all, and has riches enough for all who call on him. ¹³ For 'Everyone who calls on the name of the Lord will be saved.' ¹⁴ But how could they call on him without having faith in him? And how could they have faith without having heard of him? And how could they hear without someone to spread the news? ¹⁵ And how could anyone spread the news without being sent? As scripture says, 'How welcome are the feet of the messengers of good news!' ¹⁶ It is true that not all have responded to the good news; as Isaiah says, 'Lord, who believed when they heard us?' ¹⁷ So then faith does come from hearing, and hearing through the word of Christ.

¹⁸ I ask, then: Can it be that they never heard? Of course they did: 'Their voice has sounded all over the world, and their words to the ends of the earth.' ¹⁹ I ask again: Can it be that Israel never understood? Listen first to Moses: 'I will use a nation that is no nation to stir you to envy, and a foolish nation to rouse your anger.' ²⁰ Isaiah is still more daring: 'I was found', he says, 'by those who were not looking for me; I revealed myself to those who never asked about me'; ²¹ while of Israel he says, 'All day long I have stretched out my hands to a disobedient and defiant people.'

11 I ASK, then: Has God rejected his people? Of course not! I am an Israelite myself, of the stock of Abraham, of the tribe of Benjamin. ² God has not

rejected the people he acknowledged of old as his own. Surely you know what scripture says in the story of Elijah—how he pleads with God against Israel: ³ 'Lord, they have killed your prophets, they have torn down your altars, and I alone am left, and they are seeking my life.' ⁴ But what was the divine word to him? 'I have left myself seven thousand men who have not knelt to Baal.' ⁵ In just the same way at the present time a 'remnant' has come into being, chosen by the grace of God. ⁶ But if it is by grace, then it does not rest on deeds, or grace would cease to be grace.

⁷ What follows? What Israel sought, Israel has not attained, but the chosen few have attained it. The rest were hardened, ⁸ as it stands written: 'God has dulled their senses; he has given them blind eyes and deaf ears, and so it is to this day.' ⁹ Similarly David says:

May their table be a snare and a trap,
their downfall and their retribution!
¹⁰ May their eyes become darkened and blind!
Bow down their backs unceasingly!

¹¹ I ask, then: When they stumbled, was their fall final? Far from it! Through a false step on their part salvation has come to the Gentiles, and this in turn will stir them to envy. ¹² If their false step means the enrichment of the world, if their falling short means the enrichment of the Gentiles, how much more will their coming to full strength mean!

¹³ It is to you Gentiles that I am speaking. As an apostle to the Gentiles, I make much of that ministry, ¹⁴ yet always in the hope of stirring those of my own race to envy, and so saving some of them. ¹⁵ For if their rejection has meant the reconciliation of the world, what will their acceptance mean? Nothing less than life from the dead! ¹⁶ If the first loaf is holy, so is the whole batch. If the root is holy, so are the branches. ¹⁷ But if some of the branches have been lopped off, and you, a wild olive, have been grafted in among them, and have come to share the same root and sap as the olive, ¹⁸ do not make yourself superior to the branches. If you do, remember that you do not sustain the root: the root sustains you.

¹⁹ You will say, 'Branches were lopped

off so that I might be grafted in.' ²⁰ Very well: they were lopped off for lack of faith, and by faith you hold your place. Put away your pride, and be on your guard; ²¹ for if God did not spare the natural branches, no more will he spare you. ²² Observe the kindness and the severity of God—severity to those who fell away, divine kindness to you provided that you remain within its scope; otherwise you too will be cut off, ²³ whereas they, if they do not continue faithless, will be grafted in, since it is in God's power to graft them in again. ²⁴ For if you were cut from your native wild olive and against nature grafted into the cultivated olive, how much more readily will they, the natural olive branches, be grafted into their native stock!

²⁵ There is a divine secret here, my friends, which I want to share with you, to keep you from thinking yourselves wise: this partial hardening has come on Israel only until the Gentiles have been admitted in full strength; ²⁶ once that has happened, the whole of Israel will be saved, in accordance with scripture:

> From Zion shall come the Deliverer;
> he shall remove wickedness from
> Jacob.
²⁷ And this is the covenant I will grant
> them,
> when I take away their sins.

²⁸ Judged by their response to the gospel, they are God's enemies for your sake; but judged by his choice, they are dear to him for the sake of the patriarchs; ²⁹ for the gracious gifts of God and his calling are irrevocable. ³⁰ Just as formerly you were disobedient to God, but now have received mercy because of their disobedience, ³¹ so now, because of the mercy shown to you, they have proved disobedient, but only in order that they too may receive mercy. ³² For in shutting all mankind in the prison of their disobedience, God's purpose was to show mercy to all mankind.

³³ How deep are the wealth
> and the wisdom and the knowledge
> of God!
> How inscrutable his judgements,
> how unsearchable his ways!
³⁴ 'Who knows the mind of the Lord?
> Who has been his counsellor?'
³⁵ 'Who has made a gift to him first,

and earned a gift in return?'
³⁶ From him and through him and for
> him all things exist—
> to him be glory for ever! Amen.

Christian service and the community

12 Therefore, my friends, I implore you by God's mercy to offer your very selves to him: a living sacrifice, dedicated and fit for his acceptance, the worship offered by mind and heart. ² Conform no longer to the pattern of this present world, but be transformed by the renewal of your minds. Then you will be able to discern the will of God, and to know what is good, acceptable, and perfect.

³ By authority of the grace God has given me I say to everyone among you: do not think too highly of yourself, but form a sober estimate based on the measure of faith that God has dealt to each of you. ⁴ For just as in a single human body there are many limbs and organs, all with different functions, ⁵ so we who are united with Christ, though many, form one body, and belong to one another as its limbs and organs.

⁶ Let us use the different gifts allotted to each of us by God's grace: the gift of inspired utterance, for example, let us use in proportion to our faith; ⁷ the gift of administration to administer, the gift of teaching to teach, ⁸ the gift of counselling to counsel. If you give to charity, give without grudging; if you are a leader, lead with enthusiasm; if you help others in distress, do it cheerfully.

⁹ Love in all sincerity, loathing evil and holding fast to the good. ¹⁰ Let love of the Christian community show itself in mutual affection. Esteem others more highly than yourself.

¹¹ With unflagging zeal, aglow with the Spirit, serve the Lord. ¹² Let hope keep you joyful; in trouble stand firm; persist in prayer; ¹³ contribute to the needs of God's people, and practise hospitality. ¹⁴ Call down blessings on your persecutors—blessings, not curses. ¹⁵ Rejoice with those who rejoice, weep with those who weep. ¹⁶ Live in agreement with one another. Do not be proud, but be ready to mix with humble people. Do not keep thinking how wise you are.

¹⁷ Never pay back evil for evil. Let your aims be such as all count honourable. ¹⁸ If

possible, so far as it lies with you, live at peace with all. [19] My dear friends, do not seek revenge, but leave a place for divine retribution; for there is a text which reads, 'Vengeance is mine, says the Lord, I will repay.' [20] But there is another text: 'If your enemy is hungry, feed him; if he is thirsty, give him a drink; by doing this you will heap live coals on his head.' [21] Do not let evil conquer you, but use good to conquer evil.

13 Every person must submit to the authorities in power, for all authority comes from God, and the existing authorities are instituted by him. [2] It follows that anyone who rebels against authority is resisting a divine institution, and those who resist have themselves to thank for the punishment they will receive. [3] Governments hold no terrors for the law-abiding but only for the criminal. You wish to have no fear of the authorities? Then continue to do right and you will have their approval, [4] for they are God's agents working for your good. But if you are doing wrong, then you will have cause to fear them; it is not for nothing that they hold the power of the sword, for they are God's agents of punishment bringing retribution on the offender. [5] That is why you are obliged to submit. It is an obligation imposed not merely by fear of retribution but by conscience. [6] That is also why you pay taxes. The authorities are in God's service and it is to this they devote their energies.

[7] Discharge your obligations to everyone; pay tax and levy, reverence and respect, to those to whom they are due. [8] Leave no debt outstanding, but remember the debt of love you owe one another. He who loves his neighbour has met every requirement of the law. [9] The commandments, 'You shall not commit adultery, you shall not commit murder, you shall not steal, you shall not covet,' and any other commandment there may be, are all summed up in the one rule, 'Love your neighbour as yourself.' [10] Love cannot wrong a neighbour; therefore love is the fulfilment of the law.

[11] Always remember that this is the hour of crisis: it is high time for you to wake out of sleep, for deliverance is nearer to us now than it was when first we

believed. [12] It is far on in the night; day is near. Let us therefore throw off the deeds of darkness and put on the armour of light. [13] Let us behave with decency as befits the day: no drunken orgies, no debauchery or vice, no quarrels or jealousies! [14] Let Christ Jesus himself be the armour that you wear; give your unspiritual nature no opportunity to satisfy its desires.

14 ACCEPT anyone who is weak in faith without debate about his misgivings. [2] For instance, one person may have faith strong enough to eat all kinds of food, while another who is weaker eats only vegetables. [3] Those who eat meat must not look down on those who do not, and those who do not eat meat must not pass judgement on those who do; for God has accepted them. [4] Who are you to pass judgement on someone else's servant? Whether he stands or falls is his own Master's business; and stand he will, because his Master has power to enable him to stand.

[5] Again, some make a distinction between this day and that; others regard all days alike. Everyone must act on his own convictions. [6] Those who honour the day honour the Lord, and those who eat meat also honour the Lord, since when they eat they give thanks to God; and those who abstain have the Lord in mind when abstaining, since they too give thanks to God.

[7] For none of us lives, and equally none of us dies, for himself alone. [8] If we live, we live for the Lord; and if we die, we die for the Lord. So whether we live or die, we belong to the Lord. [9] This is why Christ died and lived again, to establish his lordship over both dead and living. [10] You, then, why do you pass judgement on your fellow-Christian? And you, why do you look down on your fellow-Christian? We shall all stand before God's tribunal; [11] for we read in scripture, 'As I live, says the Lord, to me every knee shall bow and every tongue acknowledge God.' [12] So, you see, each of us will be answerable to God.

[13] Let us therefore cease judging one another, but rather make up our minds to place no obstacle or stumbling block in a fellow-Christian's way. [14] All that I know

13:10 **the fulfilment of the law**: *or* the whole content of the law.

of the Lord Jesus convinces me that nothing is impure in itself; only, if anyone considers something impure, then for him it is impure. ¹⁵ If your fellow-Christian is outraged by what you eat, then you are no longer guided by love. Do not by your eating be the ruin of one for whom Christ died! ¹⁶ You must not let what you think good be brought into disrepute; ¹⁷ for the kingdom of God is not eating and drinking, but justice, peace, and joy, inspired by the Holy Spirit. ¹⁸ Everyone who shows himself a servant of Christ in this way is acceptable to God and approved by men.

¹⁹ Let us, then, pursue the things that make for peace and build up the common life. ²⁰ Do not destroy the work of God for the sake of food. Everything is pure in itself, but it is wrong to eat if by eating you cause another to stumble. ²¹ It is right to abstain from eating meat or drinking wine or from anything else which causes a fellow-Christian to stumble. ²² If you have some firm conviction, keep it between yourself and God. Anyone who can make his decision without misgivings is fortunate. ²³ But anyone who has misgivings and yet eats is guilty, because his action does not arise from conviction, and anything which does not arise from conviction is sin. ¹ Those of us who are strong must accept as our own burden the tender scruples of the weak, and not just please ourselves. ² Each of us must consider his neighbour and think what is for his good and will build up the common life. ³ Christ too did not please himself; to him apply the words of scripture, 'The reproaches of those who reproached you fell on me.' ⁴ The scriptures written long ago were all written for our instruction, in order that through the encouragement they give us we may maintain our hope with perseverance. ⁵ And may God, the source of all perseverance and all encouragement, grant that you may agree with one another after the manner of Christ Jesus, ⁶ and so with one mind and one voice may praise the God and Father of our Lord Jesus Christ.

⁷ In a word, accept one another as Christ accepted us, to the glory of God. ⁸ Remember that Christ became a servant of the Jewish people to maintain the faithfulness of God by making good his promises to the patriarchs, ⁹ and by giving the Gentiles cause to glorify God for his mercy. As scripture says, 'Therefore I will praise you among the Gentiles and sing hymns to your name'; ¹⁰ and again, 'Gentiles, join in celebration with his people'; ¹¹ and yet again, 'All Gentiles, praise the Lord; let all peoples praise him.' ¹² Once again, Isaiah says, 'The Scion of Jesse shall come, a ruler who rises to govern the Gentiles; on him shall they set their hope.' ¹³ And may God, who is the ground of hope, fill you with all joy and peace as you lead the life of faith until, by the power of the Holy Spirit, you overflow with hope.

¹⁴ My friends, I have no doubt in my own mind that you yourselves are full of goodness and equipped with knowledge of every kind, well able to give advice to one another; ¹⁵ nevertheless I have written to refresh your memory, and written somewhat boldly at times, in virtue of the gift I have from God. ¹⁶ His grace has made me a minister of Christ Jesus to the Gentiles; and in the service of the gospel of God it is my priestly task to offer the Gentiles to him as an acceptable sacrifice, consecrated by the Holy Spirit.

¹⁷ In Christ Jesus I have indeed grounds for pride in the service of God. ¹⁸ I will venture to speak only of what Christ has done through me to bring the Gentiles into his allegiance, by word and deed, ¹⁹ by the power of signs and portents, and by the power of the Holy Spirit. I have completed the preaching of the gospel of Christ from Jerusalem as far round as Illyricum. ²⁰ But I have always made a point of taking the gospel to places where the name of Christ has not been heard, not wanting to build on another man's foundation; ²¹ as scripture says,

Those who had no news of him shall see,
and those who never heard of him shall understand.

²² That is why I have been prevented all this time from coming to you. ²³ But now I have no further scope in these parts, and I

14:23 *See note on 16:27.*

145

have been longing for many years to visit you [24] on my way to Spain; for I hope to see you in passing, and to be sent on my way there with your support after having enjoyed your company for a while. [25] But at the moment I am on my way to Jerusalem, on an errand to God's people there. [26] For Macedonia and Achaia have resolved to raise a fund for the benefit of the poor among God's people at Jerusalem. [27] They have resolved to do so, and indeed they are under an obligation to them. For if the Jewish Christians shared their spiritual treasures with the Gentiles, the Gentiles have a clear duty to contribute to their material needs. [28] So when I have finished this business and seen the proceeds safely delivered to them, I shall set out for Spain and visit you on the way; [29] I am sure that when I come it will be with a full measure of the blessing of Christ.

[30] I implore you by our Lord Jesus Christ and by the love that the Spirit inspires, be my allies in the fight; pray to God for me [31] that I may be saved from unbelievers in Judaea and that my errand to Jerusalem may find acceptance with God's people, [32] in order that by his will I may come to you in a happy frame of mind and enjoy a time of rest with you. [33] The God of peace be with you all. Amen.

Greetings

16 I COMMEND to you Phoebe, my fellow-Christian who is a minister in the church at Cenchreae. [2] Give her, in the fellowship of the Lord, a welcome worthy of God's people, and support her in any business in which she may need your help, for she has herself been a good friend to many, including myself.

[3] Give my greetings to Prisca and Aquila, my fellow-workers in Christ Jesus. [4] They risked their necks to save my life, and not I alone but all the gentile churches are grateful to them. [5] Greet also the church that meets at their house.

Give my greetings to my dear friend Epaenetus, the first convert to Christ in Asia, [6] and to Mary, who worked so hard for you. [7] Greet Andronicus and Junia, my fellow-countrymen and comrades in captivity, who are eminent among the apostles and were Christians before I was.

[8] Greetings to Ampliatus, my dear friend in the fellowship of the Lord, [9] to Urban my comrade in Christ, and to my dear Stachys. [10] My greetings to Apelles, well proved in Christ's service, to the household of Aristobulus, [11] to my countryman Herodion, and to those of the household of Narcissus who are in the Lord's fellowship. [12] Greet Tryphaena and Tryphosa, who work hard in the Lord's service, and dear Persis who has worked hard in his service for so long. [13] Give my greetings to Rufus, an outstanding follower of the Lord, and to his mother, whom I call mother too. [14] Greet Asyncritus, Phlegon, Hermes, Patrobas, Hermas, and any other Christians who are with them. [15] Greet Philologus and Julia, Nereus and his sister, and Olympas, and all God's people who are with them.

[16] Greet one another with the kiss of peace. All Christ's churches send you their greetings.

[17] I implore you, my friends, keep an eye on those who stir up quarrels and lead others astray, contrary to the teaching you received. Avoid them; [18] such people are servants not of Christ our Lord but of their own appetites, and they seduce the minds of simple people with smooth and specious words. [19] The fame of your obedience has spread everywhere, and this makes me happy about you. I want you to be expert in goodness, but innocent of evil, [20] and the God of peace will soon crush Satan beneath your feet. The grace of our Lord Jesus be with you!

[21] Greetings to you from my colleague Timothy, and from Lucius, Jason, and Sosipater my fellow-countrymen. [22] (I Tertius, who took this letter down, add my Christian greetings.) [23] Greetings also from Gaius, my host and host of the whole congregation, and from Erastus, treasurer of this city, and our brother Quartus.

[25] To him who has power to make you stand firm, according to my gospel and the proclamation of Jesus Christ, according to the revelation of that divine secret kept in silence for long ages [26] but now

---

15:33 *See note on* 16:27.   16:1 **minister:** *or* deacon.   16:7 **Junia:** *or* Junias.   16:15 **Julia:** *or* Julias.   16:20 **The grace ... with you:** *These words are omitted at this point in some witnesses; in some, these or similar words are given as verse 24, and in some others after verse 27.*   16:23 *After this verse some witnesses add* [24] The grace of our Lord Jesus Christ be with you all! Amen.

disclosed, and by the eternal God's command made known to all nations through prophetic scriptures, to bring them to faith and obedience—²⁷ to the only wise God through Jesus Christ be glory for endless ages! Amen.

16:27 *After this verse some witnesses add* The grace of our Lord Jesus Christ be with you! *Some witnesses place verses 25–27 at the end of chapter 14, one other places them at the end of chapter 15, and others omit them altogether.*

THE FIRST LETTER OF PAUL TO THE
CORINTHIANS

1 FROM Paul, apostle of Christ Jesus by God's call and by his will, together with our colleague Sosthenes, ² to God's church at Corinth, dedicated to him in Christ Jesus, called to be his people, along with all who invoke the name of our Lord Jesus Christ wherever they may be—their Lord as well as ours.

³ Grace and peace to you from God our Father and the Lord Jesus Christ.

⁴ I am always thanking God for you. I thank him for his grace given to you in Christ Jesus; ⁵ I thank him for all the enrichment that has come to you in Christ. You possess full knowledge and you can give full expression to it, ⁶ because what we testified about Christ has been confirmed in your experience. ⁷ There is indeed no single gift you lack, while you wait expectantly for our Lord Jesus Christ to reveal himself. ⁸ He will keep you firm to the end, without reproach on the day of our Lord Jesus. ⁹ It is God himself who called you to share in the life of his Son Jesus Christ our Lord; and God keeps faith.

True and false wisdom

¹⁰ I APPEAL to you, my friends, in the name of our Lord Jesus Christ: agree among yourselves, and avoid divisions; let there be complete unity of mind and thought. ¹¹ My friends, it has been brought to my notice by Chloe's people that there are quarrels among you. ¹² What I mean is this: each of you is saying, 'I am for Paul,' or 'I am for Apollos'; 'I am for Cephas,' or 'I am for Christ.' ¹³ Surely Christ has not been divided! Was it Paul who was crucified for you? Was it in Paul's name that you were

baptized? ¹⁴ Thank God, I never baptized any of you, except Crispus and Gaius; ¹⁵ no one can say you were baptized in my name. ¹⁶ I did of course baptize the household of Stephanas; I cannot think of anyone else. ¹⁷ Christ did not send me to baptize, but to proclaim the gospel; and to do it without recourse to the skills of rhetoric, lest the cross of Christ be robbed of its effect.

¹⁸ The message of the cross is sheer folly to those on the way to destruction, but to us, who are on the way to salvation, it is the power of God. ¹⁹ Scripture says, 'I will destroy the wisdom of the wise, and bring to nothing the cleverness of the clever.' ²⁰ Where is your wise man now, your man of learning, your subtle debater of this present age? God has made the wisdom of this world look foolish! ²¹ As God in his wisdom ordained, the world failed to find him by its wisdom, and he chose by the folly of the gospel to save those who have faith. ²² Jews demand signs, Greeks look for wisdom, ²³ but we proclaim Christ nailed to the cross; and though this is an offence to Jews and folly to Gentiles, ²⁴ yet to those who are called, Jews and Greeks alike, he is the power of God and the wisdom of God.

²⁵ The folly of God is wiser than human wisdom, and the weakness of God stronger than human strength. ²⁶ My friends, think what sort of people you are, whom God has called. Few of you are wise by any human standard, few powerful or of noble birth. ²⁷ Yet, to shame the wise, God has chosen what the world counts folly, and to shame what is strong, God has chosen what the world counts weakness. ²⁸ He has chosen things without

rank or standing in the world, mere nothings, to overthrow the existing order. [29] So no place is left for any human pride in the presence of God. [30] By God's act you are in Christ Jesus; God has made him our wisdom, and in him we have our right-eousness, our holiness, our liberation. [31] Therefore, in the words of scripture, 'If anyone must boast, let him boast of the Lord.'

2 So it was, my friends, that I came to you, without any pretensions to elo-quence or wisdom in declaring the truth about God. [2] I resolved that while I was with you I would not claim to know anything but Jesus Christ—Christ nailed to the cross. [3] I came before you in weak-ness, in fear, in great trepidation. [4] The word I spoke, the gospel I proclaimed, did not sway you with clever arguments; it carried conviction by spiritual power, [5] so that your faith might be built not on human wisdom but on the power of God.

[6] Among the mature I do speak words of wisdom, though not a wisdom belonging to this present age or to its governing powers, already in decline; [7] I speak God's hidden wisdom, his secret purpose framed from the very beginning to bring us to our destined glory. [8] None of the powers that rule the world has known that wisdom; if they had, they would not have crucified the Lord of glory. [9] Scripture speaks of 'things beyond our seeing, things beyond our hearing, things beyond our imagin-ing, all prepared by God for those who love him'; [10] and these are what God has revealed to us through the Spirit. For the Spirit explores everything, even the depths of God's own nature. [11] Who knows what a human being is but the human spirit within him? In the same way, only the Spirit of God knows what God is. [12] And we have received this Spirit from God, not the spirit of the world, so that we may know all that God has lavished on us; [13] and, because we are interpreting spiritual truths to those who have the Spirit, we speak of these gifts of God in words taught us not by our human wisdom but by the Spirit. [14] An unspiritual person refuses what belongs to the Spirit of God; it is folly to him; he cannot grasp it, because it needs to be judged in the light of the Spirit. [15] But a spiritual person can judge the worth of everything, yet is not himself subject to judgement by others. [16] Scripture indeed asks, 'Who can know the mind of the Lord or be his counsellor?' Yet we possess the mind of Christ.

Servants of Christ

3 But I could not talk to you, my friends, as people who have the Spirit; I had to deal with you on the natural plane, as infants in Christ. [2] I fed you on milk, instead of solid food, for which you were not yet ready. Indeed, you are still not ready for it; [3] you are still on the merely natural plane. Can you not see that as long as there is jealousy and strife among you, you are unspiritual, living on the purely human level? [4] When one declares, 'I am for Paul,' and another, 'I am for Apollos,' are you not all too human?

[5] After all, what is Apollos? What is Paul? Simply God's agents in bringing you to faith. Each of us performed the task which the Lord assigned to him: [6] I planted the seed, and Apollos watered it; but God made it grow. [7] It is not the gardeners with their planting and water-ing who count, but God who makes it grow. [8] Whether they plant or water, they work as a team, though each will get his own pay for his own labour. [9] We are fellow-workers in God's service; and you are God's garden.

Or again, you are God's building. [10] God gave me the privilege of laying the foun-dation like a skilled master builder; others put up the building. Let each take care how he builds. [11] There can be no other foundation than the one already laid: I mean Jesus Christ himself. [12] If anyone builds on that foundation with gold, silver, and precious stones, or with wood, hay, and straw, [13] the work that each does will at last be brought to light; the day of judgement will expose it. For that day dawns in fire, and the fire will test the worth of each person's work. [14] If any-one's building survives, he will be re-warded; [15] if it burns down, he will have to bear the loss; yet he will escape with his life, though only by passing through the

---

2:1 **declaring ... God:** *some witnesses read* declaring God's secret purpose.   3:9 **We ... service:** *or* We are God's fellow-workers.

fire. [16] Surely you know that you are God's temple, where the Spirit of God dwells. [17] Anyone who destroys God's temple will himself be destroyed by God, because the temple of God is holy; and you are that temple.

[18] Make no mistake about this: if there is anyone among you who fancies himself wise—wise, I mean, by the standards of this age—he must become a fool if he is to be truly wise. [19] For the wisdom of this world is folly in God's sight. Scripture says, 'He traps the wise in their own cunning,' [20] and again, 'The Lord knows that the arguments of the wise are futile.' [21] So never make any human being a cause for boasting. For everything belongs to you—[22] Paul, Apollos, and Cephas, the world, life, and death, the present and the future, all are yours—[23] and you belong to Christ, and Christ to God.

4 We are to be regarded as Christ's subordinates and as stewards of the secrets of God. [2] Now stewards are required to show themselves trustworthy. [3] To me it matters not at all if I am called to account by you or by any human court. Nor do I pass judgement on myself, [4] for I have nothing on my conscience; but that does not prove me innocent. My judge is the Lord. [5] So pass no premature judgement; wait until the Lord comes. He will bring to light what darkness hides and disclose our inward motives; then will be the time for each to receive commendation from God.

[6] My friends, I have applied all this to Apollos and myself for your benefit, so that you may take our case as an example, and learn the true meaning of 'nothing beyond what stands written', and may not be inflated with pride as you take sides in support of one against another. [7] My friend, who makes you so important? What do you possess that was not given you? And if you received it as a gift, why take the credit to yourself?

[8] No doubt you already have all you could desire; you have come into your fortune already! Without us you have come into your kingdom. How I wish you had indeed come into your kingdom; then you might share it with us! [9] For it seems to me God has made us apostles the last act in the show, like men condemned to death in the arena, a spectacle to the

whole universe—to angels as well as men. [10] We are fools for Christ's sake, while you are sensible Christians! We are weak; you are powerful! You are honoured; we are in disgrace! [11] To this day we go hungry and thirsty and in rags; we are beaten up; we wander from place to place; [12] we wear ourselves out earning a living with our own hands. People curse us, and we bless; they persecute us, and we submit; [13] they slander us, and we try to be conciliatory. To this day we are treated as the scum of the earth, as the dregs of humanity.

[14] I am not writing this to shame you, but to bring you to reason; for you are my dear children. [15] You may have thousands of tutors in Christ, but you have only one father; for in Christ Jesus you are my offspring, and mine alone, through the preaching of the gospel. [16] I appeal to you therefore to follow my example. [17] That is why I have sent Timothy, who is a dear son to me and a trustworthy Christian, to remind you of my way of life in Christ, something I teach everywhere in all the churches. [18] There are certain persons who are filled with self-importance because they think I am not coming to Corinth. [19] I shall come very soon, if it is the Lord's will; and then I shall take the measure of these self-important people, not by what they say, but by what they can do, [20] for the kingdom of God is not a matter of words, but of power. [21] Choose, then: am I to come to you with a rod in my hand, or with love and a gentle spirit?

Sexual immorality

5 I ACTUALLY hear reports of sexual immorality among you, immorality such as even pagans do not tolerate: the union of a man with his stepmother. [2] And you are proud of yourselves! You ought to have gone into mourning; anyone who behaves like that should be turned out of your community. [3] For my part, though I am absent in body, I am present in spirit, and have already reached my judgement on the man who did this thing, as if I were indeed present: [4] when you are all assembled in the name of our Lord Jesus, and I am with you in spirit, through the power of our Lord Jesus you are [5] to consign this man to Satan for the destruction of his body, so that his spirit may be saved on the day of the Lord.

⁶ Your self-satisfaction ill becomes you. Have you never heard the saying, 'A little leaven leavens all the dough'? ⁷ Get rid of the old leaven and then you will be a new batch of unleavened dough. Indeed you already are, because Christ our Passover lamb has been sacrificed. ⁸ So we who observe the festival must not use the old leaven, the leaven of depravity and wickedness, but only the unleavened bread which is sincerity and truth.

⁹ In my letter I wrote that you must have nothing to do with those who are sexually immoral. ¹⁰ I was not, of course, referring to people in general who are immoral or extortioners or swindlers or idolaters; to avoid them you would have to withdraw from society altogether. ¹¹ I meant that you must have nothing to do with any so-called Christian who leads an immoral life, or is extortionate, idolatrous, a slanderer, a drunkard, or a swindler; with anyone like that you should not even eat. ¹²⁻¹³ What business of mine is it to judge outsiders? God is their judge. But within the fellowship, you are the judges: 'Root out the wrong-doer from your community.'

Lawsuits among Christians

6 IF one of your number has a dispute with another, does he have the face to go to law before a pagan court instead of before God's people? ² It is God's people who are to judge the world; surely you know that. And if the world is subject to your judgement, are you not competent to deal with these trifling cases? ³ Are you not aware that we are to judge angels, not to mention day to day affairs? ⁴ If therefore you have such everyday disputes, how can you entrust jurisdiction to outsiders with no standing in the church? ⁵ I write this to shame you. Can it be that there is not among you a single person wise enough to give a decision in a fellow-Christian's cause? ⁶ Must Christian go to law with Christian—and before unbelievers at that? ⁷ Indeed, you suffer defeat by going to law with one another at all. Why not rather submit to wrong? Why not let yourself be defrauded? ⁸ But instead, it is you who are wronging and defrauding, and fellow-Christians at that! ⁹ Surely you know that wrongdoers will never possess the kingdom of God. Make no mistake: no fornicator or idolater, no

adulterer or sexual pervert, ¹⁰ no thief, extortioner, drunkard, slanderer, or swindler will possess the kingdom of God. ¹¹ Such were some of you; but you have been washed clean, you have been dedicated to God, you have been justified through the name of the Lord Jesus and through the Spirit of our God.

¹² 'I am free to do anything,' you say. Yes, but not everything does good. No doubt I am free to do anything, but I for one will not let anything make free with me. ¹³ 'Food is for the belly and the belly for food,' you say. True; and one day God will put an end to both. But the body is not for fornication; it is for the Lord—and the Lord for the body. ¹⁴ God not only raised our Lord from the dead; he will also raise us by his power. ¹⁵ Do you not know that your bodies are limbs and organs of Christ? Shall I then take parts of Christ's body and make them over to a prostitute? Never! ¹⁶ You surely know that anyone who joins himself to a prostitute becomes physically one with her, for scripture says, 'The two shall become one flesh'; ¹⁷ but anyone who joins himself to the Lord is one with him spiritually. ¹⁸ Have nothing to do with fornication. Every other sin that one may commit is outside the body; but the fornicator sins against his own body. ¹⁹ Do you not know that your body is a temple of the indwelling Holy Spirit, and the Spirit is God's gift to you? You do not belong to yourselves; ²⁰ you were bought at a price. Then honour God in your body.

Sex, marriage, and divorce

7 NOW FOR the matters you wrote about. You say, 'It is a good thing for a man not to have intercourse with a woman.' ² Rather, in the face of so much immorality, let each man have his own wife and each woman her own husband. ³ The husband must give the wife what is due to her, and equally the wife must give the husband his due. ⁴ The wife cannot claim her body as her own; it is her husband's. Equally, the husband cannot claim his body as his own; it is his wife's. ⁵ Do not deny yourselves to one another, except when you agree to devote yourselves to prayer for a time, and to come together again afterwards; otherwise, through lack of self-control, you may be tempted by Satan. ⁶ I say this by way of

concession, not command. [7] I should like everyone to be as I myself am; but each person has the gift God has granted him, one this gift and another that.

[8] To the unmarried and to widows I say this: it is a good thing if like me they stay as they are; [9] but if they do not have self-control, they should marry. It is better to be married than burn with desire.

[10] To the married I give this ruling, which is not mine but the Lord's: a wife must not separate herself from her husband—[11] if she does, she must either remain unmarried or be reconciled to her husband—and the husband must not divorce his wife.

[12] To the rest I say this, as my own word, not as the Lord's: if a Christian has a wife who is not a believer, and she is willing to live with him, he must not divorce her; [13] and if a woman has a husband who is not a believer, and he is willing to live with her, she must not divorce him. [14] For the husband now belongs to God through his Christian wife, and the wife through her Christian husband. Otherwise your children would not belong to God, whereas in fact they do. [15] If however the unbelieving partner wishes for a separation, it should be granted; in such cases the Christian husband or wife is not bound by the marriage. God's call is a call to live in peace. [16] But remember: a wife may save her husband; and a husband may save his wife.

[17] However that may be, each one should accept the lot which the Lord has assigned him and continue as he was when God called him. That is the rule I give in all the churches. [18] Was a man called with the marks of circumcision on him? Let him not remove them. Was he uncircumcised when he was called? Let him not be circumcised. [19] Circumcision or uncircumcision is neither here nor there; what matters is to keep God's commands. [20] Everyone should remain in the condition in which he was called. [21] Were you a slave when you were called? Do not let that trouble you; though if a chance of freedom should

come, by all means take it. [22] Anyone who received his call to be a Christian while a slave is the Lord's freedman, and, equally, every free man who has received the call is a slave in the service of Christ. [23] You were bought at a price; do not become slaves of men. [24] So, my friends, everyone is to remain before God in the condition in which he received his call.

[25] About the unmarried, I have no instructions from the Lord, but I give my opinion as one who by the Lord's mercy is fit to be trusted. [26] I think the best way for a man to live in a time of stress like the present is this—to remain as he is. [27] Are you bound in marriage? Do not seek a dissolution. Has your marriage been dissolved? Do not seek a wife. [28] But if you do marry, you are not doing anything wrong, nor does a girl if she marries; it is only that those who marry will have hardships to endure, and my aim is to spare you.

[29] What I mean, my friends, is this: the time we live in will not last long. While it lasts, married men should be as if they had no wives; [30] mourners should be as if they had nothing to grieve them, the joyful as if they did not rejoice; those who buy should be as if they possessed nothing, [31] and those who use the world's wealth as if they did not have full use of it. For the world as we know it is passing away.

[32] I want you to be free from anxious care. An unmarried man is concerned with the Lord's business; his aim is to please the Lord. [33] But a married man is concerned with worldly affairs; his aim is to please his wife, [34] and he is pulled in two directions. The unmarried woman or girl is concerned with the Lord's business; her aim is to be dedicated to him in body as in spirit. But the married woman is concerned with worldly affairs; her aim is to please her husband.

[35] In saying this I am thinking simply of your own good. I have no wish to keep you on a tight rein; I only want you to be beyond criticism and be free from distraction in your devotion to the Lord. [36] But if

7:21 *though if ... take it:* or but even if a chance of freedom should come, choose rather to make good use of your servitude.   7:33–34 *his wife ... girl is concerned:* some witnesses read his wife. [34] There is this difference between the wife and the virgin; the unmarried woman is concerned.   7:36–38 *But if ... better:* or But if a man feels open to criticism about his daughter, because she has reached puberty and the normal course ought to be followed, he may do as he wishes: let the marriage take place; there is nothing wrong in it. [37] But if a man is steadfast in his purpose and under no obligation, if he is free to act at his own discretion, and has decided in his

151

a man feels that he is not behaving properly towards the girl to whom he is betrothed, if his passions are strong and something must be done, let him carry out his intention by getting married; there is nothing wrong in it. [37]But if a man is steadfast in his purpose and under no obligation, if he is free to act at his own discretion, and has decided in his own mind to respect her virginity, he will do well. [38]Thus he who marries his betrothed does well, and he who does not marry does better.

[39]A wife is bound to her husband as long as he lives. But if the husband dies, she is free to marry whom she will, provided the marriage is within the Lord's fellowship. [40]But she is better off as she is; that is my opinion, and I believe that I too have the Spirit of God.

Food offered to idols

8 Now ABOUT meat consecrated to heathen deities.

Of course 'We all have knowledge,' as you say. 'Knowledge' inflates a man, whereas love builds him up. [2]If anyone fancies that he has some kind of knowledge, he does not yet know in the true sense of knowing. [3]But if anyone loves God, he is known by God.

[4]Well then, about eating this consecrated meat: of course, as you say, 'A false god has no real existence, and there is no god but one.' [5]Even though there be so-called gods, whether in heaven or on earth—and indeed there are many such gods and many such lords—[6]yet for us there is one God, the Father, from whom are all things, and we exist for him; there is one Lord, Jesus Christ, through whom are all things, and we exist through him.

[7]But not everyone possesses this knowledge. There are some who have been so accustomed to idolatry that they still think of this meat as consecrated to the idol, and their conscience, being weak, is defiled by eating it. [8]Certainly food will not bring us into God's presence: if we do not eat, we are none the worse,

and if we do eat, we are none the better. [9]But be careful that this liberty of yours does not become a pitfall for the weak. [10]If one of them sees you sitting down to a meal in a heathen temple—you with your 'knowledge'—will not his conscience be emboldened to eat meat consecrated to the heathen deity? [11]This 'knowledge' of yours destroys the weak, the fellow-Christian for whom Christ died. [12]In sinning against your brothers and sisters in this way and wounding their conscience, weak as it is, you sin against Christ. [13]Therefore, if food be the downfall of a fellow-Christian, I will never eat meat again, for I will not be the cause of a fellow-Christian's downfall.

9 AM I not free? Am I not an apostle? Have I not seen Jesus our Lord? Are not you my own handiwork in the Lord? [2]If others do not accept me as an apostle, you at least are bound to do so, for in the Lord you are the very seal of my apostleship.

[3]To those who would call me to account, this is my defence: [4]Have I no right to eat and drink? [5]Have I not the right to take a Christian wife about with me, like the rest of the apostles and the Lord's brothers and Cephas? [6]Are only Barnabas and I bound to work for our living? [7]Did you ever hear of a man serving in the army at his own expense? Or planting a vineyard without eating the fruit? Or tending a flock without using the milk? [8]My case does not rest on these human analogies, for the law says the same; [9]in the law of Moses we read, 'You shall not muzzle an ox while it is treading out the grain.' Do you suppose God's concern is with oxen? [10]Must not the saying refer to us? Of course it does: the ploughman should plough and the thresher thresh in hope of sharing the produce. [11]If we have sown a spiritual crop for you, is it too much to expect from you a material harvest? [12]If you allow others those rights, have not we a stronger claim?

own mind to keep the girl unmarried, he will do well. [38] Thus he who gives his daughter in marriage does well, and he who does not does better. *Or* But if a man has a partner in celibacy and feels that he is not behaving properly towards her, if, that is, his instincts are too strong for him, and something must be done, let him do what he wishes: let them marry; there is nothing wrong in it. [37]But if a man is steadfast in his purpose and under no obligation, if he is free to act at his own discretion, and has decided in his own mind to keep his partner in her virginity, he will do well. [38]Thus he who marries his partner does well, and he who does not marry her does better.   8:12 *Some witnesses omit* weak as it is.

But I have never availed myself of any such right. On the contrary, I put up with all that comes my way rather than offer any hindrance to the gospel of Christ. [13] You must know that those who are engaged in temple service eat the temple offerings, and those who officiate at the altar claim their share of the sacrifice. [14] In the same way the Lord gave instructions that those who preach the gospel should get their living by the gospel. [15] But I have never taken advantage of any such right, nor do I intend to claim it in this letter. I had rather die! No one shall make my boast an empty boast. [16] Even if I preach the gospel, I can claim no credit for it; I cannot help myself; it would be agony for me not to preach. [17] If I did it of my own choice, I should be earning my pay; but since I have no choice, I am simply discharging a trust. [18] Then what is my pay? It is the satisfaction of preaching the gospel without expense to anyone; in other words, of waiving the rights my preaching gives me.

[19] I am free and own no master; but I have made myself everyone's servant, to win over as many as possible. [20] To Jews I behaved like a Jew, to win Jews; that is, to win those under the law I behaved as if under the law, though not myself subject to the law. [21] To win those outside that law, I behaved as if outside the law, though not myself outside God's law, but subject to the law of Christ. [22] To the weak I became weak, to win the weak. To them all I have become everything in turn, so that in one way or another I may save some. [23] All this I do for the sake of the gospel, to have a share in its blessings.

[24] At the games, as you know, all the runners take part, though only one wins the prize. [25] You also must run to win. Every athlete goes into strict training. They do it to win a fading garland; we, to win a garland that never fades. [26] For my part, I am no aimless runner; I am not a boxer who beats the air. [27] I do not spare my body, but bring it under strict control, for fear that after preaching to others I should find myself disqualified.

10 Let me remind you, my friends, that our ancestors were all under the cloud, and all of them passed through

the Red Sea; [2] so they all received baptism into the fellowship of Moses in cloud and sea. [3] They all ate the same supernatural food, [4] and all drank the same supernatural drink; for they drank from the supernatural rock that accompanied their travels—and that rock was Christ. [5] Yet most of them were not accepted by God, for the wilderness was strewn with their corpses.

[6] These events happened as warnings to us not to set our desires on evil things as they did. [7] Do not be idolaters, like some of them; as scripture says, 'The people sat down to feast and rose up to revel.' [8] Let us not commit fornication; some of them did, and twenty-three thousand died in one day. [9] Let us not put the Lord to the test as some of them did; they were destroyed by the snakes. [10] Do not grumble as some of them did; they were destroyed by the Destroyer.

[11] All these things that happened to them were symbolic, and were recorded as a warning for us, upon whom the end of the ages has come. [12] If you think you are standing firm, take care, or you may fall. [13] So far you have faced no trial beyond human endurance; God keeps faith and will not let you be tested beyond your powers, but when the test comes he will at the same time provide a way out and so enable you to endure.

[14] So THEN, my dear friends, have nothing to do with idolatry. [15] I appeal to you as sensible people; form your own judgement on what I say. [16] When we bless the cup of blessing, is it not a means of sharing in the blood of Christ? When we break the bread, is it not a means of sharing in the body of Christ? [17] Because there is one loaf, we, though many, are one body; for it is one loaf of which we all partake.

[18] Consider Jewish practice: are not those who eat the sacrificial meal partners in the altar? [19] What do I imply by this? That meat consecrated to an idol is anything more than meat, or that an idol is anything more than an idol? [20] No, I mean that pagan sacrifices are offered (in the words of scripture) 'to demons and to that which is not God'; and I will not have

10:9 **the Lord:** *some witnesses read* Christ.   10:17 **Because ... body:** *or* For we, many as we are, are one loaf, one body.

you become partners with demons. ²¹ You cannot drink the cup of the Lord and the cup of demons. You cannot partake of the Lord's table and the table of demons. ²² Are we to provoke the Lord? Are we stronger than he is?

²³ 'We are free to do anything,' you say. Yes, but not everything is good for us. We are free to do anything, but not everything builds up the community. ²⁴ You should each look after the interests of others, not your own.

²⁵ You may eat anything sold in the meat market without raising questions of conscience; ²⁶ 'for the earth is the Lord's and all that is in it'.

²⁷ If an unbeliever invites you to a meal and you accept, eat whatever is put before you, without raising questions of conscience. ²⁸ But if somebody says to you, 'This food has been offered in sacrifice,' then, out of consideration for him and for conscience' sake, do not eat it—²⁹ not your conscience, I mean, but his.

'What?' you say. 'Is my freedom to be called in question by another's conscience? ³⁰ If I partake with thankfulness, why am I blamed for eating food over which I have said grace?' ³¹ You may eat or drink, or do anything else, provided it is all done to the glory of God; ³² give no offence to Jews, or Greeks, or to the church of God. ³³ For my part I always try to be considerate to everyone, not seeking my own good but the good of the many, so

11 that they may be saved. ¹ Follow my example as I follow Christ's.

Public worship

² I COMMEND you for always keeping me in mind, and maintaining the tradition I handed on to you. ³ But I wish you to understand that, while every man has Christ for his head, a woman's head is man, as Christ's head is God. ⁴ A man who keeps his head covered when he prays or prophesies brings shame on his head; ⁵ but a woman brings shame on her head if she prays or prophesies bareheaded; it is as bad as if her head were shaved. ⁶ If a woman does not cover her head she might as well have her hair cut off; but if it is a disgrace for her to be cropped and shaved, then she should cover her head. ⁷ A man must not cover his head, because

man is the image of God, and the mirror of his glory, whereas a woman reflects the glory of man. ⁸ For man did not originally spring from woman, but woman was made out of man; ⁹ and man was not created for woman's sake, but woman for the sake of man; ¹⁰ and therefore a woman must have the sign of her authority on her head, out of regard for the angels. ¹¹ Yet in the Lord's fellowship woman is as essential to man as man to woman. ¹² If woman was made out of man, it is through woman that man now comes to be; and God is the source of all.

¹³ Judge for yourselves: is it fitting for a woman to pray to God bareheaded? ¹⁴ Does not nature herself teach you that while long hair disgraces a man, ¹⁵ it is a woman's glory? For her hair was given as a covering.

¹⁶ And if anyone still insists on arguing, there is no such custom among us, or in any of the congregations of God's people.

¹⁷ In giving you these instructions I come to something I cannot commend: your meetings tend to do more harm than good. ¹⁸ To begin with, I am told that when you meet as a congregation you fall into sharply divided groups. I believe there is some truth in it, ¹⁹ for divisions are bound to arise among you if only to show which of your members are genuine. ²⁰ The result is that when you meet as a congregation, it is not the Lord's Supper you eat; when it comes to eating, ²¹ each of you takes his own supper, one goes hungry and another has too much to drink. ²² Have you no homes of your own to eat and drink in? Or are you so contemptuous of the church of God that you shame its poorer members? What am I to say? Can I commend you? On this point, certainly not!

²³ For the tradition which I handed on to you came to me from the Lord himself: that on the night of his arrest the Lord Jesus took bread, ²⁴ and after giving thanks to God broke it and said: 'This is my body, which is for you; do this in memory of me.' ²⁵ In the same way, he took the cup after supper, and said: 'This cup is the new covenant sealed by my blood. Whenever you drink it, do this in memory of me.' ²⁶ For every time you eat this bread and drink the cup, you

11:3 **is man:** *or* is her husband.   11:7 **a woman ... man:** *or* a woman reflects her husband's glory.

proclaim the death of the Lord, until he comes.

²⁷ It follows that anyone who eats the bread or drinks the cup of the Lord unworthily will be guilty of offending against the body and blood of the Lord. ²⁸ Everyone must test himself before eating from the bread and drinking from the cup. ²⁹ For he who eats and drinks eats and drinks judgement on himself if he does not discern the body. ³⁰ That is why many of you are feeble and sick, and a number have died. ³¹ But if we examined ourselves, we should not fall under judgement. ³² When, however, we do fall under the Lord's judgement, he is disciplining us to save us from being condemned with the rest of the world.

³³ Therefore, my friends, when you meet for this meal, wait for one another. ³⁴ If you are hungry, eat at home, so that in meeting together you may not fall under judgement. The other matters I will settle when I come.

Spiritual gifts

12 ABOUT gifts of the Spirit, my friends, I want there to be no misunderstanding.

² You know how, in the days when you were still pagan, you used to be carried away by some impulse or other to those dumb heathen gods. ³ For this reason I must impress upon you that no one who says 'A curse on Jesus!' can be speaking under the influence of the Spirit of God; and no one can say 'Jesus is Lord!' except under the influence of the Holy Spirit.

⁴ There are varieties of gifts, but the same Spirit. ⁵ There are varieties of service, but the same Lord. ⁶ There are varieties of activity, but in all of them and in everyone the same God is active. ⁷ In each of us the Spirit is seen to be at work for some useful purpose. ⁸ One, through the Spirit, has the gift of wise speech, while another, by the power of the same Spirit, can put the deepest knowledge into words. ⁹ Another, by the same Spirit, is granted faith; another, by the one Spirit, gifts of healing, ¹⁰ and another miraculous powers; another has the gift of prophecy, and another the ability to distinguish true spirits from false; yet another has the gift of tongues of various kinds, and another the ability to interpret them. ¹¹ But all these gifts are the activity of one and the same Spirit, distributing them to each individual at will.

¹² Christ is like a single body with its many limbs and organs, which, many as they are, together make up one body; ¹³ for in the one Spirit we were all brought into one body by baptism, whether Jews or Greeks, slaves or free; we were all given that one Spirit to drink.

¹⁴ A body is not a single organ, but many. ¹⁵ Suppose the foot were to say, 'Because I am not a hand, I do not belong to the body,' it belongs to the body none the less. ¹⁶ Suppose the ear were to say, 'Because I am not an eye, I do not belong to the body,' it still belongs to the body. ¹⁷ If the body were all eye, how could it hear? If the body were all ear, how could it smell? ¹⁸ But, in fact, God appointed each limb and organ to its own place in the body as he chose. ¹⁹ If the whole were a single organ, there would not be a body at all; ²⁰ in fact, however, there are many different organs, but one body. ²¹ The eye cannot say to the hand, 'I do not need you,' or the head to the feet, 'I do not need you.' ²² Quite the contrary: those parts of the body which seem to be more frail than others are indispensable, ²³ and those parts of the body which we regard as less honourable are treated with special honour. The parts we are modest about are treated with special respect, ²⁴ whereas our respectable parts have no such need. But God has combined the various parts of the body, giving special honour to the humbler parts, ²⁵ so that there might be no division in the body, but that all its parts might feel the same concern for one another. ²⁶ If one part suffers, all suffer together; if one flourishes, all rejoice together.

²⁷ Now you are Christ's body, and each of you a limb or organ of it. ²⁸ Within our community God has appointed in the first place apostles, in the second place prophets, thirdly teachers; then miracle-workers, then those who have gifts of healing, or ability to help others or power to guide them, or the gift of tongues of various kinds. ²⁹ Are all apostles? All prophets? All teachers? Do all work miracles? ³⁰ Do all have gifts of healing? Do all speak in tongues of ecstasy? Can all interpret them? ³¹ The higher gifts are those you should prize.

But I can show you an even better way.

13 I may speak in tongues of men or of angels, but if I have no love, I am a sounding gong or a clanging cymbal. [2] I may have the gift of prophecy and the knowledge of every hidden truth; I may have faith enough to move mountains; but if I have no love, I am nothing. [3] I may give all I possess to the needy, I may give my body to be burnt, but if I have no love, I gain nothing by it.

[4] Love is patient and kind. Love envies no one, is never boastful, never conceited, [5] never rude; love is never selfish, never quick to take offence. Love keeps no score of wrongs, [6] takes no pleasure in the sins of others, but delights in the truth. [7] There is nothing love cannot face; there is no limit to its faith, its hope, its endurance.

[8] Love will never come to an end. Prophecies will cease; tongues of ecstasy will fall silent; knowledge will vanish. [9] For our knowledge and our prophecy alike are partial, [10] and the partial vanishes when wholeness comes. [11] When I was a child I spoke like a child, thought like a child, reasoned like a child; but when I grew up I finished with childish things. [12] At present we see only puzzling reflections in a mirror, but one day we shall see face to face. My knowledge now is partial; then it will be whole, like God's knowledge of me. [13] There are three things that last for ever: faith, hope, and love; and the greatest of the three is love.

14 Make love your aim; then be eager for the gifts of the Spirit, above all for prophecy. [2] If anyone speaks in tongues he is talking with God, not with men and women; no one understands him, for he speaks divine mysteries in the Spirit. [3] On the other hand, if anyone prophesies, he is talking to men and women, and his words have power to build; they stimulate and they encourage. [4] Speaking in tongues may build up the speaker himself, but it is prophecy that builds up a Christian community. [5] I am happy for you all to speak in tongues, but happier still for you to prophesy. The prophet is worth more than one who speaks in tongues—unless indeed he can explain its meaning, and so help to build up the community. [6] Suppose, my friends, that when I come to you I speak in tongues: what good shall I do you unless

what I say contains something by way of revelation, or enlightenment, or prophecy, or instruction?

[7] Even with inanimate things that produce sounds—a flute, say, or a lyre—unless their notes are distinct, how can you tell what tune is being played? [8] Or again, if the trumpet-call is not clear, who will prepare for battle? [9] In the same way, if what you say in tongues yields no precise meaning, how can anyone tell what is being said? You will be talking to empty air. [10] There are any number of different languages in the world; nowhere is without language. [11] If I do not know the speaker's language, his words will be gibberish to me, and mine to him. [12] You are, I know, eager for gifts of the Spirit; then aspire above all to excel in those which build up the church.

[13] Anyone who speaks in tongues should pray for the ability to interpret. [14] If I use such language in prayer, my spirit prays, but my mind is barren. [15] What then? I will pray with my spirit, but also with my mind; I will sing hymns with my spirit, but with my mind as well. [16] Suppose you are praising God with the spirit alone: how will an ordinary person who is present be able to say 'Amen' to your thanksgiving, when he does not know what you are saying? [17] Your prayer of thanksgiving may be splendid, but it is no help to the other person. [18] Thank God, I am more gifted in tongues than any of you, [19] but in the congregation I would rather speak five intelligible words, for the benefit of others as well as myself, than thousands of words in the language of ecstasy.

[20] Do not be children in your thinking, my friends; be infants in evil, but in your thinking be grown-up. [21] We read in the law: 'I will speak to this people through strange tongues, and by the lips of foreigners; and even so they will not heed me, says the Lord.' [22] Clearly then these 'strange tongues' are not intended as a sign for believers, but for unbelievers, whereas prophecy is designed not for unbelievers but for believers. [23] So if the whole congregation is assembled and all are using the 'strange tongues' of ecstasy, and some uninstructed persons or unbelievers should enter, will they not think

---

13:3 **give my ... burnt:** *some witnesses read* seek glory by self-sacrifice.

you are mad? ²⁴ But if all are uttering prophecies, the visitor, when he enters, hears from everyone something that searches his conscience and brings conviction, ²⁵ and the secrets of his heart are laid bare. So he will fall down and worship God, declaring, 'God is certainly among you!'

²⁶ To sum up, my friends: when you meet for worship, each of you contributing a hymn, some instruction, a revelation, an ecstatic utterance, or its interpretation, see that all of these aim to build up the church. ²⁷ If anyone speaks in tongues, only two should speak, or at most three, one at a time, and someone must interpret. ²⁸ If there is no interpreter, they should keep silent and speak to themselves and to God. ²⁹ Of the prophets, two or three may speak, while the rest exercise their judgement upon what is said. ³⁰ If someone else present receives a revelation, let the first speaker stop. ³¹ You can all prophesy, one at a time, so that all may receive instruction and encouragement. ³² It is for prophets to control prophetic inspiration, ³³ for God is not a God of disorder but of peace.

As in all congregations of God's people, ³⁴ women should keep silent at the meeting. They have no permission to talk, but should keep their place as the law directs. ³⁵ If there is something they want to know, they can ask their husbands at home. It is a shocking thing for a woman to talk at the meeting.

³⁶ Did the word of God originate with you? Or are you the only people to whom it came? ³⁷ If anyone claims to be inspired or a prophet, let him recognize that what I write has the Lord's authority. ³⁸ If he does not acknowledge this, his own claim cannot be acknowledged.

³⁹ In short, my friends, be eager to prophesy; do not forbid speaking in tongues; ⁴⁰ but let all be done decently and in order.

The resurrection of the dead

15 AND now, my friends, I must remind you of the gospel that I preached to you; the gospel which you received, on which you have taken your stand, ² and which is now bringing you salvation. Remember the terms in which I preached the gospel to you—for I assume that you hold it fast and that your conversion was not in vain.

³ First and foremost, I handed on to you the tradition I had received: that Christ died for our sins, in accordance with the scriptures; ⁴ that he was buried; that he was raised to life on the third day, in accordance with the scriptures; ⁵ and that he appeared to Cephas, and afterwards to the Twelve. ⁶ Then he appeared to over five hundred of our brothers at once, most of whom are still alive, though some have died. ⁷ Then he appeared to James, and afterwards to all the apostles.

⁸ Last of all he appeared to me too; it was like a sudden, abnormal birth. ⁹ For I am the least of the apostles, indeed not fit to be called an apostle, because I had persecuted the church of God. ¹⁰ However, by God's grace I am what I am, and his grace to me has not proved vain; in my labours I have outdone them all—not I, indeed, but the grace of God working with me. ¹¹ But no matter whether it was I or they! This is what we all proclaim, and this is what you believed.

¹² Now if this is what we proclaim, that Christ was raised from the dead, how can some of you say there is no resurrection of the dead? ¹³ If there is no resurrection, then Christ was not raised; ¹⁴ and if Christ was not raised, then our gospel is null and void, and so too is your faith; ¹⁵ and we turn out to have given false evidence about God, because we bore witness that he raised Christ to life, whereas, if the dead are not raised, he did not raise him. ¹⁶ For if the dead are not raised, it follows that Christ was not raised; ¹⁷ and if Christ was not raised, your faith has nothing to it and you are still in your old state of sin. ¹⁸ It follows also that those who have died within Christ's fellowship are utterly lost. ¹⁹ If it is for this life only that Christ has given us hope, we of all people are most to be pitied.

²⁰ But the truth is, Christ was raised to life—the firstfruits of the harvest of the dead. ²¹ For since it was a man who brought death into the world, a man also brought resurrection of the dead. ²² As in Adam all die, so in Christ all will be brought to life; ²³ but each in proper order: Christ the firstfruits, and afterwards,

14:38 If ... acknowledged: *some witnesses read* If he refuses to recognize this, let him refuse!

at his coming, those who belong to Christ. [24] Then comes the end, when he delivers up the kingdom to God the Father, after deposing every sovereignty, authority, and power. [25] For he is destined to reign until God has put all enemies under his feet; [26] and the last enemy to be deposed is death. [27] Scripture says, 'He has put all things in subjection under his feet.' But in saying 'all things', it clearly means to exclude God who made all things subject to him; [28] and when all things are subject to him, then the Son himself will also be made subject to God who made all things subject to him, and thus God will be all in all.

[29] Again, there are those who receive baptism on behalf of the dead. What do you suppose they are doing? If the dead are not raised to life at all, what do they mean by being baptized on their behalf?

[30] And why do we ourselves face danger hour by hour? [31] Every day I die: I swear it by my pride in you, my friends—for in Christ Jesus our Lord I am proud of you. [32] With no more than human hopes, what would have been the point of my fighting those wild beasts at Ephesus? If the dead are never raised to life, 'Let us eat and drink, for tomorrow we die.'

[33] Make no mistake: 'Bad company ruins good character.' [34] Wake up, be sober, and stop sinning: some of you have no knowledge of God—to your shame I say it.

[35] But, you may ask, how are the dead raised? In what kind of body? [36] What stupid questions! The seed you sow does not come to life unless it has first died; [37] and what you sow is not the body that shall be, but a bare grain, of wheat perhaps, or something else; [38] and God gives it the body of his choice, each seed its own particular body. [39] All flesh is not the same: there is human flesh, flesh of beasts, of birds, and of fishes—all different. [40] There are heavenly bodies and earthly bodies; and the splendour of the heavenly bodies is one thing, the splendour of the earthly another. [41] The sun has a splendour of its own, the moon another splendour, and the stars yet another; and one star differs from another in brightness. [42] So it is with the resurrection of the dead: what is sown as a perishable thing is raised imperishable. [43] Sown in humiliation, it is raised in glory; sown in weakness, it is raised in power; [44] sown a physical body, it is raised a spiritual body.

If there is such a thing as a physical body, there is also a spiritual body. [45] It is in this sense that scripture says, 'The first man, Adam, became a living creature,' whereas the last Adam has become a life-giving spirit. [46] Observe, the spiritual does not come first; the physical body comes first, and then the spiritual. [47] The first man is from earth, made of dust: the second man is from heaven. [48] The man made of dust is the pattern of all who are made of dust, and the heavenly man is the pattern of all the heavenly. [49] As we have worn the likeness of the man made of dust, so we shall wear the likeness of the heavenly man.

[50] What I mean, my friends, is this: flesh and blood can never possess the kingdom of God, the perishable cannot possess the imperishable. [51] Listen! I will unfold a mystery: we shall not all die, but we shall all be changed [52] in a flash, in the twinkling of an eye, at the last trumpet-call. For the trumpet will sound, and the dead will rise imperishable, and we shall be changed. [53] This perishable body must be clothed with the imperishable, and what is mortal with immortality. [54] And when this perishable body has been clothed with the imperishable and our mortality has been clothed with immortality, then the saying of scripture will come true: 'Death is swallowed up; victory is won!' [55] 'O Death, where is your victory? O Death, where is your sting?' [56] The sting of death is sin, and sin gains its power from the law. [57] But thanks be to God! He gives us victory through our Lord Jesus Christ.

[58] Therefore, my dear friends, stand firm and immovable, and work for the Lord always, work without limit, since you know that in the Lord your labour cannot be lost.

Plans and greetings

16 NOW ABOUT the collection in aid of God's people: you should follow the instructions I gave to our churches in Galatia. [2] Every Sunday each of you is to

---

15:54 *Some witnesses omit* this perishable body has been clothed with the imperishable and.

put aside and keep by him whatever he can afford, so that there need be no collecting when I come. [3] When I arrive, I will give letters of introduction to persons approved by you, and send them to carry your gift to Jerusalem. [4] If it seems right for me to go as well, they can travel with me.

[5] I shall come to Corinth after passing through Macedonia—for I am travelling by way of Macedonia—[6] and I may stay some time with you, perhaps even for the whole winter; and then you can help me on my way wherever I go next. [7] I do not want this to be a flying visit; I hope to spend some time with you, if the Lord permits. [8] But I shall remain at Ephesus until Pentecost, [9] for a great opportunity has opened for effective work, and there is much opposition.

[10] If Timothy comes, see that you put him at his ease; for it is the Lord's work that he is engaged on, as I am myself; [11] so no one must slight him. Speed him on his way with your blessing; for he is to join me, and I am waiting for him with our friends. [12] As for our friend Apollos, I urged him strongly to go to Corinth with the others, but he was quite determined not to go at present; he will go when the time is right.

[13] Be on the alert; stand firm in the faith; be valiant, be strong. [14] Let everything you do be done in love.

[15] One thing more, my friends. You know that the Stephanas family were the first converts in Achaia, and have devoted themselves to the service of God's people. [16] I urge you to accept the leadership of people like them, of anyone who labours hard at our common task. [17] It is a great pleasure to me that Stephanas, Fortunatus, and Achaicus have arrived, because they have done what you had no chance to do; [18] they have raised my spirits—and no doubt yours too. Such people deserve recognition.

[19] Greetings from the churches of Asia. Many greetings in the Lord from Aquila and Prisca and the church that meets in their house. [20] Greetings from the whole brotherhood. Greet one another with the kiss of peace.

[21] This greeting is in my own hand—Paul.

[22] If anyone does not love the Lord, let him be outcast.

Marana tha—Come, Lord!

[23] The grace of the Lord Jesus be with you.

[24] My love to you all in Christ Jesus.

16:12 but ... not to go: *or* but it was clearly not the will of God that he should go.

THE SECOND LETTER OF PAUL TO THE
CORINTHIANS

1 FROM Paul, apostle of Christ Jesus by God's will, and our colleague Timothy, to God's church at Corinth, together with all God's people throughout the whole of Achaia.

[2] Grace and peace to you from God our Father and the Lord Jesus Christ.

[3] Praise be to the God and Father of our Lord Jesus Christ, the all-merciful Father, the God whose consolation never fails us! [4] He consoles us in all our troubles, so that we in turn may be able to console others in any trouble of theirs and to share with them the consolation we ourselves receive from God. [5] As Christ's suffering exceeds all measure and extends to us, so too it is through Christ that our consolation has no limit. [6] If distress is our lot, it is the price we pay for your consolation and your salvation; if our lot is consolation, it is to help us to bring you consolation, and strength to face with fortitude the same sufferings we now endure. [7] And our hope for you is firmly grounded; for we know that if you share in the suffering, you share also in the consolation.

[8] In saying this, my friends, we should like you to know how serious was the trouble that came upon us in the province of Asia. The burden of it was far too heavy

for us to bear, so heavy that we even despaired of life. [9] Indeed, we felt in our hearts that we had received a death sentence. This was meant to teach us to place reliance not on ourselves, but on God who raises the dead. [10] From such mortal peril God delivered us; and he will deliver us again, he on whom our hope is fixed. Yes, he will continue to deliver us, [11] while you co-operate by praying for us. Then, with so many people praying for our deliverance, there will be many to give thanks on our behalf for God's gracious favour towards us.

Paul's concern for the church at Corinth

[12] THERE is one thing we are proud of: our conscience shows us that in our dealings with others, and above all in our dealings with you, our conduct has been governed by a devout and godly sincerity, by the grace of God and not by worldly wisdom. [13-14] There is nothing in our letters to you but what you can read and understand. You do understand us in some measure, but I hope you will come to understand fully that you have as much reason to be proud of us, as we of you, on the day of our Lord Jesus.

[15] It was because I felt so confident about all this that I had intended to come first of all to you and give you the benefit of a double visit: [16] I meant to visit you on my way to Macedonia and, after leaving Macedonia, to return to you, and you could then have sent me on my way to Judaea. [17] That was my intention; did I lightly change my mind? Or do I, when framing my plans, frame them as a worldly man might, first saying 'Yes, yes' and then 'No, no'? [18] God is to be trusted, and therefore what we tell you is not a mixture of Yes and No. [19] The Son of God, Christ Jesus, proclaimed among you by us (by Silvanus and Timothy, I mean, as well as myself), was not a mixture of Yes and No. With him it is always Yes; [20] for all the promises of God have their Yes in him. That is why, when we give glory to God, it is through Christ Jesus that we say 'Amen'. [21] And if you and we belong to Christ, guaranteed as his and anointed, it is all God's doing; [22] it is God also who has set his seal upon us and, as a pledge of

what is to come, has given the Spirit to dwell in our hearts.

[23] I appeal to God as my witness and stake my life upon it: it was out of consideration for you that I did not after all come to Corinth. [24] It is not that we have control of your faith; rather we are working with you for your happiness. For it is by that faith that you stand. [1] So I made up my mind that my next visit to you must not be another painful one. [2] If I cause pain to you, who is left to cheer me up, except you whom I have offended? [3] This is precisely the point I made in my letter: I did not want, I said, to come and be made miserable by the very people who ought to have made me happy; and I had sufficient confidence in you all to know that for me to be happy is for all of you to be happy. [4] That letter I sent you came out of great distress and anxiety; how many tears I shed as I wrote it! Not because I wanted to cause you pain; rather I wanted you to know the love, the more than ordinary love, that I have for you.

[5] Any injury that has been done has not been done to me; to some extent (I do not want to make too much of it) it has been done to you all. [6] The penalty on which the general meeting has agreed has met the offence well enough. [7] Something very different is called for now: you must forgive the offender and put heart into him; the man's distress must not be made so severe as to overwhelm him. [8] I urge you therefore to reassure him of your love for him. [9] I wrote, I may say, to see how you stood the test, whether you fully accepted my authority. [10] But anyone who has your forgiveness has mine too; and when I speak of forgiving (so far as there is anything for me to forgive), I mean that as the representative of Christ I have forgiven him for your sake. [11] For Satan must not be allowed to get the better of us; we know his wiles all too well.

[12] When I came to Troas, where I was to preach the gospel of Christ, and where an opening awaited me for serving the Lord, [13] I still found no relief of mind, for my colleague Titus was not there to meet me; so I took leave of the people and went

---

1:12 **devout:** *some witnesses read* frank.   1:17 **That was ... mind?:** *or* In forming this intention, did I act irresponsibly?   2:10 **as the representative:** *or* in the presence.

off to Macedonia. ¹⁴But thanks be to God, who continually leads us as captives in Christ's triumphal procession, and uses us to spread abroad the fragrance of the knowledge of himself! ¹⁵We are indeed the incense offered by Christ to God, both among those who are on the way to salvation, and among those who are on the way to destruction: ¹⁶to the latter it is a deadly fume that kills, to the former a vital fragrance that brings life. Who is equal to such a calling? ¹⁷We are not adulterating the word of God for profit as so many do; when we declare the word we do it in sincerity, as from God and in God's sight, as members of Christ.

Paul's commission as an apostle

3 ARE we beginning all over again to produce our credentials? Do we, like some people, need letters of introduction to you, or from you? ²No, you are all the letter we need, a letter written on our heart; anyone can see it for what it is and read it for himself. ³And as for you, it is plain that you are a letter that has come from Christ, given to us to deliver; a letter written not with ink but with the Spirit of the living God, written not on stone tablets but on the pages of the human heart.

⁴It is in full reliance upon God, through Christ, that we make such claims. ⁵There is no question of our having sufficient power in ourselves: we cannot claim anything as our own. The power we have comes from God; ⁶it is he who has empowered us as ministers of a new covenant, not written but spiritual; for the written law condemns to death, but the Spirit gives life.

⁷The ministry that brought death, and that was engraved in written form on stone, was inaugurated with such glory that the Israelites could not keep their eyes on Moses, even though the glory on his face was soon to fade. ⁸How much greater, then, must be the glory of the ministry of the Spirit! ⁹If glory accompanied the ministry that brought condemnation, how much richer in glory must be the ministry that brings acquittal! ¹⁰Indeed, the glory that once was is now no glory at all; it is outshone by a still greater glory. ¹¹For if what was to fade away had

its glory, how much greater is the glory of what endures!

¹²With such a hope as this we speak out boldly; ¹³it is not for us to do as Moses did: he put a veil over his face to keep the Israelites from gazing at the end of what was fading away. ¹⁴In any case their minds had become closed, for that same veil is there to this very day when the lesson is read from the old covenant; and it is never lifted, because only in Christ is it taken away. ¹⁵Indeed to this very day, every time the law of Moses is read, a veil lies over the mind of the hearer. ¹⁶But (as scripture says) 'Whenever he turns to the Lord the veil is removed.' ¹⁷Now the Lord of whom this passage speaks is the Spirit; and where the Spirit of the Lord is, there is liberty. ¹⁸And because for us there is no veil over the face, we all see as in a mirror the glory of the Lord, and we are being transformed into his likeness with ever-increasing glory, through the power of the Lord who is the Spirit.

4 SINCE God in his mercy has given us this ministry, we never lose heart. ²We have renounced the deeds that people hide for very shame; we do not practise cunning or distort the word of God. It is by declaring the truth openly that we recommend ourselves to the conscience of our fellow-men in the sight of God. ³If our gospel is veiled at all, it is veiled only for those on the way to destruction; ⁴their unbelieving minds are so blinded by the god of this passing age that the gospel of the glory of Christ, who is the image of God, cannot dawn upon them and bring them light. ⁵It is not ourselves that we proclaim; we proclaim Christ Jesus as Lord, and ourselves as your servants for Jesus's sake. ⁶For the God who said, 'Out of darkness light shall shine,' has caused his light to shine in our hearts, the light which is knowledge of the glory of God in the face of Jesus Christ.

⁷But we have only earthenware jars to hold this treasure, and this proves that such transcendent power does not come from us; it is God's alone. ⁸We are hard pressed, but never cornered; bewildered, but never at our wits' end; ⁹hunted, but never abandoned to our fate; struck down, but never killed. ¹⁰Wherever we go

3:18 see ... mirror: *or* reflect like a mirror.

we carry with us in our body the death that Jesus died, so that in this body also the life that Jesus lives may be revealed. [11] For Jesus' sake we are all our life being handed over to death, so that the life of Jesus may be revealed in this mortal body of ours. [12] Thus death is at work in us, but life in you.

[13] But scripture says, 'I believed, and therefore I spoke out,' and we too, in the same spirit of faith, believe and therefore speak out; [14] for we know that he who raised the Lord Jesus to life will with Jesus raise us too, and bring us to his presence, and you with us. [15] Indeed, all this is for your sake, so that, as the abounding grace of God is shared by more and more, the greater may be the chorus of thanksgiving that rises to the glory of God.

[16] No wonder we do not lose heart! Though our outward humanity is in decay, yet day by day we are inwardly renewed. [17] Our troubles are slight and short-lived, and their outcome is an eternal glory which far outweighs them, [18] provided our eyes are fixed, not on the things that are seen, but on the things that are unseen; for what is seen is transient, what is unseen is eternal. [1] We know that if the earthly frame that houses us today is demolished, we possess a building which God has provided—a house not made by human hands, eternal and in heaven. [2] In this present body we groan, yearning to be covered by our heavenly habitation put on over this one, [3] in the hope that, being thus clothed, we shall not find ourselves naked. [4] We groan indeed, we who are enclosed within this earthly frame; we are oppressed because we do not want to have the old body stripped off. What we want is to be covered by the new body put on over it, so that our mortality may be absorbed into life immortal. [5] It is for this destiny that God himself has been shaping us; and as a pledge of it he has given us the Spirit.

[6] Therefore we never cease to be confident. We know that so long as we are at home in the body we are exiles from the Lord; [7] faith is our guide, not sight. [8] We are confident, I say, and would rather be exiled from the body and make our home with the Lord. [9] That is why it is our ambition, wherever we are, at home or in exile, to be acceptable to him. [10] For we must all have our lives laid open before the tribunal of Christ, where each must receive what is due to him for his conduct in the body, good or bad.

The message of reconciliation

[11] WITH this fear of the Lord before our eyes we address our appeal to men and women. To God our lives lie open, and I hope that in your heart of hearts they lie open to you also. [12] This is not another attempt to recommend ourselves to you: we are rather giving you a chance to show yourselves proud of us; then you will have something to say to those whose pride is all in outward show and not in inward worth. [13] If these are mad words, take them as addressed to God; if sound sense, as addressed to you. [14] For the love of Christ controls us once we have reached the conclusion that one man died for all and therefore all mankind has died. [15] He died for all so that those who live should cease to live for themselves, and should live for him who for their sake died and was raised to life. [16] With us therefore worldly standards have ceased to count in our estimate of anyone; even if once they counted in our understanding of Christ, they do so now no longer. [17] For anyone united to Christ, there is a new creation: the old order has gone; a new order has already begun.

[18] All this has been the work of God. He has reconciled us to himself through Christ, and has enlisted us in this ministry of reconciliation: [19] God was in Christ reconciling the world to himself, no longer holding people's misdeeds against them, and has entrusted us with the message of reconciliation. [20] We are therefore Christ's ambassadors. It is as if God were appealing to you through us: we implore you in Christ's name, be reconciled to God! [21] Christ was innocent of sin, and yet for our sake God made him one with human sinfulness, so that in him we might be made one with the

5:13 **If these ... to you:** *or* If we speak in ecstasy, it is to God's glory; if we speak sober sense, it is to your advantage.   5:17 **For anyone ... begun:** *or* When anyone is united to Christ he is a new creature: his old life is over; a new life has already begun.   5:19 **God ... himself:** *or* God was reconciling the world to himself by Christ.

6 righteousness of God. ¹ Sharing in God's work, we make this appeal: you have received the grace of God; do not let it come to nothing. ² He has said:

In the hour of my favour I answered you;
on the day of deliverance I came to your aid.

This is the hour of favour, this the day of deliverance. ³ Lest our ministry be brought into discredit, we avoid giving any offence in anything. ⁴ As God's ministers, we try to recommend ourselves in all circumstances by our steadfast endurance: in affliction, hardship, and distress; ⁵ when flogged, imprisoned, mobbed; overworked, sleepless, starving. ⁶ We recommend ourselves by innocent behaviour and grasp of truth, by patience and kindliness, by gifts of the Holy Spirit, by unaffected love, ⁷ by declaring the truth, by the power of God. We wield the weapons of righteousness in right hand and left. ⁸ Honour and dishonour, praise and blame, are alike our lot: we are the impostors who speak the truth, ⁹ the unknown men whom all men know; dying we still live on; disciplined by suffering, we are not done to death; ¹⁰ in our sorrows we have always cause for joy; poor ourselves, we bring wealth to many; penniless, we own the world.

¹¹ We have spoken very frankly to you, friends in Corinth; we have opened our heart to you. ¹² There is no constraint on our part; any constraint there may be is in you. ¹³ In fair exchange then (if I may speak to you like a father) open your hearts to us.

Church life and discipline

¹⁴ DO NOT team up with unbelievers. What partnership can righteousness have with wickedness? Can light associate with darkness? ¹⁵ Can Christ agree with Belial, or a believer join with an unbeliever? ¹⁶ Can there be a compact between the temple of God and idols? And the temple of the living God is what we are. God's own words are: 'I will live and move about among them; I will be their God, and they shall be my people.' ¹⁷ And therefore, 'Come away and leave them, separate yourselves, says the Lord; touch nothing unclean. Then I will accept you,

¹⁸ says the Lord Almighty; I will be a father to you, and you shall be my sons 7 and daughters.' ¹ Such are the promises that have been made to us, dear friends. Let us therefore cleanse ourselves from all that can defile flesh or spirit and, in the fear of God, let us complete our consecration.

² MAKE a place for us in your hearts! We have wronged no one, ruined no one, exploited no one. ³ My words are no reflection on you. I have told you before that, come death, come life, your place in our hearts is secure. ⁴ I am speaking to you with great frankness, but my pride in you is just as great. In all our many troubles my cup is full of consolation and overflows with joy.

⁵ Even when we reached Macedonia we still found no relief; instead trouble met us at every turn, fights without and fears within. ⁶ But God, who brings comfort to the downcast, has comforted us by the arrival of Titus, ⁷ and not merely by his arrival, but by his being so greatly encouraged about you. He has told us how you long for me, how sorry you are, and how eager to take my side; and that has made me happier still.

⁸ Even if I did hurt you by the letter I sent, I do not now regret it. I did regret it; but now that I see the letter gave you pain, though only for a time, ⁹ I am happy—not because of the pain but because the pain led to a change of heart. You bore the pain as God would have you bear it, and so you came to no harm from what we did. ¹⁰ Pain borne in God's way brings no regrets but a change of heart leading to salvation; pain borne in the world's way brings death. ¹¹ You bore your pain in God's way, and just look at the results: it made you take the matter seriously and vindicate yourselves; it made you indignant and apprehensive; it aroused your longing for me, your devotion, and your eagerness to see justice done! At every point you have cleared yourselves of blame. ¹² And so, although I did send you that letter, it was not the offender or his victim that most concerned me. My aim in writing was to help to make plain to you, in the sight of God, how truly you are devoted to us. ¹³ That is why we have been so encouraged.

But besides being encouraged ourselves,

we have also been delighted beyond everything by seeing how happy Titus is: you have all helped to set his mind completely at rest. [14] Anything I may have said to him to show my pride in you has been justified. Every word we addressed to you bore the mark of truth, and the same holds of the proud boast we made in the presence of Titus; that also has proved true. [15] His heart warms all the more to you as he recalls how ready you all were to do what he asked, meeting him as you did in fear and trembling. [16] How happy I am now to have complete confidence in you!

The collection for the church in Jerusalem

8 WE must tell you, friends, about the grace that God has given to the churches in Macedonia. [2] The troubles they have been through have tried them hard, yet in all this they have been so exuberantly happy that from the depths of their poverty they have shown themselves lavishly open-handed. [3] Going to the limit of their resources, as I can testify, and even beyond that limit, [4] they begged us most insistently, and on their own initiative, to be allowed to share in this generous service to their fellow-Christians. [5] And their giving surpassed our expectations; for first of all they gave themselves to the Lord and, under God, to us. [6] The upshot is that we have asked Titus, since he has already made a beginning, to bring your share in this further work of generosity also to completion. [7] You are so rich in everything—in faith, speech, knowledge, and diligence of every kind, as well as in the love you have for us—that you should surely show yourselves equally lavish in this generous service! [8] This is not meant as an order; by telling you how keen others are I am putting your love to the test. [9] You know the generosity of our Lord Jesus Christ: he was rich, yet for your sake he became poor, so that through his poverty you might become rich.

[10] Here is my advice, and I have your interests at heart. You made a good beginning last year both in what you did and in your willingness to do it. [11] Now go on and finish it. Be as eager to complete the scheme as you were to adopt it, and give according to your means. [12] If we give eagerly according to our means, that is acceptable to God; he does not ask for what we do not have. [13] There is no question of relieving others at the cost of hardship to yourselves; [14] it is a question of equality. At the moment your surplus meets their need, but one day your need may be met from their surplus. The aim is equality; [15] as scripture has it, 'Those who gathered more did not have too much, and those who gathered less did not have too little.'

[16] I thank God that he has made Titus as keen on your behalf as we are! [17] So keen is he that he not only welcomed our request; it is by his own choice he is now leaving to come to you. [18] With him we are sending one of our company whose reputation for his services to the gospel among all the churches is high. [19] Moreover they have duly appointed him to travel with us and help in this beneficent work, by which we do honour to the Lord himself and show our own eagerness to serve. [20] We want to guard against any criticism of our handling of these large sums; [21] for our aims are entirely honourable, not only in the Lord's eyes, but also in the eyes of men and women.

[22] We are sending with them another of our company whose enthusiasm we have had repeated opportunities of testing, and who is now all the more keen because of the great confidence he has in you. [23] If there is any question about Titus, he is my partner and my fellow-worker in dealings with you; as for the others, they are delegates of the churches and bring honour to Christ. [24] So give them, and through them the churches, clear evidence of your love and justify our pride in you.

9 About this aid for God's people, it is superfluous for me to write to you. [2] I know how eager you are to help and I speak of it with pride to the Macedonians, telling them that Achaia had everything ready last year; and most of them have been fired by your zeal. [3] My purpose in sending these friends is to ensure that what we have said about you in this matter should not prove to be an empty

8:7 *the love ... us: some witnesses read* the love we have for you, *or* the love which we have kindled in your hearts.

boast. I want you to be prepared, as I told them you were; ⁴ for if I bring men from Macedonia with me and they find you are not prepared, what a disgrace it will be to us, let alone to you, after all the confidence we have shown! ⁵ I have accordingly thought it necessary to ask these friends to go on ahead to Corinth, to see that your promised bounty is in order before I come; it will then be awaiting me as genuine bounty, and not as an extortion.

⁶ Remember: sow sparingly, and you will reap sparingly; sow bountifully, and you will reap bountifully. ⁷ Each person should give as he has decided for himself; there should be no reluctance, no sense of compulsion; God loves a cheerful giver. ⁸ And it is in God's power to provide you with all good gifts in abundance, so that, with every need always met to the full, you may have something to spare for every good cause; ⁹ as scripture says: 'He lavishes his gifts on the needy; his benevolence lasts for ever.' ¹⁰ Now he who provides seed for sowing and bread for food will provide the seed for you to sow; he will multiply it and swell the harvest of your benevolence, ¹¹ and you will always be rich enough to be generous. Through our action such generosity will issue in thanksgiving to God, ¹² for as a piece of willing service this is not only a contribution towards the needs of God's people; more than that, it overflows in a flood of thanksgiving to God. ¹³ For with the proof which this aid affords, those who receive it will give honour to God when they see how humbly you obey him and how faithfully you confess the gospel of Christ; and they will thank him for your liberal contribution to their need and to the general good. ¹⁴ And as they join in prayer on your behalf, their hearts will go out to you because of the richness of the grace which God has given you. ¹⁵ Thanks be to God for his gift which is beyond all praise!

The challenge to Paul's authority

10 I, PAUL, appeal to you by the gentleness and magnanimity of Christ—I who am so timid (you say) when face to face with you, so courageous when I am away from you. ² Spare me when I come, I beg you, the need for that courage and self-assurance, which I reckon I could confidently display against those who assume my behaviour to be dictated by human weakness. ³ Weak and human we may be, but that does not dictate the way we fight our battles. ⁴ The weapons we wield are not merely human; they are strong enough with God's help to demolish strongholds. ⁵ We demolish sophistries and all that rears its proud head against the knowledge of God; we compel every human thought to surrender in obedience to Christ; ⁶ and we are prepared to punish any disobedience once your own obedience is complete.

⁷ Look facts in the face. Is someone convinced that he belongs to Christ? Let him think again and reflect that we belong to Christ as much as he does. ⁸ Indeed, if I am boasting too much about our authority—an authority given by the Lord to build your faith, not pull it down—I shall make good my boast. ⁹ So you must not think of me as one who tries to scare you by the letters he writes. ¹⁰ 'His letters', so it is said, 'are weighty and powerful; but when he is present he is unimpressive, and as a speaker he is beneath contempt.' ¹¹ People who talk in that way should reckon with this: my actions when I come will show the same man as my letters showed while I was absent.

¹² We should not dare to class ourselves or compare ourselves with any of those who commend themselves. What fools they are to measure themselves on their own, to find in themselves their standard of comparison! ¹³ As for us, our boasting will not go beyond the proper limits; and our sphere is determined by the limit God laid down for us, which permitted us to come as far as Corinth. ¹⁴ We are not overstretching our commission, as we would be if we had never come to you; but we were the first to reach as far as Corinth in the work of the gospel of Christ. ¹⁵ And we do not boast of work done where others have laboured, work beyond our proper sphere. Our hope is rather that, as your faith grows, we may attain a position among you greater than ever before, but still within the limits of our sphere. ¹⁶ Then we can carry the gospel to lands that lie beyond you, never priding ourselves on work already done in anyone else's sphere. ¹⁷ If anyone would boast, let him boast of the Lord. ¹⁸ For it is not the one who recommends himself, but the

one whom the Lord recommends, who is to be accepted.

Paul speaks as a fool

11 I SHOULD like you to bear with me in a little foolishness; please bear with me. [2] I am jealous for you, with the jealousy of God; for I betrothed you to Christ, thinking to present you as a chaste virgin to her true and only husband. [3] Now I am afraid that, as the serpent in his cunning seduced Eve, your thoughts may be corrupted and you may lose your single-hearted devotion to Christ. [4] For if some newcomer proclaims another Jesus, not the Jesus whom we proclaimed, or if you receive a spirit different from the Spirit already given to you, or a gospel different from the gospel you have already accepted, you put up with that well enough. [5] I am not aware of being in any way inferior to those super-apostles. [6] I may be no speaker, but knowledge I do have; at all times we have made known to you the full truth.

[7] Or was this my offence, that I made no charge for preaching the gospel of God, humbling myself in order to exalt you? [8] I robbed other churches—by accepting support from them to serve you. [9] If I ran short while I was with you, I did not become a charge on anyone; my needs were fully met by friends from Macedonia; I made it a rule, as I always shall, never to be a burden to you. [10] As surely as the truth of Christ is in me, nothing shall bar me from boasting about this throughout Achaia. [11] Why? Because I do not love you? God knows I do.

[12] And I shall go on doing as I am doing now, to cut the ground from under those who would seize any chance to put their vaunted apostleship on the same level as ours. [13] Such people are sham apostles, confidence tricksters masquerading as apostles of Christ. [14] And no wonder! Satan himself masquerades as an angel of light, [15] so it is easy enough for his agents to masquerade as agents of good. But their fate will match their deeds.

[16] I repeat: let no one take me for a fool; but if you must, then give me the privilege of a fool, and let me have my little boast like others. [17] In boasting so confidently I am not speaking like a Christian, but like

a fool. [18] So many people brag of their earthly distinctions that I shall do so too. [19] How gladly you put up with fools, being yourselves so wise! [20] If someone tyrannizes over you, exploits you, gets you in his clutches, puts on airs, and hits you in the face, you put up with it. [21] And you call me a weakling! I admit the reproach.

But if there is to be bravado (and I am still speaking as a fool), I can indulge in it too. [22] Are they Hebrews? So am I. Israelites? So am I. Abraham's descendants? So am I. [23] Are they servants of Christ? I am mad to speak like this, but I can outdo them: more often overworked, more often imprisoned, scourged more severely, many a time face to face with death. [24] Five times the Jews have given me the thirty-nine strokes; [25] three times I have been beaten with rods; once I was stoned; three times I have been shipwrecked, and for twenty-four hours I was adrift on the open sea. [26] I have been constantly on the road; I have met dangers from rivers, dangers from robbers, dangers from my fellow-countrymen, dangers from foreigners, dangers in the town, dangers in the wilderness, dangers at sea, dangers from false Christians. [27] I have toiled and drudged and often gone without sleep; I have been hungry and thirsty and have often gone without food; I have suffered from cold and exposure.

[28] Apart from these external things, there is the responsibility that weighs on me every day, my anxious concern for all the churches. [29] Is anyone weak? I share his weakness. If anyone brings about the downfall of another, does my heart not burn with anger? [30] If boasting there must be, I will boast of the things that show up my weakness. [31] He who is blessed for ever, the God and Father of the Lord Jesus, knows that what I say is true. [32] When I was in Damascus, the commissioner of King Aretas kept the city under observation to have me arrested; [33] and I was let down in a basket, through a window in the wall, and so escaped his clutches.

12 IT may do no good, but I must go on with my boasting; I come now to visions and revelations granted by the Lord. [2] I know a Christian man who

---

11:3 *lose … devotion: some witnesses read* lose your purity and single-hearted devotion.

fourteen years ago (whether in the body or out of the body, I do not know—God knows) was caught up as far as the third heaven. ³And I know that this same man (whether in the body or apart from the body, I do not know—God knows) ⁴ was caught up into paradise, and heard words so secret that human lips may not repeat them. ⁵About such a man I am ready to boast; but I will not boast on my own account, except of my weaknesses. ⁶If I chose to boast, it would not be the boast of a fool, for I should be speaking the truth. But I refrain, because I do not want anyone to form an estimate of me which goes beyond the evidence of his own eyes and ears. ⁷To keep me from being unduly elated by the magnificence of such revelations, I was given a thorn in my flesh, a messenger of Satan sent to buffet me; this was to save me from being unduly elated. ⁸Three times I begged the Lord to rid me of it, ⁹but his answer was: 'My grace is all you need; power is most fully seen in weakness.' I am therefore happy to boast of my weaknesses, because then the power of Christ will rest upon me. ¹⁰So I am content with a life of weakness, insult, hardship, persecution, and distress, all for Christ's sake; for when I am weak, then I am strong.

Paul's final appeal

¹¹ I AM being very foolish, but it was you who drove me to it; my credentials should have come from you. In nothing did I prove inferior to those super-apostles, even if I am a nobody. ¹²The signs of an apostle were there in the work I did among you, marked by unfailing endurance, by signs, portents, and miracles. ¹³Is there any way in which you were treated worse than the other churches—except this, that I was never a charge on you? Forgive me for being so unfair!

¹⁴I am now getting ready to pay you a third visit; and I am not going to be a charge on you. It is you I want, not your money; parents should make provision for their children, not children for their parents. ¹⁵I would gladly spend everything for you—yes, and spend myself to the limit. If I love you overmuch, am I to be loved the less? ¹⁶All very well, you say;

I did not myself prove a burden to you, but I did use a confidence trick to take you in. ¹⁷Was it one of the men I sent to you that I used to exploit you? ¹⁸I begged Titus to visit you, and I sent our friend with him. Did Titus exploit you? Have we not both been guided by the same Spirit, and followed the same course?

¹⁹Perhaps you have been thinking all this time that it is to you we are addressing our defence. No; we are speaking in God's sight, and as Christians. Our whole aim, dear friends, is to build you up. ²⁰I fear that when I come I may find you different from what I wish, and you may find me to be what you do not wish. I fear I may find quarrelling and jealousy, angry tempers and personal rivalries, backbiting and gossip, arrogance and general disorder. ²¹I am afraid that when I come my God may humiliate me again in your presence, that I may have cause to grieve over many who were sinning before and have not repented of their unclean lives, their fornication and sensuality.

13 This will be my third visit to you. As scripture says, 'Every charge must be established on the evidence of two or three witnesses': ²to those who sinned before, and to everyone else, I repeat the warning I gave last time; on my second visit I gave it in person, and now I give it while absent. It is that when I come this time, I will show no leniency. ³Then you will have the proof you seek of the Christ who speaks through me, the Christ who, far from being weak with you, makes his power felt among you. ⁴True, he died on the cross in weakness, but he lives by the power of God; so you will find that we who share his weakness shall live with him by the power of God.

⁵Examine yourselves: are you living the life of faith? Put yourselves to the test. Surely you recognize that Jesus Christ is among you? If not, you have failed the test. ⁶I hope you will come to see that we have not failed. ⁷Our prayer to God is that you may do no wrong, not that we should win approval; we want you to do what is right, even if we should seem failures. ⁸We have no power to act against the truth, but only for it. ⁹We are happy to be weak at any time if only you are strong.

12:6–7 **ears ... given**: *some witnesses read* ears, ⁷ and because of the magnificence of the revelations themselves. Therefore to keep me from being unduly elated I was given.

Our prayer, then, is for your amendment. [10] In writing this letter before I come, my aim is to spare myself, when I do come, any sharp exercise of authority—authority which the Lord gave me for building up and not for pulling down.

[11] And now, my friends, farewell. Mend your ways; take our appeal to heart; agree with one another; live in peace; and the God of love and peace will be with you. [12] Greet one another with the kiss of peace. [13] All God's people send you greetings.

[14] The grace of the Lord Jesus Christ, and the love of God, and the fellowship of the Holy Spirit, be with you all.

THE LETTER OF PAUL TO THE
GALATIANS

1 FROM Paul, an apostle commissioned not by any human authority or human act, but by Jesus Christ and God the Father who raised him from the dead. [2] I and all the friends now with me send greetings to the churches of Galatia.

[3] Grace to you and peace from God the Father and our Lord Jesus Christ, [4] who gave himself for our sins, to rescue us out of the present wicked age as our God and Father willed; [5] to him be glory for ever and ever! Amen.

One gospel for all

[6] I AM astonished to find you turning away so quickly from him who called you by grace, and following a different gospel. [7] Not that it is in fact another gospel; only there are some who unsettle your minds by trying to distort the gospel of Christ. [8] But should anyone, even I myself or an angel from heaven, preach a gospel other than the gospel I preached to you, let him be banned! [9] I warned you in the past and now I warn you again: if anyone preaches a gospel other than the gospel you received, let him be banned!

[10] Now do I sound as if I were asking for human approval and not for God's alone? Am I currying favour with men? If I were still seeking human favour, I should be no servant of Christ.

[11] I must make it clear to you, my friends, that the gospel you heard me preach is not of human origin. [12] I did not take it over from anyone; no one taught it me; I received it through a revelation of Jesus Christ.

[13] You have heard what my manner of life was when I was still a practising Jew: how savagely I persecuted the church of God and tried to destroy it; [14] and how in the practice of our national religion I outstripped most of my Jewish contemporaries by my boundless devotion to the traditions of my ancestors. [15] But then in his good pleasure God, who from my birth had set me apart, and who had called me through his grace, chose [16] to reveal his Son in and through me, in order that I might proclaim him among the Gentiles. Immediately, without consulting a single person, [17] without going up to Jerusalem to see those who were apostles before me, I went off to Arabia, and afterwards returned to Damascus.

[18] Three years later I did go up to Jerusalem to get to know Cephas, and I stayed two weeks with him. [19] I saw none of the other apostles, except James, the Lord's brother. [20] What I write is plain truth; God knows I am not lying! [21] Then I left for the regions of Syria and Cilicia. [22] I was still unknown by sight to the Christian congregations in Judaea; [23] they had simply heard it said, 'Our former persecutor is preaching the good news of the faith which once he tried to destroy,' [24] and they praised God for what had happened to me.

2 Fourteen years later, I went up again to Jerusalem with Barnabas, and we took Titus with us. [2] I went in response to a revelation from God; I explained, at a private interview with those of repute, the gospel which I preach to the Gentiles, to

1 : 3 **God . . . Christ**: *some witnesses read* God our Father and the Lord Jesus Christ.   1 : 6 **from him . . . grace**: *some witnesses read* from Christ who called you by grace, *or* from him who called you by the grace of Christ.

make sure that the race I had run and was running should not be in vain. [3] Not even my companion Titus, Greek though he is, was compelled to be circumcised. [4] That course was urged only as a concession to certain sham Christians, intruders who had sneaked in to spy on the liberty we enjoy in the fellowship of Christ Jesus. These men wanted to bring us into bondage, [5] but not for one moment did I yield to their dictation; I was determined that the full truth of the gospel should be maintained for you.

[6] As for those reputed to be something (not that their importance matters to me: God does not recognize these personal distinctions)—these men of repute, I say, imparted nothing further to me. [7] On the contrary, they saw that I had been entrusted to take the gospel to the Gentiles as surely as Peter had been entrusted to take it to the Jews; [8] for the same God who was at work in Peter's mission to the Jews was also at work in mine to the Gentiles.

[9] Recognizing, then, the privilege bestowed on me, those who are reputed to be pillars of the community, James, Cephas, and John, accepted Barnabas and myself as partners and shook hands on it: the agreement was that we should go to the Gentiles, while they went to the Jews. [10] All they asked was that we should keep in mind the poor, the very thing I have always made it my business to do.

[11] But when Cephas came to Antioch, I opposed him to his face, because he was clearly in the wrong. [12] For until some messengers came from James, he was taking his meals with gentile Christians; but after they came he drew back and began to hold aloof, because he was afraid of the Jews. [13] The other Jewish Christians showed the same lack of principle; even Barnabas was carried away and played false like the rest. [14] But when I saw that their conduct did not square with the truth of the gospel, I said to Cephas in front of the whole congregation, 'If you, a Jew born and bred, live like a Gentile, and not like a Jew, how can you insist that Gentiles must live like Jews?'

[15] We ourselves are Jews by birth, not gentile sinners; [16] yet we know that no one is ever justified by doing what the law

requires, but only through faith in Christ Jesus. So we too have put our faith in Jesus Christ, in order that we might be justified through this faith, and not through actions dictated by law; for no human being can be justified by keeping the law.

[17] If then, in seeking to be justified in Christ, we ourselves no less than the Gentiles turn out to be sinners, does that mean that Christ is a promoter of sin? Of course not! [18] On the contrary, it is only if I start building up again all I have pulled down that I prove to be one who breaks the law. [19] For through the law I died to law—to live for God. [20] I have been crucified with Christ: the life I now live is not my life, but the life which Christ lives in me; and my present mortal life is lived by faith in the Son of God, who loved me and gave himself up for me. [21] I will not nullify the grace of God; if righteousness comes by law, then Christ died for nothing.

The freedom of faith

3 YOU STUPID Galatians! You must have been bewitched—you before whose eyes Jesus Christ was openly displayed on the cross! [2] Answer me one question: did you receive the Spirit by keeping the law or by believing the gospel message? [3] Can you really be so stupid? You started with the spiritual; do you now look to the material to make you perfect? [4] Is all you have experienced to come to nothing—surely not! [5] When God gives you the Spirit and works miracles among you, is it because you keep the law, or is it because you have faith in the gospel message?

[6] Look at Abraham: he put his faith in God, and that faith was counted to him as righteousness. [7] You may take it, then, that it is those who have faith who are Abraham's sons. [8] And scripture, foreseeing that God would justify the Gentiles through faith, declared the gospel to Abraham beforehand: 'In you all nations shall find blessing.' [9] Thus it is those with faith who share the blessing with faithful Abraham.

[10] On the other hand, those who rely on obedience to the law are under a curse; for scripture says, 'Cursed is everyone who does not persevere in doing everything

2:4–5 **bondage** ... **for you**: *or, following some witnesses,* bondage; [5] I yielded to their demand for the moment, to ensure that gospel truth should not be prevented from reaching you.   2:12 **the Jews**: *or* the advocates of circumcision.

that is written in the book of the law.' ¹¹ It is evident that no one is ever justified before God by means of the law, because we read, 'He shall gain life who is justified through faith.' ¹² Now the law does not operate on the basis of faith, for we read, 'He who does this shall gain life by what he does.' ¹³ Christ bought us freedom from the curse of the law by coming under the curse for our sake; for scripture says, 'Cursed is everyone who is hanged on a gibbet.' ¹⁴ The purpose of this was that the blessing of Abraham should in Jesus Christ be extended to the Gentiles, so that we might receive the promised Spirit through faith.

¹⁵ My friends, let me give you an illustration. When a man's will and testament has been duly executed, no one else can set it aside or add a codicil. ¹⁶ Now, the promises were pronounced to Abraham and to his 'issue'. It does not say 'issues' in the plural, but 'your issue' in the singular; and by 'issue' is meant Christ. ¹⁷ My point is this: a testament, or covenant, had already been validated by God; a law made four hundred and thirty years later cannot invalidate it and so render its promises ineffective. ¹⁸ If the inheritance is by legal right, then it is not by promise; but it was by promise that God bestowed it as a free gift on Abraham.

¹⁹ Then what of the law? It was added to make wrongdoing a legal offence; it was an interim measure pending the arrival of the 'issue' to whom the promise was made. It was promulgated through angels, and there was an intermediary; ²⁰ but an intermediary is not needed for one party acting alone, and God is one.

²¹ Does the law, then, contradict the promises? Of course not! If a law had been given which had power to bestow life, then righteousness would indeed have come from keeping the law. ²² But scripture has declared the whole world to be prisoners in subjection to sin, so that faith in Jesus Christ should be the ground on which the promised blessing is given to those who believe.

²³ Before this faith came, we were close prisoners in the custody of law, pending the revelation of faith. ²⁴ The law was thus put in charge of us until Christ should come, when we should be justified through faith; ²⁵ and now that faith has come, its charge is at an end.

²⁶ It is through faith that you are all sons of God in union with Christ Jesus. ²⁷ Baptized into union with him, you have all put on Christ like a garment. ²⁸ There is no such thing as Jew and Greek, slave and freeman, male and female; for you are all one person in Christ Jesus. ²⁹ So if you belong to Christ, you are the 'issue' of Abraham and heirs by virtue of the promise.

Life under the law

4 THIS is what I mean: so long as the heir is a minor, he is no better off than a slave, even though the whole estate is his; ² he is subject to guardians and trustees until the date set by his father. ³ So it was with us: during our minority we were slaves, subject to the elemental spirits of the universe, ⁴ but when the appointed time came, God sent his Son, born of a woman, born under the law, ⁵ to buy freedom for those who were under the law, in order that we might attain the status of sons.

⁶ To prove that you are sons, God has sent into our hearts the Spirit of his Son, crying 'Abba, Father!' ⁷ You are therefore no longer a slave but a son, and if a son, an heir by God's own act.

⁸ Formerly, when you did not know God, you were slaves to gods who are not gods at all. ⁹ But now that you do acknowledge God—or rather, now that he has acknowledged you—how can you turn back to those feeble and bankrupt elemental spirits? Why do you propose to enter their service all over again? ¹⁰ You keep special days and months and seasons and years. ¹¹ I am afraid that all my hard work on you may have been wasted.

¹² PUT yourselves in my place, my friends, I beg you, as I put myself in yours. You never did me any wrong: ¹³ it was bodily illness, as you will remember, that originally led to my bringing you the gospel, ¹⁴ and you resisted any temptation to show scorn or disgust at my physical condition; on the contrary you welcomed me as if I were an angel of God, as you might have

---

3:19 added ... offence: *or* added to restrain offences. belonging to this world.   4:9 bankrupt ... spirits: *or* threadbare elementary notions.   4:3 to ... universe: *or* to elementary notions

welcomed Christ Jesus himself. [15] What
has become of the happiness you felt
then? I believe you would have torn out
your eyes and given them to me, had that
been possible! [16] Have I now made myself
your enemy by being frank with you?

[17] Others are lavishing attention on
you, but without sincerity: what they
really want is to isolate you so that you
may lavish attention on them. [18] To be the
object of sincere attentions is always
good, and not just when I am with you.
[19] You are my own children, and I am in
labour with you all over again until you
come to have the form of Christ. [20] How I
wish I could be with you now, for then I
could modify my tone; as it is, I am at my
wits' end about you.

Freedom through Christ

[21] TELL me now, you that are so anxious
to be under law, will you not listen to
what the law says? [22] It is written there
that Abraham had two sons, the one by a
slave, the other by a free-born woman.
[23] The slave's son was born in the ordinary course of nature, but the free woman's through God's promise. [24] This is
an allegory: the two women stand for two
covenants. The one covenant comes from
Mount Sinai; that is Hagar, and her
children are born into slavery. [25] Sinai is a
mountain in Arabia and represents the
Jerusalem of today, for she and her children are in slavery. [26] But the heavenly
Jerusalem is the free woman; she is our
mother. [27] For scripture says, 'Rejoice, O
barren woman who never bore a child;
break into a shout of joy, you who have
never been in labour; for the deserted wife
will have more children than she who
lives with her husband.'

[28] Now you, my friends, like Isaac, are
children of God's promise, [29] but just as in
those days the natural-born son persecuted the spiritual son, so it is today. [30] Yet
what does scripture say? 'Drive out the
slave and her son, for the son of the slave
shall not share the inheritance with the
son of the free woman.' [31] You see, then,
my friends, we are no slave's children;

5 our mother is the free woman. [1] It is
for freedom that Christ set us free.
Stand firm, therefore, and refuse to submit again to the yoke of slavery.

[2] Mark my words: I, Paul, say to you
that if you get yourself circumcised Christ

will benefit you no more. [3] I impress on you
once again that every man who accepts
circumcision is under obligation to keep
the entire law. [4] When you seek to be
justified by way of law, you are cut off from
Christ: you have put yourselves outside
God's grace. [5] For it is by the Spirit and
through faith that we hope to attain that
righteousness which we eagerly await. [6] If
we are in union with Christ Jesus, circumcision makes no difference at all, nor does
the lack of it; the only thing that counts is
faith expressing itself through love.

[7] You were running well; who was it
hindered you from following the truth?
[8] Whatever persuasion was used, it did
not come from God who called you. [9] 'A
little leaven', remember, 'leavens all the
dough.' [10] The Lord gives me confidence
that you will not adopt the wrong view;
but whoever it is who is unsettling your
minds must bear God's judgement. [11] As
for me, my friends, if I am still advocating
circumcision, then why am I still being
persecuted? To do that would be to strip
the cross of all offence. [12] Those agitators
had better go the whole way and make
eunuchs of themselves!

Guidance by the Spirit

[13] YOU, MY friends, were called to be free;
only beware of turning your freedom into
licence for your unspiritual nature. Instead, serve one another in love; [14] for the
whole law is summed up in a single
commandment: 'Love your neighbour as
yourself.' [15] But if you go on fighting one
another, tooth and nail, all you can
expect is mutual destruction.

[16] What I mean is this: be guided by the
Spirit and you will not gratify the desires
of your unspiritual nature. [17] That nature
sets its desires against the Spirit, while the
Spirit fights against it. They are in conflict
with one another so that you cannot do
what you want. [18] But if you are led by the
Spirit, you are not subject to law.

[19] Anyone can see the behaviour that
belongs to the unspiritual nature: fornication, indecency, and debauchery;
[20] idolatry and sorcery; quarrels, a contentious temper, envy, fits of rage, selfish
ambitions, dissensions, party intrigues,
[21] and jealousies; drinking bouts, orgies,
and the like. I warn you, as I warned you
before, that no one who behaves like that
will ever inherit the kingdom of God.

²² But the harvest of the Spirit is love, joy, peace, patience, kindness, goodness, fidelity, ²³ gentleness, and self-control. Against such things there is no law. ²⁴ Those who belong to Christ Jesus have crucified the old nature with its passions and desires. ²⁵ If the Spirit is the source of our life, let the Spirit also direct its course.

²⁶ We must not be conceited, inciting one another to rivalry, jealous of one another. 6 ¹ If anyone is caught doing something wrong, you, my friends, who live by the Spirit must gently set him right. Look to yourself, each one of you: you also may be tempted. ² Carry one another's burdens, and in this way you will fulfil the law of Christ.

³ If anyone imagines himself to be somebody when he is nothing, he is deluding himself. ⁴ Each of you should examine his own conduct, and then he can measure his achievement by comparing himself with himself and not with anyone else; ⁵ for everyone has his own burden to bear.

⁶ When anyone is under instruction in the faith, he should give his teacher a share of whatever good things he has.

⁷ Make no mistake about this: God is not to be fooled; everyone reaps what he sows. ⁸ If he sows in the field of his unspiritual nature, he will reap from it a harvest of corruption; but if he sows in the field of the Spirit, he will reap from it a harvest of eternal life. ⁹ Let us never tire of doing good, for if we do not slacken our efforts we shall in due time reap our harvest. ¹⁰ Therefore, as opportunity offers, let us work for the good of all, especially members of the household of the faith.

¹¹ LOOK how big the letters are, now that I am writing to you in my own hand. ¹² It is those who want to be outwardly in good standing who are trying to force circumcision on you; their sole object is to escape persecution for the cross of Christ. ¹³ Even those who do accept circumcision are not thoroughgoing observers of the law; they want you to be circumcised just in order to boast of your submission to that outward rite. ¹⁴ God forbid that I should boast of anything but the cross of our Lord Jesus Christ, through which the world is crucified to me and I to the world! ¹⁵ Circumcision is nothing; uncircumcision is nothing; the only thing that counts is new creation! ¹⁶ All who take this principle for their guide, peace and mercy be upon them, the Israel of God!

¹⁷ In future let no one make trouble for me, for I bear the marks of Jesus branded on my body.

¹⁸ The grace of our Lord Jesus Christ be with you, my friends. Amen.

6:14 which: *or* whom.   6:16 the ... God: *or* and upon the whole Israel of God.

THE LETTER OF PAUL TO THE
EPHESIANS

1 FROM Paul, by the will of God apostle of Christ Jesus, to God's people at Ephesus, to the faithful, incorporate in Christ Jesus.

² Grace to you and peace from God our Father and the Lord Jesus Christ.

The glory of Christ in the church

³ BLESSED be the God and Father of our Lord Jesus Christ, who has conferred on us in Christ every spiritual blessing in the heavenly realms. ⁴ Before the foundation of the world he chose us in Christ to be his people, to be without blemish in his sight, to be full of love; ⁵ and he predestined us to be adopted as his children through Jesus Christ. This was his will and pleasure ⁶ in order that the glory of his gracious gift, so graciously conferred on us in his Beloved, might redound to his praise. ⁷ In Christ our release is secured and our sins forgiven through the shedding of his blood. In the richness of his grace ⁸ God has lavished on us all wisdom and insight.

1:1 at Ephesus: *some witnesses omit.*   1:4–5 sight ... he: *or* sight. In his love ⁵ he.

[9] He has made known to us his secret purpose, in accordance with the plan which he determined beforehand in Christ, [10] to be put into effect when the time was ripe: namely, that the universe, everything in heaven and on earth, might be brought into a unity in Christ.

[11] In Christ indeed we have been given our share in the heritage, as was decreed in his design whose purpose is everywhere at work; for it was his will [12] that we, who were the first to set our hope on Christ, should cause his glory to be praised. [13] And in Christ you also—once you had heard the message of the truth, the good news of your salvation, and had believed it—in him you were stamped with the seal of the promised Holy Spirit; [14] and that Spirit is a pledge of the inheritance which will be ours when God has redeemed what is his own, to his glory and praise.

[15] Because of all this, now that I have heard of your faith in the Lord Jesus and the love you bear towards all God's people, [16] I never cease to give thanks for you when I mention you in my prayers. [17] I pray that the God of our Lord Jesus Christ, the all-glorious Father, may confer on you the spiritual gifts of wisdom and vision, with the knowledge of him that they bring. [18] I pray that your inward eyes may be enlightened, so that you may know what is the hope to which he calls you, how rich and glorious is the share he offers you among his people in their inheritance, [19] and how vast are the resources of his power open to us who have faith. His mighty strength was seen at work [20] when he raised Christ from the dead, and enthroned him at his right hand in the heavenly realms, [21] far above all government and authority, all power and dominion, and any title of sovereignty that commands allegiance, not only in this age but also in the age to come. [22] He put all things in subjection beneath his feet, and gave him as head over all things to the church [23] which is his body, the fullness of him who is filling the universe in all its parts.

God's grace to Gentiles

2 YOU ONCE were dead because of your sins and wickedness; [2] you followed the ways of this present world order, obeying the commander of the spiritual powers of the air, the spirit now at work among God's rebel subjects. [3] We too were once of their number: we were ruled by our physical desires, and did what instinct and evil imagination suggested. In our natural condition we lay under the condemnation of God like the rest of mankind. [4] But God is rich in mercy, and because of his great love for us, [5] he brought us to life with Christ when we were dead because of our sins; it is by grace you are saved. [6] And he raised us up in union with Christ Jesus and enthroned us with him in the heavenly realms, [7] so that he might display in the ages to come how immense are the resources of his grace, and how great his kindness to us in Christ Jesus. [8] For it is by grace you are saved through faith; it is not your own doing. It is God's gift, [9] not a reward for work done. There is nothing for anyone to boast of; [10] we are God's handiwork, created in Christ Jesus for the life of good deeds which God designed for us.

[11] Remember then your former condition, Gentiles as you are by birth, 'the uncircumcised' as you are called by those who call themselves 'the circumcised' because of a physical rite. [12] You were at that time separate from Christ, excluded from the community of Israel, strangers to God's covenants and the promise that goes with them. Yours was a world without hope and without God. [13] Once you were far off, but now in union with Christ Jesus you have been brought near through the shedding of Christ's blood. [14] For he is himself our peace. Gentiles and Jews, he has made the two one, and in his own body of flesh and blood has broken down the barrier of enmity which separated them; [15] for he annulled the law with its rules and regulations, so as to create out of the two a single new humanity in himself, thereby making peace. [16] This was his purpose, to reconcile the two in a single body to God through the cross, by which he killed the enmity. [17] So he came and proclaimed the good news: peace to you who were far off, and peace to those who were near; [18] for through him we both alike have access to the Father in the one Spirit.

1 : 12 who … Christ: *or* who already looked forward in hope to Christ.   1 : 23 body … parts: *or* body, filled as he is with the full being of God, who is imparting to all things that same fullness.   2 : 16 cross … enmity: *or* cross. Thus in his own person he put to death the enmity.

¹⁹ Thus you are no longer aliens in a foreign land, but fellow-citizens with God's people, members of God's household. ²⁰ You are built on the foundation of the apostles and prophets, with Christ Jesus himself as the corner-stone. ²¹ In him the whole building is bonded together and grows into a holy temple in the Lord. ²² In him you also are being built with all the others into a spiritual dwelling for God.

Paul's prayer

3 WITH this in mind I pray for you, I, Paul, who for the sake of you Gentiles am now the prisoner of Christ Jesus—² for surely you have heard how God's gift of grace to me was designed for your benefit. ³ It was by a revelation that his secret purpose was made known to me. I have already written you a brief account of this, ⁴ and by reading it you can see that I understand the secret purpose of Christ. ⁵ In former generations that secret was not disclosed to mankind; but now by inspiration it has been revealed to his holy apostles and prophets, ⁶ that through the gospel the Gentiles are joint heirs with the Jews, part of the same body, sharers together in the promise made in Christ Jesus. ⁷ Such is the gospel of which I was made a minister by God's unmerited gift, so powerfully at work in me. ⁸ To me, who am less than the least of all God's people, he has granted the privilege of proclaiming to the Gentiles the good news of the unfathomable riches of Christ, ⁹ and of bringing to light how this hidden purpose was to be put into effect. It lay concealed for long ages with God the Creator of the universe, ¹⁰ in order that now, through the church, the wisdom of God in its infinite variety might be made known to the rulers and authorities in the heavenly realms. ¹¹ This accords with his age-long purpose, which he accomplished in Christ Jesus our Lord, ¹² in whom we have freedom of access to God, with the confidence born of trust in him. ¹³ I beg you, then, not to lose heart over my sufferings for you; indeed, they are your glory.

¹⁴ With this in mind, then, I kneel in prayer to the Father, ¹⁵ from whom every family in heaven and on earth takes its name, ¹⁶ that out of the treasures of his glory he may grant you inward strength and power through his Spirit, ¹⁷ that through faith Christ may dwell in your hearts in love. With deep roots and firm foundations ¹⁸ may you, in company with all God's people, be strong to grasp what is the breadth and length and height and depth ¹⁹ of Christ's love, and to know it, though it is beyond knowledge. So may you be filled with the very fullness of God.

²⁰ Now to him who is able through the power which is at work among us to do immeasurably more than all we can ask or conceive, ²¹ to him be glory in the church and in Christ Jesus from generation to generation for evermore! Amen.

Christian conduct

4 I IMPLORE you then—I, a prisoner for the Lord's sake: as God has called you, live up to your calling. ² Be humble always and gentle, and patient too, putting up with one another's failings in the spirit of love. ³ Spare no effort to make fast with bonds of peace the unity which the Spirit gives. ⁴ There is one body and one Spirit, just as there is one hope held out in God's call to you; ⁵ one Lord, one faith, one baptism; ⁶ one God and Father of all, who is over all and through all and in all.

⁷ But each of us has been given a special gift, a particular share in the bounty of Christ. ⁸ That is why scripture says:

He ascended into the heights;
he took captives into captivity;
he gave gifts to men.

⁹ Now, the word 'ascended' implies that he also descended to the lowest level, down to the very earth. ¹⁰ He who descended is none other than he who ascended far above all heavens, so that he might fill the universe. ¹¹ And it is he who has given some to be apostles, some prophets, some evangelists, some pastors and teachers, ¹² to equip God's people for work in his service, for the building up of the body of Christ, ¹³ until we all attain to the unity inherent in our faith and in our knowledge of the Son of God—to mature manhood, measured by nothing less than the full stature of Christ. ¹⁴ We are no longer to be children, tossed about by the waves and whirled around by every fresh gust of teaching, dupes of cunning rogues

---

4:9 *descended ... earth: or* descended to the regions beneath the earth.

and their deceitful schemes. [15] Rather we are to maintain the truth in a spirit of love; so shall we fully grow up into Christ. He is the head, [16] and on him the whole body depends. Bonded and held together by every constituent joint, the whole frame grows through the proper functioning of each part, and builds itself up in love.

[17] Here then is my word to you, and I urge it on you in the Lord's name: give up living as pagans do with their futile notions. [18] Their minds are closed, they are alienated from the life that is in God, because ignorance prevails among them and their hearts have grown hard as stone. [19] Dead to all feeling, they have abandoned themselves to vice, and there is no indecency that they do not practise. [20] But that is not how you learned Christ. [21] For were you not told about him, were you not as Christians taught the truth as it is in Jesus? [22] Renouncing your former way of life, you must lay aside the old human nature which, deluded by its desires, is in process of decay: [23] you must be renewed in mind and spirit, [24] and put on the new nature created in God's likeness, which shows itself in the upright and devout life called for by the truth.

[25] Then have done with falsehood and speak the truth to each other, for we belong to one another as parts of one body. [26] If you are angry, do not be led into sin; do not let sunset find you nursing your anger; [27] and give no foothold to the devil. [28] The thief must give up stealing, and work hard with his hands to earn an honest living, so that he may have something to share with the needy.

[29] Let no offensive talk pass your lips, only what is good and helpful to the occasion, so that it brings a blessing to those who hear it. [30] Do not grieve the Holy Spirit of God, for that Spirit is the seal with which you were marked for the day of final liberation. [31] Have done with all spite and bad temper, with rage, insults, and slander, with evil of any kind. [32] Be generous to one another, tender-hearted, forgiving one another as God in Christ forgave you.

5 In a word, as God's dear children, you must be like him. [2] Live in love as Christ loved you and gave himself up on

your behalf, an offering and sacrifice whose fragrance is pleasing to God.

[3] Fornication and indecency of any kind, or ruthless greed, must not be so much as mentioned among you, as befits the people of God. [4] No coarse, stupid, or flippant talk: these things are out of place; you should rather be thanking God. [5] For be very sure of this: no one given to fornication or vice, or the greed which makes an idol of gain, has any share in the kingdom of Christ and of God. [6] Let no one deceive you with shallow arguments; it is for these things that divine retribution falls on God's rebel subjects. [7] Have nothing to do with them. [8] Though you once were darkness, now as Christians you are light. Prove yourselves at home in the light, [9] for where light is, there is a harvest of goodness, righteousness, and truth. [10] Learn to judge for yourselves what is pleasing to the Lord; [11] take no part in the barren deeds of darkness, but show them up for what they are. [12] It would be shameful even to mention what is done in secret. [13] But everything is shown up by being exposed to the light, and whatever is exposed to the light itself becomes light. [14] That is why it is said:

Awake, sleeper,
rise from the dead,
and Christ will shine upon you.

[15] Take great care, then, how you behave: act sensibly, not like simpletons. [16] Use the present opportunity to the full, for these are evil days. [17] Do not be foolish, but understand what the will of the Lord is. [18] Do not give way to drunkenness and the ruin that goes with it, but let the Holy Spirit fill you: [19] speak to one another in psalms, hymns, and songs; sing and make music from your heart to the Lord; [20] and in the name of our Lord Jesus Christ give thanks every day for everything to our God and Father.

Christian relationships

[21] BE subject to one another out of reverence for Christ.

[22] Wives, be subject to your husbands as though to the Lord; [23] for the man is the head of the woman, just as Christ is the head of the church. Christ is, indeed, the saviour of that body; [24] but just as

---

5:19 **hymns, and:** *some witnesses add* spiritual.

the church is subject to Christ, so must women be subject to their husbands in everything.

25 Husbands, love your wives, as Christ loved the church and gave himself up for it, 26 to consecrate and cleanse it by water and word, 27 so that he might present the church to himself all glorious, with no stain or wrinkle or anything of the sort, but holy and without blemish. 28 In the same way men ought to love their wives, as they love their own bodies. In loving his wife a man loves himself. 29 For no one ever hated his own body; on the contrary, he keeps it nourished and warm, and that is how Christ treats the church, 30 because it is his body, of which we are living parts. 31 'This is why' (in the words of scripture) 'a man shall leave his father and mother and be united to his wife, and the two shall become one flesh.' 32 There is hidden here a great truth, which I take to refer to Christ and to the church. 33 But it applies also to each one of you: the husband must love his wife as his very self, and the wife must show reverence for her husband.

6 Children, obey your parents; for it is only right that you should. 2 'Honour your father and your mother' is the first commandment to carry a promise with it: 3 'that it may be well with you and that you may live long on the earth.'

4 Fathers, do not goad your children to resentment, but bring them up in the discipline and instruction of the Lord.

5 Slaves, give single-minded obedience to your earthly masters with fear and trembling, as if to Christ. 6 Do it not merely to catch their eye or curry favour with them, but as slaves of Christ do the will of God wholeheartedly. 7 Give cheerful service, as slaves of the Lord rather than of men. 8 You know that whatever good anyone may do, slave or free, will be repaid by the Lord.

9 Masters, treat your slaves in the same spirit: give up using threats, and remember that you both have the same Master in heaven; there is no favouritism with him.

The Christian's armoury

10 FINALLY, find your strength in the Lord, in his mighty power. 11 Put on the full armour provided by God, so that you may be able to stand firm against the stratagems of the devil. 12 For our struggle is not against human foes, but against cosmic powers, against the authorities and potentates of this dark age, against the superhuman forces of evil in the heavenly realms. 13 Therefore, take up the armour of God; then you will be able to withstand them on the evil day and, after doing your utmost, to stand your ground. 14 Stand fast, I say. Fasten on the belt of truth; for a breastplate put on integrity; 15 let the shoes on your feet be the gospel of peace, to give you firm footing; 16 and, with all these, take up the great shield of faith, with which you will be able to quench all the burning arrows of the evil one. 17 Accept salvation as your helmet, and the sword which the Spirit gives you, the word of God. 18 Constantly ask God's help in prayer, and pray always in the power of the Spirit. To this end keep watch and persevere, always interceding for all God's people. 19 Pray also for me, that I may be granted the right words when I speak, and may boldly and freely make known the hidden purpose of the gospel, 20 for which I am an ambassador—in chains. Pray that I may speak of it boldly, as is my duty.

21 YOU WILL want to know how I am and what I am doing; Tychicus will give you all the news. He is our dear brother and trustworthy helper in the Lord's work. 22 I am sending him to you on purpose to let you have news of us and to put fresh heart into you.

23 Peace to the community and love with faith, from God the Father and the Lord Jesus Christ. 24 God's grace be with all who love our Lord Jesus Christ with undying love.

6:24 Christ ... love: *or* Christ, grace and immortality.

THE LETTER OF PAUL TO THE
PHILIPPIANS

1 From Paul and Timothy, servants of Christ Jesus, to all God's people at Philippi, who are incorporate in Christ Jesus, with the bishops and deacons.

2 Grace to you and peace from God our Father and the Lord Jesus Christ.

3 I thank my God every time I think of you; 4 whenever I pray for you all, my prayers are always joyful, 5 because of the part you have taken in the work of the gospel from the first day until now. 6 Of this I am confident, that he who started the good work in you will bring it to completion by the day of Christ Jesus. 7 It is only natural that I should feel like this about you all, because I have great affection for you, knowing that, both while I am kept in prison and when I am called on to defend the truth of the gospel, you all share in this privilege of mine. 8 God knows how I long for you all with the deep yearning of Christ Jesus himself. 9 And this is my prayer, that your love may grow ever richer in knowledge and insight of every kind, 10 enabling you to learn by experience what things really matter. Then on the day of Christ you will be flawless and without blame, 11 yielding the full harvest of righteousness that comes through Jesus Christ, to the glory and praise of God.

Paul in prison

12 My friends, I want you to understand that the progress of the gospel has actually been helped by what has happened to me. 13 It has become common knowledge throughout the imperial guard, and indeed among the public at large, that my imprisonment is in Christ's cause; 14 and my being in prison has given most of our fellow-Christians confidence to speak the word of God fearlessly and with extraordinary courage.

15 Some, it is true, proclaim Christ in a jealous and quarrelsome spirit, but some do it in goodwill. 16 These are moved by love, knowing that it is to defend the gospel that I am where I am; 17 the others are moved by selfish ambition and present Christ from mixed motives, meaning to cause me distress as I lie in prison. 18 What does it matter? One way or another, whether sincerely or not, Christ is proclaimed; and for that I rejoice.

Yes, and I shall go on rejoicing; 19 for I know well that the issue will be my deliverance, because you are praying for me and the Spirit of Jesus Christ is given me for support. 20 It is my confident hope that nothing will daunt me or prevent me from speaking boldly; and that now as always Christ will display his greatness in me, whether the verdict be life or death. 21 For to me life is Christ, and death is gain. 22 If I am to go on living in the body there is fruitful work for me to do. Which then am I to choose? I cannot tell. 23 I am pulled two ways: my own desire is to depart and be with Christ—that is better by far; 24 but for your sake the greater need is for me to remain in the body. 25 This convinces me: I am sure I shall remain, and stand by you all to ensure your progress and joy in the faith, 26 so that on my account you may have even more cause for pride in Christ Jesus—through seeing me restored to you.

Unity and witness

27 Whatever happens, let your conduct be worthy of the gospel of Christ, so that whether or not I come and see you for myself I may hear that you are standing firm, united in spirit and in mind, side by side in the struggle to advance the gospel faith, 28 meeting your opponents without so much as a tremor. This is a sure sign to them that destruction is in store for them and salvation for you, a sign from God himself; 29 for you have been granted the privilege not only of believing in Christ but also of suffering for him. 30 Your conflict is the same as mine; once you saw me in it, and now you hear I am in it still.

1:1 **bishops and deacons**: or overseers and assistants.   1:13 **the imperial guard**: or the Residency.

2 If then our common life in Christ yields anything to stir the heart, any consolation of love, any participation in the Spirit, any warmth of affection or compassion, [2] fill up my cup of happiness by thinking and feeling alike, with the same love for one another and a common attitude of mind. [3] Leave no room for selfish ambition and vanity, but humbly reckon others better than yourselves. [4] Look to each other's interests and not merely to your own.

[5] Take to heart among yourselves what you find in Christ Jesus: [6] 'He was in the form of God; yet he laid no claim to equality with God, [7] but made himself nothing, assuming the form of a slave. Bearing the human likeness, [8] sharing the human lot, he humbled himself, and was obedient, even to the point of death, death on a cross! [9] Therefore God raised him to the heights and bestowed on him the name above all names, [10] that at the name of Jesus every knee should bow—in heaven, on earth, and in the depths— [11] and every tongue acclaim, "Jesus Christ is Lord," to the glory of God the Father.'

[12] So you too, my friends, must be obedient, as always; even more, now that I am absent, than when I was with you. You must work out your own salvation in fear and trembling; [13] for it is God who works in you, inspiring both the will and the deed, for his own chosen purpose.

[14] Do everything without grumbling or argument. [15] Show yourselves innocent and above reproach, faultless children of God in a crooked and depraved generation, in which you shine like stars in a dark world [16] and proffer the word of life. Then you will be my pride on the day of Christ, proof that I did not run my race in vain or labour in vain. [17] But if my life-blood is to be poured out to complete the sacrifice and offering up of your faith, I rejoice and share my joy with you all. [18] You too must rejoice and share your joy with me.

Paul's plans

[19] I HOPE, in the Lord Jesus, to send Timothy to you soon; it will cheer me up to have news of you. [20] I have no one else here like him, who has a genuine concern for your affairs; [21] they are all bent on their own interests, not on those of Christ Jesus. [22] But Timothy's record is known to you: you know that he has been at my side in the service of the gospel like a son working under his father. [23] So he is the one I mean to send as soon as I see how things go with me; [24] and I am confident, in the Lord, that I shall be coming myself before long.

[25] I have decided I must also send our brother Epaphroditus, my fellow-worker and comrade, whom you commissioned to attend to my needs. [26] He has been missing you all, and was upset because you heard he was ill. [27] Indeed he was dangerously ill, but God was merciful to him; and not only to him but to me, to spare me one sorrow on top of another. [28] For this reason I am all the more eager to send him and give you the happiness of seeing him again; that will relieve my anxiety as well. [29] Welcome him then in the fellowship of the Lord with whole-hearted delight. You should honour people like him; [30] in Christ's cause he came near to death, risking his life to render me the service you could not give.

3 And now, my friends, I wish you joy in the Lord.

The Christian's goal

To REPEAT what I have written to you before is no trouble to me, and it is a safeguard for you. [2] Be on your guard against those dogs, those who do nothing but harm and who insist on mutilation— 'circumcision' I will not call it; [3] we are the circumcision, we who worship by the Spirit of God, whose pride is in Christ Jesus, and who put no confidence in the physical. [4] It is not that I am myself without grounds for such confidence. If anyone makes claims of that kind, I can make a stronger case for myself: [5] circumcised on my eighth day, Israelite by race, of the tribe of Benjamin, a Hebrew born and bred; in my practice of the law a Pharisee, [6] in zeal for religion a persecutor of the church, by the law's standard of righteousness without fault. [7] But all such assets I have written off because of Christ. [8] More than that, I count everything

---

2:20 no one ... who has: *or* no one else here who sees things as I do, and has.   3:3 who worship ... God: *some witnesses read* who worship God in the spirit; *one reads* whose worship is spiritual.

sheer loss, far outweighed by the gain of knowing Christ Jesus my Lord, for whose sake I did in fact forfeit everything. I count it so much rubbish, for the sake of gaining Christ [9] and finding myself in union with him, with no righteousness of my own based on the law, nothing but the righteousness which comes from faith in Christ, given by God in response to faith. [10] My one desire is to know Christ and the power of his resurrection, and to share his sufferings in growing conformity with his death, [11] in hope of somehow attaining the resurrection from the dead.

[12] It is not that I have already achieved this. I have not yet reached perfection, but I press on, hoping to take hold of that for which Christ once took hold of me. [13] My friends, I do not claim to have hold of it yet. What I do say is this: forgetting what is behind and straining towards what lies ahead, [14] I press towards the finishing line, to win the heavenly prize to which God has called me in Christ Jesus.

[15] We who are mature should keep to this way of thinking. If on any point you think differently, this also God will make plain to you. [16] Only let our conduct be consistent with what we have already attained.

[17] Join together, my friends, in following my example. You have us for a model; imitate those whose way of life conforms to it. [18] As I have often told you, and now tell you with tears, there are many whose way of life makes them enemies of the cross of Christ. [19] They are heading for destruction, they make appetite their god, they take pride in what should bring shame; their minds are set on earthly things. [20] We, by contrast, are citizens of heaven, and from heaven we expect our deliverer to come, the Lord Jesus Christ. [21] He will transfigure our humble bodies, and give them a form like that of his own glorious body, by that power which enables him to make all things subject to 4 himself. [1] This, my dear friends, whom I love and long for, my joy and crown, this is what it means to stand firm in the Lord.

[2] Euodia and Syntyche, I appeal to you both: agree together in the Lord. [3] Yes, and you too, my loyal comrade, I ask you to help these women, who shared my struggles in the cause of the gospel, with Clement and my other fellow-workers, who are enrolled in the book of life.

[4] I wish you joy in the Lord always. Again I say: all joy be yours.

[5] Be known to everyone for your consideration of others.

The Lord is near; [6] do not be anxious, but in everything make your requests known to God in prayer and petition with thanksgiving. [7] Then the peace of God, which is beyond all understanding, will guard your hearts and your thoughts in Christ Jesus.

[8] And now, my friends, all that is true, all that is noble, all that is just and pure, all that is lovable and attractive, whatever is excellent and admirable—fill your thoughts with these things.

[9] Put into practice the lessons I taught you, the tradition I have passed on, all that you heard me say or saw me do; and the God of peace will be with you.

Thanks and greetings

[10] It is a great joy to me in the Lord that after so long your care for me has now revived. I know you always cared; it was opportunity you lacked. [11] Not that I am speaking of want, for I have learned to be self-sufficient whatever my circumstances. [12] I know what it is to have nothing, and I know what it is to have plenty. I have been thoroughly initiated into fullness and hunger, plenty and poverty. [13] I am able to face anything through him who gives me strength. [14] All the same, it was kind of you to share the burden of my troubles.

[15] You Philippians are aware that, when I set out from Macedonia in the early days of my mission, yours was the only church to share with me in the giving and receiving; [16] more than once you contributed to my needs, even at Thessalonica. [17] Do not think I set my heart on the gift; all I care for is the interest mounting up in your account. [18] I have been paid in full; I have all I need and more, now that I have received from Epaphroditus what you sent. It is a fragrant offering, an acceptable sacrifice, pleasing to God. [19] And my God will supply all your needs out of the magnificence of his riches in Christ Jesus. [20] To our God

and Father be glory for ever and ever! Amen.

²¹ Give my greetings, in the fellowship of Christ Jesus, to each one of God's people. My colleagues send their greetings to you, ²² and so do all God's people here, particularly those in the emperor's service.

²³ The grace of our Lord Jesus Christ be with your spirit.

THE LETTER OF PAUL TO THE
COLOSSIANS

1 From Paul, by the will of God apostle of Christ Jesus, and our colleague Timothy, ² to God's people at Colossae, our fellow-believers in Christ.

Grace to you and peace from God our Father.

³ In all our prayers to God, the Father of our Lord Jesus Christ, we thank him for you, ⁴ because we have heard of your faith in Christ Jesus and the love you bear towards all God's people; ⁵ both spring from that hope stored up for you in heaven of which you learned when the message of the true gospel first ⁶ came to you. That same gospel is bearing fruit and making new growth the whole world over, as it does among you and has done since the day when you heard of God's grace and learned what it truly is. ⁷ It was Epaphras, our dear fellow-servant and a trusted worker for Christ on our behalf, who taught you this, ⁸ and it is he who has brought us news of the love the Spirit has awakened in you.

The supremacy of Christ

⁹ This is why, ever since we first heard about you, we have not ceased to pray for you. We ask God that you may receive from him full insight into his will, all wisdom and spiritual understanding, ¹⁰ so that your manner of life may be worthy of the Lord and entirely pleasing to him. We pray that you may bear fruit in active goodness of every kind, and grow in knowledge of God. ¹¹ In his glorious might may he give you ample strength to meet with fortitude and patience whatever comes; ¹² and to give joyful thanks to the Father who has made you fit to share the heritage of God's people in the realm of light.

¹³ He rescued us from the domain of darkness and brought us into the kingdom of his dear Son, ¹⁴ through whom our release is secured and our sins are forgiven. ¹⁵ He is the image of the invisible God; his is the primacy over all creation. ¹⁶ In him everything in heaven and on earth was created, not only things visible but also the invisible orders of thrones, sovereignties, authorities, and powers: the whole universe has been created through him and for him. ¹⁷ He exists before all things, and all things are held together in him. ¹⁸ He is the head of the body, the church. He is its origin, the first to return from the dead, to become in all things supreme. ¹⁹ For in him God in all his fullness chose to dwell, ²⁰ and through him to reconcile all things to himself, making peace through the shedding of his blood on the cross—all things, whether on earth or in heaven.

²¹⁻²² Formerly you yourselves were alienated from God, his enemies in heart and mind, as your evil deeds showed. But now by Christ's death in his body of flesh and blood God has reconciled you to himself, so that he may bring you into his own presence, holy and without blame or blemish. ²³ Yet you must persevere in faith, firm on your foundations and never to be dislodged from the hope offered in the gospel you accepted. This is the gospel which has been proclaimed in the whole creation under heaven, the gospel of which I, Paul, became a minister.

1:7 **our behalf:** *some witnesses read* your behalf.   whatever comes; ¹² and to give thanks.   1:16 **for him:** *or* with him as its goal.   1:11–12 **patience ... thanks:** *or* patience, and joy   1:20 **to himself:** *or* to their goal in him.

[24] It is now my joy to suffer for you; for the sake of Christ's body, the church, I am completing what still remains for Christ to suffer in my own person. [25] I became a servant of the church by virtue of the task assigned to me by God for your benefit: to put God's word into full effect, [26] that secret purpose hidden for long ages and through many generations, but now disclosed to God's people. [27] To them he chose to make known what a wealth of glory is offered to the Gentiles in this secret purpose: Christ in you, the hope of glory.

[28] He it is whom we proclaim. We teach everyone and instruct everyone in all the ways of wisdom, so as to present each one of you as a mature member of Christ's body. [29] To this end I am toiling strenuously with all the energy and power of Christ at work in me. [1] I want you to know how strenuous are my exertions for you and the Laodiceans, and for all who have never set eyes on me. [2] My aim is to keep them in good heart and united in love, so that they may come to the full wealth of conviction which understanding brings, and grasp God's secret, which is Christ himself, [3] in whom lie hidden all the treasures of wisdom and knowledge. [4] I tell you this to make sure no one talks you into error by specious arguments. [5] I may be absent in body, but in spirit I am with you, and rejoice to see your unbroken ranks and the solid front which your faith in Christ presents.

True and false teaching

[6] THEREFORE, since you have accepted Christ Jesus as Lord, live in union with him. [7] Be rooted in him, be built in him, grow strong in the faith as you were taught; let your hearts overflow with thankfulness. [8] Be on your guard; let no one capture your minds with hollow and delusive speculations, based on traditions of human teaching and centred on the elemental spirits of the universe and not on Christ.

[9] For it is in Christ that the Godhead in all its fullness dwells embodied, [10] it is in him you have been brought to fulfilment. Every power and authority in the universe is subject to him as head. [11] In him

also you were circumcised, not in a physical sense, but by the stripping away of the old nature, which is Christ's way of circumcision. [12] For you were buried with him in baptism, and in that baptism you were also raised to life with him through your faith in the active power of God, who raised him from the dead. [13] And although you were dead because of your sins and your uncircumcision, he has brought you to life with Christ. For he has forgiven us all our sins; [14] he has cancelled the bond which was outstanding against us with its legal demands; he has set it aside, nailing it to the cross. [15] There he disarmed the cosmic powers and authorities and made a public spectacle of them, leading them as captives in his triumphal procession.

[16] ALLOW no one, therefore, to take you to task about what you eat or drink, or over the observance of festival, new moon, or sabbath. [17] These are no more than a shadow of what was to come; the reality is Christ's. [18] You are not to be disqualified by the decision of people who go in for self-mortification and angel-worship and access to some visionary world. Such people, bursting with the futile conceit of worldly minds, [19] lose their hold upon the head; yet it is from the head that the whole body, with all its joints and ligaments, has its needs supplied, and thus knit together grows according to God's design.

[20] Did you not die with Christ and pass beyond reach of the elemental spirits of the universe? Then why behave as though you were still living the life of the world? Why let people dictate to you: [21] 'Do not handle this, do not taste that, do not touch the other'— [22] referring to things that must all perish as they are used? That is to follow human rules and regulations. [23] Such conduct may have an air of wisdom, with its forced piety, its self-mortification, and its severity to the body; but it is of no use at all in combating sensuality.

[1] Were you not raised to life with Christ? Then aspire to the realm above, where Christ is, seated at God's right hand, [2] and fix your thoughts on

---

2:8 **and centred ... universe:** *or* and elementary ideas belonging to this world.   2:15 **he disarmed ... of them:** *or* he stripped himself of his physical body, and thereby made a public spectacle of the cosmic powers and authorities.   2:20 **elemental ... universe:** *or* elementary ideas belonging to this world.

that higher realm, not on this earthly life. ³ You died; and now your life lies hidden with Christ in God. ⁴ When Christ, who is our life, is revealed, then you too will be revealed with him in glory.

Christian conduct

⁵ So PUT to death those parts of you which belong to the earth—fornication, indecency, lust, evil desires, and the ruthless greed which is nothing less than idolatry; ⁶ on these divine retribution falls. ⁷ This is the way you yourselves once lived; ⁸ but now have done with rage, bad temper, malice, slander, filthy talk—banish them all from your lips! ⁹ Do not lie to one another, now that you have discarded the old human nature and the conduct that goes with it, ¹⁰ and have put on the new nature which is constantly being renewed in the image of its Creator and brought to know God. ¹¹ There is no question here of Greek and Jew, circumcised and uncircumcised, barbarian, Scythian, slave and freeman; but Christ is all, and is in all.

¹² Put on, then, garments that suit God's chosen and beloved people: compassion, kindness, humility, gentleness, patience. ¹³ Be tolerant with one another and forgiving, if any of you has cause for complaint: you must forgive as the Lord forgave you. ¹⁴ Finally, to bind everything together and complete the whole, there must be love. ¹⁵ Let Christ's peace be arbiter in your decisions, the peace to which you were called as members of a single body. Always be thankful. ¹⁶ Let the gospel of Christ dwell among you in all its richness; teach and instruct one another with all the wisdom it gives you. With psalms and hymns and spiritual songs, sing from the heart in gratitude to God. ¹⁷ Let every word and action, everything you do, be in the name of the Lord Jesus, and give thanks through him to God the Father.

¹⁸ WIVES, be subject to your husbands; that is your Christian duty. ¹⁹ Husbands, love your wives and do not be harsh with them. ²⁰ Children, obey your parents in everything, for that is pleasing to God and is the Christian way. ²¹ Fathers, do not exasperate your children, in case they lose heart. ²² Slaves, give entire obedience to your earthly masters, not merely to

catch their eye or curry favour with them, but with single-mindedness, out of reverence for the Lord. ²³ Whatever you are doing, put your whole heart into it, as if you were doing it for the Lord and not for men, ²⁴ knowing that there is a master who will give you an inheritance as a reward for your service. Christ is the master you must serve. ²⁵ Wrongdoers will pay for the wrong they do; there will be no favouritism. ¹ Masters, be just and fair to your slaves, knowing that you too have a master in heaven.

4 ² Persevere in prayer, with minds alert and with thankful hearts; ³ and include us in your prayers, asking God to provide an opening for the gospel, that we may proclaim the secret of Christ, for which indeed I am in prison. ⁴ Pray that I may make the secret plain, as it is my duty to do.

⁵ Be wise in your dealings with outsiders, but use your opportunities to the full. ⁶ Let your words always be gracious, never insipid; learn how best to respond to each person you meet.

News and greetings

⁷ YOU WILL hear all my news from Tychicus, our dear brother and trustworthy helper and fellow-servant in the Lord's work. ⁸ I am sending him to you for this purpose, to let you know how we are and to put fresh heart into you. ⁹ With him comes Onesimus, our trustworthy and dear brother, who is one of yourselves. They will tell you all that has happened here.

¹⁰ Aristarchus, Christ's captive like myself, sends his greetings; so does Mark, the cousin of Barnabas (you have had instructions about him; if he comes, make him welcome), ¹¹ and Jesus Justus. Of the Jewish Christians, these are the only ones working with me for the kingdom of God, and they have been a great comfort to me. ¹² Greetings from Epaphras, servant of Christ, who is one of yourselves. He prays hard for you all the time, that you may stand fast, as mature Christians, fully determined to do the will of God. ¹³ I can vouch for him, that he works tirelessly for you and the people at Laodicea and Hierapolis. ¹⁴ Greetings to you from our dear friend Luke, the doctor, and from Demas. ¹⁵ Give our greetings to the

4: 15 Nympha ... her house: *some witnesses read* Nymphas ... his house.

Christians at Laodicea, and to Nympha and the congregation that meets at her house. [16] Once this letter has been read among you, see that it is read also to the church at Laodicea, and that you in turn read my letter to Laodicea. [17] Give Archip-pus this message: 'See that you carry out fully the duty entrusted to you in the Lord's service.'

[18] I add this greeting in my own hand—Paul. Remember I am in prison. Grace be with you.

THE FIRST LETTER OF PAUL TO THE
THESSALONIANS

1 FROM Paul, Silvanus, and Timothy to the church of the Thessalonians who belong to God the Father and the Lord Jesus Christ.

Grace to you and peace.

[2] We always thank God for you all, and mention you in our prayers. [3] We continually call to mind, before our God and Father, how your faith has shown itself in action, your love in labour, and your hope of our Lord Jesus Christ in perseverance. [4] My dear friends, beloved by God, we are certain that he has chosen you, [5] because when we brought you the gospel we did not bring it in mere words but in the power of the Holy Spirit and with strong conviction. You know what we were like for your sake when we were with you.

[6] You, in turn, followed the example set by us and by the Lord; the welcome you gave the message meant grave suffering for you, yet you rejoiced in the Holy Spirit; [7] and so you have become a model for all believers in Macedonia and in Achaia. [8] From you the word of the Lord rang out; and not in Macedonia and Achaia alone, but everywhere your faith in God has become common knowledge. No words of ours are needed; [9] everyone is spreading the story of our visit to you: how you turned from idols to be servants of the true and living God, [10] and to wait expectantly for his Son from heaven, whom he raised from the dead, Jesus our deliverer from the retribution to come.

Paul and the church at Thessalonica

2 YOU KNOW for yourselves, my friends, that our visit to you was not fruitless. [2] Far from it! After all the injury and outrage which as you know we had suffered at Philippi, by the help of our God we declared the gospel of God to you frankly and fearlessly in face of great opposition. [3] The appeal we make does not spring from delusion or sordid motive or from any attempt to deceive; [4] but God has approved us as fit to be entrusted with the gospel. So when we preach, we do not curry favour with men; we seek only the favour of God, who is continually testing our hearts. [5] We have never resorted to flattery, as you have cause to know; nor, as God is our witness, have our words ever been a cloak for greed. [6] We have never sought honour from men, not from you or from anyone else, [7] although as Christ's own envoys we might have made our weight felt; but we were as gentle with you as a nurse caring for her children. [8] Our affection was so deep that we were determined to share with you not only the gospel of God but our very selves; that is how dear you had become to us! [9] You remember, my friends, our toil and drudgery; night and day we worked for a living, rather than be a burden to any of you while we proclaimed to you the good news of God.

[10] We call you to witness, yes and God himself, how devout and just and blameless was our conduct towards you who are believers. [11] As you well know, we dealt with each one of you as a father deals with his children; [12] we appealed to you, we encouraged you, we urged you, to live lives worthy of the God who calls you into his kingdom and glory.

[13] We have reason to thank God continually because, when we handed on God's message, you accepted it, not as the word of men, but as what it truly is, the very word of God at work in you who are

183

believers. [14] You, my friends, have followed the example of the Christians in the churches of God in Judaea: you have been treated by your own countrymen as they were treated by the Jews, [15] who killed the Lord Jesus and the prophets and drove us out, and are so heedless of God's will and such enemies of their fellow-men [16] that they hinder us from telling the Gentiles how they may be saved. All this time they have been making up the full measure of their guilt. But now retribution has overtaken them for good and all!

[17] My friends, when for a short spell you were lost to us—out of sight but not out of mind—we were exceedingly anxious to see you again. [18] So we made up our minds to visit you—I, Paul, more than once—but Satan thwarted us. [19] For what hope or joy or triumphal crown is there for us when we stand before our Lord Jesus at his coming? What indeed but you? [20] You are our glory and our joy.

3 So when we could bear it no longer, we decided to stay on alone at Athens, [2] and sent Timothy, our colleague and a fellow-worker with God in the service of the gospel of Christ, to encourage you to stand firm for the faith [3] and under all these hardships remain unshaken. You know that this is our appointed lot, [4] for when we were with you we warned you that we were bound to suffer hardship; and so it has turned out, as you have found. [5] This was why I could bear it no longer and sent to find out about your faith; I was afraid that the tempter might have tempted you and our labour might be wasted.

[6] But now Timothy has just returned from his visit to you, bringing good news of your faith and love. He tells us that you always think kindly of us, and are as anxious to see us as we are to see you. [7] So amid all our difficulties and hardships we are reassured, my friends, by the news of your faith. [8] It is the breath of life to us to know that you stand firm in the Lord. [9] What thanks can we give to God in return for you? What thanks for all the joy you have brought us, making us rejoice before our God [10] while we pray most earnestly night and day to be allowed to see you again and to make good whatever is lacking in your faith?
[11] May our God and Father himself, and

our Lord Jesus, open the way for us to come to you; [12] and may the Lord make your love increase and overflow to one another and to everyone, as our love does to you. [13] May he make your hearts firm, so that you may stand before our God and Father holy and faultless when our Lord Jesus comes with all those who are his own.

Christian conduct

4 AND now, friends, we have one thing to ask of you, as fellow-Christians. We passed on to you the tradition of the way we must live if we are to please God; you are indeed already following it, but we beg you to do so yet more thoroughly. [2] You know the rules we gave you in the name of the Lord Jesus. [3] This is the will of God, that you should be holy: you must abstain from fornication; [4] each one of you must learn to gain mastery over his body, to hallow and honour it, [5] not giving way to lust like the pagans who know nothing of God; [6] no one must do his fellow-Christian wrong in this matter, or infringe his rights. As we impressed on you before, the Lord punishes all such offences. [7] For God called us to holiness, not to impurity. [8] Anyone therefore who flouts these rules is flouting not man but the God who bestows on you his Holy Spirit.
[9] About love of the brotherhood you need no words of mine, for you are yourselves taught by God to love one another, [10] and you are in fact practising this rule of love towards all your fellow-Christians throughout Macedonia. Yet we appeal to you, friends, to do better still. [11] Let it be your ambition to live quietly and attend to your own business; and to work with your hands, as we told you, [12] so that you may command the respect of those outside your own number, and at the same time never be in want.

Christ's return

[13] WE wish you not to remain in ignorance, friends, about those who sleep in death; you should not grieve like the rest of mankind, who have no hope. [14] We believe that Jesus died and rose again; so too will God bring those who died as Christians to be with Jesus.
[15] This we tell you as a word from the Lord: those of us who are still alive when the Lord comes will have no advantage

over those who have died; ¹⁶when the command is given, when the archangel's voice is heard, when God's trumpet sounds, then the Lord himself will descend from heaven; first the Christian dead will rise, ¹⁷then we who are still alive shall join them, caught up in clouds to meet the Lord in the air. Thus we shall always be with the Lord. ¹⁸Console one another, then, with these words.

5 About dates and times, my friends, there is no need to write to you, ²for you yourselves know perfectly well that the day of the Lord comes like a thief in the night. ³While they are saying, 'All is peaceful, all secure,' destruction is upon them, sudden as the pangs that come on a woman in childbirth; and there will be no escape. ⁴But you, friends, are not in the dark; the day will not come upon you like a thief. ⁵You are all children of light, children of day. We do not belong to night and darkness, ⁶and we must not sleep like the rest, but keep awake and sober. ⁷Sleepers sleep at night, and drunkards get drunk at night, ⁸but we, who belong to the daylight, must keep sober, armed with the breastplate of faith and love, and the hope of salvation for a helmet. ⁹God has not destined us for retribution, but for the full attainment of salvation through our Lord Jesus Christ. ¹⁰He died for us so that awake or asleep we might live in company with him. ¹¹Therefore encourage one another, build one another up—as indeed you do.

Final instructions and greetings

¹²WE beg you, friends, to acknowledge those who are working so hard among you, and are your leaders and counsellors in the Lord's fellowship. ¹³Hold them in the highest esteem and affection for the work they do.

Live at peace among yourselves. ¹⁴We urge you, friends, to rebuke the idle, encourage the faint-hearted, support the weak, and be patient with everyone.

¹⁵See to it that no one pays back wrong for wrong, but always aim at what is best for each other and for all.

¹⁶Always be joyful; ¹⁷pray continually; ¹⁸give thanks whatever happens; for this is what God wills for you in Christ Jesus.

¹⁹Do not stifle inspiration ²⁰or despise prophetic utterances, ²¹but test them all; keep hold of what is good ²²and avoid all forms of evil.

²³May God himself, the God of peace, make you holy through and through, and keep you sound in spirit, soul, and body, free of any fault when our Lord Jesus Christ comes. ²⁴He who calls you keeps faith; he will do it.

²⁵Friends, pray for us also.

²⁶Greet all our fellow-Christians with the kiss of peace.

²⁷I adjure you by the Lord to have this letter read to them all.

²⁸The grace of our Lord Jesus Christ be with you!

THE SECOND LETTER OF PAUL TO THE
THESSALONIANS

1 FROM Paul, Silvanus, and Timothy to the church of the Thessalonians who belong to God our Father and the Lord Jesus Christ.

²Grace to you and peace from God the Father and the Lord Jesus Christ.

³Friends, we are always bound to thank God for you, and it is right that we should, because your faith keeps on increasing and the love you all have for each other grows ever greater. ⁴Indeed we boast about you among the churches

of God, because your faith remains so steadfast under all the persecutions and troubles you endure. ⁵This points to the justice of God's judgement; you will be proved worthy of the kingdom of God, for which indeed you are suffering. ⁶It is just that God should balance the account by sending affliction to those who afflict you, ⁷and relief to you who are afflicted, and to us as well, when the Lord Jesus is revealed from heaven with his mighty angels ⁸in blazing fire. Then he will mete out punishment to those who refuse to acknowledge God and who will not obey the gospel of our Lord Jesus. [9] They will suffer the penalty of eternal destruction, cut off from the presence of the Lord and the splendour of his might, [10] when on the great day he comes to reveal his glory among his own and his majesty among all believers; and therefore among you, since you believed the testimony we brought you.

[11] With this in mind we pray for you always, that our God may count you worthy of your calling, and that his power may bring to fulfilment every good purpose and every act inspired by faith, [12] so that the name of our Lord Jesus may be glorified in you, and you in him, according to the grace of our God and the Lord Jesus Christ.

Christ's return

2 Now ABOUT the coming of our Lord Jesus Christ, when he is to gather us to himself: I beg you, my friends, [2] do not suddenly lose your heads, do not be alarmed by any prophetic utterance, any pronouncement, or any letter purporting to come from us, alleging that the day of the Lord is already here. [3] Let no one deceive you in any way. That day cannot come before the final rebellion against God, when wickedness will be revealed in human form, the man doomed to destruction. [4] He is the adversary who raises himself up against every so-called god or object of worship, and even enthrones himself in God's temple claiming to be God. [5] Do you not remember that I told you this while I was still with you? [6] You know, too, about the restraining power which ensures that he will be revealed only at his appointed time; [7] for already the secret forces of wickedness are at work, secret only for the present until the restraining hand is removed from the scene. [8] Then he will be revealed, the wicked one whom the Lord Jesus will destroy with the breath of his mouth and annihilate by the radiance of his presence. [9] The coming of the wicked one is the work of Satan; it will be attended by all the powerful signs and miracles that falsehood can devise, [10] all the deception that sinfulness can impose on those

doomed to destruction, because they did not open their minds to love of the truth and so find salvation. [11] That is why God puts them under a compelling delusion, which makes them believe what is false, [12] so that all who have not believed the truth but made sinfulness their choice may be brought to judgement.

[13] WE are always bound to thank God for you, my friends beloved by the Lord. From the beginning of time God chose you to find salvation in the Spirit who consecrates you and in the truth you believe. [14] It was for this that he called you through the gospel we brought, so that you might come to possess the splendour of our Lord Jesus Christ.

[15] Stand firm then, my friends, and hold fast to the traditions which you have learned from us by word or by letter. [16] And may our Lord Jesus Christ himself and God our Father, who has shown us such love, and in his grace has given us such unfailing encouragement and so sure a hope, [17] still encourage and strengthen you in every good deed and word.

Christian conduct

3 AND now, friends, pray for us, that the word of the Lord may have everywhere the swift and glorious success it has had among you, [2] and that we may be rescued from wrong-headed and wicked people; for not all have faith. [3] But the Lord keeps faith, and he will strengthen you and guard you from the evil one; [4] and in the Lord we have confidence about you, that you are doing and will continue to do what we tell you. [5] May the Lord direct your hearts towards God's love and the steadfastness of Christ.

[6] These are our instructions to you, friends, in the name of our Lord Jesus Christ: hold aloof from every Christian who falls into idle habits, and disregards the tradition you received from us. [7] You yourselves know how you ought to follow our example: you never saw us idling; [8] we did not accept free hospitality from anyone; night and day in toil and drudgery we worked for a living, rather than be a burden to any of you—[9] not because we do not have the right to maintenance, but to set an example for you to follow.

2:13 From ... chose you: *some witnesses read* God chose you as his firstfruits.

[10]Already during our stay with you we laid down this rule: anyone who will not work shall not eat. [11]We mention this because we hear that some of you are idling their time away, minding everybody's business but their own. [12]We instruct and urge such people in the name of the Lord Jesus Christ to settle down to work and earn a living.

[13]My friends, you must never tire of doing right. [14]If anyone disobeys the instructions given in my letter, single him out, and have nothing to do with him until he is ashamed of himself. [15]I do not mean treat him as an enemy, but admonish him as one of the family.

[16]May the Lord of peace himself give you peace at all times and in all ways. The Lord be with you all.

[17]This greeting is in my own handwriting; all genuine letters of mine bear the same signature—Paul.

[18]The grace of our Lord Jesus Christ be with you all.

THE FIRST LETTER OF PAUL TO
TIMOTHY

1 FROM Paul, apostle of Christ Jesus by command of God our Saviour and Christ Jesus our hope, [2]to Timothy his true-born son in the faith.

Grace, mercy, and peace to you from God the Father and Christ Jesus our Lord.

Paul's charge to Timothy

[3]WHEN I was starting for Macedonia, I urged you to stay on at Ephesus. You were to instruct certain people to give up teaching erroneous doctrines [4]and devoting themselves to interminable myths and genealogies, which give rise to mere speculation, and do not further God's plan for us, which works through faith.

[5]This instruction has love as its goal, the love which springs from a pure heart, a good conscience, and a genuine faith. [6]Through lack of these some people have gone astray into a wilderness of words. [7]They set out to be teachers of the law, although they do not understand either the words they use or the subjects about which they are so dogmatic.

[8]We all know that the law is an admirable thing, provided we treat it as law, [9]recognizing that it is designed not for good citizens, but for the lawless and unruly, the impious and sinful, the irreligious and worldly, for parricides and matricides, murderers [10]and fornicators, perverts, kidnappers, liars, perjurers—in fact all whose behaviour flouts the sound teaching [11]which conforms with the gospel entrusted to me, the gospel which tells of the glory of the ever-blessed God.

[12]I give thanks to Christ Jesus our Lord, who has made me equal to the task; I thank him for judging me worthy of trust and appointing me to his service—[13]although in the past I had met him with abuse and persecution and outrage. But because I acted in the ignorance of unbelief I was dealt with mercifully; [14]the grace of our Lord was lavished upon me, along with the faith and love which are ours in Christ Jesus.

[15]Here is a saying you may trust, one that merits full acceptance: 'Christ Jesus came into the world to save sinners'; and among them I stand first. [16]But I was mercifully dealt with for this very purpose, that Jesus Christ might find in me the first occasion for displaying his inexhaustible patience, and that I might be typical of all who were in future to have faith in him and gain eternal life. [17]To the King eternal, immortal, invisible, the only God, be honour and glory for ever and ever! Amen.

[18]In laying this charge upon you, Timothy my son, I am guided by those prophetic utterances which first directed me to you. Encouraged by them, fight the good fight [19]with faith and a clear conscience. It was through spurning conscience that certain persons made

1:4 **do not ... faith**: *or* do not promote the faithful discharge of God's stewardship.

shipwreck of their faith, [20] among them Hymenaeus and Alexander, whom I consigned to Satan, in the hope that through this discipline they might learn not to be blasphemous.

Christian conduct

2 FIRST of all, then, I urge that petitions, prayers, intercessions, and thanksgivings be offered for everyone, [2] for sovereigns and for all in high office so that we may lead a tranquil and quiet life, free to practise our religion with dignity. [3] Such prayer is right, and approved by God our Saviour, [4] whose will it is that all should find salvation and come to know the truth. [5] For there is one God, and there is one mediator between God and man, Christ Jesus, himself man, [6] who sacrificed himself to win freedom for all mankind, revealing God's purpose at God's good time; [7] of this I was appointed herald and apostle (this is no lie, it is the truth), to instruct the Gentiles in the true faith.

[8] It is my desire, therefore, that everywhere prayers be said by the men of the congregation, who shall lift up their hands with a pure intention, without anger or argument. [9] Women must dress in becoming manner, modestly and soberly, not with elaborate hair-styles, not adorned with gold or pearls or expensive clothes, [10] but with good deeds, as befits women who claim to be religious. [11] Their role is to learn, listening quietly and with due submission. [12] I do not permit women to teach or dictate to the men; they should keep quiet. [13] For Adam was created first, and Eve afterwards; [14] moreover it was not Adam who was deceived; it was the woman who, yielding to deception, fell into sin. [15] But salvation for the woman will be in the bearing of children, provided she continues in faith, love, and holiness, with modesty.

3 Here is a saying you may trust: 'To aspire to leadership is an honourable ambition.' [2] A bishop, therefore, must be above reproach, husband of one wife, sober, temperate, courteous, hospitable, and a good teacher; [3] he must not be given to drink or brawling, but be of a forbearing disposition, avoiding quarrels, and not avaricious. [4] He must be one who manages his own household well and controls his children without losing his dignity, [5] for if a man does not know how to manage his own family, how can he take charge of a congregation of God's people? [6] He should not be a recent convert; conceit might bring on him the devil's punishment. [7] He must moreover have a good reputation with the outside world, so that he may not be exposed to scandal and be caught in the devil's snare.

[8] Deacons, likewise, must be dignified, not indulging in double talk, given neither to excessive drinking nor to money-grubbing. [9] They must be men who combine a clear conscience with a firm hold on the mystery of the faith. [10] And they too must first undergo scrutiny, and only if they are of unimpeachable character may they serve as deacons. [11] Women in this office must likewise be dignified, not scandalmongers, but sober, and trustworthy in every way. [12] A deacon must be the husband of one wife, and good at managing his children and his own household. [13] For deacons with a good record of service are entitled to high standing and the right to be heard on matters of the Christian faith.

[14] I am hoping to come to you before long, but I write this [15] in case I am delayed, to let you know what is proper conduct in God's household, that is, the church of the living God, the pillar and bulwark of the truth. [16] And great beyond all question is the mystery of our religion:

He was manifested in flesh,
vindicated in spirit,
seen by angels;
he was proclaimed among the
  nations,
believed in throughout the world,
raised to heavenly glory.

False teaching

4 THE Spirit explicitly warns us that in time to come some will forsake the faith and surrender their minds to subversive spirits and demon-inspired doctrines, [2] through the plausible falsehoods of those whose consciences have been permanently branded, [3] They will forbid marriage, and insist on abstinence from foods

---

3:1 **Here ... trust:** *some witnesses read* There is a popular saying.   3:11 **Women ... office:** *or* Their wives.
4:1 **in time to come:** *or* in the last times.   4:2 **branded:** *or* seared.

which God created to be enjoyed with thanksgiving by believers who have come to knowledge of the truth. [4] Everything that God has created is good, and nothing is to be rejected provided it is accepted with thanksgiving, [5] for it is then made holy by God's word and by prayer.

[6] By offering such advice as this to the brotherhood you will prove to be a good servant of Christ Jesus, nurtured in the precepts of our faith and of the sound instruction which you have followed. [7] Have nothing to do with superstitious myths, mere old wives' tales. Keep yourself in training for the practice of religion; [8] for while the training of the body brings limited benefit, the benefits of religion are without limit, since it holds out promise not only for this life but also for the life to come. [9] Here is a saying you may trust, one that merits full acceptance. [10] 'This is why we labour and struggle, because we have set our hope on the living God, who is the Saviour of all'—the Saviour, above all, of believers.

[11] Insist on these things in your teaching. [12] Let no one underrate you because you are young, but be to believers an example in speech and behaviour, in love, fidelity, and purity. [13] Until I arrive devote yourself to the public reading of the scriptures, to exhortation, and to teaching. [14] Do not neglect the spiritual endowment given you when, under the guidance of prophecy, the elders laid their hands on you.

[15] Make these matters your business, make them your absorbing interest, so that your progress may be plain to all. [16] Persevere in them, keeping close watch on yourself and on your teaching; by doing so you will save both yourself and your hearers.

Church discipline

5 NEVER be harsh with an older man; appeal to him as if he were your father. Treat the younger men as brothers, [2] the older women as mothers, and the younger as your sisters, in all purity. [3] Enrol as widows only those who are widows in the fullest sense. [4] If a widow

has children or grandchildren, they should learn as their first duty to show loyalty to the family and so repay what they owe to their parents and grandparents; for that has God's approval. [5] But a widow in the full sense, one who is alone in the world, puts all her trust in God, and regularly, night and day, attends the meetings for prayer and worship. [6] A widow given to self-indulgence, however, is as good as dead. [7] Add these instructions to the rest, so that the widows may be above reproach. [8] And if anyone does not make provision for his relations, and especially for members of his own household, he has denied the faith and is worse than an unbeliever.

[9] A widow under sixty years of age should not be put on the roll. An enrolled widow must have been the wife of one husband, [10] and must have gained a reputation for good deeds, by taking care of children, by showing hospitality, by washing the feet of God's people, by supporting those in distress—in short, by doing good at every opportunity.

[11] Do not admit younger widows to the roll; for if they let their passions distract them from Christ's service they will want to marry again, [12] and so be guilty of breaking their earlier vow to him. [13] Besides, in going round from house to house they would learn to be idle, indeed worse than idle, gossips and busybodies, speaking of things better left unspoken. [14] For that reason it is my wish that young widows should marry again, have children, and manage a household; then they will give the enemy no occasion for scandal. [15] For there have in fact been some who have taken the wrong turning and gone over to Satan.

[16] If a Christian woman has widows in her family, she must support them; the congregation must be relieved of the burden, so that it may be free to support those who are widows in the full sense.

[17] Elders who give good service as leaders should be reckoned worthy of a double stipend, in particular those who work hard at preaching and teaching. [18] For scripture says, 'You shall not muzzle an

---

4:8–10 **for while ... Saviour of all':** *or* for 'While the training of the body brings limited benefit, the benefits of religion are without limit, since it holds out promise not only for this life but also for the life to come.' [9] That is a saying you may trust, one that merits full acceptance. [10] This is why we labour and struggle, because we have set our hope on the living God, who is the Saviour of all.   4:14 **prophecy ... on you:** *or* prophecy, you were ordained as an elder.

ox while it is treading out the grain';
besides, 'The worker earns his pay.'

[19] Do not entertain a charge against an
elder unless it is supported by two or three
witnesses. [20] Those who do commit sins
you must rebuke in public, to put fear into
the others. [21] Before God and Christ Jesus
and the angels who are his chosen, I
solemnly charge you: maintain these
rules, never prejudging the issue, but
acting with strict impartiality. [22] Do not be
over-hasty in the laying on of hands, or
you may find yourself implicated in other
people's misdeeds; keep yourself above
reproach.

[23] Stop drinking only water; in view of
your frequent ailments take a little wine
to help your digestion.

[24] There are people whose offences are
so obvious that they precede them into
court, and others whose offences have not
yet caught up with them. [25] So too with
good deeds; they may be obvious, but,
even if they are not, they cannot be concealed for ever.

6 All who wear the yoke of slavery
must consider their masters worthy
of all respect, so that the name of God and
the Christian teaching are not brought
into disrepute. [2] Slaves of Christian
masters must not take liberties with them
just because they are their brothers. Quite
the contrary: they must do their work all
the better because those who receive the
benefit of their service are one with them
in faith and love.

Final instructions

THIS is what you are to teach and preach.
[3] Anyone who teaches otherwise, and
does not devote himself to sound precepts—that is, those of our Lord Jesus
Christ—and to good religious teaching,
[4] is a pompous ignoramus with a morbid
enthusiasm for mere speculations and
quibbles. These give rise to jealousy, quarrelling, slander, base suspicions, [5] and
endless wrangles—all typical of those
whose minds are corrupted and who have
lost their grip of the truth. They think
religion should yield dividends; [6] and of
course religion does yield high dividends,
but only to those who are content with
what they have. [7] We brought nothing
into this world, and we can take nothing
out; [8] if we have food and clothing let us
rest content. [9] Those who want to be rich
fall into temptations and snares and into
many foolish and harmful desires which
plunge people into ruin and destruction.
[10] The love of money is the root of all evil,
and in pursuit of it some have wandered
from the faith and spiked themselves on
many a painful thorn.

[11] But you, man of God, must shun all
that, and pursue justice, piety, integrity,
love, fortitude, and gentleness. [12] Run the
great race of faith and take hold of eternal
life, for to this you were called, when you
confessed your faith nobly before many
witnesses. [13] Now in the presence of God,
who gives life to all things, and of Jesus
Christ, who himself made that noble
confession in his testimony before Pontius
Pilate, I charge you [14] to obey your orders
without fault or failure until the appearance of our Lord Jesus Christ [15] which God
will bring about in his own good time. He
is the blessed and only Sovereign, King
of kings and Lord of lords; [16] he alone
possesses immortality, dwelling in unap-
proachable light; him no one has ever
seen or can ever see; to him be honour
and dominion for ever! Amen.

[17] Instruct those who are rich in this
world's goods not to be proud, and to fix
their hopes not on so uncertain a thing as
money, but on God, who richly provides
all things for us to enjoy. [18] They are to do
good and to be rich in well-doing, to be
ready to give generously and to share
with others, [19] and so acquire a treasure
which will form a good foundation for the
future. Then they will grasp the life that is
life indeed.

[20] Timothy, keep safe what has been
entrusted to you. Turn a deaf ear to empty
and irreligious chatter, and the contra-
dictions of 'knowledge' so-called, [21] for by
laying claim to it some have strayed far
from the faith.

Grace be with you all!

THE SECOND LETTER OF PAUL TO

TIMOTHY

1 FROM Paul, apostle of Christ Jesus by the will of God, whose promise of life is fulfilled in Christ Jesus, ² to Timothy his dear son.

Grace, mercy, and peace to you from God the Father and Christ Jesus our Lord.

³ I give thanks to the God of my fore-fathers, whom I worship with a clear conscience, when I mention you in my prayers as I do constantly night and day; ⁴ when I remember the tears you shed, I long to see you again and so make my happiness complete. ⁵ I am reminded of the sincerity of your faith, a faith which was alive in Lois your grandmother and Eunice your mother before you, and which, I am confident, now lives in you.

The gospel of Jesus Christ

⁶ THAT is why I remind you to stir into flame the gift from God which is yours through the laying on of my hands. ⁷ For the spirit that God gave us is no cowardly spirit, but one to inspire power, love, and self-discipline. ⁸ So never be ashamed of your testimony to our Lord, nor of me imprisoned for his sake, but through the power that comes from God accept your share of suffering for the sake of the gospel. ⁹ It is he who has brought us salvation and called us to a dedicated life, not for any merit of ours but for his own purpose and of his own grace, granted to us in Christ Jesus from all eternity, ¹⁰ and now at length disclosed by the appear-ance on earth of our Saviour Jesus Christ. He has broken the power of death and brought life and immortality to light through the gospel.

¹¹ Of this gospel I have been appointed herald, apostle, and teacher. ¹² That is the reason for my present plight; but I am not ashamed of it, because I know whom I have trusted, and am confident of his power to keep safe what he has put into my charge until the great day. ¹³ Hold to the outline of sound teaching which you

heard from me, living by the faith and love which are ours in Christ Jesus. ¹⁴ Keep safe the treasure put into our charge, with the help of the Holy Spirit dwelling within us.

¹⁵ As you are aware, everyone in the province of Asia deserted me, including Phygelus and Hermogenes. ¹⁶ But may the Lord's mercy rest on the house of Onesiphorus! He has often relieved me in my troubles; he was not ashamed to visit a prisoner, ¹⁷ but when he came to Rome took pains to search me out until he found me. ¹⁸ The Lord grant that he find mercy from the Lord on the great day! You know as well as anyone the many services he rendered at Ephesus.

Charge to Timothy

2 TAKE strength, my son, from the grace of God which is ours in Christ Jesus. ² You heard my teaching in the presence of many witnesses; hand on that teaching to reliable men who in turn will be qualified to teach others.

³ Take your share of hardship, like a good soldier of Christ Jesus. ⁴ A soldier on active service must not let himself be involved in the affairs of everyday life if he is to give satisfaction to his commanding officer. ⁵ Again, no athlete wins a prize unless he abides by the rules. ⁶ The farmer who does the work has first claim on the crop. ⁷ Reflect on what I am saying, and the Lord will help you to full understand-ing.

⁸ Remember the theme of my gospel: Jesus Christ, risen from the dead, born of David's line. ⁹ For preaching this I am exposed to hardship, even to the point of being fettered like a criminal; but the word of God is not fettered. ¹⁰ All this I endure for the sake of God's chosen ones, in the hope that they too may attain the glorious and eternal salvation which is in Christ Jesus.

¹¹ Here is a saying you may trust:

1:12 what ... charge: or what I have put into his charge. the sound teaching.

1:13 Hold ... teaching: or Take as your model

If we died with him, we shall live
with him;
[12] if we endure, we shall reign with him;
if we disown him, he will disown us;
[13] if we are faithless, he remains
faithful,
for he cannot disown himself.

[14] Keep on reminding people of this, and
charge them solemnly before God to stop
disputing about mere words; it does no
good, and only ruins those who listen.
[15] Try hard to show yourself worthy of
God's approval, as a worker with no cause
for shame; keep strictly to the true gospel,
[16] avoiding empty and irreligious chatter;
those who indulge in it will stray farther
and farther into godless ways, [17] and the
infection of their teaching will spread like
gangrene. Such are Hymenaeus and Phile-
tus; [18] in saying that our resurrection has
already taken place they are wide of the
truth and undermine people's faith. [19] But
God has laid a foundation-stone, and it
stands firm, bearing this inscription: 'The
Lord knows his own' and 'Everyone who
takes the Lord's name upon his lips must
forsake wickedness.' [20] Now in any great
house there are not only utensils of gold
and silver, but also others of wood or
earthenware; the former are valued, the
latter held cheap. [21] Anyone who cleanses
himself from all this wickedness will be a
vessel valued and dedicated, a thing useful
to the master of the house, and fit for any
honourable purpose.

[22] Turn from the wayward passions of
youth, and pursue justice, integrity, love,
and peace together with all who worship
the Lord in singleness of mind; [23] have
nothing to do with foolish and wild speculations. You know they breed quarrels,
[24] and a servant of the Lord must not be
quarrelsome; he must be kindly towards
all. He should be a good teacher, tolerant,
[25] and gentle when he must discipline
those who oppose him. God may then
grant them a change of heart and lead
them to recognize the truth; [26] thus they
may come to their senses and escape from
the devil's snare in which they have been
trapped and held at his will.

3 Remember, the final age of this world
is to be a time of turmoil! [2] People will
love nothing but self and money; they

will be boastful, arrogant, and abusive;
disobedient to parents, devoid of gratitude, piety, [3] and natural affection; they
will be implacable in their hatreds, scandalmongers, uncontrolled and violent,
hostile to all goodness, [4] perfidious, fool-
hardy, swollen with self-importance.
They will love their pleasures more than
their God. [5] While preserving the outward
form of religion, they are a standing
denial of its power. Keep clear of them.
[6] They are the sort that insinuate themselves into private houses and there get
silly women into their clutches, women
burdened with sins and carried away by
all kinds of desires, [7] always wanting to be
taught but incapable of attaining to a
knowledge of the truth. [8] As Jannes and
Jambres opposed Moses, so these men
oppose the truth; their warped minds
disqualify them from grasping the faith.
[9] Their successes will be short-lived; like
those opponents of Moses, they will come
to be recognized by everyone for the fools
they are.

[10] But you, my son, have observed
closely my teaching and manner of life,
my resolution, my faithfulness, patience,
and spirit of love, and my fortitude
[11] under persecution and suffering—all I
went through at Antioch, at Iconium, at
Lystra, and the persecutions I endured;
and from all of them the Lord rescued me.
[12] Persecution will indeed come to everyone who wants to live a godly life as a
follower of Christ Jesus, [13] whereas evildoers and charlatans will progress from
bad to worse, deceiving and deceived.
[14] But for your part, stand by the truths
you have learned and are assured of.
Remember from whom you learned
them; [15] remember that from early childhood you have been familiar with the
sacred writings which have power to
make you wise and lead you to salvation
through faith in Christ Jesus. [16] All inspired scripture has its use for teaching
the truth and refuting error, or for refor-
mation of manners and discipline in right
living, [17] so that the man of God may be
capable and equipped for good work of
every kind.

4 Before God, and before Christ Jesus
who is to judge the living and the
dead, I charge you solemnly by his coming

2:26 **trapped ... will:** *or* trapped, and be made subject to God's will.

appearance and his reign, [2] proclaim the message, press it home in season and out of season, use argument, reproof, and appeal, with all the patience that teaching requires. [3] For the time will come when people will not stand sound teaching, but each will follow his own whim and gather a crowd of teachers to tickle his fancy. [4] They will stop their ears to the truth and turn to fables. [5] But you must keep your head whatever happens; put up with hardship, work to spread the gospel, discharge all the duties of your calling.

[6] As for me, my life is already being poured out on the altar, and the hour for my departure is upon me. [7] I have run the great race, I have finished the course, I have kept the faith. [8] And now there awaits me the garland of righteousness which the Lord, the righteous Judge, will award to me on the great day, and not to me alone, but to all who have set their hearts on his coming appearance.

Final instructions

[9] Do YOUR best to join me soon. [10] Demas, his heart set on this present world, has deserted me and gone to Thessalonica; Crescens is away in Galatia, Titus in Dalmatia; apart from Luke [11] I have no one with me. Get hold of Mark and bring him with you; he is a great help to me.

[12] Tychicus I have sent to Ephesus. [13] When you come, bring the cloak I left with Carpus at Troas, and the books, particularly my notebooks.

[14] Alexander the coppersmith did me a great deal of harm. The Lord will deal with him as he deserves, [15] but you had better be on your guard against him, for he is bitterly opposed to everything we teach. [16] At the first hearing of my case no one came into court to support me; they all left me in the lurch; I pray that it may not be counted against them. [17] But the Lord stood by me and lent me strength, so that I might be his instrument in making the full proclamation of the gospel for the whole pagan world to hear; and thus I was rescued from the lion's jaws. [18] The Lord will rescue me from every attempt to do me harm, and bring me safely into his heavenly kingdom. Glory to him for ever and ever! Amen.

[19] Greetings to Prisca and Aquila, and the household of Onesiphorus.

[20] Erastus stayed behind at Corinth, and Trophimus I left ill at Miletus. [21] Do try to get here before winter.

Greetings from Eubulus, Pudens, Linus, and Claudia, and from all the brotherhood here.

[22] The Lord be with your spirit. Grace be with you all!

4:10 **Galatia**: *or* Gaul.

THE LETTER OF PAUL TO
TITUS

1 FROM Paul, servant of God and apostle of Jesus Christ, marked as such by the faith of God's chosen people and the knowledge of the truth enshrined in our religion [2] with its hope of eternal life, which God, who does not lie, promised long ages ago, [3] and now in his own good time has openly declared in the proclamation entrusted to me by command of God our Saviour.

[4] To Titus, my true-born son in the faith which we share. Grace and peace to you from God the Father and Jesus Christ our Saviour.

Christian discipline

[5] MY intention in leaving you behind in Crete was that you should deal with any outstanding matters, and in particular should appoint elders in each town in accordance with the principles I have laid down: [6] Are they men of unimpeachable character? Is each the husband of one wife? Are their children believers, not

1:1 **apostle ... knowledge**: *or* apostle of Jesus Christ, to bring God's chosen people to faith and to knowledge.

open to any charge of dissipation or indiscipline? [7] For as God's steward a bishop must be a man of unimpeachable character. He must not be overbearing or short-tempered or given to drink; no brawler, no money-grubber, [8] but hospitable, right-minded, temperate, just, devout, and self-controlled. [9] He must keep firm hold of the true doctrine, so that he may be well able both to appeal to his hearers with sound teaching and to refute those who raise objections.

[10] There are many, especially among Jewish converts, who are undisciplined, who talk wildly and lead others astray. [11] Such men must be muzzled, because they are ruining whole families by teaching what they should not, and all for sordid gain. [12] It was a Cretan prophet, one of their own countrymen, who said, 'Cretans were ever liars, vicious brutes, lazy gluttons'—[13] and how truly he spoke! All the more reason why you should rebuke them sharply, so that they may be restored to a sound faith, [14] instead of paying heed to Jewish myths and to human commandments, the work of those who turn their backs on the truth.

[15] To the pure all things are pure; but nothing is pure to tainted disbelievers, tainted both in reason and in conscience. [16] They profess to know God but by their actions deny him; they are detestable and disobedient, disqualified for any good work.

2 For your part, what you say must be in keeping with sound doctrine. [2] The older men should be sober, dignified, and temperate, sound in faith, love, and fortitude. [3] The older women, similarly, should be reverent in their demeanour, not scandalmongers or slaves to excessive drinking; they must set a high standard, [4] and so teach the younger women to be loving wives and mothers, [5] to be temperate, chaste, busy at home, and kind, respecting the authority of their husbands. Then the gospel will not be brought into disrepute.

[6] Urge the younger men, similarly, to be temperate [7] in all things, and set them an example of good conduct yourself. In your teaching you must show integrity and seriousness, [8] and offer sound instruction

to which none can take exception. Any opponent will be at a loss when he finds nothing to say to our discredit.

[9] Slaves are to respect their masters' authority in everything and to give them satisfaction; they are not to answer back, [10] nor to pilfer, but are to show themselves absolutely trustworthy. In all this they will add lustre to the doctrine of God our Saviour.

[11] For the grace of God has dawned upon the world with healing for all mankind; [12] and by it we are disciplined to renounce godless ways and worldly desires, and to live a life of temperance, honesty, and godliness in the present age, [13] looking forward to the happy fulfilment of our hope when the splendour of our great God and Saviour Christ Jesus will appear. [14] He it is who sacrificed himself for us, to set us free from all wickedness and to make us his own people, pure and eager to do good.

[15] These are your themes; urge them and argue them with an authority which no one can disregard.

3 Remind everyone to be submissive to the government and the authorities, and to obey them; to be ready for any honourable work; [2] to slander no one, to avoid quarrels, and always to show forbearance and a gentle disposition to all.

[3] There was a time when we too were lost in folly and disobedience and were slaves to passions and pleasures of every kind. Our days were passed in malice and envy; hateful ourselves, we loathed one another. [4] But when the kindness and generosity of God our Saviour dawned upon the world, [5] then, not for any good deeds of our own, but because he was merciful, he saved us through the water of rebirth and the renewing power of the Holy Spirit, [6] which he lavished upon us through Jesus Christ our Saviour, [7] so that, justified by his grace, we might in hope become heirs to eternal life.' [8] That is a saying you may trust.

Final instructions

SUCH are the points I want you to insist on, so that those who have come to believe in God may be sure to devote themselves to good works. These precepts

2:13 **of our great … Saviour:** *or* of the great God and our Saviour.   3:5 **water … power of:** *or* water of rebirth and of renewal by.   3:8 **devote … good in themselves:** *or* engage in honest employment. This is good in itself.

are good in themselves and also useful to society. [9] But avoid foolish speculations, genealogies, quarrels, and controversies over the law; they are unprofitable and futile.

[10] If someone is contentious, he should be allowed a second warning; after that, have nothing more to do with him, [11] recognizing that anyone like that has a distorted mind and stands self-condemned in his sin.

[12] Once I have sent Artemas or Tychicus to you, join me at Nicopolis as soon as you can, for that is where I have decided to spend the winter. [13] Do your utmost to help Zenas the lawyer and Apollos on their travels, and see that they are not short of anything. [14] And our own people must be taught to devote themselves to good works to meet urgent needs; they must not be unproductive.

[15] All who are with me send you greetings. My greetings to our friends in the faith. Grace be with you all!

3:14 **devote ... needs:** *or* engage in honest employment to produce the necessities of life.

THE LETTER OF PAUL TO
PHILEMON

FROM Paul, a prisoner of Christ Jesus, and our colleague Timothy, to Philemon our dear friend and fellow-worker, [2] together with Apphia our sister, and Archippus our comrade-in-arms, and the church that meets at your house.

[3] Grace to you and peace from God our Father and the Lord Jesus Christ.

[4] I thank my God always when I mention you in my prayers, [5] for I hear of your love and faith towards the Lord Jesus and for all God's people. [6] My prayer is that the faith you hold in common with us may deepen your understanding of all the blessings which belong to us as we are brought closer to Christ. [7] Your love has brought me much joy and encouragement; through you God's people have been much refreshed.

A runaway slave

[8] ACCORDINGLY, although in Christ I might feel free to dictate where your duty lies, [9] yet, because of that same love, I would rather appeal to you. Ambassador as I am of Christ Jesus, and now his prisoner, [10] I, Paul, appeal to you about my child, whose father I have become in this prison. I mean Onesimus, [11] once so useless to you, but now useful indeed, both to you and to me. [12] In sending him back to you I am sending my heart. [13] I should have liked to keep him with me, to look after me on your behalf, here in prison for the gospel, [14] but I did not want to do anything without your consent, so that your kindness might be a matter not of compulsion, but of your own free will. [15] Perhaps this is why you lost him for a time to receive him back for good— [16] no longer as a slave, but as more than a slave: as a dear brother, very dear to me, and still dearer to you, both as a man and as a Christian.

[17] If, then, you think of me as your partner in the faith, welcome him as you would welcome me. [18] If he did you any wrong and owes you anything, put it down to my account. [19] Here is my signature: Paul. I will repay you—not to mention that you owe me your very self. [20] Yes, brother, I am asking this favour of you as a fellow-Christian; set my mind at rest.

[21] I write to you confident that you will meet my wishes; I know that you will in fact do more than I ask. [22] And one last thing: have a room ready for me, for I hope through the prayers of you all to be restored to you.

[23] Epaphras, a captive of Christ Jesus like myself, sends you greetings. [24] So do my fellow-workers Mark, Aristarchus, Demas, and Luke.

[25] The grace of the Lord Jesus Christ be with your spirit!

A LETTER TO
HEBREWS

Jesus, divine and human

1 WHEN in times past God spoke to our forefathers, he spoke in many and varied ways through the prophets. ² But in this the final age he has spoken to us in his Son, whom he has appointed heir of all things; and through him he created the universe. ³ He is the radiance of God's glory, the stamp of God's very being, and he sustains the universe by his word of power. When he had brought about purification from sins, he took his seat at the right hand of God's Majesty on high, ⁴ raised as far above the angels as the title he has inherited is superior to theirs.

⁵ To which of the angels did God ever say, 'You are my son; today I have become your father,' or again, 'I shall be his father, and he will be my son'? ⁶ Again, when he presents the firstborn to the world, he says, 'Let all God's angels pay him homage.' ⁷ Of the angels he says:

He makes his angels winds,
and his ministers flames of fire;

⁸ but of the Son:

Your throne, O God, is for ever and
ever,
and the sceptre of his kingdom is the
sceptre of justice.
⁹ You have loved right and hated
wrong;
therefore, O God, your God has set
you above your fellows
by anointing you with oil, the token
of joy.

¹⁰ And again:

By you, Lord, were earth's
foundations laid of old,
and the heavens are the work of
your hands.
¹¹ They will perish, but you remain;
like clothes they will all wear out.
¹² You will fold them up like a cloak,
they will be changed like any
garment.

But you are the same, and your
years will have no end.

¹³ To which of the angels has he ever said, 'Sit at my right hand until I make your enemies your footstool'? ¹⁴ Are they not all ministering spirits sent out in God's service, for the sake of those destined to receive salvation?

2 That is why we are bound to pay all the more heed to what we have been told, for fear of drifting from our course. ² For if God's word spoken through angels had such force that any violation of it, or any disobedience, met with its proper penalty, ³ what escape can there be for us if we ignore so great a deliverance? This deliverance was first announced through the Lord, and those who heard him confirmed it to us, ⁴ God himself adding his testimony by signs and wonders, by miracles of many kinds, and by gifts of the Holy Spirit distributed at his own will.

⁵ For it is not to angels that he has subjected the world to come, which is our theme. ⁶ There is somewhere this solemn assurance:

What is man, that you should
remember him,
a man, that you should care for
him?
⁷ You made him for a short while
subordinate to the angels;
with glory and honour you crowned
him;
⁸ you put everything in subjection
beneath his feet.

For in subjecting everything to him, God left nothing that is not made subject. But in fact we do not yet see everything in subjection to man. ⁹ What we do see is Jesus, who for a short while was made subordinate to the angels, crowned now with glory and honour because he suffered death, so that, by God's gracious will, he should experience death for all mankind.

1:6 **Again ... presents:** *or* And when he again presents. 1:9 **therefore ... your God:** *or* therefore God who is your God. 2:9 **so that ... will:** *some witnesses read* so that, apart from God.

[10] In bringing many sons to glory it was fitting that God, for whom and through whom all things exist, should make the pioneer of their salvation perfect through sufferings; [11] for he who consecrates and those who are consecrated are all of one stock. That is why he does not shrink from calling men his brothers, [12] when he says, 'I will make your fame known to my brothers; in the midst of the assembly I will praise you'; [13] and again, 'I will keep my trust fixed on him'; and again, 'Here am I, and the children whom God has given me.' [14] Since the children share in flesh and blood, he too shared in them, so that by dying he might break the power of him who had death at his command, that is, the devil, [15] and might liberate those who all their life had been in servitude through fear of death. [16] Clearly they are not angels whom he helps, but the descendants of Abraham. [17] Therefore he had to be made like his brothers in every way, so that he might be merciful and faithful as their high priest before God, to make expiation for the sins of the people. [18] Because he himself has passed through the test of suffering, he is able to help those who are in the midst of their test.

Jesus, the faithful high priest

3 THEREFORE, brothers in the family of God, partners in a heavenly calling, think of Jesus, the apostle and high priest of the faith we profess: [2] he was faithful to God who appointed him, as Moses also was faithful in God's household; [3] but Jesus has been counted worthy of greater honour than Moses, as the founder of a house enjoys more honour than his household. [4] Every house has its founder; and the founder of all is God. [5] Moses indeed was faithful as a servant in God's whole household; his task was to bear witness to the words that God would speak; [6] but Christ is faithful as a son, set over the household. And we are that household, if only we are fearless and keep our hope high.

[7] 'TODAY', therefore, as the Holy Spirit says—

Today if you hear his voice,
[8] do not grow stubborn as in the rebellion,
at the time of testing in the desert,

[9] where your forefathers tried me and tested me,
though for forty years they saw the things I did.
[10] Therefore I was incensed with that generation
and said, Their hearts are for ever astray;
they would not discern my ways;
[11] so I vowed in my anger,
they shall never enter my rest.

[12] See to it, my friends, that no one among you has the wicked and faithless heart of a deserter from the living God. [13] Rather, day by day, as long as that word 'today' sounds in your ears, encourage one another, so that no one of you is made stubborn by the wiles of sin. [14] For we have become partners with Christ, if only we keep our initial confidence firm to the end. [15] When scripture says, 'Today if you hear his voice, do not grow stubborn as in the rebellion,' [16] who was it that heard and yet rebelled? All those, surely, whom Moses had led out of Egypt. [17] And with whom was God indignant for forty years? With those, surely, who had sinned, whose bodies lay where they fell in the desert. [18] And to whom did he vow that they should not enter his rest, if not to those who had refused to believe? [19] We see, then, it was unbelief that prevented their entering.

4 What we must fear, therefore, is that, while the promise of entering his rest remains open, any one of you should be found to have missed his opportunity. [2] For indeed we have had the good news preached to us, just as they had. But the message they heard did them no good, for it was not combined with faith in those who heard it. [3] Because we have faith, it is we who enter that rest of which he has said: 'As I vowed in my anger, they shall never enter my rest.' Yet God's work had been finished ever since the world was created. [4] Scripture somewhere says of the seventh day: 'God rested from all his work on the seventh day'— [5] and in the passage above we read: 'They shall never enter my rest.' [6] This implies that some are to enter it, and since those who first heard the good news failed to enter through unbelief, [7] once more God sets a day. 'Today', he says, speaking so many years later in the words already quoted from the

Psalms: 'Today if you hear his voice, do not grow stubborn.' [8] If Joshua had given them rest, God would not have spoken afterwards of another day. [9] Therefore, a sabbath rest still awaits the people of God; [10] anyone who enters God's rest, rests from his own work, as God did from his. [11] Let us, then, make every effort to enter that rest, so that no one may fall by following the old example of unbelief.

[12] The word of God is alive and active. It cuts more keenly than any two-edged sword, piercing so deeply that it divides soul and spirit, joints and marrow; it discriminates among the purposes and thoughts of the heart. [13] Nothing in creation can hide from him; everything lies bare and exposed to the eyes of him to whom we must render account.

[14] Since therefore we have a great high priest who has passed through the heavens, Jesus the Son of God, let us hold fast to the faith we profess. [15] Ours is not a high priest unable to sympathize with our weaknesses, but one who has been tested in every way as we are, only without sinning. [16] Let us therefore boldly approach the throne of grace, in order that we may receive mercy and find grace to give us timely help.

5 FOR every high priest is taken from among men and appointed their representative before God, to offer gifts and sacrifices for sins. [2] He is able to bear patiently with the ignorant and erring, since he too is beset by weakness; [3] and because of this he is bound to make sin-offerings for himself as well as for the people. [4] Moreover nobody assumes the office on his own authority: he is called by God, just as Aaron was. [5] So it is with Christ: he did not confer on himself the glory of becoming high priest; it was granted by God, who said to him, 'You are my son; today I have become your father'; [6] as also in another place he says, 'You are a priest for ever, in the order of Melchizedek.' [7] In the course of his earthly life he offered up prayers and petitions, with loud cries and tears, to God who was able to deliver him from death. Because of his devotion his prayer was heard: [8] son though he was, he learned obedience through his sufferings, [9] and, once per-

fected, he became the source of eternal salvation for all who obey him, [10] and by God he was designated high priest in the order of Melchizedek.

Jesus and Melchizedek

[11] ABOUT Melchizedek we have much to say, much that is difficult to explain to you, now that you have proved so slow to learn. [12] By this time you ought to be teachers, but instead you need someone to teach you the ABC of God's oracles over again. It comes to this: you need milk instead of solid food. [13] Anyone who lives on milk is still an infant, with no experience of what is right. [14] Solid food is for adults, whose perceptions have been trained by long use to discriminate between good and evil.

6 [1-2] Let us stop discussing the rudiments of Christianity. We ought not to be laying the foundation all over again: repentance from the deadness of our former ways and faith in God, by means of instruction about cleansing rites and the laying on of hands, the resurrection of the dead and eternal judgement. Instead, let us advance towards maturity; [3] and so we shall, if God permits. [4] For when people have once been enlightened, when they have tasted the heavenly gift and have shared in the Holy Spirit, [5] when they have experienced the goodness of God's word and the spiritual power of the age to come, [6] and then after all this have fallen away, it is impossible to bring them afresh to repentance; for they are crucifying to their own hurt the Son of God and holding him up to mockery. [7] When the soil drinks in the rain that falls often upon it, and yields a crop for the use of those who cultivate it, it receives its blessing from God; [8] but if it bears thorns and thistles, it is worthless and a curse hangs over it; it ends by being burnt.

[9] Yet although we speak as we do, we are convinced that you, dear friends, are in a better state, which makes for your salvation. [10] For God is not so unjust as to forget what you have done for love of his name in rendering service to his people, as you still do. [11] But we should dearly like each one of you to show the same keenness to the end, until your hope is fully realized. [12] We want you not to be lax, but

6:6 **crucifying:** *or* crucifying again.

198

to imitate those who, through faith and patience, receive the promised inheritance. ¹³ When God made his promise to Abraham, because he had no one greater to swear by he swore by himself: ¹⁴ 'I vow that I will bless you abundantly and multiply your descendants.' ¹⁵ Thus it was that Abraham, after patient waiting, obtained the promise. ¹⁶ People swear by what is greater than themselves, and making a statement on oath sets a limit to what can be called in question; ¹⁷ and so, since God desired to show even more clearly to the heirs of his promise how immutable was his purpose, he guaranteed it by an oath. ¹⁸ Here, then, are two irrevocable acts in which God could not possibly play us false. They give powerful encouragement to us, who have laid claim to his protection by grasping the hope set before us. ¹⁹ We have that hope as an anchor for our lives, safe and secure. It enters the sanctuary behind the curtain, ²⁰ where Jesus has entered on our behalf as forerunner, having become high priest for ever in the order of Melchizedek.

7 THIS Melchizedek, king of Salem, priest of God Most High, met Abraham returning from the defeat of the kings and blessed him; ² and Abraham gave him a tithe of everything as his share. His name, in the first place, means 'king of righteousness'; next he is king of Salem, that is, 'king of peace'. ³ He has no father, no mother, no ancestors; his life has no beginning and no end. Bearing the likeness of the Son of God, he remains a priest for all time.

⁴ Consider now how great he must be for the patriarch Abraham to give him his tithe from the finest of the spoil. ⁵ The descendants of Levi who succeed to the priestly office are required by the law to tithe the people, that is, their fellow-countrymen, although they too are descendants of Abraham. ⁶ But Melchizedek, though he does not share their ancestry, tithed Abraham himself and gave his blessing to the man who had been given the promises; ⁷ and, beyond all dispute, it is always the lesser who is blessed by the greater. ⁸ Moreover, in the one instance tithes are received by men who must die; but in the other, by one whom scripture affirms to be alive. ⁹ It might even be said that Levi, the receiver of tithes, was himself tithed through Abraham; ¹⁰ for he was still in his ancestor's loins when Melchizedek met him.

¹¹ Now if perfection had been attainable through the levitical priesthood (on the basis of which the people were given the law), there would have been no need for another kind of priest to arise, described as being in the order of Melchizedek, instead of in the order of Aaron. ¹² But a change of priesthood must mean a change of law; ¹³ for he who is spoken of here belongs to a different tribe, no member of which has ever served at the altar. ¹⁴ It is beyond all doubt that our Lord is sprung from Judah, a tribe to which Moses made no reference in speaking of priests.

¹⁵ What makes this still clearer is that a new priest has arisen, one like Melchizedek; ¹⁶ he owes his priesthood not to a system of rules relating to descent but to the power of a life that cannot be destroyed. ¹⁷ For here is the testimony: 'You are a priest for ever, in the order of Melchizedek.' ¹⁸ The earlier rules are repealed as ineffective and useless, ¹⁹ since the law brought nothing to perfection; and a better hope is introduced, through which we draw near to God.

²⁰⁻²² Notice also that no oath was sworn when the other men were made priests; but for this priest an oath was sworn in the words addressed to him: 'The Lord has sworn and will not go back on his word, "You are a priest for ever."' In the same way, God's oath shows how superior is the covenant which Jesus guarantees. ²³ There have been many levitical priests, because death prevents them from continuing in office; ²⁴ but Jesus holds a perpetual priesthood, because he remains for ever. ²⁵ That is why he is able to save completely those who approach God through him, since he is always alive to plead on their behalf.

²⁶ Such a high priest is indeed suited to our need: he is holy, innocent, undefiled, set apart from sinners, and raised high above the heavens. ²⁷ He has no need to

6:18 They give ... grasping: *or* They give to us, who have laid claim to his protection, a powerful encouragement to grasp. 7:25 completely: *or* for all time.

offer sacrifices daily, as the high priests do, first for their own sins and then for those of the people; he did this once for all when he offered up himself. [28] The high priests appointed by the law are men in all their weakness; but the priest appointed by the words of the oath which supersedes the law is the Son, who has been made perfect for ever.

8 MY main point is: this is the kind of high priest we have, and he has taken his seat at the right hand of the throne of Majesty in heaven, [2] a minister in the real sanctuary, the tent set up by the Lord, not by man. [3] Every high priest is appointed to offer gifts and sacrifices; hence, of necessity, this one too had something to offer. [4] If he were on earth, he would not be a priest at all, since there are already priests to offer the gifts prescribed by the law, [5] although the sanctuary in which they minister is only a shadowy symbol of the heavenly one. This is why Moses, when he was about to put up the tent, was instructed by God: 'See to it that you make everything according to the pattern shown you on the mountain.' [6] But in fact the ministry which Jesus has been given is superior to theirs, for he is the mediator of a better covenant, established on better promises.

[7] Had that first covenant been faultless, there would have been no occasion to look for a second to replace it. [8] But God finds fault with his people when he says, 'The time is coming, says the Lord, when I shall conclude a new covenant with the house of Israel and the house of Judah. [9] It will not be like the covenant I made with their forefathers when I took them by the hand to lead them out of Egypt; because they did not abide by the terms of that covenant, and so I abandoned them, says the Lord. [10] For this is the covenant I shall make with Israel after those days, says the Lord: I shall set my laws in their understanding and write them on their hearts; I shall be their God, and they will be my people. [11] They will not teach one another, each saying to his fellow-citizen and his brother, "Know the Lord!" For all of them will know me, high and low alike; [12] I shall pardon their wicked deeds, and their sins I shall remember no more.' [13] By speaking of a new covenant, he has

pronounced the first one obsolete; and anything that is becoming obsolete and growing old will shortly disappear.

9 THE first covenant had its ordinances governing divine service and its sanctuary, but it was an earthly sanctuary. [2] An outer tent, called the Holy Place, was set up to contain the lampstand, the table, and the Bread of the Presence. [3] Beyond the second curtain was the tent called the Most Holy Place. [4] Here were a gold incense-altar and the Ark of the Covenant plated all over with gold, in which were kept a gold jar containing the manna, and Aaron's staff which once budded, and the tablets of the covenant; [5] and above the Ark were the cherubim of God's glory, overshadowing the place of expiation. These we need not discuss in detail now.

[6] Under this arrangement, the priests are continually entering the first tent in the performance of their duties; [7] but the second tent is entered by the high priest alone, and that only once a year. He takes with him the blood which he offers for himself and for the people's inadvertent sins. [8] By this the Holy Spirit indicates that so long as the outer tent still stands, the way into the sanctuary has not been opened up. [9] All this is symbolic, pointing to the present time. It means that the prescribed offerings and sacrifices cannot give the worshipper a clear conscience and so bring him to perfection; [10] they are concerned only with food and drink and various rites of cleansing—external ordinances in force until the coming of the new order.

[11] But now Christ has come, high priest of good things already in being. The tent of his priesthood is a greater and more perfect one, not made by human hands, that is, not belonging to this created world; [12] the blood of his sacrifice is his own blood, not the blood of goats and calves; and thus he has entered the sanctuary once for all and secured an eternal liberation. [13] If sprinkling the blood of goats and bulls and the ashes of a heifer consecrates those who have been defiled and restores their ritual purity, [14] how much greater is the power of the blood of Christ; through the eternal Spirit he offered himself without blemish to God. His blood will cleanse our conscience from the deadness of our former ways to serve the living God.

9:11 things ... being: *some witnesses read* things to be.

15 That is why the new covenant or testament of which he is mediator took effect once a death had occurred, to bring liberation from sins committed under the former covenant; its purpose is to enable those whom God has called to receive the eternal inheritance he has promised them. 16 Now where there is a testament it is necessary for the death of the testator to be established; 17 for a testament takes effect only when a death has occurred: it has no force while the testator is still alive. 18 Even the former covenant itself was not inaugurated without blood, 19 for when Moses had told the assembled people all the commandments as set forth in the law, he took the blood of calves, with water, scarlet wool, and marjoram, and sprinkled the law book itself and all the people, 20 saying, 'This is the blood of the covenant which God commanded you to keep.' 21 In the same way he sprinkled the blood over the tent and all the vessels of divine service. 22 Indeed, under the law, it might almost be said that everything is cleansed by blood, and without the shedding of blood there is no forgiveness.

Jesus, the final sacrifice

23 If, then, the symbols of heavenly things required those sacrifices to cleanse them, the heavenly things themselves required still better sacrifices; 24 for Christ has not entered a sanctuary made by human hands which is only a pointer to the reality; he has entered heaven itself, to appear now before God on our behalf. 25 It was not his purpose to offer himself again and again, as the high priest enters the sanctuary year after year with blood not his own; 26 for then he would have had to suffer repeatedly since the world was created. But as it is, he has appeared once for all at the climax of history to abolish sin by the sacrifice of himself. 27 Just as it is our mortal lot to die once, with judgement to follow, 28 so Christ was offered once to bear the sins of mankind, and will appear a second time, not to deal with sin, but to bring salvation to those who eagerly await him.

10 THE law contains but a shadow of the good things to come, not the true picture. With the same sacrifices offered year after year for all time, it can never bring the worshippers to perfection. 2 If it could, these sacrifices would surely have ceased to be offered, because the worshippers, cleansed once for all, would no longer have any sense of sin. 3 Instead, by these sacrifices sins are brought to mind year after year, 4 because they can never be removed by the blood of bulls and goats.

5 That is why, at Christ's coming into the world, he says:

Sacrifice and offering you did not desire,
but you have prepared a body for me.
6 Whole-offerings and sin-offerings you did not delight in.
7 Then I said, 'Here I am: as it is written of me in the scroll,
I have come, O God, to do your will.'

8 First he says, 'Sacrifices and offerings, whole-offerings and sin-offerings, you did not desire or delight in,' although the law prescribes them. 9 Then he adds, 'Here I am: I have come to do your will.' He thus abolishes the former to establish the latter. 10 And it is by the will of God that we have been consecrated, through the offering of the body of Jesus Christ once for all.

11 Daily every priest stands performing his service and time after time offering the same sacrifices, which can never remove sins. 12 Christ, having offered for all time a single sacrifice for sins, took his seat at God's right hand, 13 where he now waits until his enemies are made his footstool. 14 So by one offering he has perfected for ever those who are consecrated by it. 15 To this the Holy Spirit also adds his witness. First he says, 16 'This is the covenant which I will make with them after those days, says the Lord: I will set my laws in their hearts and write them on their understanding'; 17 then he adds, 'and their sins and wicked deeds I will remember no more.' 18 And where these have been forgiven, there are no further offerings for sin.

19 So NOW, my friends, the blood of Jesus makes us free to enter the sanctuary with

9:28 to bear the sins: *or* to remove the sins.   10:1 sacrifices ... perfection: *or* sacrifices offered year after year it can never bring the worshippers to perfection for all time.   10:12 for all time ... seat: *or* a single sacrifice for sins, took his seat for all time.

confidence [20] by the new and living way which he has opened for us through the curtain, the way of his flesh. [21] We have a great priest set over the household of God; [22] so let us make our approach in sincerity of heart and the full assurance of faith, inwardly cleansed from a guilty conscience, and outwardly washed with pure water. [23] Let us be firm and unswerving in the confession of our hope, for the giver of the promise is to be trusted. [24] We ought to see how each of us may best arouse others to love and active goodness. [25] We should not stay away from our meetings, as some do, but rather encourage one another, all the more because we see the day of the Lord drawing near.

[26] For if we deliberately persist in sin after receiving the knowledge of the truth, there can be no further sacrifice for sins; there remains [27] only a terrifying expectation of judgement, of a fierce fire which will consume God's enemies. [28] Anyone who flouts the law of Moses is put to death without mercy on the evidence of two or three witnesses. [29] Think how much more severe a penalty will be deserved by anyone who has trampled underfoot the Son of God, profaned the blood of the covenant by which he was consecrated, and insulted God's gracious Spirit! [30] For we know who it is that said, 'Justice is mine: I will repay'; and again, 'The Lord will judge his people.' [31] It is a terrifying thing to fall into the hands of the living God.

[32] Remember those early days when, newly enlightened, you met the test of great suffering and held firm. [33] Some of you were publicly exposed to abuse and tormented, while others stood loyally by those who were so treated. [34] For indeed you shared the sufferings of those who were in prison, and you cheerfully accepted the seizure of your possessions, knowing that you had a better, more lasting possession. [35] Do not, therefore, throw away your confidence, for it carries a great reward. [36] You need endurance in order to do God's will and win what he has promised. [37] For, in the words of scripture,

very soon he who is to come will
come;

he will not delay;
[38] and by faith my righteous servant
shall find life;
but if anyone shrinks back,
I take no pleasure in him.

[39] But we are not among those who shrink back and are lost; we have the faith to preserve our life.

Faith in times past

11 FAITH gives substance to our hopes and convinces us of realities we do not see.

[2] It was for their faith that the people of old won God's approval.

[3] By faith we understand that the universe was formed by God's command, so that the visible came forth from the invisible.

[4] By faith Abel offered a greater sacrifice than Cain's; because of his faith God approved his offerings and attested his goodness; and through his faith, though he is dead, he continues to speak.

[5] By faith Enoch was taken up to another life without passing through death; he was not to be found, because God had taken him, and it is the testimony of scripture that before he was taken he had pleased God. [6] But without faith it is impossible to please him, for whoever comes to God must believe that he exists and rewards those who seek him.

[7] By faith Noah took good heed of the divine warning about the unseen future, and built an ark to save his household. Through his faith he put the whole world in the wrong, and made good his own claim to the righteousness which comes of faith.

[8] By faith Abraham obeyed the call to leave his home for a land which he was to receive as a possession; he went away without knowing where he was to go. [9] By faith he settled as an alien in the land which had been promised him, living in tents with Isaac and Jacob, who were heirs with him to the same promise. [10] For he was looking forward to a city with firm foundations, whose architect and builder is God.

[11] By faith even Sarah herself was enabled to conceive, though she was past the age, because she judged that God who

10:20 **curtain ... flesh:** *or* curtain of his flesh.
was: *some witnesses add* barren and.   11:1 **substance:** *or* assurance.   11:11 **though she**

had promised would keep faith. ¹²Therefore from one man, a man as good as dead, there sprang descendants as numerous as the stars in the heavens or the countless grains of sand on the seashore.

¹³All these died in faith. Although they had not received the things promised, yet they had seen them far ahead and welcomed them, and acknowledged themselves to be strangers and aliens without fixed abode on earth. ¹⁴Those who speak in that way show plainly that they are looking for a country of their own. ¹⁵If their thoughts had been with the country they had left, they could have found opportunity to return. ¹⁶Instead, we find them longing for a better country, a heavenly one. That is why God is not ashamed to be called their God; for he has a city ready for them.

¹⁷By faith Abraham, when put to the test, offered up Isaac: he had received the promises, and yet he was ready to offer his only son, ¹⁸of whom he had been told, 'Through the line of Isaac your descendants shall be traced.' ¹⁹For he reckoned that God had power even to raise from the dead—and it was from the dead, in a sense, that he received him back.

²⁰By faith Isaac blessed Jacob and Esau and spoke of things to come. ²¹By faith Jacob, as he was dying, blessed each of Joseph's sons, and bowed in worship over the top of his staff.

²²By faith Joseph, at the end of his life, spoke of the departure of Israel from Egypt, and gave instructions about his burial.

²³By faith, when Moses was born, his parents hid him for three months, because they saw what a fine child he was; they were not intimidated by the king's edict. ²⁴By faith Moses, when he grew up, refused to be called a son of Pharaoh's daughter, ²⁵preferring to share hardship with God's people rather than enjoy the transient pleasures of sin. ²⁶He considered the stigma that rests on God's Anointed greater wealth than the treasures of Egypt, for his eyes were fixed on the coming reward. ²⁷By faith he left Egypt, with no fear of the king's anger; for he was resolute, as one who saw the invisible God.

²⁸By faith he celebrated the Passover and the sprinkling of blood, so that the destroying angel might not touch the firstborn of Israel. ²⁹By faith they crossed the Red Sea as though it were dry land, whereas the Egyptians, when they attempted the crossing, were engulfed.

³⁰By faith the walls of Jericho were made to fall after they had been encircled on seven successive days. ³¹By faith the prostitute Rahab escaped the fate of the unbelievers, because she had given the spies a kindly welcome.

³²Need I say more ? Time is too short for me to tell the stories of Gideon, Barak, Samson, and Jephthah, of David and Samuel and the prophets. ³³Through faith they overthrew kingdoms, established justice, saw God's promises fulfilled. They shut the mouths of lions, ³⁴quenched the fury of fire, escaped death by the sword. Their weakness was turned to strength, they grew powerful in war, they put foreign armies to rout. ³⁵Women received back their dead raised to life. Others were tortured to death, refusing release, to win resurrection to a better life. ³⁶Others, again, had to face jeers and flogging, even fetters and prison bars. ³⁷They were stoned to death, they were sawn in two, they were put to the sword, they went about clothed in skins of sheep or goats, deprived, oppressed, ill-treated. ³⁸The world was not worthy of them. They were refugees in deserts and on the mountains, hiding in caves and holes in the ground. ³⁹All these won God's approval because of their faith ; and yet they did not receive what was promised, ⁴⁰because, with us in mind, God had made a better plan, that only with us should they reach perfection.

Faith today

12 WITH this great cloud of witnesses around us, therefore, we too must throw off every encumbrance and the sin that all too readily restricts us, and run with resolution the race which lies ahead of us, ²our eyes fixed on Jesus, the pioneer and perfecter of faith. For the sake of the joy that lay ahead of him, he endured the cross, ignoring its disgrace, and has taken his seat at the right hand of the throne of God.

³Think of him who submitted to such

11:37 **stoned to death**: *some witnesses add* they were tested.   12:1 **restricts**: *some witnesses read* distracts.
12:2 **For the sake ... him**: *or* In place of the joy that was open to him.

opposition from sinners: that will help you not to lose heart and grow faint. ⁴ In the struggle against sin, you have not yet resisted to the point of shedding your blood. ⁵ You have forgotten the exhortation which addresses you as sons:

My son, do not think lightly of the
  Lord's discipline,
or be discouraged when he corrects
  you;
⁶ for whom the Lord loves he
  disciplines;
he chastises every son whom he
  acknowledges.

⁷ You must endure it as discipline: God is treating you as sons. Can anyone be a son and not be disciplined by his father? ⁸ If you escape the discipline in which all sons share, you must be illegitimate and not true sons. ⁹ Again, we paid due respect to our human fathers who disciplined us; should we not submit even more readily to our spiritual Father, and so attain life? ¹⁰ They disciplined us for a short time as they thought best; but he does so for our true welfare, so that we may share his holiness. ¹¹ Discipline, to be sure, is never pleasant; at the time it seems painful, but afterwards those who have been trained by it reap the harvest of a peaceful and upright life. ¹² So brace your drooping arms and shaking knees, ¹³ and keep to a straight path; then the weakened limb will not be put out of joint, but will regain its former powers.

The fruit of righteousness

¹⁴ AIM at peace with everyone and a holy life, for without that no one will see the Lord. ¹⁵ Take heed that there is no one among you who forfeits the grace of God, no bitter, noxious weed growing up to contaminate the rest, ¹⁶ no immoral person, no one worldly-minded like Esau. He sold his birthright for a single meal, ¹⁷ and you know that afterwards, although he wanted to claim the blessing, he was rejected; though he begged for it to the point of tears, he found no way open for a change of mind.

¹⁸ IT is not to the tangible, blazing fire of Sinai that you have come, with its darkness, gloom, and whirlwind, ¹⁹ its trumpet-blast and oracular voice, which the people heard and begged to hear no

more; ²⁰ for they could not bear the command, 'If even an animal touches the mountain, it must be stoned to death.' ²¹ So appalling was the sight that Moses said, 'I shudder with fear.'

²² No, you have come to Mount Zion, the city of the living God, the heavenly Jerusalem, to myriads of angels, ²³ to the full concourse and assembly of the firstborn who are enrolled in heaven, and to God the judge of all, and to the spirits of good men made perfect, ²⁴ and to Jesus. the mediator of a new covenant, whose sprinkled blood has better things to say than the blood of Abel. ²⁵ See that you do not refuse to hear the voice that speaks. Those who refused to hear the oracle speaking on earth found no escape; still less shall we escape if we reject him who speaks from heaven. ²⁶ Then indeed his voice shook the earth, but now he has promised, 'Once again I will shake not only the earth, but the heavens also.' ²⁷ The words 'once again' point to the removal of all created things, of all that is shaken, so that what cannot be shaken may remain. ²⁸ The kingdom we are given is unshakeable; let us therefore give thanks to God for it, and so worship God as he would be worshipped, with reverence and awe; ²⁹ for our God is a devouring fire.

13 NEVER cease to love your fellow-Christians. ² Do not neglect to show hospitality; by doing this, some have entertained angels unawares. ³ Remember those in prison, as if you were there with them, and those who are being maltreated, for you are vulnerable too.

⁴ Marriage must be honoured by all, and the marriage bond be kept inviolate; for God's judgement will fall on fornicators and adulterers.

⁵ Do not live for money; be content with what you have, for God has said, 'I will never leave you or desert you.' ⁶ So we can take courage and say, 'The Lord is my helper, I will not fear; what can man do to me?'

⁷ Remember your leaders, who spoke God's message to you. Keep before you the outcome of their life and follow the example of their faith.

⁸ Jesus Christ is the same yesterday, today, and for ever. ⁹ So do not be swept off your course by all sorts of outlandish

teachings; it is good that we should gain inner strength from the grace of God, and not from rules about food, which have never benefited those who observed them.

¹⁰ Our altar is one from which the priests of the sacred tent have no right to eat. ¹¹ As you know, the animals whose blood is brought by the high priest into the sanctuary as a sin-offering have their bodies burnt outside the camp. ¹² Therefore, to consecrate the people by his own blood, Jesus also suffered outside the gate. ¹³ Let us then go to him outside the camp, bearing the stigma that he bore. ¹⁴ For here we have no lasting city, but we are seekers after the city which is to come. ¹⁵ Through Jesus let us continually offer up to God a sacrifice of praise, that is, the tribute of lips which acknowledge his name.

¹⁶ Never neglect to show kindness and to share what you have with others; for such are the sacrifices which God approves.

¹⁷ Obey your leaders and submit to their authority; for they are tireless in their care for you, as those who must render an account. See that their work brings them happiness, not pain and grief, for that would be no advantage to you.

¹⁸ Pray for us. We are sure that our conscience is clear, and our desire is always to do what is right. ¹⁹ I specially ask for your prayers, so that I may be restored to you the sooner.

²⁰ May the God of peace, who brought back from the dead our Lord Jesus, the great Shepherd of the sheep, through the blood of an eternal covenant, ²¹ make you perfect in all goodness so that you may do his will; and may he create in us what is pleasing to him, through Jesus Christ, to whom be glory for ever and ever! Amen.

²² I beg you, friends, bear with my appeal; for this is after all a short letter. ²³ I have news for you: our friend Timothy has been released; and if he comes in time he will be with me when I see you.

²⁴ Greet all your leaders and all God's people. Greetings to you from our Italian friends.

²⁵ God's grace be with you all!

A LETTER OF
JAMES

1 FROM James, a servant of God and the Lord Jesus Christ. Greetings to the twelve tribes dispersed throughout the world.

Faith under trial

[2] MY friends, whenever you have to face all sorts of trials, count yourselves supremely happy [3] in the knowledge that such testing of your faith makes for strength to endure. [4] Let endurance perfect its work in you that you may become perfected, sound throughout, lacking in nothing. [5] If any of you lacks wisdom, he should ask God and it will be given him, for God is a generous giver who neither grudges nor reproaches anyone. [6] But he who asks must ask in faith, with never a doubt in his mind; for the doubter is like a wave of the sea tossed hither and thither by the wind. [7] A man like that should not think he will receive anything from the Lord. [8] He is always in two minds and unstable in all he does.

[9] The church member in humble circumstances does well to take pride in being exalted; [10] the wealthy member must find his pride in being brought low, for the rich man will disappear like a wild flower; [11] once the sun is up with its scorching heat, it parches the plant, its flower withers, and what was lovely to look at is lost for ever. So shall the rich man fade away as he goes about his business.

[12] Happy is the man who stands up to trial! Having passed that test he will receive in reward the life which God has promised to those who love him. [13] No one when tempted should say, 'I am being tempted by God'; for God cannot be tempted by evil and does not himself tempt anyone. [14] Temptation comes when anyone is lured and dragged away by his own desires; [15] then desire conceives and gives birth to sin, and sin when it is full-grown breeds death.

[16] Make no mistake, my dear friends. [17] Every good and generous action and every perfect gift come from above, from the Father who created the lights of heaven. With him there is no variation, no play of passing shadows. [18] Of his own choice, he brought us to birth by the word of truth to be a kind of firstfruits of his creation.

[19] Of that you may be certain, my dear friends. But everyone should be quick to listen, slow to speak, and slow to be angry. [20] For human anger does not promote God's justice. [21] Then discard everything sordid, and every wicked excess, and meekly accept the message planted in your hearts, with its power to save you.

[22] Only be sure you act on the message, and do not merely listen and so deceive yourselves. [23] Anyone who listens to the message but does not act on it is like somebody looking in a mirror at the face nature gave him; [24] he glances at himself and goes his way, and promptly forgets what he looked like. [25] But he who looks into the perfect law, the law that makes us free, and does not turn away, remembers what he hears; he acts on it, and by so acting he will find happiness.

[26] If anyone thinks he is religious but does not bridle his tongue, he is deceiving himself; that man's religion is futile. [27] A pure and faultless religion in the sight of God the Father is this: to look after orphans and widows in trouble and to keep oneself untarnished by the world.

Love your neighbour as yourself

2 MY friends, you believe in our Lord Jesus Christ who reigns in glory and you must always be impartial. [2] For instance, two visitors may enter your meeting, one a well-dressed man with gold rings, and the other a poor man in grimy clothes. [3] Suppose you pay special attention to the well-dressed man and say to him, 'Please take this seat,' while to the

---

1:17 no variation ... shadows: *some witnesses read* no variation, or shadow caused by change.   1:21 Then discard ... and meekly accept: *or* Then meekly discard ... and accept.   2:3 Please ... seat: *or* Do take this comfortable seat.

poor man you say, 'You stand over there, or sit here on the floor by my footstool,' [4] do you not see that you are discriminating among your members and judging by wrong standards? [5] Listen, my dear friends: has not God chosen those who are poor in the eyes of the world to be rich in faith and to possess the kingdom he has promised to those who love him? [6] And yet you have humiliated the poor man. Moreover, are not the rich your oppressors? Is it not they who drag you into court [7] and pour contempt on the honoured name by which God has claimed you?

[8] If, however, you are observing the sovereign law laid down in scripture, 'Love your neighbour as yourself,' that is excellent. [9] But if you show partiality, you are committing a sin and you stand convicted by the law as offenders. [10] For if a man breaks just one commandment and keeps all the others, he is guilty of breaking all of them. [11] For he who said, 'You shall not commit adultery,' said also, 'You shall not commit murder.' If you commit murder you are a breaker of the law, even if you do not commit adultery as well. [12] Always speak and act as men who are to be judged under a law which makes them free. [13] In that judgement there will be no mercy for the man who has shown none. Mercy triumphs over judgement.

[14] WHAT good is it, my friends, for someone to say he has faith when his actions do nothing to show it? Can that faith save him? [15] Suppose a fellow-Christian, whether man or woman, is in rags with not enough food for the day, [16] and one of you says, 'Goodbye, keep warm, and have a good meal,' but does nothing to supply their bodily needs, what good is that? [17] So with faith; if it does not lead to action, it is by itself a lifeless thing.

[18] But someone may say: 'One chooses faith, another action.' To which I reply: 'Show me this faith you speak of with no actions to prove it, while I by my actions will prove to you my faith.' [19] You have faith and believe that there is one God. Excellent! Even demons have faith like that, and it makes them tremble. [20] Do you have to be told, you fool, that faith divorced from action is futile? [21] Was it not by his action, in offering his son Isaac

upon the altar, that our father Abraham was justified? [22] Surely you can see faith was at work in his actions, and by these actions his faith was perfected? [23] Here was fulfilment of the words of scripture: 'Abraham put his faith in God, and that faith was counted to him as righteousness,' and he was called 'God's friend'. [24] You see then it is by action and not by faith alone that a man is justified. [25] The same is true also of the prostitute Rahab. Was she not justified by her action in welcoming the messengers into her house and sending them away by a different route? [26] As the body is dead when there is no breath left in it, so faith divorced from action is dead.

Christian speaking

3 MY friends, not many of you should become teachers, for you may be certain that we who teach will ourselves face severer judgement. [2] All of us go wrong again and again; a man who never says anything wrong is perfect and is capable of controlling every part of his body. [3] When we put a bit into a horse's mouth to make it obey our will, we can direct the whole animal. [4] Or think of a ship: large though it may be and driven by gales, it can be steered by a very small rudder on whatever course the helmsman chooses. [5] So with the tongue; it is small, but its pretensions are great.

What a vast amount of timber can be set ablaze by the tiniest spark! [6] And the tongue is a fire, representing in our body the whole wicked world. It pollutes our whole being, it sets the whole course of our existence alight, and its flames are fed by hell. [7] Beasts and birds of every kind, creatures that crawl on the ground or swim in the sea, can be subdued and have been subdued by man; [8] but no one can subdue the tongue. It is an evil thing, restless and charged with deadly venom. [9] We use it to praise our Lord and Father; then we use it to invoke curses on our fellow-men, though they are made in God's likeness. [10] Out of the same mouth come praise and curses. This should not be so, my friends. [11] Does a fountain flow with both fresh and brackish water from the same outlet? [12] My friends, can a fig tree produce olives, or a grape vine produce figs? No more can salt water produce fresh.

The sin of envy

13 WHICH of you is wise or learned? Let him give practical proof of it by his right conduct, with the modesty that comes of wisdom. 14 But if you are harbouring bitter jealousy and the spirit of rivalry in your hearts, stop making false claims in defiance of the truth. 15 This is not the wisdom that comes from above; it is earth-bound, sensual, demonic. 16 For with jealousy and rivalry come disorder and the practice of every kind of evil. 17 But the wisdom from above is in the first place pure; and then peace-loving, considerate, and open-minded; it is straightforward and sincere, rich in compassion and in deeds of kindness that are its fruit. 18 Peace is the seed-bed of righteousness, and the peacemakers will reap its harvest.

4 What causes fighting and quarrels among you? Is not their origin the appetites that war in your bodies? 2 You want what you cannot have, so you murder; you are envious, and cannot attain your ambition, so you quarrel and fight. You do not get what you want, because you do not pray for it. 3 Or, if you do, your requests are not granted, because you pray from wrong motives, in order to squander what you get on your pleasures. 4 Unfaithful creatures! Surely you know that love of the world means enmity to God? Whoever chooses to be the world's friend makes himself God's enemy. 5 Or do you suppose that scripture has no point when it says that the spirit which God implanted in us is filled with envious longings? 6 But the grace he gives is stronger; thus scripture says, 'God opposes the arrogant and gives grace to the humble.' 7 Submit then to God. Stand up to the devil, and he will turn and run. 8 Come close to God, and he will draw close to you. Sinners, make your hands clean; you whose motives are mixed, see that your hearts are pure. 9 Be sorrowful, mourn, and weep. Turn your laughter into mourning and your gaiety into gloom. 10 Humble yourselves before the Lord, and he will exalt you.

11 Friends, you must never speak ill of one another. He who speaks ill of a brother or passes judgement on him speaks ill of the law and judges the law. But if you judge the law, you are not keeping it but sitting in judgement upon it. 12 There is only one lawgiver and judge: he who is able to save life or destroy it. So who are you to judge your neighbour?

The danger of wealth

13 Now A word with all who say, 'Today or the next day we will go off to such and such a town and spend a year there trading and making money.' 14 Yet you have no idea what tomorrow will bring. What is your life after all? You are no more than a mist, seen for a little while and then disappearing. 15 What you ought to say is: 'If it be the Lord's will, we shall live to do so and so.' 16 But instead, you boast and brag, and all such boasting is wrong. 17 What it comes to is that anyone who knows the right thing to do and does not do it is a sinner.

5 Next a word to you who are rich. Weep and wail over the miserable fate overtaking you: 2 your riches have rotted away; your fine clothes are motheaten; 3 your silver and gold have corroded, and their corrosion will be evidence against you and consume your flesh like fire. You have piled up wealth in an age that is near its close. 4 The wages you never paid to the men who mowed your fields are crying aloud against you, and the outcry of the reapers has reached the ears of the Lord of Hosts. 5 You have lived on the land in wanton luxury, gorging yourselves—and that on the day appointed for your slaughter. 6 You have condemned and murdered the innocent one, who offers no resistance.

Patience and prayer

7 YOU MUST be patient, my friends, until the Lord comes. Consider: the farmer looking for the precious crop from his land can only wait in patience until the early and late rains have fallen. 8 You too must be patient and stout-hearted, for the coming of the Lord is near. 9 My friends, do not blame your troubles on one another, or you will fall under judgement; and there at the door stands the Judge. 10 As a pattern of patience under ill-treatment, take the prophets who spoke in the name of the Lord. 11 We count those happy who stood firm. You have heard how Job stood firm, and you have seen how the Lord treated him in the end, for the Lord is merciful and compassionate.

[12] ABOVE all things, my friends, do not use oaths, whether 'by heaven' or 'by earth' or by anything else. When you say 'Yes' or 'No', let it be plain Yes or No, for fear you draw down judgement on yourselves.

[13] Is anyone among you in trouble? Let him pray. Is anyone in good heart? Let him sing praises. [14] Is one of you ill? Let him send for the elders of the church to pray over him and anoint him with oil in the name of the Lord; [15] the prayer offered in faith will heal the sick man, the Lord will restore him to health, and if he has committed sins they will be forgiven. [16] Therefore confess your sins to one another, and pray for one another, that you may be healed. A good man's prayer is very powerful and effective. [17] Elijah was a man just like us; yet when he prayed fervently that there should be no rain, the land had no rain for three and a half years; [18] when he prayed again, the rain poured down and the land bore crops once more.

[19] My friends, if one of you strays from the truth and another succeeds in bringing him back, [20] you may be sure of this: the one who brings a sinner back from his erring ways will be rescuing a soul from death and cancelling a multitude of sins.

THE FIRST LETTER OF
PETER

1 FROM Peter, apostle of Jesus Christ, to the scattered people of God now living as aliens in Pontus, Galatia, Cappadocia, Asia, and Bithynia, [2] chosen in the foreknowledge of God the Father, by the consecrating work of the Holy Spirit, for obedience to Jesus Christ and sprinkling with his blood.

Grace and peace to you in fullest measure.

Peter gives thanks

[3] PRAISED be the God and Father of our Lord Jesus Christ! In his great mercy by the resurrection of Jesus Christ from the dead, he gave us new birth into a living hope, [4] the hope of an inheritance, reserved in heaven for you, which nothing can destroy or spoil or wither. [5] Because you put your faith in God, you are under the protection of his power until the salvation now in readiness is revealed at the end of time.

[6] This is cause for great joy, even though for a little while you may have had to suffer trials of many kinds. [7] Even gold passes through the assayer's fire, and much more precious than perishable gold is faith which stands the test. These trials come so that your faith may prove itself worthy of all praise, glory, and honour when Jesus Christ is revealed.

[8] You have not seen him, yet you love him; and trusting in him now without seeing him, you are filled with a glorious joy too great for words, [9] while you are reaping the harvest of your faith, that is, salvation for your souls.

The calling of a Christian

[10] THIS salvation was the subject of intense search by the prophets who prophesied about the grace of God awaiting you. [11] They tried to find out the time and the circumstances to which the spirit of Christ in them pointed, when it foretold the sufferings in Christ's cause and the glories to follow. [12] It was disclosed to them that these matters were not for their benefit but for yours. Now they have been openly announced to you through preachers who brought you the gospel in the power of the Holy Spirit sent from heaven. These are things that angels long to glimpse.

[13] Your minds must therefore be stripped for action and fully alert. Fix your hopes on the grace which is to be yours when Jesus Christ is revealed. [14] Be obedient to God your Father, and do not let your characters be shaped any longer by the desires you cherished in your days of ignorance. [15] He who called you is holy; like him, be holy in all your conduct. [16] Does not scripture say, 'You shall be holy, for I am holy'?

[17] If you say 'Father' to him who judges everyone impartially on the basis of what they have done, you must live in awe of him during your time on earth. [18] You know well that it was nothing of passing value, like silver or gold, that bought your freedom from the futility of your traditional ways. [19] You were set free by Christ's precious blood, blood like that of a lamb without mark or blemish. [20] He was predestined before the foundation of the world, but in this last period of time he has been revealed for your sake. [21] Through him you have come to trust in God who raised him from the dead and gave him glory, and so your faith and hope are fixed on God.

[22] Now that you have purified your souls by obedience to the truth until you feel sincere affection towards your fellow-Christians, love one another wholeheartedly with all your strength. [23] You have been born again, not of mortal but of immortal parentage, through the living and enduring word of God. [24] As scripture says:

All mortals are like grass;
all their glory like the flower of the field;
the grass withers, the flower falls;
[25] but the word of the Lord endures for evermore.

1:11 **the time:** *or* the person.

And this 'word' is the gospel which was preached to you.

2 Then away with all wickedness and deceit, hypocrisy and jealousy and malicious talk of any kind! [2] Like the new-born infants you are, you should be craving for pure spiritual milk so that you may thrive on it and be saved; for [3] surely you have tasted that the Lord is good.

[4] So come to him, to the living stone which was rejected by men but chosen by God and of great worth to him. [5] You also, as living stones, must be built up into a spiritual temple, and form a holy priesthood to offer spiritual sacrifices acceptable to God through Jesus Christ. [6] For you will find in scripture:

I am laying in Zion a chosen corner-
    stone of great worth.
Whoever has faith in it will not be
    put to shame.

[7] So for you who have faith it has great worth; but for those who have no faith 'the stone which the builders rejected has become the corner-stone', [8] and also 'a stone to trip over, a rock to stumble against'. They trip because they refuse to believe the word; this is the fate appointed for them.

[9] But you are a chosen race, a royal priesthood, a dedicated nation, a people claimed by God for his own, to proclaim the glorious deeds of him who has called you out of darkness into his marvellous light. [10] Once you were not a people at all; but now you are God's people. Once you were outside his mercy; but now you are outside no longer.

The Christian household

[11] DEAR friends, I appeal to you, as aliens in a foreign land, to avoid bodily desires which make war on the soul. [12] Let your conduct among unbelievers be so good that, although they now malign you as wrongdoers, reflection on your good deeds will lead them to give glory to God on the day when he comes in judgement. [13] Submit yourselves for the sake of the Lord to every human authority, whether to the emperor as supreme, [14] or to governors as his deputies for the punishment of those who do wrong and the commenda-tion of those who do right. [15] For it is God's will that by doing right you should silence ignorance and stupidity.

[16] Live as those who are free; not however as though your freedom provided a cloak for wrongdoing, but as slaves in God's service. [17] Give due honour to everyone: love your fellow-Christians, reverence God, honour the emperor.

[18] Servants, submit to your masters with all due respect, not only to those who are kind and forbearing, but even to those who are unjust. [19] It is a sign of grace if, because God is in his thoughts, someone endures the pain of undeserved suffering. [20] What credit is there in enduring the beating you deserve when you have done wrong? On the other hand, when you have behaved well and endured suffering for it, that is a sign of grace in the sight of God. [21] It is your vocation because Christ himself suffered on your behalf, and left you an example in order that you should follow in his steps. [22] 'He committed no sin, he was guilty of no falsehood.' [23] When he was abused he did not retaliate, when he suffered he uttered no threats, but delivered himself up to him who judges justly. [24] He carried our sins in his own person on the gibbet, so that we might cease to live for sin and begin to live for righteousness. By his wounds you have been healed. [25] You were straying like sheep, but now you have turned towards the Shepherd and Guardian of your souls.

3 In the same way you women must submit to your husbands, so that if there are any of them who disbelieve the gospel they may be won over without a word being said, [2] by observing your chaste and respectful behaviour. [3] Your beauty should lie, not in outward adorn-ment—braiding the hair, wearing gold ornaments, or dressing up in fine clothes—[4] but in the inmost self, with its imperishable quality of a gentle, quiet spirit, which is of high value in the sight of God. [5] This is how in past days the women of God's people, whose hope was in him, used to make themselves attract-ive, submitting to their husbands. [6] Such was Sarah, who obeyed Abraham and called him master. By doing good and

2:19, 20 **a sign of grace:** *or* creditable.   2:21 **suffered:** *some witnesses read* died.   2:24 **on the gibbet:** *or* to the gibbet.

showing no fear, you have become her daughters.

[7] In the same way, you husbands must show understanding in your married life: treat your wives with respect, not only because they are physically weaker, but also because God's gift of life is something you share together. Then your prayers will not be impeded.

[8] Finally, be united, all of you, in thought and feeling; be full of brotherly affection, kindly and humble. [9] Do not repay wrong with wrong, or abuse with abuse; on the contrary, respond with blessing, for a blessing is what God intends you to receive. As scripture says:

[10] If anyone wants to love life
     and see good days
   he must restrain his tongue from evil
     and his lips from deceit;
[11] he must turn from wrong and do
     good,
   seek peace and pursue it.
[12] The Lord has eyes for the righteous,
     and ears open to their prayers;
   but the face of the Lord is set against
     wrongdoers.

[13] Who is going to do you harm if you are devoted to what is good? [14] Yet if you should suffer for doing right you may count yourselves happy. Have no fear of other people: do not be perturbed, [15] but hold Christ in your hearts in reverence as Lord. Always be ready to make your defence when anyone challenges you to justify the hope which is in you. But do so with courtesy and respect, [16] keeping your conscience clear, so that when you are abused, those who malign your Christian conduct may be put to shame. [17] It is better to suffer for doing right, if such should be the will of God, than for doing wrong.

[18] Christ too suffered for our sins once and for all, the just for the unjust, that he might bring us to God; put to death in the body, he was brought to life in the spirit. [19] In the spirit also he went and made his proclamation to the imprisoned spirits, [20] those who had refused to obey in the past, while God waited patiently in the days when Noah was building the ark; in

it a few people, eight in all, were brought to safety through the water. [21] This water symbolized baptism, through which you are now brought to safety. Baptism is not the washing away of bodily impurities but the appeal made to God from a good conscience; and it brings salvation through the resurrection of Jesus Christ, [22] who is now at the right hand of God, having entered heaven and received the submission of angels, authorities, and powers.

The final testing

4 SINCE Christ endured bodily suffering, you also must arm yourselves with the same disposition. When anyone has endured bodily suffering he has finished with sin, [2] so that for the rest of his days on earth he may live, not to satisfy human appetites, but to do what God wills. [3] You have spent time enough in the past doing what pagans are doing. You lived then in licence and debauchery, drunkenness, orgies and carousal, and the forbidden worship of idols. [4] Now, when you no longer plunge with the pagans into all this reckless dissipation, they cannot understand it and start abusing you; [5] but they will have to give account of themselves to him who is ready to pass judgement on the living and the dead. [6] That was why the gospel was preached even to the dead: in order that, although in the body they were condemned to die as everyone dies, yet in the spirit they might live as God lives.

[7] The end of all things is upon us; therefore to help you to pray you must lead self-controlled and sober lives. [8] Above all, maintain the fervour of your love for one another, because love cancels a host of sins. [9] Be hospitable to one another without grumbling. [10] As good stewards of the varied gifts given you by God, let each use the gift he has received in service to others. [11] Are you a speaker? Speak as one who utters God's oracles. Do you give service? Give it in the strength which God supplies. In all things let God be glorified through Jesus Christ; to him belong glory and power for ever and ever. Amen.

3:14 Have ... people: *or* Do not fear what other people fear.   3:18 suffered: *some witnesses read* died. for our sins: *some witnesses read* for sins.   3:21 from a good conscience: *or* for a good conscience.   4:6 although ... lives: *or* although in the body they suffered judgement by human standards, in the spirit they might be given life in accordance with God's purpose.

[12] DEAR friends, do not be taken aback by the fiery ordeal which has come to test you, as though it were something extraordinary. [13] On the contrary, in so far as it gives you a share in Christ's sufferings, you should rejoice; and then when his glory is revealed, your joy will be unbounded. [14] If you are reviled for being Christians, count yourselves happy, because the Spirit of God in all his glory rests upon you. [15] If you do suffer, it must not be for murder, theft, or any other crime, nor should it be for meddling in other people's business. [16] But if anyone suffers as a Christian, he should feel it no disgrace, but confess that name to the honour of God.

[17] The time has come for the judgement to begin; it is beginning with God's own household. And if it is starting with us, how will it end for those who refuse to obey the gospel of God? [18] Scripture says: 'It is hard enough for the righteous to be saved; what then will become of the impious and sinful?' [19] So let those who suffer according to God's will entrust their souls to him while continuing to do good; their Maker will not fail them.

The Christian community

5 NOW I APPEAL to the elders of your community, as a fellow-elder and a witness to Christ's sufferings, and as one who has shared in the glory to be revealed: [2] look after the flock of God whose shepherds you are; do it, not under compulsion, but willingly, as God would have it; not for gain but out of sheer devotion; [3] not

lording it over your charges, but setting an example to the flock. [4] So when the chief shepherd appears, you will receive glory, a crown that never fades.

[5] In the same way the younger men should submit to the older. You should all clothe yourselves with humility towards one another, because 'God sets his face against the arrogant but shows favour to the humble.' [6] Humble yourselves, then, under God's mighty hand, and in due time he will lift you up. [7] He cares for you, so cast all your anxiety on him.

[8] Be on the alert! Wake up! Your enemy the devil, like a roaring lion, prowls around looking for someone to devour. [9] Stand up to him, firm in your faith, and remember that your fellow-Christians in this world are going through the same kinds of suffering. [10] After your brief suffering, the God of all grace, who called you to his eternal glory in Christ, will himself restore, establish, and strengthen you on a firm foundation. [11] All power belongs to him for ever and ever! Amen.

Final greetings

[12] I WRITE you this brief letter through Silvanus, whom I know to be a trustworthy colleague, to encourage you and to testify that this is the true grace of God; in this stand fast.

[13] Greetings from your sister church in Babylon, and from my son Mark. [14] Greet one another with a loving kiss.

Peace to you all who belong to Christ!

THE SECOND LETTER OF
PETER

1 FROM Simeon Peter, servant and apostle of Jesus Christ, to those who share equally with us in the privileges of faith through the righteousness of our God and Saviour Jesus Christ.
[2] Grace and peace be yours in fullest measure, through knowledge of God and of Jesus our Lord.

Living in the last days

[3] GOD'S divine power has bestowed on us everything that makes for life and true

religion, through our knowledge of him who called us by his own glory and goodness. [4] In this way he has given us his promises, great beyond all price, so that through them you may escape the corruption with which lust has infected the world, and may come to share in the very being of God.

[5] With all this in view, you should make every effort to add virtue to your faith, knowledge to virtue, [6] self-control to knowledge, fortitude to self-control, piety

to fortitude, [7] brotherly affection to piety, and love to brotherly affection.

[8] If you possess and develop these gifts, you will grow actively and effectively in knowledge of our Lord Jesus Christ. [9] Whoever lacks them is wilfully blind; he has forgotten that his past sins were washed away. [10] All the more then, my friends, do your utmost to establish that God has called and chosen you. If you do this, you will never stumble, [11] and there will be rich provision for your entry into the eternal kingdom of our Lord and Saviour Jesus Christ.

[12] I shall keep reminding you of all this, although you know it and are well grounded in the truth you possess; [13] yet I think it right to keep on reminding you as long as I still lodge in this body. [14] I know I must soon leave it, as our Lord Jesus Christ told me. [15] But I will do my utmost to ensure that after I am gone you will always be able to call these things to mind.

[16] It was not on tales, however cleverly concocted, that we relied when we told you about the power of our Lord Jesus Christ and his coming; rather with our own eyes we had witnessed his majesty. [17] He was invested with honour and glory by God the Father, and there came to him from the sublime Presence a voice which said: 'This is my Son, my Beloved, on whom my favour rests.' [18] We ourselves heard this voice when it came from heaven, for we were with him on the sacred mountain.

[19] All this confirms for us the message of the prophets, to which you will do well to attend; it will go on shining like a lamp in a murky place, until day breaks and the morning star rises to illuminate your minds.

[20] BUT first note this: no prophetic writing is a matter for private interpretation. [21] It was not on any human initiative that prophecy came; rather, it was under the compulsion of the Holy Spirit that people spoke as messengers of God.

God's judgement on false teaching

2 IN the past there were also false prophets among the people, just as you also will have false teachers among you. They will introduce their destructive views, disowning the very Master who redeemed them, and bringing swift destruction on their own heads. [2] They will gain many adherents to their dissolute practices, through whom the way of truth will be brought into disrepute. [3] In their greed for money they will trade on your credulity with sheer fabrications.

But judgement has long been in preparation for them; destruction waits for them with unsleeping eyes. [4] God did not spare the angels who sinned, but consigned them to the dark pits of hell, where they are held for judgement. [5] Nor did he spare the world in ancient times (except for Noah, who proclaimed righteousness, and was preserved with seven others), but brought the flood upon that world with its godless people. [6] God reduced the cities of Sodom and Gomorrah to ashes, condemning them to total ruin as an object-lesson for the ungodly in future days. [7] But he rescued Lot, a good man distressed by the dissolute habits of the lawless society in which he lived; [8] day after day every sight and sound of their evil ways tortured that good man's heart. [9] The Lord knows how to rescue the godly from their trials, and to keep the wicked under punishment until the day of judgement.

[10] Above all he will punish those who follow their abominable lusts and flout authority. Reckless and headstrong, they are not afraid to insult celestial beings, [11] whereas angels, for all their superior strength and power, employ no insults in seeking judgement against them before the Lord.

[12] These men are like brute beasts, mere creatures of instinct, born to be caught and killed. They pour abuse upon things they do not understand; they will perish like the beasts, [13] suffering hurt for the hurt they have inflicted. To carouse in broad daylight is their idea of pleasure; while they sit with you at table they are an ugly blot on your company, because they revel in their deceits.

[14] They have eyes for nothing but loose women, eyes never resting from sin. They lure the unstable to their ruin; experts in mercenary greed, God's curse is on them!

1:17 **This . . . Beloved:** *or* This is my only Son.   2:4 **consigned . . . hell:** *some witnesses read* consigned them to darkness and chains in hell.

214

¹⁵ They have abandoned the straight road and gone astray. They have followed in the steps of Balaam son of Bosor, who eagerly accepted payment for doing wrong, ¹⁶ but had his offence brought home to him when a dumb beast spoke with a human voice and checked the prophet's madness.

¹⁷ These men are springs that give no water, mists driven by a storm; the place reserved for them is blackest darkness. ¹⁸ They utter empty bombast; they use sensual lusts and debauchery as a bait to catch people who have only just begun to escape from their pagan associates. ¹⁹ They promise them freedom, but are themselves slaves of corruption; for people are the slaves of whatever has mastered them. ²⁰ If they escaped the world's defilements through coming to know our Lord and Saviour Jesus Christ and entangled themselves in them again, and were mastered by them, their last state would be worse than the first. ²¹ Better for them never to have known the right way, than, having known it, to turn back and abandon the sacred commandment entrusted to them! ²² In their case the proverb has proved true: 'The dog returns to its vomit,' and 'The washed sow wallows in the mud again.'

The coming end

3 THIS, dear friends, is now my second letter to you. In both I have been recalling to you what you already know, to rouse you to honest thought. ² Remember the predictions made by God's own prophets, and the commandment given by the Lord and Saviour through your apostles.

³ First of all, note this: in the last days there will come scoffers who live self-indulgent lives; they will mock you and say: ⁴ 'What has happened to his promised coming? Our fathers have been laid to rest, but still everything goes on exactly as it always has done since the world began.'

⁵ In maintaining this they forget that there were heavens and earth long ago, created by God's word out of water and with water; ⁶ and that the first world was destroyed by water, the water of the flood. ⁷ By God's word the present heavens and earth are being reserved for burning; they are being kept until the day of judgement when the godless will be destroyed.

⁸ Here is something, dear friends, which you must not forget: in the Lord's sight one day is like a thousand years and a thousand years like one day. ⁹ It is not that the Lord is slow in keeping his promise, as some suppose, but that he is patient with you. It is not his will that any should be lost, but that all should come to repentance.

¹⁰ But the day of the Lord will come like a thief. On that day the heavens will disappear with a great rushing sound, the elements will be dissolved in flames, and the earth with all that is in it will be brought to judgement.

¹¹ Since the whole universe is to dissolve in this way, think what sort of people you ought to be, what devout and dedicated lives you should live! ¹² Look forward to the coming of the day of God, and work to hasten it on; that day will set the heavens ablaze until they fall apart, and will melt the elements in flames. ¹³ Relying on his promise we look forward to new heavens and a new earth, in which justice will be established.

¹⁴ In expectation of all this, my friends, do your utmost to be found at peace with him, unblemished and above reproach. ¹⁵ Bear in mind that our Lord's patience is an opportunity for salvation, as Paul, our dear friend and brother, said when he wrote to you with the wisdom God gave him. ¹⁶ He does the same in all his other letters, wherever he speaks about this, though they contain some obscure passages, which the ignorant and unstable misinterpret to their own ruin, as they do the other scriptures.

¹⁷ So, dear friends, you have been forewarned. Take care not to let these unprincipled people seduce you with their errors; do not lose your own safe foothold. ¹⁸ But grow in grace and in the knowledge of our Lord and Saviour Jesus Christ. To him be glory both now and for all eternity!

2:15 Bosor: *some witnesses read* Beor.   3:10 **will be brought to judgement:** *lit.* will be found.

THE FIRST LETTER OF

JOHN

1 It was there from the beginning; we have heard it; we have seen it with our own eyes; we looked upon it, and felt it with our own hands: our theme is the Word which gives life. ² This life was made visible; we have seen it and bear our testimony; we declare to you the eternal life which was with the Father and was made visible to us. ³ It is this which we have seen and heard that we declare to you also, in order that you may share with us in a common life, that life which we share with the Father and his Son Jesus Christ. ⁴ We are writing this in order that our joy may be complete.

Fellowship, obedience, and forgiveness

⁵ Here is the message we have heard from him and pass on to you: God is light, and in him there is no darkness at all. ⁶ If we claim to be sharing in his life while we go on living in darkness, our words and our lives are a lie. ⁷ But if we live in the light as he himself is in the light, then we share a common life, and the blood of Jesus his Son cleanses us from all sin.

⁸ If we claim to be sinless, we are self-deceived and the truth is not in us. ⁹ If we confess our sins, he is just and may be trusted to forgive our sins and cleanse us from every kind of wrongdoing. ¹⁰ If we say we have committed no sin, we make him out to be a liar and his word has no place in us.

2 My children, I am writing this to you so that you should not commit sin. But if anybody does, we have in Jesus Christ one who is acceptable to God and will plead our cause with the Father. ² He is himself a sacrifice to atone for our sins, and not ours only but the sins of the whole world.

³ It is by keeping God's commands that we can be sure we know him. ⁴ Whoever says, 'I know him,' but does not obey his commands, is a liar and the truth is not in him; ⁵ but whoever is obedient to his word, in him the love of God is truly made

perfect. This is how we can be sure that we are in him: ⁶ whoever claims to be dwelling in him must live as Christ himself lived.

⁷ Dear friends, it is no new command that I am sending you, but an old command which you have had from the beginning; the old command is the instruction which you have already received. ⁸ Yet because the darkness is passing away and the true light already shining, it is a new command that I write and it is true in Christ's life and in yours.

⁹ Whoever says, 'I am in the light,' but hates his fellow-Christian, is still in darkness. ¹⁰ He who loves his fellow-Christian dwells in light: there is no cause of stumbling in him. ¹¹ But anyone who hates his fellow is in darkness; he walks in the dark and has no idea where he is going, because the darkness has made him blind.

¹² I write to you, children, because your
   sins have been forgiven for his
   sake.
¹³ I write to you, fathers, because you
   know him who is and has been
   from the beginning.
I write to you, young men, because
   you have conquered the evil one.

I have written to you, children,
   because you know the Father.
¹⁴ I have written to you, fathers,
   because you know him who is and
   has been from the beginning.
I have written to you, young men,
   because you are strong; God's
   word remains in you, and you
   have conquered the evil one.

¹⁵ Do not set your hearts on the world or what is in it. Anyone who loves the world does not love the Father. ¹⁶ Everything in the world, all that panders to the appetites or entices the eyes, all the arrogance based on wealth, these spring not from the Father but from the world. ¹⁷ That

2:9 **fellow-Christian**: *lit.* brother.

world with all its allurements is passing away, but those who do God's will remain for ever.

The danger of false teaching

[18] CHILDREN, this is the last hour! You were told that an antichrist was to come. Well, many antichrists have already appeared, proof to us that this is indeed the last hour. [19] They left our ranks, but never really belonged to us; if they had, they would have stayed with us. They left so that it might be clear that none of them belong to us.

[20] What is more, you have been anointed by the Holy One, and so you all have knowledge. [21] It is not because you are ignorant of the truth that I have written to you, but because you do know it, and know that lies never come from the truth.

[22] Anyone who denies that Jesus is the Christ is nothing but a liar. He is the antichrist, for he denies both the Father and the Son: [23] to deny the Son is to be without the Father; to acknowledge the Son is to have the Father too. [24] You must therefore keep hold of what you heard at the beginning; if what you heard then still dwells in you, you will yourselves dwell both in the Son and in the Father. [25] And this is the promise that he himself gave us, the promise of eternal life.

[26] So much for those who would mislead you. [27] But as for you, the anointing which you received from him remains with you; you need no other teacher, but you learn all you need to know from his anointing, which is true and no lie. Dwell in him as he taught you to do.

[28] Even now, children, dwell in him, so that when he appears we may be confident and unashamed before him at his coming. [29] You know that God is righteous; then recognize that everyone who does what is right is his child.

How Christians live together

3 CONSIDER how great is the love which the Father has bestowed on us in calling us his children! For that is what we are. The reason why the world does not recognize us is that it has not known

him. [2] Dear friends, we are now God's children; what we shall be has not yet been disclosed, but we know that when Christ appears we shall be like him, because we shall see him as he is. [3] As he is pure, everyone who has grasped this hope makes himself pure.

[4] To commit sin is to break God's law: for sin is lawlessness. [5] You know that Christ appeared in order to take away sins, and in him there is no sin. [6] No one who dwells in him sins any more; the sinner has neither seen him nor known him.

[7] Children, do not be misled: anyone who does what is right is righteous, just as Christ is righteous; [8] anyone who sins is a child of the devil, for the devil has been a sinner from the first; and the Son of God appeared for the very purpose of undoing the devil's work. [9] No child of God commits sin, because the divine seed remains in him; indeed because he is God's child he cannot sin. [10] This is what shows who are God's children and who are the devil's: anyone who fails to do what is right or love his fellow-Christians is not a child of God.

[11] The message you have heard from the beginning is that we should love one another. [12] Do not be like Cain, who was a child of the evil one and murdered his brother. And why did he murder him? Because his own actions were wrong, and his brother's were right.

[13] Friends, do not be surprised if the world hates you. [14] We know we have crossed over from death to life, because we love our fellow-Christians. Anyone who does not love is still in the realm of death, [15] for everyone who hates a fellow-Christian is a murderer, and murderers, as you know, do not have eternal life dwelling within them. [16] This is how we know what love is: Christ gave his life for us. And we in our turn must give our lives for our fellow-Christians. [17] But if someone who possesses the good things of this world sees a fellow-Christian in need and withholds compassion from him, how can it be said that the love of God dwells in him?

[18] Children, love must not be a matter of theory or talk; it must be true love which

2:19 **none of them:** *or* not all of them.　　2:20 **you all have knowledge:** *some witnesses read* you have all knowledge.　　3:2 **we are ... like him:** *or* we are God's children, though he has not yet appeared; what we shall be we know, for when he does appear we shall be like him. **when Christ appears:** *or* when it is disclosed.

shows itself in action. [19] This is how we shall know that we belong to the realm of truth, and reassure ourselves in his sight [20] where conscience condemns us; for God is greater than our conscience and knows all.

[21] My dear friends, if our conscience does not condemn us, then we can approach God with confidence, [22] and obtain from him whatever we ask, because we are keeping his commands and doing what he approves. [23] His command is that we should give our allegiance to his Son Jesus Christ and love one another, as Christ commanded us. [24] Those who keep his commands dwell in him and he dwells in them. And our certainty that he dwells in us comes from the Spirit he has given us.

Spirits of truth and error

4 My dear friends, do not trust every spirit, but test the spirits, to see whether they are from God; for there are many false prophets about in the world. [2] The way to recognize the Spirit of God is this: every spirit which acknowledges that Jesus Christ has come in the flesh is from God, [3] and no spirit is from God which does not acknowledge Jesus. This is the spirit of antichrist; you have been warned that it was to come, and now here it is, in the world already!

[4] Children, you belong to God's family, and you have the mastery over these false prophets, because God who inspires you is greater than the one who inspires the world. [5] They belong to that world, and so does their teaching; that is why the world listens to them. [6] But we belong to God and whoever knows God listens to us, while whoever does not belong to God refuses to listen to us. That is how we can distinguish the spirit of truth from the spirit of error.

Love one another

[7] My dear friends, let us love one another, because the source of love is God. Everyone who loves is a child of God and knows God, [8] but the unloving know nothing of God, for God is love. [9] This is how he showed his love among us: he sent his only Son into the world that we might have life through him. [10] This is what love really is: not that we have loved God, but that he loved us and sent his Son as a sacrifice to atone for our sins. [11] If God thus loved us, my dear friends, we also must love one another. [12] God has never been seen by anyone, but if we love one another, he himself dwells in us; his love is brought to perfection within us.

[13] This is how we know that we dwell in him and he dwells in us: he has imparted his Spirit to us. [14] Moreover, we have seen for ourselves, and we are witnesses, that the Father has sent the Son to be the Saviour of the world. [15] If anyone acknowledges that Jesus is God's Son, God dwells in him and he in God. [16] Thus we have come to know and believe in the love which God has for us.

God is love; he who dwells in love is dwelling in God, and God in him. [17] This is how love has reached its perfection among us, so that we may have confidence on the day of judgement; and this we can have, because in this world we are as he is. [18] In love there is no room for fear; indeed perfect love banishes fear. For fear has to do with punishment, and anyone who is afraid has not attained to love in its perfection. [19] We love because he loved us first. [20] But if someone says, 'I love God,' while at the same time hating his fellow-Christian, he is a liar. If he does not love a fellow-Christian whom he has seen, he is incapable of loving God whom he has not seen. [21] We have this command from Christ: whoever loves God must love his fellow-Christian too.

Obedience to the truth

5 Everyone who believes that Jesus is the Christ is a child of God. To love the parent means to love his child. [2] It follows that when we love God and obey his commands we love his children too. [3] For to love God is to keep his commands; and these are not burdensome, [4] because every child of God overcomes the world. Now, the victory by which the world is overcome is our faith, [5] for who is victor over the world but he who believes that Jesus is the Son of God? [6] This is he whose coming was with water and blood: Jesus Christ. He came,

---

3:19–20 reassure ... than our conscience: or convince ourselves in his sight that even if our conscience condemns us, God is greater than our conscience.

not by the water alone, but both by the water and by the blood; and to this the Spirit bears witness, because the Spirit is truth. 7–8 In fact there are three witnesses, the Spirit, the water, and the blood, and these three are in agreement. 9 We accept human testimony, but surely the testimony of God is stronger, and the testimony of God is the witness he has borne to his Son. 10 He who believes in the Son of God has the testimony in his own heart, but he who does not believe God makes him out to be a liar by refusing to accept God's witness to his Son. 11 This is the witness: God has given us eternal life, and this life is found in his Son. 12 He who possesses the Son possesses life; he who does not possess the Son of God does not possess life.

Final instructions and encouragement

13 YOU HAVE given your allegiance to the Son of God; this letter is to assure you that you have eternal life.

14 We can approach God with this confidence: if we make requests which accord with his will, he listens to us; 15 and if we know that our requests are heard, we also know that all we ask of him is ours.

16 If anyone sees a fellow-Christian committing a sin which is not a deadly sin, he should intercede for him, and God will grant him life—that is, to those who are not guilty of deadly sin. There is such a thing as deadly sin, and I do not suggest that he should pray about that. 17 Although all wrongdoing is sin, not all sin is deadly sin.

18 We know that no child of God commits sin; he is kept safe by the Son of God, and the evil one cannot touch him.

19 We know that we are of God's family, but that the whole world lies in the power of the evil one.

20 We know that the Son of God has come and given us understanding to know the true God; indeed we are in him who is true, since we are in his Son Jesus Christ. He is the true God and eternal life. 21 Children, be on your guard against idols.

THE SECOND LETTER OF
JOHN

Truth and love

THE Elder to the Lady chosen by God and to her children whom I love in the truth, and not I alone but all who know the truth. 2 We love you for the sake of the truth that dwells among us and will be with us for ever.

3 Grace, mercy, and peace will be with us from God the Father and from Jesus Christ the Son of the Father, in truth and love.

4 I was very glad to find that some of your children are living by the truth, in accordance with the command we have received from the Father. 5 And now, Lady, I have a request to make of you. Do not think I am sending a new command; I am recalling the one we have had from the beginning: I ask that we love one another. 6 What love means is to live according to the commands of God. This is the command that was given you from the beginning, to be your rule of life.

7 Many deceivers have gone out into the world, people who do not acknowledge Jesus Christ as coming in the flesh. Any such person is the deceiver and antichrist. 8 See to it that you do not lose what we have worked for, but receive your reward in full.

9 Anyone who does not stand by the teaching about Christ, but goes beyond it, does not possess God; he who stands by it possesses both the Father and the Son. 10 If anyone comes to you who does not bring this teaching, do not admit him to your house or give him any greeting; 11 for he who greets him becomes an accomplice in his evil deeds.

12 I have much to write to you, but I do not care to put it down on paper. Rather, I hope to visit you and talk with you face to face, so that our joy may be complete. 13 The children of your Sister, chosen by God, send you greetings.

THE THIRD LETTER OF
JOHN

Trouble in the church

THE Elder to dear Gaius, whom I love in the truth.

[2] Dear friend, above all I pray that things go well with you, and that you may enjoy good health: I know it is well with your soul. [3] I was very glad when some fellow-Christians arrived and told me of your faithfulness to the truth; indeed you live by the truth. [4] Nothing gives me greater joy than to hear that my children are living by the truth.

[5] Dear friend, you show a fine loyalty in what you do for our fellow-Christians, though they are strangers to you. [6] They have testified to your kindness before the congregation here. Please help them on their journey in a manner worthy of the God we serve. [7] It was for love of Christ's name that they went out; and they would accept nothing from unbelievers. [8] Therefore we ought to support such people, and so play our part in spreading the truth.

[9] I wrote to the congregation, but Diotrephes, who enjoys taking the lead, will have nothing to do with us. [10] So when I come, I will draw attention to the things he is doing: he lays nonsensical and spiteful charges against us; not content with that, he refuses to receive fellow-Christians himself, and interferes with those who would receive them, and tries to expel them from the congregation.

[11] Dear friend, follow good examples, not bad ones. The well-doer is a child of God; the evildoer has never seen God.

[12] Demetrius is well spoken of by everyone, and even by the truth itself. I add my testimony, and you know that my testimony is true.

[13] I had much to write to you, but I do not care to set it down with pen and ink. [14] I hope to see you very soon, when we will talk face to face. Peace be with you. Your friends here send you greetings. Greet each of our friends by name.

A LETTER OF
JUDE

The danger of false belief

FROM Jude, servant of Jesus Christ and brother of James, to those whom God has called, who live in the love of God the Father and are kept safe for the coming of Jesus Christ.

[2] Mercy, peace, and love be yours in fullest measure.

[3] My friends, I was fully intending to write to you about the salvation we share, when I found it necessary to take up my pen and urge you to join in the struggle for that faith which God entrusted to his people once for all. [4] Certain individuals have wormed their way in, the very people whom scripture long ago marked down for the sentence they are now incurring. They are enemies of religion; they pervert the free favour of our God into licentiousness, disowning Jesus Christ, our only Master and Lord.

[5] You already know all this, but let me remind you how the Lord, having once for all delivered his people out of Egypt, later destroyed those who did not believe. [6] Remember too those angels who were not content to maintain the dominion assigned to them, but abandoned their proper dwelling-place; God is holding them, bound in darkness with everlasting

1 kept ... coming: *or* in the safe keeping.   4 disowning ... Lord: *or* disowning our one and only Master, and Jesus Christ our Lord.   5 the Lord: *some witnesses read* Jesus; *others read* God.

chains, for judgement on the great day. [7] Remember Sodom and Gomorrah and the neighbouring towns; like the angels, they committed fornication and indulged in unnatural lusts; and in eternal fire they paid the penalty, a warning for all.

[8] In the same way these deluded dreamers continue to defile their bodies, flout authority, and insult celestial beings. [9] Not even the archangel Michael, when he was disputing with the devil for possession of Moses' body, presumed to condemn him in insulting words, but said, 'May the Lord rebuke you!'

[10] But these people pour abuse on whatever they do not understand; the things that, like brute beasts, they do understand by their senses prove their undoing. [11] Alas for them! They have followed the way of Cain; for profit they have plunged into Balaam's error; they have rebelled like Korah, and they share his fate.

[12] These people are a danger at your love-feasts with their shameless carousals. They are shepherds who take care only of themselves. They are clouds carried along by a wind without giving rain, trees fruitless in autumn, dead twice over and pulled up by the roots. [13] They are wild sea waves, foaming with disgraceful deeds; they are stars that have wandered from their courses, and the place reserved for them is an eternity of blackest darkness.

[14] It was against them that Enoch, the seventh in descent from Adam, prophesied when he said: 'I saw the Lord come with his myriads of angels, [15] to bring all mankind to judgement and to convict all the godless of every godless deed they had committed, and of every defiant word they had spoken against him, godless sinners that they are.'

[16] They are a set of grumblers and malcontents. They follow their lusts. Bombast comes rolling from their lips, and they court favour to gain their ends. [17] But you, my friends, should remember the predictions made by the apostles of our Lord Jesus Christ. [18] They said to you: 'In the final age there will be those who mock at religion and follow their own ungodly lusts.'

[19] These people create divisions; they are worldly and unspiritual. [20] But you, my friends, must make your most sacred faith the foundation of your lives. Continue to pray in the power of the Holy Spirit. [21] Keep yourselves in the love of God, and look forward to the day when our Lord Jesus Christ in his mercy will give eternal life.

[22] There are some doubting souls who need your pity. [23] Others you should save by snatching them from the flames. For others your pity must be mixed with fear; hate the very clothing that is contaminated with sensuality.

[24] Now to the One who can keep you from falling and set you in the presence of his glory, jubilant and above reproach, [25] to the only God our Saviour, be glory and majesty, power and authority, through Jesus Christ our Lord, before all time, now, and for evermore. Amen.

9 to condemn...words: *or* to charge him with blasphemy.   19 These...unspiritual: *or* These people draw a line between spiritual and unspiritual persons, although they themselves are unspiritual, not spiritual. 23 Others you...fear: *some witnesses read* There are some whom you should snatch from the flames. Show pity to doubting souls with fear.

THE
REVELATION
OF JOHN

1 THIS is the revelation of Jesus Christ, which God gave him so that he might show his servants what must soon take place. He made it known by sending his angel to his servant John, ² who in telling all that he saw has borne witness to the word of God and to the testimony of Jesus Christ.

³ Happy is the one who reads aloud the words of this prophecy, and happy those who listen if they take to heart what is here written; for the time of fulfilment is near.

Christ's messages to seven churches

⁴ JOHN, to the seven churches in the province of Asia.

Grace be to you and peace, from him who is, who was, and who is to come, from the seven spirits before his throne, ⁵ and from Jesus Christ, the faithful witness, the firstborn from the dead and ruler of the kings of the earth.

To him who loves us and has set us free from our sins with his blood, ⁶ who has made of us a royal house to serve as the priests of his God and Father—to him be glory and dominion for ever! Amen.

⁷ Look, he is coming with the clouds; everyone shall see him, including those who pierced him; and all the peoples of the world shall lament in remorse. So it shall be. Amen.

⁸ 'I am the Alpha and the Omega,' says the Lord God, who is, who was, and who is to come, the sovereign Lord of all.

⁹ I, John, your brother, who share with you in the suffering, the sovereignty, and the endurance which are ours in Jesus, was on the island called Patmos because I had preached God's word and borne my testimony to Jesus. ¹⁰ On the Lord's day the Spirit came upon me; and I heard behind me a loud voice, like the sound of a trumpet, ¹¹ which said, 'Write down in a book what you see and send it to the seven churches: to Ephesus, Smyrna, Pergamum, Thyatira, Sardis, Philadelphia, and Laodicea.' ¹² I turned to see whose voice it was that spoke to me; and when I turned I saw seven lampstands of gold. ¹³ Among the lamps was a figure like a man, in a robe that came to his feet, with a golden girdle round his breast. ¹⁴ His hair was as white as snow-white wool, and his eyes flamed like fire; ¹⁵ his feet were like burnished bronze refined in a furnace, and his voice was like the sound of a mighty torrent. ¹⁶ In his right hand he held seven stars, and from his mouth came a sharp, two-edged sword; his face shone like the sun in full strength.

¹⁷ When I saw him, I fell at his feet as though I were dead. But he laid his right hand on me and said, 'Do not be afraid. I am the first and the last, ¹⁸ and I am the living One; I was dead and now I am alive for evermore, and I hold the keys of death and Hades. ¹⁹ Write down therefore what you have seen, what is now, and what is to take place hereafter.

²⁰ 'This is the secret meaning of the seven stars you saw in my right hand, and of the seven gold lamps: the seven stars are the angels of the seven churches, and the seven lamps are the seven churches themselves.

2 'TO THE angel of the church at Ephesus write:

' "These are the words of the One who holds the seven stars in his right hand, who walks among the seven gold lamps: ² I know what you are doing, how you toil and endure. I know you cannot abide wicked people; you have put to the test those who claim to be apostles but are not, and you have found them to be false. ³ Endurance you have; you have borne up in my cause and have never become weary. ⁴ However, I have this against you: the love you felt at first you have now lost. ⁵ Think from what a height you have fallen; repent, and do as once you did. If you do not, I will come to you and remove your lamp from its place. ⁶ Yet you have this much in your favour: you detest as I do the practices of the Nicolaitans. [7] You have ears, so hear what the Spirit says to the churches! To those who are victorious I will give the right to eat from the tree of life that stands in the garden of God."

[8] 'To the angel of the church at Smyrna write:

' "These are the words of the First and the Last, who was dead and came to life again: [9] I know how hard pressed and poor you are, but in reality you are rich. I know how you are slandered by those who claim to be Jews but are not; they are really a synagogue of Satan. [10] Do not be afraid of the sufferings to come. The devil will throw some of you into prison, to be put to the test, and for ten days you will be hard pressed. Be faithful till death, and I will give you the crown of life. [11] You have ears, so hear what the Spirit says to the churches! Those who are victorious cannot be harmed by the second death."

[12] 'To the angel of the church at Pergamum write:

' "These are the words of the One who has the sharp, two-edged sword: [13] I know where you live; it is where Satan is enthroned. Yet you are holding fast to my cause, and did not deny your faith in me even at the time when Antipas, my faithful witness, was put to death in your city, where Satan has his home. [14] But I have a few matters to bring against you. You have in Pergamum some that hold to the teaching of Balaam, who taught Balak to put temptation in the way of the Israelites; he encouraged them to eat food sacrificed to idols and to commit fornication. [15] In the same way you also have some who hold to the teaching of the Nicolaitans. [16] So repent! If you do not, I will come to you quickly and make war on them with the sword that comes out of my mouth. [17] You have ears, so hear what the Spirit says to the churches! To anyone who is victorious I will give some of the hidden manna; I will also give him a white stone, and on it will be written a new name, known only to him who receives it."

[18] 'To the angel of the church at Thyatira write:

' "These are the words of the Son of God, whose eyes flame like fire, and whose feet are like burnished bronze: [19] I know

what you are doing, your love and faithfulness, your service and your endurance; indeed of late you have done even better than you did at first. [20] But I have this against you: you tolerate that Jezebel, the woman who claims to be a prophetess, whose teaching lures my servants into fornication and into eating food sacrificed to idols. [21] I have given her time to repent, but she refuses to repent of her fornication. [22] So I will throw her on a bed of pain, and I will plunge her lovers into terrible suffering, unless they renounce what she is doing; [23] and her children I will kill with pestilence. This will teach all the churches that I am the searcher of men's hearts and minds, and that I will give to each of you what his deeds deserve. [24] And now I speak to the rest of you in Thyatira, all who do not accept this teaching and have had no experience of what they call the deep secrets of Satan. On you I impose no further burden; [25] only hold fast to what you have, until I come. [26] To him who is victorious, to him who perseveres in doing my will to the end, I will give authority over the nations—[27] that same authority which I received from my Father—and he will rule them with a rod of iron, smashing them to pieces like earthenware; [28] and I will give him the star of dawn. [29] You have ears, so hear what the Spirit says to the churches!"

3 'To the angel of the church at Sardis write:

' "These are the words of the One who has the seven spirits of God and the seven stars: I know what you are doing; people say you are alive, but in fact you are dead. [2] Wake up, and put some strength into what you still have, because otherwise it must die! For I have not found any work of yours brought to completion in the sight of my God. [3] Remember therefore the teaching you received; observe it, and repent. If you do not wake up, I will come upon you like a thief, and you will not know the moment of my coming. [4] Yet you have a few people in Sardis who have not polluted their clothing, and they will walk with me in white, for so they deserve. [5] Anyone who is victorious will be robed in white like them, and I shall never strike his name off the roll of the living; in the presence of my Father and his angels I shall acknowledge him as mine. [6] You have ears, so hear what the Spirit says to the churches!"

[7] 'To the angel of the church at Philadelphia write:

' "These are the words of the Holy One, the True One, who has David's key, so that when he opens the door, no one can shut it, and when he shuts it, no one can open it: [8] I know what you are doing. I have set before you an open door which no one can shut. I know your strength is small, yet you have observed my command and have not disowned my name. [9] As for those of Satan's synagogue, who falsely claim to be Jews, I will make them come and fall at your feet; and they will know that you are my beloved people. [10] Because you have kept my command to stand firm, I will also keep you from the ordeal that is to fall upon the whole world to test its inhabitants. [11] I am coming soon; hold fast to what you have, and let no one rob you of your crown. [12] Those who are victorious I shall make pillars in the temple of my God; they will remain there for ever. I shall write on them the name of my God, and the name of the city of my God, that new Jerusalem which is coming down out of heaven from my God, and my own new name. [13] You have ears, so hear what the Spirit says to the churches!"

[14] 'To the angel of the church at Laodicea write:

' "These are the words of the Amen, the faithful and true witness, the source of God's creation: [15] I know what you are doing; you are neither cold nor hot. How I wish you were either cold or hot! [16] Because you are neither one nor the other, but just lukewarm, I will spit you out of my mouth. [17] You say, 'How rich I am! What a fortune I have made! I have everything I want.' In fact, though you do not realize it, you are a pitiful wretch, poor, blind, and naked. [18] I advise you to buy from me gold refined in the fire to make you truly rich, and white robes to put on to hide the shame of your nakedness, and ointment for your eyes so that you may see. [19] All whom I love I reprove and discipline. Be wholehearted therefore in your repentance. [20] Here I stand knocking at the door; if anyone hears my voice and opens the door, I will come in and he and I will eat together. [21] To anyone who is victorious I will grant

a place beside me on my throne, as I myself was victorious and sat down with my Father on his throne. [22] You have ears, so hear what the Spirit says to the churches!"'

Visions of heaven

4 AFTER this I had a vision: a door stood open in heaven, and the voice that I had first heard speaking to me like a trumpet said, 'Come up here, and I will show you what must take place hereafter.' [2] At once the Spirit came upon me. There in heaven stood a throne. On it sat One [3] whose appearance was like jasper or cornelian, and round it was a rainbow, bright as an emerald. [4] In a circle about this throne were twenty-four other thrones, and on them were seated twenty-four elders, robed in white and wearing gold crowns. [5] From the throne came flashes of lightning and peals of thunder. Burning before the throne were seven flaming torches, the seven spirits of God, [6] and in front of it stretched what looked like a sea of glass or a sheet of ice.

In the centre, round the throne itself, were four living creatures, covered with eyes in front and behind. [7] The first creature was like a lion, the second like an ox, the third had a human face, and the fourth was like an eagle in flight. [8] Each of the four living creatures had six wings, and eyes all round and inside them. Day and night unceasingly they sing:

'Holy, holy, holy is God the sovereign Lord of all, who was, and is, and is to come!'

[9] Whenever the living creatures give glory and honour and thanks to the One who sits on the throne, who lives for ever and ever, [10] the twenty-four elders prostrate themselves before the One who sits on the throne and they worship him who lives for ever and ever. As they lay their crowns before the throne they cry:

[11] 'You are worthy, O Lord our God, to receive glory and honour and power, because you created all things; by your will they were created and have their being!'

5 I saw in the right hand of the One who sat on the throne a scroll with writing on both sides, and sealed with seven seals. [2] And I saw a mighty angel

proclaiming in a loud voice, 'Who is worthy to break the seals and open the scroll?' ³ But there was no one in heaven or on earth or under the earth able to open the scroll to look inside it. ⁴ And because no one was found worthy to open the scroll and look inside, I wept bitterly. ⁵ One of the elders said to me: 'Do not weep; the Lion from the tribe of Judah, the shoot growing from David's stock, has won the right to open the scroll and its seven seals.'

⁶ Then I saw a Lamb with the marks of sacrifice on him, standing with the four living creatures between the throne and the elders. He had seven horns and seven eyes, the eyes which are the seven spirits of God sent to every part of the world. ⁷ The Lamb came and received the scroll from the right hand of the One who sat on the throne. ⁸ As he did so, the four living creatures and the twenty-four elders prostrated themselves before the Lamb. Each of the elders had a harp; they held golden bowls full of incense, the prayers of God's people, ⁹ and they were singing a new song:

'You are worthy to receive the scroll and break its seals, for you were slain and by your blood you bought for God people of every tribe and language, nation and race. ¹⁰ You have made them a royal house of priests for our God, and they shall reign on earth.'

¹¹ As I looked I heard, all round the throne and the living creatures and the elders, the voices of many angels, thousands on thousands, myriads on myriads. ¹² They proclaimed with loud voices:

'Worthy is the Lamb who was slain, to receive power and wealth, wisdom and might, honour and glory and praise!'

¹³ Then I heard all created things, in heaven, on earth, under the earth, and in the sea, crying:

'Praise and honour, glory and might, to him who sits on the throne and to the Lamb for ever!'

¹⁴ The four living creatures said, 'Amen,' and the elders prostrated themselves in worship.

The seven seals

6 I WATCHED as the Lamb broke the first of the seven seals, and I heard one of the four living creatures say in a voice like thunder, 'Come!' ² There before my eyes was a white horse, and its rider held a bow. He was given a crown, and he rode forth, conquering and to conquer.

³ The Lamb broke the second seal, and I heard the second creature say, 'Come!' ⁴ Out came another horse, which was red. Its rider was given power to take away peace from the earth that men might slaughter one another; and he was given a great sword.

⁵ He broke the third seal, and I heard the third creature say, 'Come!' There, as I looked, was a black horse, and its rider was holding in his hand a pair of scales. ⁶ I heard what sounded like a voice from among the four living creatures; it said, 'A day's wage for a quart of flour, a day's wage for three quarts of barley-meal! But do not damage the olive and the vine!'

⁷ He broke the fourth seal, and I heard the fourth creature say, 'Come!' ⁸ There, as I looked, was another horse, sickly pale; its rider's name was Death, and Hades followed close behind. To them was given power over a quarter of the earth, power to kill by sword and famine, by pestilence and wild beasts.

⁹ He broke the fifth seal, and I saw beneath the altar the souls of those who had been slaughtered for God's word and for the testimony they bore. ¹⁰ They gave a great cry: 'How long, sovereign Lord, holy and true, must it be before you will vindicate us and avenge our death on the inhabitants of the earth?' ¹¹ They were each given a white robe, and told to rest a little longer, until the number should be complete of all their brothers in Christ's service who were to be put to death, as they themselves had been.

¹² I watched as the Lamb broke the sixth seal. There was a violent earthquake; the sun turned black as a funeral pall and the moon all red as blood; ¹³ the stars in the sky fell to the earth, like figs blown off a tree in a gale; ¹⁴ the sky vanished like a scroll being rolled up, and every mountain and island was dislodged from its place. ¹⁵ The kings of the earth,

---

5:6 **standing ... elders:** *or* standing in the middle of the throne, inside the circle of living creatures and the circle of elders.   6:9 **beneath:** *or* at the foot of.

the nobles and the commanders, the rich and the powerful, and all men, slave or free, hid themselves in caves and under mountain crags; [16] and they called out to the mountains and the crags, 'Fall on us, hide us from the One who sits on the throne and from the wrath of the Lamb, [17] for the great day of their wrath has come, and who can stand?'

7 After that I saw four angels stationed at the four corners of the earth, holding back its four winds so that no wind should blow on land or sea or on any tree. [2] I saw another angel rising from the east, bearing the seal of the living God. To the four angels who had been given the power to ravage land and sea, he cried out: [3] 'Do no damage to land or sea or to the trees until we have set the seal of our God upon the foreheads of his servants.' [4] I heard how many had been marked with the seal—a hundred and forty-four thousand from all the tribes of Israel: [5] twelve thousand from the tribe of Judah, twelve thousand from the tribe of Reuben, twelve thousand from the tribe of Gad, [6] twelve thousand from the tribe of Naphtali, twelve thousand from the tribe of Manasseh, [7] twelve thousand from the tribe of Simeon, twelve thousand from the tribe of Levi, twelve thousand from the tribe of Issachar, [8] twelve thousand from the tribe of Zebulun, twelve thousand from the tribe of Joseph, and twelve thousand from the tribe of Benjamin.

[9] After that I looked and saw a vast throng, which no one could count, from all races and tribes, nations and languages, standing before the throne and the Lamb. They were robed in white and had palm branches in their hands, [10] and they shouted aloud:

'Victory to our God who sits on the throne, and to the Lamb!'

[11] All the angels who stood round the throne and round the elders and the four living creatures prostrated themselves before the throne and worshipped God, [12] crying:

'Amen! Praise and glory and wisdom, thanksgiving and honour, power and might, be to our God for ever! Amen.'

[13] One of the elders turned to me and asked, 'Who are these all robed in white, and where do they come from?' [14] I answered, 'My lord, it is you who know.' He said to me, 'They are those who have passed through the great ordeal; they have washed their robes and made them white in the blood of the Lamb. [15] That is why they stand before the throne of God and worship him day and night in his temple; and he who sits on the throne will protect them with his presence. [16] Never again shall they feel hunger or thirst; never again shall the sun beat on them or any scorching heat, [17] because the Lamb who is at the centre of the throne will be their shepherd and will guide them to springs of the water of life; and God will wipe every tear from their eyes.'

8 Now when the Lamb broke the seventh seal, there was silence in heaven for about half an hour.

The seven trumpets

[2] I SAW the seven angels who stand in the presence of God: they were given seven trumpets.

[3] Another angel came and stood at the altar, holding a golden censer. He was given much incense to offer with the prayers of all God's people on the golden altar in front of the throne, [4] and the smoke of the incense from the angel's hand went up before God with his people's prayers. [5] The angel took the censer, filled it with fire from the altar, and threw it down on the earth; and there came peals of thunder, lightning-flashes, and an earthquake.

[6] THE seven angels who held the seven trumpets prepared to blow them.

[7] The first angel blew his trumpet. There came hail and fire mingled with blood, and this was hurled upon the earth; a third of the earth was burnt, a third of the trees, and all the green grass.

[8] The second angel blew his trumpet. What looked like a great mountain flaming with fire was hurled into the sea; a third of the sea was turned to blood, [9] a third of the living creatures in it died, and a third of the ships on it were destroyed.

[10] The third angel blew his trumpet. A great star shot from the sky, flaming like a torch, and fell on a third of the rivers and springs; [11] the name of the star was Wormwood. A third of the water turned

to wormwood, and great numbers of people died from drinking the water because it had been made bitter.

¹² The fourth angel blew his trumpet. A third part of the sun was struck, a third of the moon, and a third of the stars, so that a third part of the light failed to appear by day or by night.

¹³ As I looked, I heard an eagle calling with a loud cry as it flew in mid-heaven: 'Woe, woe, woe to the inhabitants of the earth at the sound of the other trumpets which the next three angels must now blow!'

9 The fifth angel blew his trumpet. I saw a star that had fallen from heaven to earth, and the star was given the key to the shaft of the abyss. ² He opened it, and smoke came up from it like smoke from a great furnace and darkened the sun and the air. ³ Out of the smoke came locusts over the earth, and they were given the powers of scorpions. ⁴ They were told not to do damage to the grass or to any plant or tree, but only to those people who had not received God's seal on their foreheads. ⁵ They were given permission to torment them for five months with torment like a scorpion's sting; but they were not to kill them. ⁶ During that time people will seek death, but will not find it; they will long to die, but death will elude them.

⁷ In appearance the locusts were like horses equipped for battle. On their heads were what looked like gold crowns; their faces were like human faces ⁸ and their hair like women's hair; they had teeth like lions' teeth ⁹ and chests like iron breastplates; the sound of their wings was like the noise of many horses and chariots charging into battle; ¹⁰ they had tails like scorpions, with stings in them, and in their tails lay their power to injure people for five months. ¹¹ They had for their king the angel of the abyss, whose name in Hebrew is Abaddon, and in Greek Apollyon, the Destroyer.

¹² The first woe has now passed; but there are still two more to come.

¹³ The sixth angel blew his trumpet. I heard a voice coming from the horns of the golden altar that stood in the presence of God. ¹⁴ To the sixth angel, who held the trumpet, the voice said: 'Release the four angels held bound at the Great River, the

Euphrates!' ¹⁵ So the four angels were let loose, to kill a third of mankind; they had been held in readiness for this very year, month, day, and hour. ¹⁶ And their squadrons of cavalry numbered twice ten thousand times ten thousand; this was the number I heard.

¹⁷ This was how I saw the horses and their riders in my vision: they wore breastplates, fiery red, turquoise, and sulphur-yellow; the horses had heads like lions' heads, and from their mouths issued fire, smoke, and sulphur. ¹⁸ By these three plagues, the fire, the smoke, and the sulphur that came from their mouths, a third of mankind was killed. ¹⁹ The power of the horses lay in their mouths and in their tails; for their tails had heads like serpents, and with them they inflicted injuries.

²⁰ The rest of mankind who survived these plagues still did not renounce the gods their hands had made, or cease their worship of demons and of idols fashioned from gold, silver, bronze, stone, and wood, which cannot see or hear or walk; ²¹ nor did they repent of their murders, their sorcery, their fornication, or their robberies.

10 I SAW another mighty angel coming down from heaven. He was wrapped in cloud, with a rainbow over his head; his face shone like the sun and his legs were like pillars of fire. ² In his hand he held a little scroll which had been opened. He planted his right foot on the sea and his left on the land, ³ and gave a great shout like the roar of a lion; when he shouted, the seven thunders spoke. ⁴ I was about to write down what the seven thunders had said, but I heard a voice from heaven saying, 'Put under seal what the seven thunders have said; do not write it down.' ⁵ Then the angel whom I saw standing on the sea and the land raised his right hand towards heaven ⁶ and swore by him who lives for ever, who created heaven and earth and the sea and everything in them: 'There shall be no more delay; ⁷ when the time comes for the seventh angel to sound his trumpet, the hidden purpose of God will have been fulfilled, as he promised to his servants the prophets.'

⁸ The voice which I had heard from heaven began speaking to me again; it

said, 'Go and take the scroll which is open in the hand of the angel who stands on the sea and the land.' ⁹ I went to the angel and asked him to give me the little scroll. He answered, 'Take it, and eat it. It will turn your stomach sour, but in your mouth it will taste as sweet as honey.' ¹⁰ I took the scroll from the angel's hand and ate it, and in my mouth it did taste as sweet as honey, but when I swallowed it my stomach turned sour.

¹¹ Then I was told, 'Once again you must utter prophecies over many nations, races, languages, and kings.'

11 I was given a long cane to use as a measuring rod, and was told: 'Go and measure the temple of God and the altar, and count the worshippers. ² But leave the outer court of the temple out of your measurements; it has been given over to the Gentiles, and for forty-two months they will trample the Holy City underfoot. ³ I will give my two witnesses authority to prophesy, dressed in sackcloth, for those twelve hundred and sixty days.' ⁴ They are the two olive trees and the two lamps that stand in the presence of the Lord of the earth. ⁵ If anyone tries to injure them, fire issues from their mouths and consumes their enemies; so shall anyone die who tries to do them injury. ⁶ These two have the power to shut up the sky, so that no rain falls during the time of their prophesying; and they have power to turn water into blood and to afflict the earth with every kind of plague whenever they like. ⁷ But when they have completed their testimony, the beast that comes up from the abyss will wage war on them and will overcome and kill them. ⁸ Their bodies will lie in the street of the great city, whose name in prophetic language is Sodom, or Egypt, where also their Lord was crucified. ⁹ For three and a half days people from every nation and tribe, language, and race, gaze on their corpses and refuse them burial. ¹⁰ The earth's inhabitants gloat over them; they celebrate and exchange presents, for these two prophets were a torment to them. ¹¹ But at the end of the three and a half days the breath of life from God came into their bodies, and they rose to their feet, to the terror of those who saw them. ¹² A loud voice from heaven was heard saying to them, 'Come up here!' and they ascended to heaven in

a cloud, in full view of their enemies. ¹³ At that moment there was a violent earthquake, and a tenth of the city collapsed. Seven thousand people were killed in the earthquake; the rest, filled with fear, did homage to the God of heaven.

¹⁴ The second woe has now passed; but the third is soon to come.

¹⁵ Then the seventh angel blew his trumpet. Voices in heaven were heard crying aloud:

'Sovereignty over the world has passed to our Lord and his Christ, and he shall reign for ever!'

¹⁶ The twenty-four elders, who sit on their thrones before God, prostrated themselves before him in adoration, ¹⁷ saying:

'O Lord God, sovereign over all, you are and you were; we give you thanks because you have assumed full power and entered upon your reign. ¹⁸ The nations rose in wrath, but your day of wrath has come. Now is the time for the dead to be judged; now is the time for rewards to be given to your servants the prophets, to your own people, and to all who honour your name, both small and great; now is the time to destroy those who destroy the earth.'

¹⁹ God's sanctuary in heaven was opened, and within his sanctuary was seen the ark of his covenant. There came flashes of lightning and peals of thunder, an earthquake, and a violent hailstorm.

Seven visions

12 AFTER that there appeared a great sign in heaven: a woman robed with the sun, beneath her feet the moon, and on her head a crown of twelve stars. ² She was about to bear a child, and in the anguish of her labour she cried out to be delivered. ³ Then a second sign appeared in heaven: a great, fiery red dragon with seven heads and ten horns. On his heads were seven diadems, ⁴ and with his tail he swept down a third of the stars in the sky and hurled them to the earth. The dragon stood in front of the woman who was about to give birth, so that when her child was born he might devour it. ⁵ But when she gave birth to a male child, who is destined to rule all nations with a rod of iron, the child was snatched up to God and to his throne. ⁶ The woman herself

fled into the wilderness, where she was to be looked after for twelve hundred and sixty days in a place prepared for her by God.

⁷ Then war broke out in heaven; Michael and his angels fought against the dragon. The dragon with his angels fought back, ⁸ but he was too weak, and they lost their place in heaven. ⁹ The great dragon was thrown down, that ancient serpent who led the whole world astray, whose name is the Devil, or Satan; he was thrown down to the earth, and his angels with him.

¹⁰ I heard a loud voice in heaven proclaim: 'This is the time of victory for our God, the time of his power and sovereignty, when his Christ comes to his rightful rule! For the accuser of our brothers, he who day and night accused them before our God, is overthrown. ¹¹ By the sacrifice of the Lamb and by the witness they bore, they have conquered him; faced with death they did not cling to life. ¹² Therefore rejoice, you heavens and you that dwell in them! But woe to you, earth and sea, for the Devil has come down to you in great fury, knowing that his time is short!'

¹³ When the dragon saw that he had been thrown down to the earth, he went in pursuit of the woman who had given birth to the male child. ¹⁴ But she was given the wings of a mighty eagle, so that she could fly to her place in the wilderness where she was to be looked after for three and a half years, out of reach of the serpent. ¹⁵ From his mouth the serpent spewed a flood of water after the woman to sweep her away with its spate. ¹⁶ But the earth came to her rescue: it opened its mouth and drank up the river which the dragon spewed from his mouth. ¹⁷ Furious with the woman, the dragon went off to wage war on the rest of her offspring, those who keep God's commandments and maintain their witness to

13 Jesus. ¹ He took his stand on the seashore.

Then I saw a beast rising out of the sea. It had ten horns and seven heads; on the horns were ten diadems, and on each head was a blasphemous name. ² The beast I saw resembled a leopard, but its feet were like a bear's and its mouth like a lion's. The dragon conferred on it his own power, his throne, and great authority. ³ One of the heads seemed to have been given a death blow, yet its mortal wound was healed. The whole world went after the beast in wondering admiration, ⁴ and worshipped the dragon because he had conferred his authority on the beast; they worshipped the beast also. 'Who is like the beast?' they said. 'Who can fight against it?'

⁵ The beast was allowed to mouth bombast and blasphemy, and was granted permission to continue for forty-two months. ⁶ It uttered blasphemies against God, reviling his name and his dwelling-place, that is, those who dwell in heaven. ⁷ It was also allowed to wage war on God's people and to defeat them, and it was granted authority over every tribe, nation, language, and race. ⁸ All the inhabitants of the earth will worship it, all whose names have not been written in the book of life of the Lamb, slain since the foundation of the world.

⁹ You have ears, so hear! ¹⁰ Whoever is to be made prisoner, to prison he shall go; whoever is to be slain by the sword, by the sword he must be slain. This calls for the endurance and faithfulness of God's people.

¹¹ Then I saw another beast; it came up out of the earth, and had two horns like a lamb's, but spoke like a dragon. ¹² It wielded all the authority of the first beast in its presence, and made the earth and its inhabitants worship this first beast, whose mortal wound had been healed. ¹³ It worked great miracles, even making fire come down from heaven to earth, where people could see it. ¹⁴ By the miracles it was allowed to perform in the presence of the beast it deluded the inhabitants of the earth, and persuaded them to erect an image in honour of the beast which had been wounded by the sword and yet lived. ¹⁵ It was allowed to give breath to the image of the beast, so that it could even speak and cause all who would not worship the image to be put to death. ¹⁶ It caused everyone, small and great, rich and poor, free man and slave, to have a mark put on his right hand or

---

12:11 **the witness they bore:** *or* the word of God to which they bore witness. 13:8 **written ... world:** *or* written, since the foundation of the world, in the book of life of the slain Lamb. 13:10 **whoever ... slain by the sword:** *or* whoever takes the sword to slay.

his forehead, [17] and no one was allowed to buy or sell unless he bore this beast's mark, either name or number. [18] (This calls for skill; let anyone who has intelligence work out the number of the beast, for the number represents a man's name, and the numerical value of its letters is six hundred and sixty-six.)

14 I LOOKED, and there on Mount Zion stood the Lamb, and with him were a hundred and forty-four thousand who had his name and the name of his Father written on their foreheads. [2] I heard a sound from heaven like a mighty torrent or a great peal of thunder; what I heard was like harpists playing on their harps. [3] They were singing a new song before the throne and the four living creatures and the elders, and no one could learn it except the hundred and forty-four thousand ransomed from the earth. [4] These are men who have kept themselves chaste and have not defiled themselves with women; these follow the Lamb wherever he goes. They have been ransomed as the firstfruits of mankind for God and the Lamb. [5] No lie was found on their lips; they are without fault.

[6] Then I saw an angel flying in midheaven, with an eternal gospel to proclaim to those on earth, to every race, tribe, language, and nation. [7] He spoke in a loud voice: 'Fear God and pay him homage, for the hour of his judgement has come! Worship him who made heaven and earth, the sea and the springs of water!'

[8] A second angel followed, saying, 'Fallen, fallen is Babylon the great, who has made all nations drink the wine of God's anger roused by her fornication!'

[9] A third angel followed, saying in a loud voice, 'Whoever worships the beast and its image and receives its mark on his forehead or hand, [10] he too shall drink the wine of God's anger, poured undiluted into the cup of his wrath. He shall be tormented in sulphurous flames in the sight of the holy angels and the Lamb. [11] The smoke of their torment will rise for ever; there will be no respite day or night for those who worship the beast and its image, or for anyone who receives the mark of its name.' [12] This calls for the endurance of God's people, all those who keep his commands and remain loyal to Jesus.

[13] I heard a voice from heaven say, 'Write this: "Happy are the dead who henceforth die in the faith of the Lord!" "Yes," says the Spirit, "let them rest from their labours, for the record of their deeds goes with them."'

[14] As I looked there appeared a white cloud, on which was seated a figure like a man; he had a gold crown on his head and a sharp sickle in his hand. [15] Another angel came out of the temple and called in a loud voice to him who sat on the cloud: 'Put in your sickle and reap, for harvest time has come and earth's crop is fully ripe.' [16] So the one who sat on the cloud swept over the earth with his sickle and the harvest was reaped.

[17] Another angel came out of the heavenly sanctuary, and he also had a sharp sickle. [18] Then from the altar came yet another, the angel who has authority over fire, and he called aloud to the one with the sharp sickle: 'Put in your sharp sickle, and gather in earth's grape harvest, for its clusters are ripe.' [19] So the angel swept over the earth with his sickle and gathered in its grapes, and threw them into the great winepress of God's wrath. [20] The winepress was trodden outside the city, and for a distance of two hundred miles blood flowed from the press to the height of horses' bridles.

The seven bowls

15 THEN I saw in heaven another great and astonishing sign: seven angels with seven plagues, the last plagues of all, for with them the wrath of God was completed.

[2] I saw what looked like a sea of glass shot through with fire. Standing beside it and holding the harps which God had given them were those who had been victorious against the beast, its image, and the number of its name.

[3] They were singing the song of Moses, the servant of God, and the song of the Lamb:

'Great and marvellous are your deeds,

13:18 the numerical ... letters: *lit.* his number.   14:13 the dead ... the Spirit: *some witnesses read* the dead who die trusting in the Lord! Henceforth", says the Spirit.

O Lord God, sovereign over all;
just and true are your ways,
O King of the ages.
4 Who shall not fear you, Lord,
and do homage to your name?
For you alone are holy.
All nations shall come and worship
before you,
for your just decrees stand revealed.'

5 After this, as I looked, the sanctuary of the heavenly Tent of Testimony was opened, 6 and from it came the seven angels with the seven plagues. They were robed in fine linen, pure and shining, and had golden girdles round their breasts. 7 One of the four living creatures gave to the seven angels seven golden bowls full of the wrath of God who lives for ever. 8 The sanctuary was filled with smoke from the glory of God and from his power, so that no one could enter it until the seven plagues of the seven angels were completed.

16 I heard a loud voice from the sanctuary say to the seven angels, 'Go and pour out the seven bowls of God's wrath on the earth.'

2 The first angel went and poured out his bowl on the earth; and foul malignant sores appeared on the men that wore the mark of the beast and worshipped its image.

3 The second angel poured out his bowl on the sea; and the sea turned to blood like the blood from a dead body, and every living thing in it died.

4 The third angel poured out his bowl on the rivers and springs, and they turned to blood.

5 And I heard the angel of the waters say, 'You are just in these your judgements, you who are, and were, O Holy One; 6 for they shed the blood of your people and your prophets, and blood you have given them to drink. They have what they deserve!' 7 I heard a voice from the altar cry, 'Yes, Lord God, sovereign over all, true and just are your judgements!'

8 The fourth angel poured out his bowl on the sun; and it was allowed to burn people with its flames. 9 They were severely burned, and cursed the name of God who had the power to inflict such plagues, but they did not repent and do him homage.

10 The fifth angel poured out his bowl on the throne of the beast; and its kingdom was plunged into darkness. Men gnawed their tongues in agony, 11 and cursed the God of heaven for their pain and sores, but they would not repent of what they had done.

12 The sixth angel poured out his bowl on the Great River, the Euphrates; and its water was dried up to prepare a way for the kings from the east.

13 I saw three foul spirits like frogs coming from the mouths of the dragon, the beast, and the false prophet. 14 These are demonic spirits with power to work miracles, sent out to muster all the kings of the world for the battle on the great day of God the sovereign Lord. 15 ('See, I am coming like a thief! Happy the man who stays awake, and keeps his clothes at hand so that he will not have to go naked and ashamed for all to see!') 16 These spirits assembled the kings at the place called in Hebrew Armageddon.

17 The seventh angel poured out his bowl on the air; and out of the sanctuary came a loud voice from the throne, which said, 'It is over!' 18 There followed flashes of lightning and peals of thunder, and a violent earthquake, so violent that nothing like it had ever happened in human history.

The destruction of Babylon

19 THE great city was split in three, and the cities of the nations collapsed in ruin. God did not forget Babylon the great, but made her drink the cup which was filled with the fierce wine of his wrath. 20 Every island vanished, and not a mountain was to be seen. 21 Huge hailstones, weighing as much as a hundredweight, crashed down from the sky on the people; and they cursed God because the plague of hail was so severe.

17 ONE of the seven angels who held the seven bowls came and spoke to me; 'Come,' he said, 'I will show you the verdict on the great whore, she who is enthroned over many waters. 2 The kings of the earth have committed fornication with her, and people the world over have made themselves drunk on the wine of her fornication.' 3 He carried me in spirit into the wilderness, and I saw a woman mounted on a scarlet beast which was

231

covered with blasphemous names and had seven heads and ten horns. ⁴ The woman was clothed in purple and scarlet, and decked out with gold and precious stones and pearls. In her hand she held a gold cup full of obscenities and the foulness of her fornication. ⁵ Written on her forehead was a name with a secret meaning: 'Babylon the great, the mother of whores and of every obscenity on earth.' ⁶ I saw that the woman was drunk with the blood of God's people, and with the blood of those who had borne their testimony to Jesus.

At the sight of her I was greatly astonished. ⁷ But the angel said to me, 'Why are you astonished? I will tell you the secret of the woman and of the beast she rides, with the seven heads and the ten horns. ⁸ The beast you saw was once alive, and is alive no longer, but has yet to ascend out of the abyss before going to be destroyed. All the inhabitants of the earth whose names have not been written in the book of life since the foundation of the world will be astonished to see the beast, which once was alive, and is alive no longer, and has still to appear.

⁹ 'This calls for a mind with insight. The seven heads are seven hills on which the woman sits enthroned. ¹⁰ They also represent seven kings: five have already fallen, one is now reigning, and the other has yet to come. When he does come, he is to last for only a little while. ¹¹ As for the beast that once was alive and is alive no longer, he is an eighth—and yet he is one of the seven, and he is going to destruction. ¹² The ten horns you saw are ten kings who have not yet begun to reign, but who for a brief hour will share royal authority with the beast. ¹³ They have a single purpose and will confer their power and authority on the beast. ¹⁴ They will wage war on the Lamb, but the Lamb will conquer them, for he is Lord of lords and King of kings, and those who are with him are called and chosen and faithful.'

¹⁵ He continued: 'The waters you saw, where the great whore sat enthroned, represent nations, populations, races, and languages. ¹⁶ As for the ten horns you saw, and the beast, they will come to hate the whore. They will strip her naked and leave her destitute; they will devour her flesh and burn her up. ¹⁷ For God has put it into their minds to carry out his purpose, by making common cause and conferring their sovereignty on the beast until God's words are fulfilled. ¹⁸ The woman you saw is the great city that holds sway over the kings of the earth.'

18 After this I saw another angel coming down from heaven; he possessed great authority and the earth shone with his splendour. ² In a mighty voice he proclaimed, 'Fallen, fallen is Babylon the great! She has become a dwelling for demons, a haunt for every unclean spirit, for every unclean and loathsome bird. ³ All the nations have drunk the wine of God's anger roused by her fornication; the kings of the earth have committed fornication with her, and merchants the world over have grown rich on her wealth and luxury.'

⁴ I heard another voice from heaven saying: 'Come out from her, my people, lest you have any part in her sins and you share in her plagues, ⁵ for her sins are piled high as heaven, and God has not forgotten her crimes. ⁶ Pay her back in her own coin, repay her twice over for her deeds! Give her a potion twice as strong as the one she mixed! ⁷ Measure out torment and grief to match her pomp and luxury! "I am a queen on my throne!" she says to herself. "No widow's weeds for me, no mourning!" ⁸ That is why plagues shall strike her in a single day, pestilence, bereavement, and famine, and she shall perish in flames; for mighty is the Lord God who has pronounced her doom!'

⁹ The kings of the earth who committed fornication with her and wallowed in her luxury will weep and wail over her, as they see the smoke of her burning. ¹⁰ In terror at her torment they will keep their distance and say, 'Alas, alas for you great city, mighty city of Babylon! In a moment your doom has come upon you!'

¹¹ The merchants of the world will weep and mourn for her, because no one buys their cargoes any more, ¹² cargoes of gold and silver, precious stones and pearls, purple and scarlet cloth, silks and fine linens; all sorts of fragrant wood, and all kinds of objects made of ivory or of costly woods, bronze, iron, or marble; ¹³ cinnamon and spice, incense, perfumes, and

17:10 **kings:** *or* emperors.

frankincense; wine, oil, flour and wheat, cattle and sheep, horses, chariots, slaves, and human lives. ¹⁴ 'The harvest you longed for', they will say, 'is gone from you; all the glitter and glamour are lost, never to be found again!' ¹⁵ The traders in all these goods, who grew rich on her, will keep their distance in terror at her torment; weeping and mourning ¹⁶ they will say: 'Alas, alas for the great city that was clothed in fine linen and purple and scarlet, decked out with gold and precious stones and pearls! ¹⁷ So much wealth laid waste in a moment!'

All the sea-captains and voyagers, the sailors and those who made a living on the sea, stayed at a distance; ¹⁸ as they saw the smoke of her burning, they cried out, 'Was there ever a city like the great city?' ¹⁹ They threw dust on their heads and, weeping and mourning, they cried aloud: 'Alas, alas for the great city, where all who had ships at sea grew rich from her prosperity! In a single hour she has been laid waste!'

²⁰ But let heaven exult over her; exult, God's people, apostles and prophets, for he has imposed on her the sentence she passed on you!

²¹ Then a mighty angel picked up a stone like a great millstone and hurled it into the sea, saying, 'Thus shall Babylon, the great city, be sent hurtling down, never to be seen again! ²² The sound of harpists and minstrels, flute-players and trumpeters, shall no more be heard in you; no more shall craftsmen of any trade be found in you, or the sound of the mill be heard in you; ²³ no more shall the light of the lamp appear in you, no more the voices of the bridegroom and bride be heard in you! Your traders were once the merchant princes of the world, and with your sorcery you deceived all the nations.' ²⁴ The blood of the prophets and of God's people was found in her, the blood of all who had been slain on earth.

19 After this I heard what sounded like a vast throng in heaven shouting:

'Hallelujah! Victory and glory and power belong to our God, ² for true and just are his judgements! He has condemned the great whore who corrupted the earth with her fornication; he has taken vengeance on her for the blood of his servants.'

³ Once more they shouted:

'Hallelujah! The smoke from her burning will rise for ever!'

⁴ The twenty-four elders and the four living creatures bowed down and worshipped God who sits on the throne; they cried: 'Amen! Hallelujah!'

⁵ THERE came a voice from the throne saying: 'Praise our God, all you his servants, you that fear him, both small and great!' ⁶ And I heard what sounded like a vast throng, like the sound of a mighty torrent or of great peals of thunder, and they cried:

'Hallelujah! The Lord our God, sovereign over all, has entered on his reign! ⁷ Let us rejoice and shout for joy and pay homage to him, for the wedding day of the Lamb has come! His bride has made herself ready, ⁸ and she has been given fine linen, shining and clean, to wear.'

(The fine linen signifies the righteous deeds of God's people.)

⁹ THE angel said to me, 'Write this: "Happy are those who are invited to the wedding banquet of the Lamb!"' He added, 'These are the very words of God.' ¹⁰ I prostrated myself to worship him, but he said, 'You must not do that! I am a fellow-servant with you and your brothers who bear their witness to Jesus. It is God you must worship. For those who bear witness to Jesus have the spirit of prophecy.'

More visions

¹¹ I SAW heaven wide open, and a white horse appeared; its rider's name was Faithful and True, for he is just in judgement and just in war. ¹² His eyes flamed like fire, and on his head were many diadems. Written on him was a name known to none but himself; ¹³ he was robed in a garment dyed in blood, and he was called the Word of God. ¹⁴ The armies of heaven followed him, riding on white horses and clothed in fine linen, white and clean. ¹⁵ Out of his mouth came a sharp sword to smite the nations; for it is he who will rule them with a rod of iron, and tread the winepress of the fierce wrath of God the sovereign Lord.

[16] On his robe and on his thigh was written the title: 'King of kings and Lord of lords'.

[17] I saw an angel standing in the sun. He cried aloud to all the birds flying in mid-heaven: 'Come, gather together for God's great banquet, [18] to eat the flesh of kings, commanders, and warriors, the flesh of horses and their riders, the flesh of all, the free and the slave, the small and the great!' [19] I saw the beast and the kings of the earth with their armies mustered to do battle against the rider and his army. [20] The beast was taken prisoner, along with the false prophet who had worked miracles in its presence and deluded those who had received the mark of the beast and worshipped its image. The two of them were thrown alive into the lake of fire with its sulphurous flames. [21] The rest were killed by the sword which came out of the rider's mouth, and the birds all gorged themselves on their flesh.

20 I saw an angel coming down from heaven with the key to the abyss and a great chain in his hand. [2] He seized the dragon, that ancient serpent who is the Devil, or Satan, and chained him up for a thousand years; [3] he threw him into the abyss, shutting and sealing it over him, so that he might not seduce the nations again till the thousand years were ended. After that he must be let loose for a little while.

[4] I saw thrones, and on them sat those to whom judgement was committed. I saw the souls of those who, for the sake of God's word and their witness to Jesus, had been beheaded, those who had not worshipped the beast and its image or received its mark on forehead or hand. They came to life again and reigned with Christ for a thousand years, [5] though the rest of the dead did not come to life until the thousand years were ended. This is the first resurrection. [6] Blessed and holy are those who share in this first resurrection! Over them the second death has no power; but they shall be priests of God and of Christ, and shall reign with him for the thousand years.

[7] When the thousand years are ended, Satan will be let loose from his prison, [8] and he will come out to seduce the nations in the four quarters of the earth. He will muster them for war, the hosts of Gog and Magog, countless as the sands of the sea. [9] They marched over the breadth of the land and laid siege to the camp of God's people and the city that he loves. But fire came down on them from heaven and consumed them. [10] Their seducer, the Devil, was flung into the lake of fire and sulphur, where the beast and the false prophet had been flung to be tormented day and night for ever.

[11] I saw a great, white throne, and the One who sits upon it. From his presence earth and heaven fled away, and there was no room for them any more. [12] I saw the dead, great and small, standing before the throne; and books were opened. Then another book, the book of life, was opened. The dead were judged by what they had done, as recorded in these books. [13] The sea gave up the dead that were in it, and Death and Hades gave up the dead in their keeping. Everyone was judged on the record of his deeds. [14] Then Death and Hades were flung into the lake of fire. This lake of fire is the second death; [15] into it were flung any whose names were not to be found in the book of life.

21 I SAW a new heaven and a new earth, for the first heaven and the first earth had vanished, and there was no longer any sea. [2] I saw the Holy City, new Jerusalem, coming down out of heaven from God, made ready like a bride adorned for her husband. [3] I heard a loud voice proclaiming from the throne: 'Now God has his dwelling with mankind! He will dwell among them and they shall be his people, and God himself will be with them. [4] He will wipe every tear from their eyes. There shall be an end to death, and to mourning and crying and pain, for the old order has passed away!'

[5] The One who sat on the throne said, 'I am making all things new!' ('Write this down,' he said, 'for these words are trustworthy and true.') [6] Then he said to me, 'It is done! I am the Alpha and the Omega, the beginning and the end. To the thirsty I will give water from the spring of life as a gift. [7] This is the victors' heritage; and I will be their God and they will be my children. [8] But as for the cowardly, the faithless, and the obscene, the murderers, fornicators, sorcerers, idolaters, and liars of every kind, the lake that burns with sulphurous flames will be their portion, and that is the second death.'

The new Jerusalem

⁹ ONE of the seven angels who held the seven bowls full of the seven last plagues came and spoke to me. 'Come,' he said, 'and I will show you the bride, the wife of the Lamb.' ¹⁰ So in the spirit he carried me away to a great and lofty mountain, and showed me Jerusalem, the Holy City, coming down out of heaven from God. ¹¹ It shone with the glory of God; it had the radiance of some priceless jewel, like a jasper, clear as crystal. ¹² It had a great and lofty wall with twelve gates, at which were stationed twelve angels; on the gates were inscribed the names of the twelve tribes of Israel. ¹³ There were three gates to the east, three to the north, three to the south, and three to the west. ¹⁴ The city wall had twelve foundation-stones, and on them were the names of the twelve apostles of the Lamb.

¹⁵ The angel who spoke with me carried a gold measuring rod to measure the city, its gates, and its wall. ¹⁶ The city had four sides, and it was as wide as it was long. Measured by his rod, it was twelve thousand furlongs, its length and breadth and height being equal. ¹⁷ Its wall was one hundred and forty-four cubits high, by human measurements, which the angel used. ¹⁸ The wall was built of jasper, while the city itself was of pure gold, bright as clear glass. ¹⁹ The foundations of the city wall were adorned with precious stones of every kind, the first of the foundation-stones being jasper, the second lapis lazuli, the third chalcedony, the fourth emerald, ²⁰ the fifth sardonyx, the sixth cornelian, the seventh chrysolite, the eighth beryl, the ninth topaz, the tenth chrysoprase, the eleventh turquoise, and the twelfth amethyst. ²¹ The twelve gates were twelve pearls, each gate fashioned from a single pearl. The great street of the city was of pure gold, like translucent glass.

²² I saw no temple in the city, for its temple was the sovereign Lord God and the Lamb. ²³ The city did not need the sun or the moon to shine on it, for the glory of God gave it light, and its lamp was the Lamb. ²⁴ By its light shall the nations walk, and to it the kings of the earth shall bring their splendour. ²⁵ The gates of the city shall never be shut by day, nor will there be any night there. ²⁶ The splendour and wealth of the nations shall be brought into it, ²⁷ but nothing unclean shall enter, nor anyone whose ways are foul or false; only those shall enter whose names are inscribed in the Lamb's book of life.

22 Then the angel showed me the river of the water of life, sparkling like crystal, flowing from the throne of God and of the Lamb ² down the middle of the city's street. On either side of the river stood a tree of life, which yields twelve crops of fruit, one for each month of the year. The leaves of the trees are for the healing of the nations. ³ Every accursed thing shall disappear. The throne of God and of the Lamb will be there, and his servants shall worship him; ⁴ they shall see him face to face and bear his name on their foreheads. ⁵ There shall be no more night, nor will they need the light of lamp or sun, for the Lord God will give them light; and they shall reign for ever.

Conclusion

⁶ HE said to me, 'These words are trustworthy and true. The Lord God who inspires the prophets has sent his angel to show his servants what must soon take place. ⁷ And remember, I am coming soon!'

Happy is the man who takes to heart the words of prophecy contained in this book! ⁸ It was I, John, who heard and saw these things. When I had heard and seen them, I prostrated myself to worship the angel who had shown them to me. ⁹ But he said, 'You must not do that! I am a fellow-servant with you and your brothers the prophets and with those who take to heart the words of this book. It is God you must worship.' ¹⁰ He told me, 'Do not seal up the words of the prophecy that are in this book, for the time of fulfilment is near. ¹¹ Meanwhile, let the evildoers persist in doing evil and the filthy-minded continue in their filth, but let the good persevere in their goodness and the holy continue in holiness.'

¹² 'I am coming soon, and bringing with me my recompense to repay everyone according to what he has done! ¹³ I am the Alpha and the Omega, the first and the last, the beginning and the end.'

¹⁴ Happy are those who wash their robes clean! They shall be free to eat from the tree of life and may enter the city by

the gates. [15] Outside are the perverts, the sorcerers and fornicators, the murderers and idolaters, and all who love and practise deceit.

[16] 'I, Jesus, have sent my angel to you with this testimony for the churches. I am the offspring of David, the shoot growing from his stock, the bright star of dawn.'

[17] 'Come!' say the Spirit and the bride.

'Come!' let each hearer reply.

Let the thirsty come; let whoever wishes accept the water of life as a gift.

[18] I, John, give this warning to every-one who is listening to the words of prophecy in this book: if anyone adds to them, God will add to him the plagues described in this book; [19] if anyone takes away from the words in this book of prophecy, God will take away from him his share in the tree of life and in the Holy City, which are described in this book.

[20] He who gives this testimony says: 'Yes, I am coming soon!'

Amen. Come, Lord Jesus!

[21] The grace of the Lord Jesus be with all.

22:15 **perverts:** *lit.* dogs.